Palgrave Studies in Prisons and Penology

This is a unique and innovative series, the first of its kind dedicated entirely to prison scholarship. At a historical point in which the prison population has reached an all-time high, the series seeks to analyse the form, nature and consequences of incarceration and related forms of punishment. Palgrave Studies in Prisons and Penology provides an important forum for burgeoning prison research across the world.

Helene De Vos

Beyond Scandinavian Exceptionalism

Normalization, Imprisonment and Society

palgrave
macmillan

Helene De Vos
Leuven Institute of Criminology
KU Leuven
Leuven, Belgium

ISSN 2753-0604 ISSN 2753-0612 (electronic)
Palgrave Studies in Prisons and Penology
ISBN 978-3-031-28634-6 ISBN 978-3-031-28635-3 (eBook)
https://doi.org/10.1007/978-3-031-28635-3

Cover credit: Francesco Vaninetti Photo/Moment/Getty

This Palgrave Macmillan imprint is published by the registered company Springer Nature Switzerland AG
The registered company address is: Gewerbestrasse 11, 6330 Cham, Switzerland

Acknowledgments

This book would never have been possible without the scientific guidance and the generous support of many people, to whom I am greatly indebted.

I am especially grateful to my supervisor Ivo Aertsen for advising and supporting me with trust and patience, and for never ceasing to challenge 'traditional' views on punishment and imprisonment. I am certain that his passion for justice will continue to inspire me for the rest of my career. Special thanks are also due to my co-supervisor Frank Verbruggen for the challenging but very enjoyable discussions that always led to new insights.

I would like to thank Sonja Snacken, Stefaan Pleysier and Thomas Ugelvik for their contribution as members of my doctoral supervisory committee, and the members of the examination committee, Tom Daems, Miranda Boone and Annabel Cerezo, for their kind and helpful feedback.

I wish to thank the Research Foundation - Flanders (FWO) for granting me the scholarship without which this work could not have been done.

I am very grateful to the staff and incarcerated people of the prisons of Trondheim (Nermarka and Leira), Leuven and Hoogstraten for all their practical support, and even more for all the thoughts and insights they shared with me.

Further I want to thank my colleagues of the Leuven Institute of Criminology (KU Leuven), many of whom have become good friends. It has been a privilege to work together with such wonderful people and I am very thankful for all the support, feedback and encouragement.

I also owe thanks to Lise Træland for the memorable Norwegian classes.

Many thanks to you, Jef and Masj, for your generous hospitality. You made me feel at home in your spacious apartment after long observation days in Hoogstraten.

My greatest gratitude goes to Kirsti, Svenn Erik, Andreas and Hannah. Thank you for sharing your home with me during my fieldwork in Trondheim. Thank you so much for all the joy and laughter, which made this an unforgettable experience for me.

Many many thanks to you, Liv Terese, for welcoming me in your home for several months and for treating me like family. Thank you so much for all the evenings that you waited for me to eat together, even when I returned quite late from the prison.

Words can never express my gratitude to my family. This research has made me realize even more how valuable it is to be unconditionally loved and supported. I am therefore incredibly grateful to have two warm, loving families, whom I can always count on.

Finally, Hendrik, I can never thank you enough for all our talks about normalization and all our walks miles away from everything that had anything to do with normalization. Thank you for your help, inspiration and encouragement. I am so lucky to have you. Thank you for everything.

Leuven
January 2023

Helene De Vos

Contents

1
Introduction

In history, Vikings are not known as the most peaceful people. Popular stories—more sensational caricature than solid history—tell the tales of how their longships brought them to the coasts of Western Europe and thence inland, where they pillaged villages and burned entire cities. Leuven, the seat of my Alma Mater, still has in its coat of arms the blood (red) and the river Dyle (white) where the Vikings were beaten and repelled during the Battle of the Dyle (891 AD). The cruelty towards their enemies was supposedly also reflected in the brutal punishments inflicted on their own criminals. Today's story is entirely different. Scandinavian countries rank among the most peaceful and wealthy in the world, and all citizens are said to benefit from high levels of welfare. At the same time, Scandinavian countries are looked at with envy for their seemingly exceptional status in penal performance: low incarceration rates, humane treatment of prisoners and low rates of recidivism. This is particularly remarkable given the so-called 'punitive turn' witnessed in other late modern societies (Pratt, 2008a, 2008b; Ugelvik & Dullum, 2012). Since the 1970s, imprisonment rates have been rising in many countries, despite declining or stable crime rates (Body-Gendrot et al., 2014; Lappi-Seppälä, 2012, 2014; Pakes, 2010). Furthermore, concepts

H. De Vos, *Beyond Scandinavian Exceptionalism*, Palgrave Studies in Prisons and Penology, https://doi.org/10.1007/978-3-031-28635-3_1

such as the *new punitiveness*, the *new penology* and the *culture of control* suggest that also the nature of punishment has changed over the last decades (Feeley & Simon, 1992; Garland, 2001; Pratt, 1998).

It was the New Zealand criminologist John Pratt who coined the term 'Scandinavian exceptionalism', referring to the comparatively low detention rates as well as humane prison conditions in the Nordic countries (Dullum & Ugelvik, 2012; Pratt, 2008a, 2008b). Based on his 2006 research undertaken in Finland, Norway and Sweden, he also argued that the exceptionally humane prison conditions resulted from the normalization principle underpinning the organization of prison life:

> Generally speaking, in this region, it is recognized that going to prison is itself the punishment for crime; prison conditions can then approximate to life outside as far as possible, rather than being allowed to degrade and debase all within. (Pratt, 2008a: 119, my emphasis)

Pratt thus draws a direct link between 'Scandinavian exceptionalism' and the normalization principle, reaching this conclusion by comparing Scandinavian countries to Anglophone countries (at first implicitly, but explicitly in Pratt & Eriksson, 2013). And he is not alone. Shammas (2016) also reassures his readers, after sketching the rising punitiveness in Norway, that prison conditions in Norwegian prisons remain more generous than those in many other Western societies, since '*the principle of "normalization" holds a dominant position in official discourse on imprisonment, and a strong commitment to replicating "normal" conditions within prison does give the prison system a peculiar character*' (Shammas, 2016: 64). Although the analytical value of this exceptionalism claim has already been questioned (see e.g. Cavadino & Dignan, 2006; Daems, 2007), it still offers food for thought. Do countries with relatively low incarceration rates and humane prison conditions tend to be more effective in resisting political pushes to increase punitiveness? Can and should the normalization principle be seen as a 'shield' against the 'punitive turn' or possible excesses? How does a principle like normalization translate into practice and to which extent does this 'translation' affect the penal performance? Do Scandinavian countries achieve their exceptional position thanks to a unique interpretation and implementation of normalization; or rather because the quality of prison life mirrors the quality of life in the Scandinavian society in general? And perhaps most interestingly, would Pratt's claim be upheld if a Scandinavian country, like Norway, were to be compared to another European country, like Belgium, which (at least nominally) relies equally strongly on the normalization principle? Before addressing these questions, let us first take a closer look at the origins and the meaning of the normalization principle itself.

1.1 Emergence of the Principle: Differing Interpretations from the Start

The idea of normalizing the living conditions of certain groups of people emerged in the context of the post-war welfare state. With various groups of citizens, such as women, black and gay people, starting to claim equal rights, the idea arose that all people, including those labelled as 'deviant', should have the same fundamental rights and their living conditions should be 'as normal as possible' (Bronston, 1974; Garland, 2001; Nirje, 1985; Whitehead, 1992). In this societal climate, the two 'founding fathers' of the normalization principle, the Swedish jurist and philosopher Bengt Nirje (1969) and the German-American psychologist Wolf Wolfensberger (1972), aimed at improving the living conditions of people with mental disabilities. Despite their common starting point, however, they formulated two different interpretations of the principle. These different interpretations are still relevant here because the questions that arose from their debates are the same as those arising in the prison context: Should normalization be considered an intrinsic or an instrumental principle? Should its rationale be based on empiricism or on values and ideological beliefs? If used instrumentally, should it be oriented towards discipline or towards emancipation?

Nirje was the first to define the principle of normalization as '*making available to all mentally retarded people* [sic] *patterns of life and conditions of everyday living which are as close as possible to the regular circumstances and ways of life of society*' (1969, 1980: 33). This formulation of the normalization principle reflected his opposition to the inhumane living conditions in large institutions for people with disabilities (Nirje, 1985). But more substantially, Nirje was also fully aware that providing legal rights for those people would not suffice to improve their living conditions. In his view, the realization of human rights and humane living conditions required more than merely a legal framework. In this respect, he argued that normalization could not be detached from its ethical aspects because problems regarding human rights '*relate to what might be right or wrong in making and taking decisions and actions concerning other people*' (Nirje, 1985: 65). Thus, his interpretation of the normalization principle was indeed explicitly value-based, aimed at emancipating and including people with disabilities in society. For Nirje, the added value of normalization did not lie in its effectiveness but rather in its 'consciousness-raising', to change beliefs about differentness of people who were labelled 'retarded' (Bronston, 1974: 492). Further developing his idea of normalization, Nirje (1999) identified eight aspects of life that were to be normalized: (1) the rhythm of the day, (2) of the week and (3) of the year, (4) experiences of the life cycle, (5) respect for the individual and the right to self-determination, (6) sexual patterns, (7) economic patterns and rights and (8) environment patterns and standards. This attempt of operationalizing the meaning of 'normal life' was supported by Ericsson (1985), adding another six aspects that were considered crucial to living a normal life: (1) the right to a house and a home in community; (2) a place for daily activity; (3) participation in or utilization of what the local community has to offer; (4) economic and material standards that enable individuals to personally purchase what they need to form their home; (5) the ability to influence their daily lives; and (6) respect for personal integrity in all social relationships.

A commonly heard criticism of identifying particular aspects of life in this way is that their normalization leads to standardization (Culham & Nind, 2003). However, Nirje (1999) was convinced of the opposite. In his opinion, normalization should result in individualization rather than standardization in order to stimulate participation in society. He furthermore emphasized that respect for the individual and the right to self-determination should be the basis for normalization (Nirje, 1999). Some authors have followed Nirje on this point and have strongly defended his statement that normalization and standardization should be considered opposites (see e.g. Bronston, 1974). Other authors, however, still criticize the normalization principle for intentionally or unintentionally provoking standardization and denying differences between people. Nirje (1999: 17) in turn wondered explicitly whether these authors did actually read his work before criticizing it.

Partly endorsing the critical response to Nirje's interpretation, psychologist Wolf Wolfensberger re-interpreted the normalization principle in 1972, aiming to make it more empirically based and more influential in practice (Flynn & Lemay, 1999). He shifted the principle's focus from the person's living conditions to the person's social role, which he thought could be more empirically valued. Therefore, the creation of '*valued social roles*' was the highest goal of normalization, '*because if a person's social role were a societally valued one, then other desirable things would be accorded to that person almost automatically*' (Wolfensberger, 1983/ 2011a: 436). To increase the chances for a valued social role, he proposed two complementary strategies: first, reducing the '*differentness [...] which may make a person devalued in the eyes of observers*' and second, changing '*societal perceptions and values in regard to a devalued person or group so that a given characteristic or person is no longer seen as devalued*' (Wolfensberger, 1983/ 2011a: 437).

In his attempt to make the concept of normalization more scientific, in 1983 Wolfensberger (1983/ 2011a: 436) abandoned the term normalization in favour of '*social role valorization*', convincingly arguing that the term normalization had been unfortunate, given the fact that a vast majority of readers '*assume—usually wrongly—that they know "what it means"*'. The new term was indeed a more accurate reflection of his interpretation of normalization (Wolfensberger, 1983/2011a: 435–440). Content-wise, Wolfensberger's conceptual shift also implied a dissociation from the promotion of human rights, which was in his opinion still a mixture of ideology and empirical social science (Wolfensberger, 2002/2011b). He argued that the fundamental difference between social role valorization and 'ideologies' like empowerment, autonomy, self-determination, democracy and human rights, is that the former is empiricism-based, whereas ideologies are not (Wolfensberger, 2002/2011b: 470). In this context, Culham and Nind (2003) questioned to what extent a human rights discourse excludes the need for empiricism and the other way around, and whether '*With inclusion, as with normalisation, is the human rights agenda in danger of being lost all over again?*' (Culham & Nind, 2003: 75). This question remains relevant to today's penological debate.

In the same societal climate of the post-war welfare state, prisoners' rights were formally recognized by international and European penal policies (Dumortier et al., 2012; Fransen, 2017; Kaminski, 2010). To make the prison sentence more humane, it was argued that the punishment should consist only of the deprivation of liberty without any additional 'pains' or deprivations. In other words, '*men should go to prison as punishment, not for punishment*' (Alexander Paterson, as cited in McConville, 2012: 3, emphasis in original). This human rights discourse, which advocates a full legal status for prisoners, apart from their right to liberty, has now become part of the official European discourse, even though there is still resistance to its implementation in practice (see e.g. Shea, 2005).

As early as in 1955, the idea of normalizing the living conditions in prison was expressed by the UN Standard Minimum Rules for the Treatment of Prisoners:

> The regime of the institution should seek to minimize any differences between prison life and life at liberty which tend to lessen the responsibility of the prisoners or the respect due to their dignity as human beings. (art. 60)

The same words were adopted verbatim by the European Prison Rules of 1973, which thus introduced the idea of normalization in European penal policy. The 1987 European Prison Rules (EPR) further developed the normalization principle, prescribing that harmful effects of imprisonment and the differences between prison life and life in society should be limited, that prisoners' human dignity should be respected, that prisoners should be able to sustain or strengthen their personal links with the outside world, and that prisoners should develop skills in order to facilitate their reintegration (rule 65 EPR 1987). More specifically, the Council of Europe member states were recommended to lodge prisoners *normally* in individual cells during the night (rule 14.1), to offer them the opportunity to eat at *normal* times (rule 25.1), to do useful work in conditions that resemble as closely as possible those in the society so that they have *normal* working days (rules 71.3 and 72.1), and prisoners who work in cooperation with private companies should be paid *normal* wages (rule 73.1). In this context, the Council of Europe explained that the view of imprisonment as an expectation to reform prisoners had now changed to '*an emphasis on normalising life and activity within the prisons—the so-called "reality prisons"*' (explanatory memorandum of the EPR of 1987: 82).

Normalization was brought to the fore even more in the fifth basic principle of the 2006 European Prison Rules: '*Life in prison shall approximate as closely as possible the positive aspects of life in the community*' (see also van Zyl Smit & Snacken, 2009). Moreover, the European Court of Human Rights is promoting its implementation in prison practice by referring explicitly to the European Prison Rules in addition to the European Convention on Human Rights itself (see Hirst v. UK, 6 October 2005; Dickson v. UK, 4 December 2007; Smaers, 2005; Snacken, 2006). Although it is acknowledged that prison life will always differ from life outside prison, the 2006 European Prison Rules call for active steps towards the normalization of prison life, without ever resulting in less humane prison conditions. As Engbo (2017) has observed, these Prison Rules embrace two complementary approaches to normalization. The proactive approach, on the one hand, entails the obligations to create conditions in which prisoners can live a normal life, which he finds reflected in this fifth basic principle. The defensive approach, on the other hand, requires authorities to avoid unnecessary interventions with prisoners' possibilities of living a normal life (Engbo, 2017). This is for example reflected in the second basic principle of these Prison Rules prescribing that '*Persons deprived of their liberty retain all rights that are not lawfully taken away by the decision sentencing them or remanding them in custody*'.

This brief overview of the emergence of the normalization principle in relation to the post-war societal and penal developments shows that the different interpretations and applications are not always easy to disentangle, as everybody has his or her own intuitive view on normalization (Wolfensberger, 1983/ 2011a: 436). What is 'normal' in one context is not necessarily in another. Given its apparent simplicity, it is not surprising that the normalization principle has been widely applied ever since its first usage by Nirje and Wolfensberger. At the same time, it is not surprising either that normalization has met with criticism or that it has been the subject of misunderstandings. A common source of criticism to normalization is voiced by scholars who associate the human rights principle with Foucault's (1977) concept of normalization that is linked to *disciplinary techniques*. Other scholars have pointed out that the Foucauldian and human rights interpretations are opposites (Feest, 1999; Snacken, 2002, see also Chapter 2). Another fundamental question that has elicited further debate is what should be perceived as normal in a society and what as peripheral, deviant or not-normal. Especially in the disability studies, normalization has raised concerns that it would eliminate the visibility, respectability and societal contribution of 'deviant' groups (see e.g. Culham & Nind, 2003). Even the very notions of 'deviant' and 'mainstream' have been challenged (Christie, 1989). Applied to the prison context, an abolitionist approach has surfaced that dismisses the idea of normalization as a new legitimization of the prison sentence (see e.g. Mathiesen, 1974, 2015). Without being able to elaborate each of the above-mentioned streams of literature for reasons of time and space, we need to further clarify one issue before focusing on the different interpretations in Norwegian and Belgian prison policy and practice, and that is the scope of the normalization principle and its limits in the prison context.

1.2 Normalization of Prison Life: Its Scope and Limits

Even if the pursuit of normal living conditions in prison reflects the broader trend towards more humane prison conditions with increased attention to prisoners' rights, the implementation of the normalization principle in the prison context is not at all self-evident. It remains paradoxical to physically exclude prisoners from society, while at the same time making their living conditions approximate those in society as closely as possible (see also Snacken, 2002). Similarly, it is paradoxical to reduce the 'pains of imprisonment' after deliberate 'pain delivery' (Christie, 1982) or 'pain manipulation' (Hayes, 2016). In Norwegian jurisprudence, for example, punishment has been defined as '*an evil that the state imposes on an offender because of the offense, with the intention to be experienced as an evil*' (Andenæs, 1962 cited in Fredwall, 2017, my translation and emphasis). Indeed, as punishment for a crime, the deprivation of liberty is the *intentional* infliction of something negative, imposed by the competent authority (Kellens, 2000).

Although it is generally accepted in Europe that the prison sentence should consist only of the deprivation of liberty, the 'pure deprivation of liberty' is a theoretical understanding of imprisonment that is not easily implemented in practice, certainly not within a penal institution. The pains and frustrations associated with the physically, socially and virtually restricted or even distorted nature of the prison environment have been outlined in detail by the growing body of prison literature (see e.g. Clemmer, 1940/1958; Crewe, 2011; Goffman, 1961; Hancock & Jewkes, 2011; Huey Dye, 2010; Irwin & Owen, 2005; Neumann, 2012; Rocheleau, 2013; Shammas, 2014; Smith, 2012; Sykes 1958/2007; Ugelvik, 2014). Classic works like Goffman's 'Asylums' (On the Characteristics of Total Institutions) and Sykes' 'The Society of Captives' are still commonly cited to point out the abnormal or distorted nature of the prison. Yet at the same time, it is increasingly acknowledged that despite some '*essential similarities*', prisons differ in significant and numerous ways (Crewe, 2021; Drake et al., 2015; Liebling, 2004: 462; 2011; Pratt, 2008a, 2008b; van Zyl Smit & Snacken, 2009). The same is true for the effects they have on the prison experience and prisoners' and prison staff's well-being. Put more strongly, '*some prison environments are more survivable than others*' (Liebling, 2011: 535). Along the same lines, the living conditions in some prisons differ more strongly from life outside than those in other.

These insights have caused the shift in focus from the *intended pains* that are to be produced by the prison sentence, to the *unintended pains* that are to be prevented in order to achieve the aims of imprisonment.[1] Back in the eighteenth century, utilitarian thinkers like Cesare

[1] Parts of this section have already been published in De Vos and Gilbert (2017).

Beccaria and Jeremy Bentham thought about punishment in terms of the *intended pains*. Beccaria found the justification of punishment in his ideal societal objective: '*the greatest happiness shared among the greater number*' (Beccaria, cited in Draper, 2000: 181). The pursuit of this happiness required the deterrence of citizens from committing crimes. This choice for deterrence as a suitable means to reduce future crimes was the logical consequence of his belief that human behaviour, including delinquent behaviour, could be explained by a reasonable cost–benefit analysis (Fijnaut, 2014). Beccaria was convinced that efficient deterrence firstly requires that the nature of the punishment reflects the nature of the crime, and secondly that the severity of this punishment is in proportion to the severity of the crime. This means that the disadvantages of the punishment should slightly outweigh the advantages of the crime (Fijnaut, 2014).

Over time, the focus has shifted from deterrence to incapacitation and rehabilitation (Cullen & Gendreau, 2001; Fijnaut, 2014) and to managing and controlling crime (Feeley & Simon, 1992; Garland, 2001; Pratt et al., 2005). According to O'Donnell (2016: 47), '*it could be argued that there has been shrinkage over time in the breadth of ambition associated with the expressed aims of imprisonment*'. O'Donnell (2016) further states that the aims of imprisonment, as defined by prison administrations, are increasingly focused on the internal organization of the prison rather than on its social function, such as the reduction of future crime. Thus, he defines the aim of imprisonment in a minimalist way, which is '*to reconstitute the prisoner's spatiotemporal world without causing avoidable collateral damage*' (O'Donnell, 2016: 39). Although the official aims of imprisonment are in many countries still more ambitious than the mere reconstitution of prisoners' '*spatiotemporal world*', the knowledge about the unintended painful and harmful effects of imprisonment has resulted in an increased focus on the reduction of these effects rather than hoping for any positive effects. This is where the normalization principle comes into play. In the explanatory memorandum of the European Prison Rules of 1987, the acceptance of less-ambitious aims of imprisonment was explained as follows:

> the findings of evaluative research, that have demonstrated that penal treatments differ very little in their capacity to reform, have led to an emphasis on normalising life and activity within the prisons—the so-called 'reality prisons'. Proponents of that approach have held too that it can be important in diminishing the deleterious effects of imprisonment, that is, as yet, imperfectly understood and remains to be tested in pragmatic and objective terms. (Council of Europe, 1987: 82)

It is still true, however, that punishment, and more specifically the liberty deprivation, is meant to be something negative. This means that the normalization of the living conditions in prison is not able, and not intended, to reduce *all* frustrations related to the liberty deprivation. This brings us to two conceptual distinctions that help understand the scope and limits of the normalization principle. First, the distinction between the *intended* effects of the infliction of punishment and the *unintended* effects of imprisonment. Sykes (1958, 2007: 64) described this distinction as follows:

> In part, the deprivations or frustrations of prison life today might be viewed as punishments which the free community deliberately inflicts on the offender for violating the law; in part, they might be seen as the unplanned (or, as some would argue, the unavoidable) concomitants of confining large groups of criminals for prolonged periods.

However, despite the obviousness of this distinction, and despite the fact that there is little dispute about the deprivation of liberty being the intentional frustration or 'pain', it is still open to debate as to what consequences are inextricably linked to this liberty deprivation and therefore considered to be part of the actual intended punishment (see e.g. ECtHR, 6 October 2005, Hirst/UK; Bronsteen et al., 2009; Feest, 1999: 100; Hayes, 2016; Markel et al., 2011; Snacken, 2002; van Ginneken & Hayes, 2017).

Second, the *painful effects* of imprisonment should be distinguished from its *harmful effects*. Whereas the painful effects include the negative experiences that are directly or indirectly caused by the prison sentence (such as feelings of loneliness or frustrations about the loss of autonomy), harmful effects refer to the negative consequences that last longer than the prison term itself (such as traumatization, broken relationships or loss of professional skills). These harmful effects may hamper a successful reintegration (Irwin & Owen, 2005; O'Donnell, 2016). In this respect, Neumann (2012: 148) points out that one '*cannot remedy the stigmatizing effects of imprisonment by offering offenders progressive prison conditions due to good behaviour in prison [...]—having been in prison does not look good on your CV*'. Although there is a considerable overlap between those two categories, not all painful effects are harmful. Normalization is then to be understood as the endeavour to reduce the unintended harmful effects of imprisonment, while the prison sentence itself still entails painful effects directly caused by the deprivation of liberty.

Without these conceptual distinctions, misunderstandings and contradictions arise, as illustrated by the following debate between Bronsteen et al. and Markel et al. In their article on Happiness and Punishment, Bronsteen et al., (2009: 1038) argue that prisoners are able to adapt surprisingly well to their incarceration, which means that '*their happiness drops at the beginning and they expect it to remain at that low ebb, but it ascends as they adjust to their new surroundings*'. This process of regaining a level of happiness that is more closely to their pre-incarceration level is called '*hedonic adaptation*'. Adapting to the post-prison situation often characterized by health problems, unemployment and broken relationships, on the other hand, appears to be much more difficult. Following this line of reasoning, the authors argue that imprisonment is *less* painful than expected, while reintegration after imprisonment is *more* painful than expected (Bronsteen et al., 2009). For the purpose of their argument, however, Bronsteen et al. (2009) do not distinguish between painful and harmful effects, confusingly defining punishment as 'harm infliction'. Nor do they make a clear distinction between the intended and unintended pains. The absence of these conceptual distinctions leads them to conclude that the harmful effects of imprisonment should be taken into account by the judge when determining the proportionality between crime and punishment. Refuting this argument, Markel et al., (2011: 618) use a more narrow definition of punishment, which only includes the *intended pains* caused by liberty deprivation:

> If the hardship endured by the offender is not authorized, intentionally imposed, and proximately caused by the state, then it is a conceptual error to call it 'punishment', even if it involves negative experience to the offender after his offense.

Although this implies that the unintended and harmful effects of imprisonment should not affect the proportionality between crime and liberty deprivation, Markel et al. (2011) do take these harmful effects seriously, explaining that '*if the harms experienced are actionable constitutional torts, then they likely deserve some remedy, not because these harms are punishment but precisely because they are not*' (Markel et al., 2011: 620, emphasis in original). Hence, any consistent and seriously thought-through implementation of normalization in the prison context requires a clear view of the actual punishment, which will determine the scope and limits of the normalization process.

1.3 Normalization Through a Comparative and holistic Lens

As already suggested, the aim of this book is to gain a deeper understanding of the normalization principle in the prison context, in relation to the broader penal and societal context. In order to make this endeavour feasible and tangible, two countries are at the centre of this research: Belgium and Norway. The comparative methodology is discussed in the next chapter, but the point being made here is that the comparison of these two countries offers a unique angle to study this principle. As a principle used in the prison context, it is an equation with two equally important parts: society and prison, and normalization as the link between those two. For prison researchers, prison life may be the most obvious part in the equation, but it means nothing without a society to which prison life should '*approximate as closely as possible*' (European Prison Rules 2006, rule no. 5). As such, the normalization of prison life touches on important normative questions. What should be considered 'a normal life' in society? And which aspects of prison life should be normalized and in what ways, given the fact that living conditions outside prison greatly differ?

These assessments of 'normality' are at least partly culturally defined, since values and standards vary between countries. This means that we can assume that what is considered normal in Belgium is not necessarily normal in Norway, and the other way around. A classic example are national eating habits: Belgian prisoners receive food three times a day (or two, since dinner is distributed with the bread for the following day's breakfast), hot meals include soup and a dessert, and very often fries are served on Sundays, or another fixed day. Norwegian prisoners eat four times a day, usually drink milk and often get *rømmegrøt*[2] on Saturdays. It also means that developments in prison conditions should be considered in relation to developments in society (see e.g. Liebling, 2004: 484). In the present context of digitalization, for example, Engbo (2017: 347) has rightly pointed out that '*Abnormalisation increases every day*' (emphasis in original) as prisons do not follow the digital evolutions in society (see also Smith, 2012). A comparison of the normalization principle in Belgium and Norway therefore compares the *relationship* between the living conditions in Belgian prisons and living conditions in Belgian society on the one hand with the *relationship* between living conditions in Norwegian prisons and those in Norwegian society on the other. To put it bluntly, looking through the lens of normalization, one would expect 'exceptional prisons' in 'exceptional societies' and 'less exceptional prisons' in 'less exceptional societies'. Following the same line of thinking, and if the normalization principle is consistently implemented, one would expect that strong welfare states, which are inclined to interfere with citizens' lives 'for their own good' (Smith & Ugelvik, 2017), are also more inclined to have prisons strongly interfering with prisoners' lives.

Indeed, normalization's fundamental link with society is important and any study on normalization will have to devote attention to the broad penal and social context of the country in which normalization is applied. This is one of the reasons why this research was focused on two

---

[2] '*Rømmegraut (sometimes rømmegrøt in Bokmål and amongst Norwegian Americans) is Norwegian porridge made with sour cream, whole milk, wheat flour, butter, and salt*' (https://en.wikipedia.org/wiki/Rømmegraut).

countries. By comparing two specific countries, instead of comparing clusters of countries or looking for general trends in all late modern societies, it attempts to avoid some of the overgeneralizations that affect the accuracy of the current debates in comparative penology. Another reason for comparing these two countries is that both in Belgium and in Norway, the normalization principle is considered one of the guiding principles of imprisonment. In the Belgian prison policy, and more specifically in the explanatory memorandum of the Prison Act of 12 January 2005, the importance of the principle is explained as follows: '*The reduction of harmful effects of imprisonment requires at least an attempt to create living conditions in prison that resemble as much as possible living conditions in society, except for the fact that one is deprived of his liberty*' (Final report Prison Act Commission, 2001: 8, my translation). In Norway, normalization is one of the five pillars on which the organization of the Correctional Service is built, and consists of three aspects: first, '*the punishment is the restriction of liberty; no other rights have been removed by the sentencing court. Therefore the sentenced offender has all the same rights as all other who live in Norway*'; second, '*no-one shall serve their sentence under stricter circumstances than necessary for the security in the community. Therefore offenders shall be placed in the lowest possible security regime*'; and third, '*during the serving of a sentence, life inside will resemble life outside as much as possible*' (www.kriminalomsorgen.no/information-in-english.265199.no.html, original in English; St. meld. no. 37, 2007–2008).

Given the prominence of the principle in both countries' prison policies, the comparison of these two countries is helpful to gain a deeper understanding of the interpretation and implementation of the normalization principle. At the same time, this comparison can shed new light on the 'Scandinavian exceptionalism thesis'. Even though 'Scandinavian exceptionalism' suggests that Scandinavian penal policies and practices are qualitatively different from all other late modern societies, this should be understood first and foremost in relation to the punitive trends that have been thoroughly described for the Anglo-Saxon world (Pratt & Eriksson, 2013). A striking example in this respect relates to the age of criminal responsibility. Downes (2012: 29–30) has noticed that '*In both the USA and England and Wales, the age threshold for criminal prosecution is as low as 10. By contrast, in the Nordic social democracies, it is 15*'. In Belgium, however, the age threshold for criminal responsibility is 18. Moreover, in contrast to most Anglophone countries, Belgium is a strong welfare state with a consensual (multiparty) and corporatist political culture, which has been associated with penal leniency (Cavadino & Dignan, 2006; Lacey, 2008; Lappi-Seppälä, 2012, 2014; Walgrave & Varone, 2008). Whereas neo-liberal states tend to exclude certain social groups, both conservative corporatist states, like Belgium, and social-democratic corporatist states, like Norway, have been characterized as community-oriented societies, seeking to include all citizens (although this is most strongly evidenced in social democracies) (Cavadino & Dignan, 2006). In addition, Belgian penal policy is explicitly built upon a human rights ideology and its judges are not elected, two factors which have also been identified as protective against the rising punitiveness (Snacken, 2010; Snacken & Dumortier, 2012; van Zyl Smit & Snacken, 2009).

These features are also reflected in the incarceration rates. Based on incarceration rates of 2012, Lappi-Seppälä (2014: 298) demonstrates that the Nordic countries have the lowest level of prisoners in Europe, with Norway having 73 prisoners per 100,000 inhabitants, followed by Western European countries, with Belgium having around 100 prisoners per 100,000 inhabitants. Similar trends emerge when looking at attitudinal punitivity (Lappi-Seppälä, 2014). On the basis of the results of the International Crime Victim Survey (ICVS) and European Social Survey (ESS), which assessed the punitive attitudes of the general public towards a young recidivist burglar who had stolen a TV set, Lappi-Seppälä (2014: 303–304) shows that respondents from the Nordic countries have the least punitive attitudes, followed by Western European respondents. However, when considering the countries separately, the attitudinal punitiveness was found to be lower in Belgium than in Norway.

It is fair to note, however, that this optimistic picture of Belgian penal policy fades away when using Google as a source to gain a first impression of both penal systems. When searching for the '*Norwegian prison system*',[3] a picture emerges of a very humane and successful prison system with headlines such as '*Why Norway's prison system is so successful*' (Sterbenz, 2014). The same impression is given by the Global Post, The Guardian and The Economist: '*Where convicts lead the good life. In Norway, even murders and rapists have a shot at landing in "open prison"*' (Fouche, 2009); '*The Norwegian prison where inmates are treated like people*' (James, 2013) and '*Plush and unusual punishment*' (W., 2011). A search for the '*Belgian prison system*',[4] by contrast, leads to '*Belgian prison chaos prompts fears of national malaise*' (Scholfield, 2016), '*Belgian prisoners released from "inhumane" jails*' (Krever, 2016) and '*A Cold Place, With No Curves: Life Inside Belgian Prisons*' (Laurent, 2014). While it is right to question the scientific value of these sources, they give a good indication of the perception that exists about Norwegian and Belgian prisons. Moreover, these impressions are at least to a certain extent confirmed by Langford et al. (2017). The findings of their analysis of the reviews by international human rights bodies (CAT and CPT) are remarkably worrying for Belgium, both when compared to Scandinavian countries and to other Western European countries like Germany. Hence, comparing Norway and Belgium will show that either the Scandinavian countries are less exceptional than generally assumed (both in penal performance and perception), or that the normalization principle produces different effects in different contexts, and that the role of the principle *as such* should not be overestimated, but rather understood in relation to other societal factors.

At the same time, however, it is also worth noting here that Scandinavian scholars have responded rather critically to the overly positive image of the Scandinavian prison systems, albeit without denying their comparatively low imprisonment rates (stock rates) and humane prison conditions. In addition to the methodological criticism, roughly four

[3] Search term used on 1 May 2017.

[4] Search term used on 1 May 2017.

types of critical insiders' responses to Pratt's 'Scandinavian exceptionalism' can be distinguished.[5] First, many Nordic authors stress the differences between the Nordic countries, which tend to be overlooked by a macro perspective and by the 'Scandinavian exceptionalism thesis' in particular (see e.g. Ugelvik, 2013; Ugelvik & Dullum, 2012). Second, the Nordic countries also display a tendency towards more punitiveness (see e.g. Smith, 2012; Shammas, 2016; Bruhn et al., 2017). According to Shammas (2016), Norway is gradually turning more punitive and thus less 'exceptional', which he associates with three broad developments in Norwegian society: (1) the growing importance of symbolic politics; (2) diminishing investments in rehabilitative politics and (3) the tendency towards neo-liberalism. Similar tendencies have been described for Denmark, including trends towards penal populism (Smith, 2012) and 'marketization' and an increased focus on efficiency and cost control (Fransen, 2017). Third, several Scandinavian scholars have pointed out the highly worrying aspects of Scandinavian penal systems, or so-called '*dark side*', which have been largely neglected or downplayed by Pratt's outsiders' view. This dark side refers to, for example, the inhumane practice of systematically isolating remand prisoners, the long sentences for drug offences and the discrimination of foreign nationals (see e.g. Langford et al., 2017; Mathiesen, 2012; Smith, 2012; Ugelvik, 2012; Smith & Ugelvik, 2017).

The fourth and last type of insiders' concerns discussed here is probably the most difficult to grasp from an outsider's perspective, but at the same time the most crucial for a good understanding of the Scandinavian penal systems. These concerns relate to the worrying aspects described above, but instead of interpreting these aspects as signifying a declining welfare state or a rising punitiveness, it is argued that these aspects should be considered as *central to* a strong but intrusive Scandinavian welfare state (Andersson, 2012; Barker, 2013; Smith, 2012; Smith & Ugelvik, 2017). Andersson (2012), for example, explains that the strong Scandinavian welfare state is built on a '*culture of interventionism*'. Along the

[5] 'Insider' and 'outsider' refer in this context to the question whether or not the person who makes certain claims about a society belongs himself to this society (see also Ugelvik & Dullum, 2012).

same line, Smith (2012: 54) points out that the problematic use of pre-trial solitary confinement could be considered the '*result of some sort of systemic Nordic welfare state problem—i.e. the arguably anti-liberal social control tendencies*'. This dualism inherent to Scandinavian penal systems, being mild and benign but at the same time 'intrusive, disciplining and oppressive' has been captured by Barker's (2013: 5) concept of the 'Janus-faced penal regime' and by Smith and Ugelvik's (2017) concept of 'Big Mother penal welfare state', which are both explained below.

While Barker does not dismiss Pratt's findings as entirely untrue, she argues that he overstated the mildness and humaneness, while leaving the intrusive and repressive character strikingly undertheorized (Barker, 2013: 7). Elaborating on this argument, she argues, contra Pratt (2008b) and Shammas (2016), that what has been called the '*dark side*' of the Scandinavian welfare state (in particular the tendency towards 'welfare nationalism' involving an exclusive attitude towards foreign nationals) should not be considered a sign of declining welfare state or neo-liberalization, but on the contrary, a '*part of the deep structure of the society itself*' (Barker, 2013: 18). Thus, Barker (2013) makes a strong argument for taking the dualities inherent to the Swedish welfare state more seriously: mild but at the same time intrusive, inclusive but at the time exclusive towards 'outsiders' and ensuring individual autonomy and material well-being without strong individual rights. Another point of disagreement between Barker and Pratt relates to the roots of the generous Swedish (and perhaps Scandinavian) welfare state: whereas Pratt emphasizes the importance of social solidarity and strong group cohesion, Barker underlines that the Swedish society is in the first place an individualistic society, rather than group-based. This individualism is crucial to her understanding of the interconnection between the mild and intrusive aspects of the Swedish welfare state, since the Swedish individual autonomy is not linked to individual rights: '*In Sweden then, individual freedom is constructed <u>through</u> the State rather than conceived as freedom <u>from</u> the State*' (Barker, 2013; 11, emphasis in original). This has resulted in a weak legal tradition of individual rights and greater possibilities for state intrusion 'for the public good'. Put even more strongly, '*"everyone has a right to dignity" even if that dignity must be forced onto them*' (Tham, 2005: 70 as cited in Barker, 2013: 13). The same duality emerges from Smith and Ugelvik's (2017: 513) reflection about the connection between rehabilitation, welfare, rights and power in Scandinavian countries, aptly summarized by their concept of '*the Big Mother penal welfare state*': '*being embraced by Big Mother can be something of a mixed blessing. Her embrace is simultaneously loving and forceful, and she both wants and knows what is best for you*'. Indeed, the strong welfare-oriented and highly trusted '*Big Mother State*' smoothly merges individualized rehabilitative measures with intrusive authoritarian interventions, the legitimacy of which is generally taken for granted (Smith & Ugelvik, 2017).

In sum, this *different* nature of the Scandinavian penal policies, as part of an intrusive and disciplinary welfare state, has made several Scandinavian authors doubt whether these societies can be considered *less* punitive (Neumann, 2012; Smith & Ugelvik, 2017; Ugelvik, 2013). Responding to these criticisms and in defence of Scandinavian exceptionalism, Pratt, together with Eriksson, criticizes these Scandinavian scholars for overly focusing on the most problematic aspects and most punitive trends (Pratt & Eriksson, 2012: 255; see also Barker, 2013: 19). Their argument seems to be reinforced by the fact that even these 'critical insiders', when looking from a comparative perspective, have to admit that the '*prisoners in these institutions are given opportunities, resources and living conditions that are not available to prisoners in most other jurisdictions*' (Ugelvik, 2016: 398), thereby referring to the important role of the normalization principle in Scandinavian prisons (Shammas, 2016; Smith & Ugelvik, 2017).

The authors' perspective has certainly proven to be relevant for the debate about Scandinavian exceptionalism, but not *all* insiders share the same view. Besides the authors' background, it is also the scope of the perspective which differs: whereas Pratt considers these penal systems from a macro, and in a way comparative, perspective, his findings have been mainly criticized from a micro perspective. Therefore, it is not surprising that Lappi-Seppälä (2012: 35), who can be considered an 'insider' in this debate, confirms the exceptionalism claim to a certain degree, on the basis of his macro analyses:

> Alongside general growth in cultures of control, there are divergent trends and country-specific deviations. The Scandinavian countries with their more restrained penal policies serve as one important counter-example, but there are others. The Scandinavian countries differ from many other European as well as non-European countries both in terms of stability and leniency of penal policy.

Of course, macro analyses are prone to criticism from a micro perspective since they downplay national differences by definition (see e.g. Daems, 2008; Lynch, 2011). Thus, the two perspectives are complementary rather than competing. This is true for various interpretations of micro- and macro-level, such as a local perspective versus a global one, the penal practice versus the official discourse and prisoners' experiences versus the general penal climate (Kruttschnitt & Dirkzwager, 2011; Sexton, 2015). The complementarity of these perspectives is shown by Shammas (2016), pointing out that two different perspectives lead to different conclusions: on the one hand, a comparative approach of various countries at one moment in time, and on the other hand, a focus on one country but taking into account evolutions over time:

> While a synchronic, cross-national comparisons [sic] may suggest the continued existence of an exceptional penal regime in Norway, an internal, diachronic assessment of the country's mode of punishment suggests that the trajectory of the penal regime as a whole seems geared more towards expansion than contraction, towards growing penalization rather than greater lenience, and towards the growth of policing, security, and surveillance. (Shammas, 2016: 65)

No one will deny that these different approaches have their merit, but it is only by combining them that normalization can be assessed as a whole, in its policy utterances as well as in its practical application on the ground. To estimate the role of normalization as a leading policy principle—the extent to which it achieves its underlying aims formulated by legislators and policymakers—it is not enough just to study normalization from a policy perspective, it is equally important to include prisoners' experiences in practice. Similarly, it is not enough just to compare specific aspects of the living conditions inside and outside prison. As much as prisons differ from each other in all kinds of aspects, they will also be different in the ways in which and the extent to which the living conditions *inside* correspond to those *outside* prison. If prison life is a *gestalt experience* (Johnsen & Granheim, 2012: 205), normalization is arguably affecting not just one but the many aspects of that experience. Understanding the prison as a set of interrelated dimensions will hence automatically imply that the normalization of one dimension cannot be fully understood without insight into the other dimensions. A holistic approach, therefore, seems vital to understand normalization in the prison context.

The holistic and comparative approach of this research is reflected in the structure of this book and in its chapters. Before diving into a detailed comparison of normalization in Belgian and Norwegian prison legislation and practice, Chapter 2 first presents the methodological and contextual background of this study. Chapter 3 then outlines the penal philosophies underlying the normalization principle in both countries, pointing out the different logics in Belgium and Norway. The following four chapters provide a more detailed analysis of the normalization principle in policy and practice through a comparative and holistic lens. Each of the four chapters addresses one broad dimension of prison life: the material environment (Chapter 4), security (Chapter 5), the social environment (Chapter 6) and the use of time (Chapter 7). Together these four broadly defined dimensions aim to capture the living conditions in prison and their normalization in a holistic way. These dimensions emerged bottom-up from the observations conducted in two Belgian and two Norwegian prisons and from the analysis of the Belgian and Norwegian policy documents and legislation. In each of these chapters, the focus is on how the efforts towards normalization, or what is claimed to be normalization, affect these dimensions, first from a legislative point of view, in both countries, and then from a practical point of view, in the two Belgian and two Norwegian prisons. It is only after thoroughly observing and analysing these four dimensions of prison life and their normalization in both legislation and practice, that we can reflect on their interaction and interconnectedness and thus, ultimately, on normalization itself. And it is only after having assessed how normalization is reflected in legislation and in practice, that we can understand how the normalization principle relates to the broader comparative penological debate concerning the 'Scandinavian exceptionalism'. Therefore, turning to the four dimensions in Chapters 4 to 7, and systematically comparing the legislation and practice of both countries, is necessary to finally link the role of the normalization principle in Belgian and Norwegian prison policies and practices to the broader comparative penological debate in the concluding chapter of this book.

References

Andersson, R. (2012). A blessing in disguise: Attention deficit hyperactivity disorder diagnosis and Swedish correctional treatment policy in the twenty-first century. In T. Ugelvik & J. Dullum (Eds.), *Penal Exceptionalism? Nordic Prison Policy and Practice* (pp. 156–171). Routledge.

Barker, V. (2013). Nordic Exceptionalism revisited: Explaining the paradox of a Janus-faced penal regime. *Theoretical Criminology, 17*(1), 5–25.

Bruhn, A., Lindberg, O., & Nylander, P. Å. (2017). Treating drug abusers in prison: Competing paradigms anchored in different welfare ideologies: The case of Sweden. In P. S. Smith & T. Ugelvik (Eds.), *Scandinavian penal history, culture and prison practice: Embraced by the welfare state?* (pp. 177–204). Palgrave Macmillan.

Body-Gendrot, S., Hough, M., Kerezsi, K., Lévy, R., & Snacken, S. (2014). Introduction. In S. Body-Gendrot, M. Hough, K. Kerezsi, R. Lévy, & S. Snacken (Eds.), *The Routledge handbook of European criminology* (pp. 1–20). Routledge.

Bronsteen, J., Buccafusco, C., & Masur, J. (2009). Happiness and punishment. *The University of Chicago Law Review, 76*(3), 1037–1082.

Bronston, W. G. (1974, September 30). Concepts and theory of normalization. Presented to the Down's Syndrome Congress, Milwaukee. Wisconsin.

Cavadino, M., & Dignan, J. (2006). *Penal systems. A comparative approach.* Sage Publications Ltd.

Christie, N. (1982). *Limits to pain.* Robertson.

Christie, N. (1989). *Beyond loneliness and institutions: Communes for extraordinary people.* Norwegian University Press.

Clemmer, D. (1958). *The prison community.* Holt, Rinehart and Winston.

Council of Europe. (1987, February 12). *Recommendation rec(87)3 of the committee of ministers to member states on the European prison rules*. https://rm.coe.int/16804f856c

Crewe, B. (2011). Depth, weight, tightness: Revisiting the pains of imprisonment. *Punishment & Society, 13*(5), 509–529.

Crewe, B. (2021). The depth of imprisonment. *Punishment & Society, 23*(3), 335–354. https://doi.org/10.1177/1462474520952153

Culham, A., & Nind, M. (2003). Deconstructing normalisation: Clearing the way for inclusion. *Journal of Intellectual & Developmental Disability, 28*(1), 65–78.

Cullen, F. T., & Gendreau, P. (2001). From nothing works to what works: Changing professional ideology in the 21st century. *The Prison Journal, 81*(3), 313–338.

Daems, T. (2007). *Making sense of penal change: Punishment, victimization & society*. K.U.Leuven. Faculteit Rechtsgeleerdheid.

Daems, T. (2008). *Making sense of penal change. Clarendon Studies in Criminology.* Oxford University Press.

De Vos, H., & Gilbert, E. (2017). Freedom, so close but yet so far: The impact of the ongoing confrontation with freedom on the perceived severity of punishment. *European Journal of Probation, 9*(2), 132–148.

Downes, D. (2012). Political economy, welfare and punishment in comparative perspective. In S. Snacken & E. Dumortier (Eds.), *Resisting punitiveness in Europe? Welfare, human rights and democracy* (pp. 23–34). Routledge.

Drake, D. H., Earle, R., & Sloan, J. (2015). General introduction: What ethnography tells us about prisons. In D. H. Drake, R. Earle, & J. Sloan (Eds.), *The Palgrave handbook of prison ethnography* (pp. 1–16). Palgrave Macmillan.

Draper, A. J. (2000). Cesare Beccaria's influence on English discussions of punishment, 1764–1789. *History of European Ideas, 26*(3–4), 177–199.

Dullum, J., & Ugelvik, T. (2012). Introduction. Exceptional prisons, exceptional societies? In T. Ugelvik & J. Dullum (eds.), *Penal exceptionalism? Nordic prison policy and practice* (pp. 1–10). Routledge.

Dumortier, E., Gutwith, S., Snacken, S., & De Hert, P. (2012). The rise of the penal state: What can human rights do about it? In S. Snacken & E. Dumortier (Eds.), *Resisting punitiveness in Europe? Welfare, Human Rights and Democracy* (pp. 107–132). Routledge.

Engbo, H. J. (2017). Normalisation in nordic prisons – From a prison governor's perspective. In T. Ugelvik & P. S. Smith (Eds.), *Scandinavian penal history, culture and prison practice: Embraced by the welfare state?* (pp. 327–352). Palgrave Macmillan.

Ericsson, K. (1985). The principle of normalization: history and experiences in Scandinavian countries, Presentation, ILSMH Congress, Hamburg.

Feeley, M. M., & Simon, J. (1992). The new penology: Notes on the emerging strategy of corrections and its implications. *Criminology, 30*(4), 449–474.

Feest, J. (1999). Imprisonment and prisoners' work: Normalization or less eligibility? *Punishment & Society, 1*(1), 99–107.

Fijnaut, F. (2014). *Criminologie en strafrechtsbedeling*. Intersentia.

Flynn, R. J., & Lemay, R. A. (1999). Normalization and social role valorization at a quarter-century: Evolution, impact, and renewal. In R. J. Flynn & R. A. Lemay (Eds.), *A quarter-century of normalization and social role valorization: Evolution and impact* (pp. 3–13). University of Ottawa Press.

Foucault, M. (1977). *Discipline and punish: The birth of the prison*. Pantheon Books.

Fouche, G. (2009, October 19). Where convicts lead the good life. *GlobalPost*. www.globalpost.com/dispatch/europe/091017/norway-open-prison. Last accessed on 19 April 2021.

Fransen, P. (2017). The rise of the open prisons and the breakthrough of the principle of normalization from the 1930s until today. In T. Ugelvik & P. S. Smith (Eds.), *Scandinavian penal history, culture and prison practice: Embraced by the welfare state?* (pp. 77–99). Palgrave Macmillan.

Fredwall, T. E. (2017). Straff som pine. *Retfærd: Nordisk juridisk tidsskrift, 40*(3–4), 24–37.

Garland, D. (2001). *The culture of control. Crime and social order in contemporary society*. Oxford University Press.

Goffman, E. (1961). *Asylums. Essays on the social situation of mental patients and other inmates*. Penguin Books Ltd.

Hancock, P., & Jewkes, Y. (2011). Architectures of incarceration: The spatial pains of imprisonment. *Punishment & Society, 13*(5), 611–629.

Hayes, D. (2016). Penal impact: Towards a more intersubjective measurement of penal severity. *Oxford Journal of Legal Studies, 36*(4), 724–750.

Huey Dye, M. (2010). Deprivation, importation, and prison suicide: Combined effects of institutional conditions and inmate composition. *Journal of Criminal Justice, 38*(4), 796–806.

Irwin, J., & Owen, B. (2005). Harm and the contemporary prison. In. A. Liebling & S. Maruna (Eds.), *The Effects of Imprisonment* (pp. 94–117). Willan Publishing.

James, E. (2013, February 25). The Norwegian prison where inmates are treated like people. *The Guardian*. www.theguardian.com/society/2013/feb/25/norwegian-prison-inmates-treated-like-people. Last accessed on 19 April 2021.

Johnsen, B., & Granheim, P. K. (2012). Prison size and the quality of life in Norwegian closed prisons in late modernity. In T. Ugelvik & J. Dullum (Eds.), *Penal exceptionalism? Nordic prison policy and practice* (pp. 199–214). Routledge.

Kaminski, D. (2010). Droits des détenus, normalisation et moindre éligibilité. *Criminologie, 43*(1), 199–226.

Kellens, G. (2000). *Punir. Pénologie & droit des sanctions pénales.* juridiques de l'Université de Liège.

Krever, M. (2016, May 24). Belgian prisoners released from 'inhumane' jails. *CNN*. http://edition.cnn.com/2016/05/24/europe/belgium-prisons/. Last accessed on 19 April 2021.

Kruttschnitt, C., & Dirkzwager, A. (2011). Are there still contrasts in tolerance? Imprisonment in the Netherlands and England 20 years later. *Punishment & Society, 13*(3), 283–306.

Lacey, N. (2008). *The prisoners' dilemma. Political economy and punishment in contemporary democracies*. Cambridge University Press.

Langford, M., Fisher, A. D., Karlsson Schaffer, J., & Pareus, F. (2017). The view from elsewhere: Scandinavian penal practices and international critique. In P. S. Smith & T. Ugelvik (Eds.), *Embraced by the welfare state? Scandinavian penal history, culture and prison practice* (Palgrave studies in prisons and penology) (pp. 451–479). Palgrave Macmillan UK.

Lappi-Seppälä, T. (2012). Explaining national differences in the use of imprisonment. In S. Snacken & E. Dumortier (Eds.), *Resisting punitiveness in Europe?: Welfare, human rights and democracy* (pp. 35–72). Routledge.

Lappi-Seppälä, T. (2014). Imprisonment and penal demands. Exploring the dimensions and drivers of systemic and attitudinal punitivity. In S. Body-Gendrot, M. Hough, K. Kerezsi, R. Lévy, & S. Snacken (Eds.), *The Routledge handbook of European criminology* (pp. 295–336). Routledge.

Laurent, O. (2014, October 13). A cold place, with no curves: Life inside Belgian prisons. *Time*. http://time.com/3597834/a-cold-place-with-no-curves-life-inside-belgian-prisons/. Last accessed on 19 April 2021.

Liebling, A., assisted by Arnold, H. (2004). *Prisons and their moral performance. A study of values, quality and prison life*. Oxford University Press.

Liebling, A. (2011). Moral performance, inhuman and degrading treatment and prison pain. *Punishment & Society, 13*(5), 530–550.

Lynch, M. (2011). Theorizing punishment: Reflections on Wacquant's punishing the poor. *Critical Sociology, 37*(2), 237–244.

Markel, D., Flanders, C., & Gray, D. (2011). Beyond experience: Getting retributive justice right. *California Law Review, 99*(2), 605–628.

Mathiesen, T. (1974). *The politics of abolition (Scandinavian studies in criminology).* Robertson.

Mathiesen, T. (2012). Scandinavian exceptionalism in penal matters. Reality or wishful thinking? In T. Ugelvik & J. Dullum (Eds.), *Penal exceptionalism? Nordic prison policy and practice* (pp. 13–37). Routledge.

Mathiesen, T. (2015). *The politics of abolition revisited*. Routledge.

McConville, S. (2012). *The use of punishment*. Routledge.

Neumann, C. B. (2012). Imprisoning the soul. In T. Ugelvik & J. Dullum (Eds.), *Penal exceptionalism? Nordic prison policy and practice* (pp. 139–155). Routledge.

Nirje, B. (1969). The normalization principle and its human management implications. In R. Kugel & W. Wolfensberger (Eds.), *Changing patterns in residential services for the mentally retarded* (pp. 179–195). President's Committee on Mental Retardation.

Nirje, B. (1980). The normalization principle. In R. J. Flynn & K. E. Nitsch (Eds.), *Normalization, social integration and community services* (pp. 31–49). University Park Press.

Nirje, B. (1985). The basis and logic of the normalization principle. *Australia and New Zealand Journal of Developmental Disabilities, 11*(2), 65–68.

Nirje, B. (1999). How I came to formulate the Normalization principle. In R. J. Flynn & R. A. Lemay (Eds.), *A quarter-century of normalization and social role valorization: Evolution and impact* (pp. 17–50). University of Ottawa Press.

O'Donnell, I. (2016). The aims of imprisonment. In Y. Jewkes, J. Bennett, & B. Crewe (Eds.), *Handbook on prisons* (2nd ed., pp. 39–54). Routledge.

Pakes, F. (2010). *Comparative criminal justice*. Willan publishing.

Pratt, J. (1998). Dangerousness, risk and technologies of power. In P. O'Malley (Ed.), *Crime and the risk society* (pp. 300–327). Ashgate.

Pratt, J. (2008a). Scandinavian exceptionalism in an era of penal excess, Part I: The nature and roots of Scandinavian exceptionalism. *The British Journal of Criminology, 48*(2), 119–137.

Pratt, J. (2008b). Scandinavian exceptionalism in an era of penal excess, Part II: Does Scandinavian exceptionalism have a future? *The British Journal of Criminology, 48*(3), 275–292.

Pratt, J., Brown, D., Brown, M., Hallsworth, S., & Morrison, W. (Eds.). (2005). *The new punitiveness. Trends, theories, perspectives*. Willan Publishing.

Pratt, J., & Eriksson, A. (2012). In defence of Scandinavian exceptionalism. In T. Ugelvik & J. Dullum (Eds.), *Penal exceptionalism? Nordic prison policy and practice* (pp. 235–260). Routledge.

Pratt, J., & Eriksson, A. (2013). *Contrasts in punishment. An explanation of anglophone excess and nordic exceptionalism*. Routledge.

Prison Act Commission. (2001). Eindverslag van de commissie 'basiswet gevangeniswezen en rechtspositie van gedetineerden'. *Verslag namens de commissie voor de Justitie uitgebracht door de heren Vincent Decroly en Tony Van Parys, Parl.St. Kamer, 2000–2001*(1076), 001.

Rocheleau, A. M. (2013). An empirical exploration of the 'Pains of imprisonment' and the level of prison misconduct and violence. *Criminal Justice Review, 38*(3), 354–374.

Scholfield, P. (2016, May 21). Belgian prison chaos prompts fears of national malaise. *BBC News*. www.bbc.com/news/world-europe-36348389. Last accessed on 19 April 2021.

Sexton, L. (2015). Penal subjectivities: Developing a theoretical framework for penal consciousness. *Punishment & Society, 17*(1), 114–136.

Shammas, V. L. (2014). The pains of freedom: Assessing the ambiguity of Scandinavian penal exceptionalism on Norway's Prison Island. *Punishment & Society, 16*(1), 104–123.

Shammas, V. L. (2016). The rise of a more punitive state: On the attenuation of Norwegian penal exceptionalism in an era of welfare state transformation. *Critical Criminology, 24*(1), 57–74.

Shea, E. (2005). Les paradoxes de la normalisation du travail pénitentiaire en France et en Allemagne. *Déviance Et Société, 29*(3), 349–365.

Smaers, G. (2005). De basiswet in het licht van de internationale mensenrechten. In F. Verbruggen, R. Verstraeten, D. Van Daele, & B. Spriet (Eds.), *Strafrecht als roeping, Liber amicorum Lieven Dupont* (pp. 521–537). Universitaire Pers Leuven.

Smith, P. S. (2012). Imprisonment and internet-access. Human rights, the principle of normalization and the question of prisoners access to digital communications technology. *Nordic Journal of Human Rights, 30*(4), 454–482.

Smith, P. S., & Ugelvik, T. (2017). *Embraced by the welfare state? Scandinavian penal history, culture and prison practice* (Palgrave studies in prisons and penology). Palgrave Macmillan UK.

Snacken, S. (2002). Normalisation en prison: concept et défis. In O. De Schutter & D. Kaminski (Eds.), *L'institution du droit pénitentiaire. Enjeux de la reconnaissance de droits aux détenus* (pp. 133–152). Librairie Générale de Droit et de Jurisprudence et Bruylant.

Snacken, S. (2006). A reductionist penal policy and European human rights standards. *European Journal on Criminal Policy and Research, 12*(2), 143–164.

Snacken, S. (2010). Resisting punitiveness in Europe? *Theoretical Criminology, 14*, 273–292.

Snacken, S., & Dumortier, E. (Eds.). (2012). *Resisting punitiveness in Europe?: Welfare, human rights and democracy.* Routledge.

Sterbenz, C. (2014, December 11). Why Norway's prison system is so successful. *Business Insider*. http://uk.businessinsider.com/why-norways-prison-system-is-so-successful-2014-12?r=US&IR=T. Last accessed on 19 April 2021.

Sykes, G. (2007). *The society of captives: A study of a maximum security prison* (First Princeton classic ed., Princeton classic editions). Princeton University Press.

Ugelvik, T. (2012). The dark side of a culture of equality: Reimagining communities in a Norwegian remand prison. In T. Ugelvik & J. Dullum (Eds.), *Penal exceptionalism? Nordic prison policy and practice* (pp. 121–138). Routledge.

Ugelvik, T., & Dullum, J. (Eds.). (2012). *Penal exceptionalism?* Routledge.

Ugelvik, T. (2013). Book review: John Pratt and Anna Eriksson, contrasts in punishment: An explanation of anglophone excess and nordic exceptionalism. *Theoretical Criminology, 17*(4), 580–582.

Ugelvik, T. (2014). *Power and resistance in prison: Doing time, doing freedom* (Palgrave studies in prisons and penology). Palgrave Macmillan.

Ugelvik, T. (2016). Prisons as welfare institutions? Punishment and the nordic model. In Y. Jewkes, J. Bennett & B. Crewe (Eds.), *Handbook on prisons* (second edition) (pp.388–402). Routledge.

van Ginneken, E. F. J. C., & Hayes, D. (2017). 'Just' punishment? Offenders' views on the meaning and severity of punishment. *Criminology & Criminal Justice, 17*(1), 62–78.

van Zyl Smit, D., & Snacken, S. (2009). *Principles of European prison law and policy. Penology and human rights.* Oxford University Press.

Walgrave, S., & Varone, F. (2008). Punctuated equilibrium and agenda-setting: Bringing parties back in: Policy change after the Dutroux crisis in

Belgium. *Governance: An International Journal of Policy, Administration, and Institutions, 21*(3), 365–395.

Whitehead, S. (1992). The social origins of normalisation. In H. Brown & H. Smith (Eds.), *Normalisation. A reader for the nineties* (pp. 47–59). Routledge.

Wolfensberger, W. (1972). *The principle of normalization in human services.* National Institute on Mental Retardation.

Wolfensberger, W. (2011a). Social role valorization: A proposed new term for the principle of normalization. *Intellectual and Developmental Disabilities, 49*(6), 435–440.

Wolfensberger, W. (2011b). Social role valorization and or versus, "empowerment." *Intellectual and Developmental Disabilities, 49*(6), 469–476.

2

Normal, Normality and Normalization: Towards a Context-Based Analysis

This research starts from the premise that the abstract principle of normalization can be interpreted and implemented in many different ways, despite its general objective to reduce the differences between the living conditions inside and those outside prison. For example, both the provision of accessible health care and the abolition of free health care in prison can be justified by the pursuit of *normal* or more humane living conditions. These two different, and potentially conflicting, implementations result from different reasonings. Having to pay a normal price can prevent prisoners from losing touch with the prices charged outside prison. At the same time, however, free health care is arguably more 'normal' as long as prisoners' income is not normalized. This shows that the seemingly straightforward principle of normalization becomes increasingly challenging when thinking about its concrete 'translation' into prison legislation or prison practice.

The aim of this book is to understand how normalization *is* reflected in Belgian and Norwegian prison policy, legislation and practice, and not how it *should* be interpreted and implemented. Instead of proposing a pre-defined notion of normalization, this chapter will introduce three components of any normalization process, i.e. its aims, focus areas and

H. De Vos, *Beyond Scandinavian Exceptionalism*, Palgrave Studies in Prisons and Penology, https://doi.org/10.1007/978-3-031-28635-3_2

results, which together can be used as a framework to better understand the different interpretations of normalization in different contexts. It is argued here that all three components need to be made explicit for one context, before they can be meaningfully compared *between* various contexts. All the more because we cannot fully understand one component without understanding the other two, and understanding one of them will increase our understanding of the other. After having introduced these three components of the normalization process, this chapter will continue with a detailed description of the four prisons that provide the context for this research. Together, the two parts of this chapter will provide the foundation for the subsequent chapters.

2.1 Three Components of the Normalization process: Aims, Focus areas and Results

2.1.1 Aims of the Normalization Process: Intrinsic versus Instrumental

The first component of the normalization process discussed here is the aim (or aims) of normalization and its relationship with the aims of imprisonment. Depending on the understanding of this relationship, normalization can be approached in two different ways: intrinsically and instrumentally. Whereas advocates of the intrinsic approach argue that the normalization of prison conditions is a valuable objective in itself, advocates of the instrumental approach consider normalization as a means to another end, such as reintegration, rehabilitation, recidivism reduction or responsibilization. Accordingly, the role of normalization will differ significantly.

The intrinsic approach to normalization is not based on empiricism but on normative beliefs. Its justification lies in human dignity and its link with human rights. Constantijn Kelk (2008), Dan Kaminski (2010) and Hans Jørgen Engbo (2017) strongly advocate this intrinsic approach. They do not only consider the normalization of prison conditions a valuable objective in itself, but also argue that prisoners' rights lose their value if they are used for any additional purpose. Kelk's reasoning is captured in his concept of *full legal citizenship*. In his view, prisoners are to be respected as full-fledged citizens and therefore able to actively participate in the execution of punishment, as part of the wider judicial system:

> The essence of full legal citizenship is participating in the legal system, legal principles, and legal values, and making these legally valid in the form of discussion [...] consisting of demand and dissent, the right of both parties to be heard, and to appeal to the belief in fairness of arguments. (Kelk, 2008: 15, my translation)

Being able to participate then requires a legal status that consists of three elements: (1) a material legal status resulting from clear prison rules, (2) a procedural legal status which is given shape by a contradictory procedure with due respect for legal guarantees and (3) adequate and sufficient information about one's material and procedural legal status (Kelk, 2008: 36). Along the same lines, Kaminski argues that the use of normalization as a guiding principle for prison policy implies that prisoners' rights are to be protected '*parce qu'ils ont en eux-même une valeur*' (Kaminski, 2010: 208–209). Prisoners should be able to use their rights as '*forces d'opposition*', which becomes impossible when these rights are used for another purpose such as rehabilitation (Kaminski, 2010: 203–204). In his view, the latter is particularly problematic when this other purpose is not made explicit (Kaminski, 2010: 202). Finally, an equally strong plea for the intrinsic approach to normalization is articulated by Engbo (2017: 351):

> The principle of normalisation is not built on speculative considerations of utility. Normalisation is an essential element of a democratically based prison regime which is opposed to totalitarian prison regimes in which inmates only have the rights and conditions of life—the 'benefits'—that the powerful prison management opts to bestow on them.

According to Engbo (2017: 342), this also means that normalization is valuable without any evidence of its effectiveness because it is '*not intended to "work"*'. While acknowledging that normalization can indeed positively impact the reintegration of prisoners and prevent some of the negative effects of detention, he underlines that these effects should merely be considered side effects of normalization (Engbo, 2017).

The instrumental approach, on the other hand, links the aims of normalization to the aims of imprisonment. Following this approach, normalization is aimed at directly or indirectly influencing prisoners' behaviour. This is the case when, for example, prison life is being normalized *with the view of* facilitating the transition from prison to freedom; or when, for example, '[t]*he organisation and methods of work in the institutions [...] resemble as closely as possible those of similar work in the community in order to prepare prisoners for the conditions of normal occupational life*' (European prison rules, 2006, rule 26.7). Indeed, European and national prison policies tend to link normalization to various aims, including encouraging prisoners' responsibility, limiting the harmful effects of detention, and facilitating the rehabilitation and reintegration.

Depending on the underlying views and aims, the instrumental approach can become disciplinary to a greater or lesser degree. This is true despite clear warnings of several scholars not to confuse the human rights-based principle, which entails the normalization of the prison conditions, with the disciplinary process of normalizing the individual prisoner. Noteworthy in this context is Johannes Feest's (1999) sharp distinction between the penological principle of normalization and Michel Foucault's use of the same term, pointing out that the former '*has nothing to do with the "dispositifs de normalisation"* (Foucault, 1977: 313), *with the normalizing effect of the disciplinary techniques*' (Feest, 1999: 100). Indeed, Foucault (1977) uses the term 'normalization' to refer to the process of disciplining or 'normalizing' the individuals in prison. More specifically, in his book *Discipline and Punish* (1977: 248), he has argued that the *penitentiary* entails everything that goes beyond the pure liberty deprivation and that this involves disciplinary techniques that are intended to 'normalize' the persons subject to these techniques. In line with Feest's reasoning, also Snacken (2002) and Hammerlin (2008) have both pointed out the distinction between normalizing the prisoner and normalizing the prison conditions. Although they acknowledge that these two processes can be found in the prison practice, in their view, it is only the former that is associated with disciplining prisoners in order for them to become law-abiding citizens after having served their sentence (Hammerlin, 2008; Snacken, 2002).

Nevertheless, the distinction between these disciplinary and rights-based processes becomes increasingly blurred when the normalization of the prison conditions is also intended to facilitate the reintegration of prisoners, ideally as law-abiding citizens. The fact that prisoners are (or should be) given the opportunity to work, to exercise, to study and to participate in therapy is not only the result of a human rights-based approach but also an implicit expression of what society, or the prison system, expects of its citizens and its prisoners. For this reason, Engbo (2017) has criticized the instrumental interpretations of the Nordic prison administrations, which he considers '*forced social education*' and '*educational paternalism*'. He uses the example of self-catering to illustrate his point. While self-catering is generally considered a good example of normalization from a policy perspective, not all prisoners experience this as a normal practice:

> I have met several inmates to whom it would be normal to satisfy their hunger at a hot dog stand or a takeaway. Other inmates have spent a considerable part of their lives at institutions, and to them institution food service is normal. [...] I also recall a first-time offender aged 66 convicted of bank robberies. He had been married for 40 years and had never boiled an egg. What was normal to him was to sit down at the table and eat the meal prepared by his wife. (Engbo, 2017: 344)

Engbo's criticism is built on an intrinsic approach to normalization that also takes into account prisoners' subjective experiences of normality. From an instrumental perspective, however, it can of course still be argued that the reintegration is likely to be more successful when prisoners know how to make themselves a meal, regardless of whether the individual prisoner considers this a normal aspect of life. The point being made here is that such underlying views must be made explicit for a good understanding of the role of normalization in a given context.

Another example that shows the importance of making the underlying aims explicit, is linked to the aim of responsibilization. Responsibilization can be understood as giving prisoners the opportunities and tools to take responsibility for their own lives. However, when normalization is implicitly aimed at fostering prisoners' responsibility, it can cause side effects linked to risk management, *soft power* and *less eligibility* (Bosworth, 2007; Crewe, 2011; Kaminski, 2010). This is explained by Bosworth (2007), for instance, in the context of her analysis of the booklets that prisoners receive on their arrival in US federal prisons. Based on this analysis, she points out the rhetorical shift from rehabilitation and care, in the booklets that were used fifty or sixty years ago, towards risk and accountability, in the contemporary booklets. The contemporary rhetoric addresses prisoners as responsible '*proto-customers*' (Bosworth, 2007: 72), whose rational choices and actions are expected to lead to self-improvement. Bosworth problematizes the normalization of this official discourse, i.e. bringing it in line with the language used by other institutions and corporations, because it seems to ignore the fact that prisoners are deprived of their liberty and that they are constantly reminded of the disciplinary sanctions that will be applied when this '*language of "responsibilization" fails*' (Bosworth, 2007: 74).

> Each articulation of the power of the prison paradoxically undermines and simultaneously reinforces the broader view presented by these documents that prisoners act rationally, make their own choices and are thus fully responsible for their actions. The threat of sanctions makes it all the more necessary for inmates to monitor their behaviour while simultaneously reminding them that they are constantly under review. (Bosworth, 2007: 76)

Also outside prison, citizens are increasingly expected to actively take responsibilities, and their rights are more strongly connected to duties (Vander Laenen et al., 2012: 18). For instance, unemployment benefits have been made dependent on the active search for work and it has been suggested to make the income from unemployment benefits consistently lower than the lowest income from work (Dufaux, 2010; Feest, 1999; Kaminski, 2010: 218). This argument is known as the principle of less eligibility. In the prison context, this less eligibility logic entails that living conditions in prison should be worse than those of the poorest people living outside prison, in order for the prison to have a deterrent effect (Bentham, cited in Fijnaut, 2014: 75; Kaminski, 2010; Rusche & Kirchheimer, 1939; Shea, 2005). The principles of less eligibility and normalization are therefore traditionally considered opposites. However, since the principle of less eligibility is gaining importance outside prison, it could be introduced into prisons through a consistent implementation of the normalization principle (Kaminski, 2010). This is especially true when the normalization process is aimed at fostering prisoners' responsibility.

2.1.2 Focus areas of the Normalization process: Narrowly Focused versus Holistic

The second component are the aspects of prison life on which the normalization process is focused, or the '*focus areas of normalization*', to use Engbo's words. Engbo (2017) distinguishes three categories of '*focus areas*': conditions and framework for prison life, framework for personal life and personal development and civil rights. Since prison life is significantly impacted by factors beyond the prison walls, the scope of the normalization process is not limited to life *inside* prison, but can also include prison leave and early release opportunities, distance between prison and prisoners' home communities, the length of prison sentences and the use of imprisonment as last resort (rule 17.1 of the European prison rules of 2006; Downes, 1992: 201, cited in Kruttschnitt & Dirkzwager, 2011: 289; King & Morgan, 1980: 38–39; Snacken, 2002: 152; Smith, 2012; van Zyl Smit & Snacken, 2009). The 'focus areas' of normalization found in policy and legislative documents usually take the form of prisoners' rights. The European Prison Rules of 1987 determine, for instance, that prisoners should be given food at *normal* times (rule 25.1) and enabled to do useful work in conditions that resemble as closely as possible to those in society so that they have *normal* working days (rule 71.3 and 72.1). Other examples of aspects that are generally expected to be normalized are social contact opportunities (see e.g. rule 24.4 EPR 2006), accommodation, health care and educational programmes (see e.g. King & Morgan, 1980: 38–39). It should be noted, however, that some aspects are not translatable into prisoners' rights but equally or even more fundamental to the experience of prison life (see e.g. Liebling, 2004).

Looking beyond a purely rights-based approach, Snacken (2002) distinguishes between an individual and a collective level of normalization (see also van Zyl Smit & Snacken, 2009: 104). The latter is described as '*offering services inside prison that are as similar as possible to those offered in outside society, especially with regard to the nature and quality of these services*' (van Zyl Smit & Snacken, 2009: 105), and can therefore be interpreted as a common policy and rights-based approach to normalization. Normalization at an individual level, on the other hand, promotes the recognition of the various social roles of each individual prisoner. This is expected to reduce the harmful effects caused by the *role-dispossessing* process described by Goffman (1961) (Snacken, 2002).

> Normalization at the individual level thus aims to develop prison regimes that recognize to as great an extent as possible these other social roles of the prisoner. Recognizing and effectively implementing the exercise of prisoners' fundamental human rights, both material and procedural, are important means of doing so. (van Zyl Smit & Snacken, 2009: 104)

By referring in the first place to the legal position of prisoners as a means to recognize their various social roles, however, this understanding of 'normalization at the individual level' risks again to be narrowed down to the aspects that are translatable into prisoners' rights.

Indeed, identifying specific aspects on which the normalization process should focus, unavoidably raises the risk of normalizing only part of the prison reality, thereby failing to effectively address the harmful effects of the prison experience as a whole, or to actually contribute to any other purpose. Prison research shows that the various aspects of the prison reality significantly affect each other. Different material conditions have been linked to differences in social atmosphere and in security and safety (Goffman, 1961; Hancock & Jewkes, 2011; Knight, 2016, Morris & Worral, 2014; Sykes, 1958/2007; Wener, 2012). Poor physical prison conditions (noise, clutter, dilapidation and lack of privacy) were found to correspond to significantly higher rates of serious violence

(Bierie, 2012). Prisoners housed in a prison with panoptic design, in older units, and in units with more double cells assessed their relationship with prison staff less positively (Beijersbergen et al., 2016). Similarly, Molleman and van Ginneken (2015) found cell sharing associated with lower perceived prison quality, partially explained by a reduction in perceived quality of the prisoner-prison staff relationship. Thus, the prison experience is to be understood as '*a more general or gestalt experience rather than the unique experience of every dimension of prison life by prisoners*' (Johnsen & Granheim, 2012: 205).

This also means that the normalization of the above-mentioned aspects needs to be understood in relation to their context and to the way in which and the extent to which this context is normalized, because this as a whole will shape the *gestalt experience* of prison life. Normalization is then conceived not just as the mere *sum* of normalizing various prison dimensions, but also as the *interplay* of these dimensions. Following the same line of thinking, any study of the normalization that focuses on a priori defined aspects of prison life risks failing to understand the actual nature and degree of normalization, even though previous research has identified the aspects of prison life that 'matter most' (Liebling,) as well as those that are experienced as most painful (e.g. Rocheleau, 2013). Moreover, understanding the nature and degree of normalization requires not only insight into the aspects that are included in the normalization process, but also into those that have been excluded, be it intentionally or unintentionally, for practical or for ideological reasons. This is the reason why this research does not specify the aspects that should be covered in advance in a limitative way, but rather pursues an open and holistic approach of the prison conditions.

The next chapters present this holistic approach as a combination of four broadly defined dimensions of prison life: material environment (Chapter 4), security (Chapter 5), social environment (Chapter 6) and the use of time (Chapter 7). Of course, the focus on four dimensions in separate chapters could be considered as the restriction of a truly holistic view, understating their interdependence and overlap, but this choice was made for the sake of clarity. It is also fair to acknowledge that the scope of this holistic approach is limited to the prison conditions, and the way in which and the extent to which they have been normalized, and does not include the impact of normalization on the prison experience. Of course, as the normalization process is reflected in the prison conditions, it does have an *indirect* effect on prisoners', prison staff's and visitors' experiences, behaviour and well-being. For instance, a context can promote opportunities to keep in touch with family and friends, but it can only *indirectly* impact the quality and the experiences of these relationships. Therefore, prisoners' and prison staff's experiences have an *indirect* relevance for this research insofar as they contribute to a better understanding of the prison conditions and their normalization. Prisoners' complaints about the lack of privacy or untasty food are *in themselves* no indicators of the degree of normalization. All of this must be understood in the light of the normalization process as reducing the differences between life inside and outside, and thus creating a living context that resembles the context outside prison, and not an ideal context, in which everyone is perfectly happy. This brings us to the intended and actual result of the normalization process.

2.1.3 Results of the Normalization process: Intended Versus Actual

The third and last component of the normalization process consists of the intended or desired result and the result in practice. The intended result refers to the chosen reference point in society that represents the 'normal counterpart' of a given aspect of prison life. The selection of these reference points unavoidably entails a subjective process and will differ according to the societal and penological views of policymakers. Part of these underlying views can already be derived from the reluctance to introduce certain aspects of 'normal life' into prison. The implementation of the normalization principle is not intended to introduce violence, unemployment or drugs, even though many prisoners have been facing these living conditions outside prison (see also Dufaux, 2010). To some degree, this view has been made explicit by the European Prison Rules of 2006, which specify that the normalization principle aims at making prison life as similar as possible to '*the positive aspects of life in the community*'. Building on the commentary on these prison rules, Engbo (2017:

335) argues that the words 'positive aspects' refer to article 3 of the European Convention of Human Rights, and are '*intended to ensure that normalisation does not lead to "inhumane prison conditions"*'. Yet, even with this minimum standard, different societal and penological views will lead to different understandings and implementations of the normalization principle.

Moreover, the intention to normalize certain aspects of prison life does not necessarily imply a desire to make these aspects completely similar to the chosen reference point in the outside world. This is often indicated by wordings such as 'to the extent possible', 'as far as resources allow',[1] or 'consistent with the constraints of secure custody'. By defining normalization as '*as far as resources allow, and consistent with the constraints of secure custody, the same general standards which govern the life of offenders in the community should be held to apply to offenders in prison*', King and Morgan (1980: 37) limit the intended result in two ways. First, by accepting the constraints due to security considerations and limited resources, and second, by defining the intended result of normalization as '*the life of offenders in the community*'. Although this seems to reflect a very narrow interpretation of normalization, King and Morgan (1980: 129) explain further in their book that

> when offenders are sentenced to imprisonment, however, they do not cease to be citizens. Basic services within prison should, whenever possible, be similar to those considered necessary or desirable in the community because prisoners, despite their temporary loss of liberty, continue to be members of the community.

Two considerations are crucial to the understanding of the intended result. The first consideration is that life in prison will always differ from life in society for at least two reasons: on the one hand, penological views, institutional characteristics and security considerations will continue to impact life in prison and, on the other hand, freedom, or the idea of being free, is a fundamental aspect of life in society. The restricted use of internet in prison is an example of how the results of the normalization

[1] However, the fourth rule of the European Prison Rules of 2006, states that '*Prison conditions that infringe prisoners' human rights are not justified by lack of resources*'.

process are heavily restricted in policy and in practice by institutional and security concerns (see for more detail Smith, 2012; Engbo, 2017). Although certain limitations to this virtual freedom could be justifiable for certain prisoners (e.g. restricted access to certain websites or monitoring online activities in order to prevent the continuation of criminal acts), these limitations can become so disturbing that they undermine the initial normalizing merit.

The second consideration is that the reference point for 'normal' life in society is inevitably determined from a particular normative perspective. This means that the intended result of normalization will only be considered 'normal' from this particular perspective. In this process, the normative and cultural considerations of policymakers will usually outweigh the customs and habits of individual prisoners. Moreover, the term 'normal' is ambiguous in itself, and can for example be understood as 'as usual' (referring to a prisoner's personal habits before incarceration), 'like an "average" citizen', or 'like the ideal norm in society'. In this respect, van Zyl Smit and Snacken (2009: 105) argue for taking social equality as general reference point for normalization, implying that the intended result should ensure an average standard of living for each prisoner rather than maintain or augment inequalities between prisoners.

> Collective normalization does not mean that negative aspects of life in the community, such as social inequality or the inadequacy of the provision of food or medical care, should also be a feature of life inside the prison... Normalization then rather justifies guaranteeing all prisoners a good 'average' standard of living rather than accepting extreme differences between prisoners. (van Zyl Smit & Snacken, 2009: 105)

This reasoning shows the normative character of determining the intended results of normalization. While it sounds justifiable to put social equality forward as the intended result, Engbo (2017) is convinced of the opposite. He refutes the argument that the pursuit of social equality is covered by the idea of 'positive aspects of life in community'. As already mentioned, in his opinion the words 'positive aspects' should be interpreted much more narrowly, in the sense of avoiding inhumanity. In support of his argument, he refers to the debate about prisoners being obliged to wear the prison uniform versus being allowed to wear their own clothes. In his view, only the latter reflects 'normalized' living conditions, even though it creates visual differences between prisoners wearing brand-name clothing and those wearing second-hand clothing. He therefore argues that artificially imposing social equality in prison is at odds with normalization:

> Unless certain adjustments of the natural social inequality among inmates can be justified for security reasons, a forced order of social equality deviating from the social order in the free society would involve a violation of the requirement of normality. (Engbo, 2017: 345)

More essentially, Engbo's (2017: 342) criticism is targeted at the very idea that the prison system would determine the 'intended result' of normalization in detail, since '*the authorities cannot decide what the individual inmate is to consider normal (or useful)*'. Instead of enforcing a '*state-authorised normality*', prison authorities should '*facilitate the individual inmate's endeavours to achieve (his or her own) normality while in prison*' (Engbo, 2017: 342). This would mean that the intended result of normalization is determined by each prisoner individually. Whether or not we agree with Engbo, his point does lay bare a potential tension: when the intended result imposes an essentially subjective normality, not necessarily shared by the one experiencing this result, it may have unintended side effects in practice, in addition to security restrictions or practical limitations. For this reason, a good understanding of the normalization process requires insight into both the intended results (the chosen reference point as well as the desired or accepted limitations) and the actual results in practice.

As explained above, the aim of this research is to grasp how normalization *is* reflected in prison policy and practice, and not how it *should* be interpreted and implemented. In practice, entering the four prisons showed in the first place how different living conditions inside are to those outside. That is why the next section will describe each of the four prisons in detail and explain how they have been studied, thus providing the context for the analysis in the next chapters.

2.2 From Theory to Practice: Two Countries and Four Prisons

2.2.1 A Collective Case study

With the aim of gaining an in-depth understanding of the normalization principle, two Belgian and two Norwegian prisons, four cases, were studied through a combination of a document analysis, participant observation and semi-structured interviews. Both in Belgium and in Norway, an open and a closed prison were selected: the prisons of Hoogstraten (open prison in Belgium), Leuven (closed prison in Belgium), Leira (open prison in Norway) and Nermarka (closed prison in Norway). The choice for prisons with different security levels was based on the hypothesis that the normalization principle can be implemented more extensively in a prison with a lower security level. However, none of these prisons can be considered representative of *the* Belgian or *the* Norwegian prisons, or of *the* open or *the* closed prisons, which was never the intention anyway. This collective case study was designed to contribute to a deeper understanding of normalization, i.e. '*analytic generalization*' (Yin, 2003: 10), and not to result in general statements about a particular type of prison.

The comparison of these four cases was conducted at two levels: first, the policy and legislative documents were compared at the level of the countries, and second, the prison practice was compared at the level of the prisons. The starting point for both countries was the prison law and the regulations directly linked to this law. This means for Belgium, the Prison Act of 12 January 2005, the Act of 17 May 2006 regarding the *Extra Muros* Legal Status of Convicted Prisoners and the Rights of Victims in the Context of the Execution of the Prison Sentence, and the relevant Royal Decrees; and for Norway, the Act on the Execution of Sentences of 18 May 2001, the Regulations relating to the Execution of Sentences, and the Guidelines concerning the Act on the Execution of Sentences and the Regulations. The views underlying the legal understanding of normalization are derived from the final report of the Belgian Prison Act Commission of 2001 and the Norwegian White Paper no. 37 (2007–2008) 'Punishment that works—less crime—safer society'. The analysis also includes the relevant legislation regarding social services in prison. For the Belgian context, and more specifically for the Flemish context,[2] this is the Flemish Decree of 8 March 2013 concerning the Organisation of Social Assistance and Services for Detainees and the related policy documents, and for Norway, this includes the Health Act, the Education Act and the Social Services Act. Excerpts from these legislative documents that are used as illustrations in the following chapters, have been translated from Dutch or Norwegian to English.

Documents on which the analysis is based	English translation
Basiswet van 12 januari 2005 betreffende het gevangeniswezen en de rechtspositie van de gedetineerden, *BS* 1 februari 2005	Belgian Prison Act of 12 January 2005
Wet van 17 mei 2006 betreffende de externe rechtspositie van de veroordeelden tot een vrijheidsstraf en de aan het slachtoffer toegekende rechten in het raam van de strafuitvoeringsmodaliteiten, *BS* 15 juni 2006	Belgian Act of 17 May 2006 regarding the 'Extra Muros' Legal Status of Convicted Prisoners and the Rights of Victims in the Context of the Execution of the Prison Sentence
Eindverslag van de commissie 'basiswet gevangeniswezen en rechtspositie van gedetineerden', Verslag namens de commissie voor de Justitie uitgebracht door de heren Vincent Decroly en Tony Van Parys, *Parl.St.* Kamer, 2000–2001, 1076/001	Final report of the Prison Act Commission of 2001
Decreet van 8 maart 2013 betreffende de organisatie van hulp- en dienstverlening aan gedetineerden, *BS* 11 april 2013	Flemish Decree of 8 March 2013 concerning the Organisation of Social Assistance and Services for Detainees
Strategisch Plan Hulp- en Dienstverlening aan gedetineerden van 2000	Flemish Strategic Plan concerning Social Assistance and Services for Detainees
Strategisch Plan Hulp- en Dienstverlening aan gedetineerden, 2015–2020	Flemish Strategic Plan concerning Social Assistance and Services for Detainees, 2015–2020

(continued)

[2] The social assistance and services for detainees do not fall within the remit of the federal government but of the Communities. For practical reasons, only the Flemish Community will be considered, hence excluding the French Community and the German-speaking Community from this analysis.

(continued)

Documents on which the analysis is based	English translation
Samenwerkingsakkoord van 8 juli 2014 tussen de Federale Staat en de Vlaamse Gemeenschap en het Vlaams Gewest inzake de hulp- en dienstverlening aan gedetineerden	Cooperation Agreement of 8 July 2014 between the Federal State and the Flemish Community and the Flemish Region regarding Social Assistance and Services for Detainees
Lov om gjennomføring av straff mv. av 18. mai 2001 (Straffegjennomføringsloven)	Norwegian Act on the Execution of Sentences of 18 May 2001
Forskrift om straffegjennomføring	Regulations relating to the Execution of Sentences
Retningslinjer til lov om gjennomføring av straff mv (straffegjennomføringsloven) og til forskrift til loven	Guidelines concerning the Act on the Execution of Sentences and the Regulations
Stortingsmelding nr. 37 (2007–2008) Straff som virker—mindre kriminalitet—tryggere samfunn St. meld. no. 37 (2007–2008)	White Paper no. 37 (2007–2008) Punishment that works—less crime—safer society
Innstilling nr. 72 (2004–2005) til Odelstinget fra justiskomiteen om lov om straff (straffeloven) Innst. O. no. 72 (2004–2005	Recommendation no. 72 (2004–2005) by the justice committee to the Parliament about the criminal law
Odelstingsproposisjon nr. 5 (2000–2001). Om lov om gjennomføring av straff mv. (straffegjennomføringsloven) Ot. prp. no. 5 (2000–2001)	Bill no. 5 (2000–2001). On the Act on the Execution of Sentences
Lov om kommunale helse- og omsorgstjenester m.m. (helse- og omsorgstjenesteloven) av 24. juni 2011	Health Act of 24 June 2011
Lov om grunnskolen og den vidaregåande opplæringa (opplæringslova) av 17. juli 1998	Education Act of 17 July 1998
Lov om sosiale tjenester i arbeids- og velferdsforvaltningen (sosialtjenesteloven) av 8. desember 2009	Social Services Act of 8 December 2009

The prison practice was studied through participant observation and semi-structured interviews. The observations consisted of 'being present' in each of the four prisons for eight months in total, which meant hanging around on the landings, making observations, and seizing every opportunity for informal conversations with prisoners and staff, while also participating as much as possible in daily activities (see also Gobo, 2008). The nature and the level of participation differed, as well as the contact opportunities with prisoners and with staff, the amount, content and depth of informal conversations and the number and types of activities in which I was allowed to participate. In this regard, Spradly (2016: 58) distinguishes five types of participant observation, ranging from no involvement to high involvement: nonparticipation, passive, moderate, active and complete participation. Although the aim in the four prisons was to participate as much as possible (albeit very cautiously in the first prison, so as not to interrupt the normal course of events), the types of participant observation ranged from 'moderate' in the prisons of Hoogstraten and Leuven to 'active' in the prison of Leira, and something in between the two in Nermarka prison. These differences were mainly due to the regime and the freedom of movement inside the prison.

During the observations, also twenty-five prisoners were interviewed in a semi-structured way. These interviews were more formal and more private than most daily conversations, and were aimed at triangulating the data from the observations. The interviews lasted between twenty minutes and two hours, and all but one were recorded and transcribed verbatim. The interviews that were not conducted in English were also translated. In Leira prison, the many opportunities for spontaneous and more or less private conversations during work or leisure activities did result in informal conversations that were more personal and in-depth than the formal interviews, which thus became redundant. For similar reasons, I did not conduct formal interviews with staff members because there were many opportunities in each prison to have individual conversations with staff members outside the 'formal setting' of an interview. In all four prisons, prisoners gave their informed consent before the start of the interviews. While some prisoners declared not to care about confidentiality, all names used in this work are pseudonyms to protect their privacy. Only one prisoner was very much concerned about his privacy and expressed his objection to the recording of the interview. Before the start of the research, the Social and Societal Ethics Committee of KU Leuven and the Belgian Commission for the Protection of Privacy were informed about ethical choices in this research.

2.2.2 Four Prisons

Entering each of the four prisons with the broadest possible view of normalization in all its possible interpretations, I wanted to find out precisely which interpretations or applications would emerge in practice. This also meant that I did not limit myself to any particular aspect, e.g. the normalization of architecture or the normalization of social relations in prison, which research nevertheless suggests would be important factors, but also looked at the influence that the material context had on that atmosphere; how that atmosphere was created; how the security measures and the attitude of the staff affected the atmosphere. I wondered how far the normalization process could reach. What are the limits? How are these boundaries perceived? Are the boundaries more of practical or principled nature? With that open mind, I wanted to understand how normalization is reflected in the policies and in the practices of the four prisons. In what follows, the four cases are introduced in detail with two aims: first, to provide the context of this research and the background against which the analysis in the following chapters is to be understood, and second, to illustrate how my role as participant-observer differed in each prison, depending on the material conditions, security arrangements and social climate in the prison. Since these influencing factors are all related to the normalization of prison life, the degree and nature of normalization was not only the focus of the observations but also affected them. It should be noted that the detailed descriptions presented here and further in this book reflect the prison practices as they were observed between 2014 and 2016, and may well have changed since then. The descriptions are only meant to illustrate and support the analysis of the normalization process, and not to make claims about a particular prison.

Hoogstraten

Hoogstraten prison is an open prison, situated in the north of Belgium, a few kilometres from the Dutch border. It is one of the four open prisons in Belgium, and one of the two in the Dutch-speaking part of the country. The prison accommodates more or less 170 convicted male prisoners, making it a fairly small prison by Belgian standards. As indicated by its official name, the *Penitentiary School Centre* of Hoogstraten provides an extensive range of educational and work programmes. The regime is officially referred to as 'open communal regime', which implies that prisoners are spending a great deal of time in association. Because of the particular characteristics in terms of openness and wide range of programmes, this prison is '*only suitable for prisoners that do not abuse the open character of the prison*' (website of Hoogstraten prison). This means that prisoners are selected on the basis of their progression towards release, their knowledge of the Dutch language and their behaviour in prison.

It was on 25 September 2014 that I entered a prison for the first time, at least for longer than a two-hour 'guided tour'. The weather was nice and I was pleasantly surprised by the peaceful silence upon my arrival at the prison, aside from the chatter of some ducks. I walked down the entranceway towards the iron gate. Two prison officers were monitoring the access to the prison, meaning that they checked every person's identity and entrance authorization before opening the gate. After having exchanged my identity card for a piece of paper with my name and photo, one of the prison officers came out of the gatehouse to open the gate manually, laughing and asking in a friendly tone of voice: '*first time, right?*'—apparently that was obvious. At the same time, I heard the other prison officer making a phone call, saying '*that girl is here*'. I walked down the cobblestoned path towards the bridge that led to the gate of an ancient castle. This castle can be traced back to the ninth century and has been a 'penitentiary school centre' since 1931 (according to the website of Hoogstraten prison). The castle is still protected heritage, which makes it difficult or even impossible to renovate certain parts of the building or, for example, to build bars in front of the windows. This also means that all doors and gates are still opened manually. I knocked loudly on the castle's wooden gate, which was opened by the prisoner whose job it was to open and close this gate.

In addition to the 125 individual cells, several services and workplaces are located within the castle. Entering through the wooden gate, the prison's registry (prisoners' administration) is located on the left-hand side, as well as the Catholic chapel, the kitchen and the bakery, in which prisoners are employed. Still on the ground floor, one also finds the showers, the visitors' room, the cinema room (also used for other activities), the gym and a large room with a television, telephones and a pool table. The door on the right-hand side leads to the offices of the prison governors, the prison administration, social workers and psychologists, on the first floor. In addition, there is a library, which is linked to the municipal library of the city of Turnhout, a classroom and a Protestant chapel, also used as meeting room. The castle's courtyard is quite large, and the grass and the flowers create the impression of a garden with basketball and volleyball courts. The cells are grouped together in sections B (B1 and B2) and C (C1, C2 and C3) and are located on the first and second floors, at both sides of the round corridors of the castle. This means that the cells differ in size and that it is impossible to oversee the entire corridor at once. In addition, several prison officers' offices are located in these sections, as well as a conversation room, the administrative centre that coordinates the daily activities of all prisoners, the prisoners' toilets and a room in which toilet buckets are to be emptied every morning. The stone steps leading to these sections have worn out through heavy use, making them slippery.

Outside the castle, but still inside the outer fence, there are two other sections with room for around fifty prisoners: sections A and D. These sections share a visitors' room and a small courtyard separate from B and C. Section A is considered the closed section of this prison, which is used for observation of incoming prisoners, and is equipped with the prison's safety and punishment cells.[3] In contrast to the cells in the castle, the cells in these sections do have toilets. At the time of observation, however, section D was being renovated, implying that most cells on section A had

---

[3] The same bare cells are used for two different purposes, following two different articles of the Prison Act: for safety reasons and for punishment:

Art. 112. § 1 of the Belgian Prison Act: '*If special safety measures are permitted, separately or in combination, as long as they are only used for this purpose and for the time necessary [...] 5° confining to a secured cell, with no objects that are dangerous if used*'; Art. 132 of the Belgian Prison Act: '*Regardless of the nature of the disciplinary offence the following disciplinary sanctions may be imposed: [...] 4° confinement in a punishment cell, as defined hereafter in section III, for a maximum duration of nine days for a first-category offence and for a maximum duration of three days for a second-category offence*' (my translation and emphasis).

been 'transformed' into two-person cells by putting a second mattress on the floor. The other buildings on the prison grounds outside of the castle are the former houses of prison governors (from the time that prison governors had to live next to their prison), the farm with 120 cows, the workhouses for the production of pallets, carpentry and printing work, and for professional trainings to become a mechanic or bricklayer, and a large room in which the children's visits are organized, with a small outdoor playground. At the time of observation, a container with little more than a double bed inside was placed in front of the A building, which was used as temporary solution for conjugal visits. The small officer's booth next to the container was intended to ensure the safety of the visiting partner during this visit.

At first glance, the atmosphere in this prison seemed relaxed. Interaction between prisoners and prison staff appeared to be friendly, first names were usually used for both prisoners and staff, and sounds of laughing and music could often be heard on the sections. The open nature of the prison, however, was somewhat relative. Whereas prisons are generally considered 'open' when there are no physical barriers to prevent escape or when prisoners can freely walk around on the prison site, this is only partially the case for the prison of Hoogstraten. The work, educational and leisure programmes are held in groups, but the remaining time is spent inside the cell (note that in Norway, this would fit the definition of a closed prison). This means, for example, that all prisoners eat individually inside their cells and that 'unemployed' prisoners spend the majority of their time inside their cells. Moreover, the entrance gate of the prison is monitored day and night and all 'movements' of prisoners on the prison site (e.g. from the cells to the workplaces) are closely monitored.

According to Spradly (2016: 60), '*moderate participation*' occurs '*when the ethnographer seeks to maintain a balance between being an insider and an outsider, between participation and observation*'. Whereas this definition suggests that the level of participation is a deliberate strategy of the researcher, my moderate involvement in this prison resulted in the first place from the fact that there was no room for association on the sections. This hampered both informal conversation and participation in daily activities. Informal conversations with prisoners were rather superficial and concerned complaints about various aspects of the prison (e.g. decisions on conditional release or the toilet buckets) or the significant differences with other, 'real' prisons (e.g. the availability of work and educational programmes and the more relaxed atmosphere in Hoogstraten, which was contrasted with stories about violent prison officers in other prisons). The activities in which I did participate were mainly staff tasks, such as counting the goods bought by prisoners before they were delivered to the cells, or joining a prison officer at his or her checkpoint, during 'movements' from or towards the workhouses or during the 'walk' in the courtyard. As a consequence, I was highly involved in social interaction with prison staff. Most informal and personal conversations were with staff members. This means that I mostly understood their views on normalization and on the functioning of the prison in general, and that I mainly observed the 'image' that was constructed for staff members, involving very few tensions or arguments between prisoners. Although both prisoners and prison officers stated that the tensions between the two groups were almost non-existent in this prison compared to 'real' prisons, these tensions played out in more subtle ways, like the well-intentioned suggestion of a prison officer not to use the 'dirty' coffee mugs that had been touched by prisoners.

Establishing trust relationships with prisoners and prison staff remained an ongoing struggle in this prison. While one-to-one conversations with prison officers often became very personal without any effort, because I would spend hours with one prison officer on a section (or three officers, depending on the section), scepticism easily became the dominant discourse in a group setting. For example, prison officers had a habit of waiting together for the start of their shift, before going to the specific section for which they were responsible during that shift. As I joined this group of prison officers at the start of every observation day, there was always the potential for uncomfortable situations.

> The weather is nice, so all prison officers are waiting together, in a large circle, for the evening shift to start. I walk towards the group and join them as usual. Some of them greet me. After a few minutes, the prison officer standing next to me turns to me with: 'Well, miss, introduce yourself!' Suddenly everyone is looking at me, so I introduce myself (although

> most of them knew me already): 'I'm Helene, I'm from the University of Leuven and I will be here for several days a week. I'm trying to understand how this prison works.' They all start laughing, while suggesting what I should write in my book: 'badly'... oh well, you can't fill your book with one word... oh wait, two words: 'not good', 'could be better', or wait, you can fill your book with 'veeeeeeeery bad'. (Field notes 18 October 2014, Hoogstraten prison, my translation)

In this prison, the scepticism of prison officers was reinforced by my personal characteristics: being young (24), female and a criminologist. For many of them, a criminologist is a person who *thinks* that he or she (mostly 'she', which makes it even more difficult to accept) knows how things work in prison.

Leira

Leira prison is small-scale and very open, and according to the manager, probably one of the most *normalized* prisons in Norway (Field notes, 3 June 2015, Leira prison). It is the low-security unit of Trondheim prison and is located at 7 km (or 15 minutes by bus) from the centre of Trondheim. The prison has room for twenty-nine convicted people: twenty-five men and four women. All prisoners can apply to spend the last part of their sentence in this prison, regardless of the type of conviction, by expressing their personal motivation and by presenting a clean drug test. Only exceptionally prisoners are sent directly to this open prison. This resulted in a turnover of 87 prisoners over the course of 2014. There are twenty-five staff members, including four who are not directly employed by the Norwegian prison system: a teacher (from the nearby secondary school), two drug therapists (from Stavne gård, see also Breivik & Thorisdottir, 2007) and a psychologist (from the nearby hospital).

The functioning of this prison is partly determined by its recognition as one of Norway's fourteen 'drug managing units', which are prisons or units of prisons with a special focus on drug rehabilitation (see circular of 4.10.2013 on the organization of drug managing units in prison). In practice, this means that the prison has two drug therapists and a strict drug policy. Every day, one or two prisoners are randomly selected to undergo a urine test. According to the manager, it is very plausible that Leira prison carries out the most drug tests of all Norwegian prisons, in proportion to the number of prisoners. Moreover, a prisoner with a positive test can be sent back to a closed prison. Despite this focus on drug rehabilitation, the manager prefers the term 'life managing' [*livsmestring*] to 'drug managing' [*rusmestring*], because all prisoners are encouraged to deal with their personal problems, including much more than drug problems.

In addition, the functioning of this prison is both ideologically and practically based on the principles of the 'consequence pedagogy method' (Information booklet for prisoners at Leira; Hammerlin & Larsen, 1997; Steiro et al., 2013). This philosophy was conceived by the Danish philosopher-pedagogue, Jens Bay, and is aimed to strengthen prisoners' capacity to make their own choices in life and to enable them to live a life without crime (Information booklet for prisoners at Leira; Hammerlin & Larsen, 1997; Steiro et al., 2013). More concretely, this future-oriented approach is based on two premises: first, that every person is responsible for his or her actions and for the consequences of these actions, and second, that choosing the right actions will lead to positive consequences (Information booklet for prisoners at Leira: 3). Following this logic, it is important that prisoners gain insight into the consequences of their actions so that they can take them into account before acting (idem: 3–5). This does not mean, however, that Leira prison provides therapy in the strict sense; it rather offers opportunities to develop the social and professional skills that are needed to live an independent and law-abiding life (idem: 2). These skills are primarily expected to be developed through working together and participating in other social activities, which require interaction and communication (idem: 4; 6). Therefore, all staff members are trained in this philosophy (idem: 9) and the prison's policy consists of clear rules and expectations, as well as clear consequences for non-compliance. Prisoners are informed beforehand about the fact that their stay at Leira prison involves participation in the prison activities, including work or education, social activities, compulsory walks on Tuesdays and Thursdays and group meetings, and that they are expected to show a positive attitude towards these activities (idem: 2).

In order to ensure that prisoners understand these expectations, candidates are invited for an intake interview and a guided tour around the prison (idem: 2). In this respect, the manager underlined the importance of following the fundamental principles from the first contact with prisoners: respect for each other and being explicit about the consequences of their choice for Leira prison.

It was on 2 June 2015 that I first walked down the entranceway towards Leira prison's main building. Neither the building nor its surroundings displayed any signs of being a prison (even the bus stop right in front of the prison is called 'Leira skole', *school* not *prison*, in contrast to the bus stop at Nermarka prison). Only after I entered the front door did a symbol indicating that mobile phones are not permitted in the area reveal that I had just entered a prison. The door on the left-hand side of the entrance hall led to a living room, which was furnished with some couches, a small table with board games and three other doors, each leading to another living room with couches and a television, giving these rooms a homey appearance. The largest living room also had a pool table. The door on the right-hand side led to the dining room and the kitchen, where coffee and tea were always available (and waffles on a regular basis), which made a pleasant first impression. Next to the kitchen was the staff office, which was easily accessible for prisoners since the door between the kitchen and the office was usually open, except during staff meetings. The stairs in the entrance hall led to the first floor, with 21 individual rooms, several conversation rooms and a room for urine tests (equipped with a urinal and a mirror, which makes it impossible to cheat as a staff member watches over the prisoner's shoulder); and to the basement floor with an exercise room, showers, a room for crafts and a laundry service.

Since I did not immediately see anyone upon my arrival, I entered the staff office. The woman in the office was well informed about my presence during the coming month, and welcomed me in Norwegian, so I introduced myself—first in English, but she kindly encouraged me to do it in Norwegian. The prison manager, who had joined this conversation, invited me for a brief explanation about the prison and for the daily staff meeting in his office at 9:30. After I had introduced myself and my research to the six other staff members who had joined this meeting, all prisoners were briefly discussed individually, which happened twice a day (in the morning and afternoon meetings), and some particular problems were discussed in more depth in order to find a solution on which everyone could agree. The manager kindly reminded everyone to speak clearly, so that I could follow the discussion.

The staff meeting was followed by a guided tour around the prison, and an information session for all prisoners and staff members, as announced on the white board in the dining room (in Norwegian): '12:00 information meeting: Meet Helene'. I introduced myself very briefly to the group of people that had gathered in the dining room. One of the men laughingly concluded my introduction with a brief quiz, as he called it: What is the capital of Belgium? How many inhabitants? How many prisoners? National sport? Only the answer to the latter question seemed to be general knowledge: 'Football, with Eden Hazard!' The atmosphere was relaxed. Afterwards I was advised to start my observations in the garden centre of the prison. I was given a red t-shirt and sweater with the logo of *Leira gartneriet*, which made me look like any other employee of the centre, and I got my first task: moving the flowers from one place to another. I was working with one of the staff members, who admitted that she first thought that I was a new prisoner, which is usually the case with new people. She recalled that this had also happened when she started working there herself, which led in her view to very funny situations.

The area around the main building consists of a large lawn, with a small playground and several separate buildings. The largest building is the garden centre, including a shop that is easily accessible for clients from outside prison and several greenhouses, in which I would be working with most prisoners and several staff members. The three smaller houses are the apartments for four female prisoners, for four male prisoners and for visitors (i.e. family members who have to travel a long distance). Indeed, the four female prisoners have their own house, but work together with the male prisoners and make use of the facilities in the main building. The other buildings are the classroom, the stable (with several horses, whose owners have an agreement with Leira prison for their care) and the car repair shop.

The first impression of this prison was dominated by its homelike character, not only in terms of material living conditions, but also in terms of its welcoming atmosphere. At first sight, there were no visible differences between staff members and prisoners: no prison uniforms, everyone was called by his or her first name and my introductions were made without making a distinction between prisoners and staff members (although most of them helped me by adding whether they were prisoners or staff). This atmosphere is exemplified by two things that struck me that first day: prisoners and staff were eating together at the small round tables in the dining room, and they took their shoes off when entering the building. The small scale and open character of this prison facilitated my observations. I could independently enter and leave the prison and was allowed to fully participate in the daily activities, including working in the garden centre or in the kitchen, joining in with lunch and dinner, and participating in leisure activities inside and outside prison after work and on the weekends (mostly playing cards and watching television, but also joining a barbecue or campfire at the edge of a lake). This easily led to more or less individual and more personal conversations with prisoners. The small scale of this prison had the advantage that everyone knew who I was and what I was doing in the prison, and that I quickly learned most of their names.

My role in this prison was determined by my being a guest, both in this prison and in Norway, an employee of the garden centre, and a prison researcher. My gender and age seemed to play a different and less decisive role than in the Belgian prisons. Although some prisoners seemed to feel somewhat responsible for me, which I believe was at least partly due to my gender and age, I never got the impression that it compromised my role as a prison researcher. Prisoners made jokes about it rather than uncomfortable comments.

> It was almost 8 p.m. and we were playing cards in the living room when Eirik explained to me that all Norwegian prisons have naked hour between 8 and 10 p.m.— 'you should definitely describe this in your book because this is very characteristic of all Norwegian prisons. Naked hour, or happy hour as it is also called, means that no one is allowed to wear clothes between 20:00 and 22:00 and when the alarm goes off, we

> all get in the shower together'. The two other card players didn't hesitate to confirm the importance of this tradition. When I assured them that there was no reason to change this tradition and that I was just doing observations, they stressed that it was absolutely necessary that everyone participates. (Field notes 26 June 2015, Leira prison, my translation)

Despite these kinds of jokes, both prisoners and prison staff showed interest in my research and in the Belgian prison system. This was not only out of curiosity about the kind of information I was collecting, but also to provide me with their own reflections upon the prison system and the advantages of and potential improvements to open prisons.

Leuven

The closed prison studied in Belgium is the prison of Leuven, which is located in the city centre at approximately 400 metres from the train station. This old prison has been operational since 1869 and is conceived as a radial 'Ducpétiaux design'[4] with a central control point that connects the three prison wings, consisting of three landings each (see Ducpétiaux, 1838: 364). It housed 170 to 200 prisoners, and in spite of being a remand prison, approximately 40% of the population was pre-trial in 2014, about 40% was convicted and about 20% was interned (annual report of 2014 concerning the social services in Leuven prison). With its great walls, several gates and camera surveillance, which are clearly visible from the street, the impressive building leaves no doubt that it serves as a prison.

I started my observations on 19 October 2015, alternating early shifts (from 6:00 to 14:00) with late shifts (14:00 to 22:00) and day shifts (8:00 to 16:00). At the beginning of each shift, I would present myself to the highest-ranking prison officer, so that he could send me to a particular prison officer and corresponding landing. However, after some weeks, this schedule as well as the allocation to a particular landing became more and more flexible, thanks to two features of the prison.

[4] Edouard Ducpétiaux (1804–1868) was the first Belgian Inspector-General of prisons and charitable institutions.

First, the doors between the entrance of the prison and the landings were monitored and unlocked from a small control room, meaning that I did not depend on a prison officer to open and close the doors manually for me, and thus, I could seemingly independently enter and leave the prison. Second, the open construction of the landings gave me a good overview of the prison, regardless of the particular landing I was assigned to, and enabled me to move around independently from one landing to another. This means that, despite the closed character of the prison, I was less dependent on the prison officers for my observations than I was in Hoogstraten prison, and that I had more opportunities for informal conversations with prisoners (although this was again mainly with the prisoners who enjoyed more freedom thanks to their work on the wings or in the library).

More specifically, the prison consists of three wings, A, B and C, with three landings each (1-2-3, 4-5-6 and 7-8-9). The landings are designed in such a way that there are cells at both outer sides of the wing, while the open space in the middle ensures that all cell doors of wings A and B are visible from the ground floor. Each landing is equipped with several telephones and showers. Wing C has a slightly different design because the *annex* for interned prisoners is located in this wing. This annex is equipped with a living room and a kitchen, with the aim to provide an adequate regime for this group of vulnerable prisoners. The chapel and the library are located on the third landing (second floor). While this first room is still called 'the chapel', it is also used for Islamic and humanist services. The library is furnished with book and DVD shelves, a large meeting table, several armchairs and computers, which are supposed to have access to the website of the municipal library of Leuven (which however was inaccessible during my observation period). Since the prison library is linked to the municipal library, prisoners can borrow all books that are available in the municipal library as well. The classroom and the offices of the Flemish staff members[5] who are responsible for education, sports and cultural activities are located on the second landing. On landing 6, which is located on the same floor as landing 3, there

[5] The relevance of the distinction between federal staff members and Flemish staff members will be explained in more detail in Chapter 6.

is an exercise room and the cinema room, which despite its name is used for all kinds of activities. Back on the ground floor (landing 1), we passed through two grilled doors towards the C wing, while also passing the prison's medical service on the right-hand side, and subsequently the three punishment cells on our left-hand side, which were dark and smelly. The prison kitchen, which employs several prisoners, and the staff mess are located further down the corridor. On the first and second floor of the C wing are the *annex* and the psychosocial service. The prison has also an attic and a cellar. Whereas the former is not used, the latter is used for part of the paid work that is available in this prison.

The three wings are connected by the central control point of the prison, which was designed to oversee the three wings but is no longer used for this purpose since it is in need of renovation. This control function has been moved to the 'new centre' on the ground floor between landings 4 and 1, and is largely based on camera surveillance. From this new centre, the daily activities in the prison are managed and coordinated in a centralized way, to ensure both the practical organization and security. For example, the beginning and the end of all activities are announced through the speakers (so that staff members hear when they should open certain cell doors), the surveillance screens are monitored and the regular counts of all prisoners are coordinated from this centre. Finally, the prison has a stone-tiled courtyard with a football court, two ping-pong tables and outdoor training equipment, to which prisoners usually have access twice a day. Interned prisoners 'walk' separately from the other prisoners.

The first impression of this prison was surprisingly similar to that of Hoogstraten prison. In addition to the uniforms of prisoners and staff, the security measures and working methods were also very familiar. As was the case in Hoogstraten, the prison of Leuven was regularly compared to 'real' Belgian prisons, given the relatively small-scale and relaxed atmosphere, and even jokingly referred to by prison officers as 'Plopsaleuven', a wordplay on the children's theme park called 'Plopsaland'. My role as a participant-observer in this prison was also similar to that in Hoogstraten prison. Informal conversations with prisoners were again limited to those who were spending some time outside of their cells, e.g. to clean the wing, to work in the library or to deliver food to the cells. Yet, there were subtle differences. In Leuven, staff members, and the prison officers in particular, had the habit of shaking hands at the beginning of each shift. By participating in this habit, I showed not only my respect for and connection with prison officers, but also my distance from prisoners. At the same time, the greater freedom of movement enabled me to distance myself a bit more from the prison officers, physically but as a consequence also in prisoners' perceptions. I also participated in several activities which enabled me to establish a closer contact with prisoners such as the circus, drawing lessons, Dutch for non-natives, and I assisted the prisoner working in the library. These activities were the only opportunities to truly *participate*, whereas the rest of the observations were rather passive, involving little participation.

Nermarka

Nermarka prison is the high-security prison in Trondheim and is located at 5 km from the city centre or 25 minutes by bus. With a capacity for 148 male and 6 female prisoners, it is a relatively large prison by Norwegian standards. Moreover, it is the only Norwegian prison with both pre-trial and convicted male and female prisoners and *forvaring*[6] prisoners. More specifically, about one-third of the prisoners were pre-trial, two-thirds were convicted and there were ten places for *forvaringsdømte* (Falkanger, 2015). From the bus stop called '*Tunga kretsfengsel*', which is the former name of the prison, the enormous prison wall, surrounded by a fence with barbed wire, is immediately visible. It is also immediately clear that the only way to enter this prison is through the large metal gate a few hundred metres down the street. Upon my first arrival, however, it was less clear how to open this gate, so I was happy that the gate was opened for a car that was leaving the prison. Later I would learn that this gate is controlled by the two gatekeepers who check the incoming persons by means of camera surveillance and intercom. After walking

[6] '*Preventive Detention is an indefinite sentence that may be given to dangerous, accountable offenders with the purpose of protecting the community against new serious crime. Legislation on preventive detention came into force on 01.01.2002, and replaced previous legislation on a similar type of sentence called "sikring"*' (www.kriminalomsorgen.no/getfile.php/2176634.823.cqufrcrbwq/Preventive+Detention.pdf).

through the gate, down the parking lot to the entrance of the building, the door indicating 'visitors/prisoners' opened seemingly automatically. This door led to the entrance hall, which was strikingly similar to that of Leuven prison, with two gatekeepers behind a window, some lockers for mobile phones, a metal detector and an X-ray system. I spontaneously gave them my identity card, but there seemed to raise confusion about my identity: '*Are you the translator*?' When I explained that I would conduct observations in this prison for a period of three months, it became clear: '*oh, are you Belgian?*' I received a visitor badge and left my mobile phone in one of the lockers. Without any further security check, the next door opened automatically, leading to an outdoor passage surrounded by fences.

The enormous outer wall encloses several smaller buildings and a large open area with grass and trees, making the prison look much less like a deterrent on the inside than on the outside. The outdoor area of Nermarka prison, where prisoners get their daily doses of fresh air, is remarkably large, with grass and benches, a field for football and courts for basketball, volleyball and tennis. The prisoners are housed in four separate buildings: the A building, the E building, the M building (*Modulen,* rehabilitation unit) and a building for *forvaring*. The prison opened in 1971, but the *Modulen* and *forvaring* buildings were constructed more recently and have been in use since 2004 and 2010, respectively (Holsvik Høyem, 2010). In addition, there are separate buildings with a classroom, workshops, the shop and the multifunctional room used for all kinds of activities, and a small library building with book and DVD shelves as well as a seating area with armchairs. Like in the Belgian prisons, this library is connected to the municipal library, making it possible to order all books that are available in that library. The shop was conceived in such a way that it resembled as much as possible a 'normal shop' outside prison, albeit without cash.

The regime in the A building is based on isolation, meaning that the fifty prisoners of A1 and A2 spend the majority of their time inside their cells, without being involved in work or educational programmes. All prisoners start their prison term in the A building, before being sent to the E building. Moreover, from the E building they can be sent back to this A building by means of disciplinary sanction. Apart from these isolation sections, the A building also has a unit for six female prisoners (A3). The E building consists of four units (E1, E2, E3 and E4) for 73 prisoners in total. E1 and E2 are on the ground floor, each on another side of the staff office. E3 and E4 are located on the first floor, similarly separated by a staff office. The four units look very similar, consisting of a living room, a kitchen, and a corridor with cells at both sides, showers and two toilets. At first, the living room and the kitchen look fairly homelike: several couches, a small table, a television, board games and a ping-pong table in the living room and wooden tables and chairs in the kitchen. The kitchen has a stove, an oven, a microwave, an electric kettle, a dishwasher, refrigerators and there is fresh milk. Almost all prisoners of the E building were at work or at school when we arrived there around eleven o'clock. Nevertheless, two door handles on E1 were turned down, indicating that these cell doors had been locked by the prisoners themselves and that they were either inside their cells or away for a short time (e.g. to the doctor or the shop). Indeed, prisoners have keys to their own cells so that they can avoid having other prisoners entering their cells. Unit E4 differs slightly from the other units: the couches are of better quality and it is equipped with a pool table and a washing machine. My contact person explained in this respect that the prisoners of E4 have signed a contract declaring that they will help to create a good atmosphere for both prisoners and staff, and that the prison aims at rewarding this good behaviour by making their living conditions slightly better.

Modulen is a rehabilitation unit for fifteen prisoners. Similarly to Leira prison, these prisoners are expected to participate in group and individual conversations, led by specialized drug therapists, and to undergo urine tests on a regular basis. In return, they are granted more privileges than the other prisoners, involving, for example, weekly activities outside of the prison. The relatively small building consists of two floors. The fifteen individual cells are located on the ground floor at both sides of the central corridor. The cells are larger than those in the E building and each has a shower and toilet. On the first floor, there is a staff office, a large kitchen with a dining table, two living rooms (one with a pool table and a couch, and one with several couches and a television), a room for urine tests, a conversation room, exercise room and toilets. The building is surrounded by a lawn with a picnic table and volleyball net, which is separated from the greater prison area by a fence (and therefore only accessible for the *Modulen* prisoners, although still visible for all others). When entering the *Modulen* building, the first thing I noticed was a shoe rack with a notice to take off outdoor shoes, which reminded me of Leira prison, and the fresh smell of washing powder.

The *forvaring* building, finally, is the most secured but also the most modern building of this prison, also referred to as 'prison within the prison'. There is room for ten male '*forvaringsdømte*', who live together in two groups of five prisoners (starting on the ground floor and moving upstairs when they show positive attitudinal or behavioural changes), and each group has its own living room, kitchen, workplace and outdoor space, separated from the other prisoners. My contact person did not show me around this building on my first day, but I entered it later with another staff member. When we walked down the secured corridor towards the building, she joked, '*The way to hell*' (Field notes 7 April 2016, Nermarka prison, original in English). Before we entered the staff office in which three staff members were monitoring the cameras that covered the unit, we had to pass through several doors, which were all locked. It was immediately clear that the focus in this unit was on security.

The general arrangements in this prison were simple: I was given permission to visit the prison between 7 a.m. and 8 p.m. This was the only prison in which I was given a belt with an alarm to ensure my security. Since I was not given a key, I depended on the prison officers to let me enter and leave the units, but inside the units, I could hang around independently for as long as I wanted: eating together, playing cards, chess or ping-pong, watching television and engaging in many informal conversations. In the E building, the prison officers entered the unit now and then (some entered only when it was necessary to give or ask someone something, while a few entered to eat together with the prisoners or to talk or play cards), but they spent most of the time inside the staff office. For this reason, I spent the majority of the time chatting with prisoners in the unit, and joined the staff members in their offices when prisoners were at work or inside their cells during the staff's break. In *Modulen*, these everyday activities were complemented by the organized activities outside of the prison. The observations in the A building were completely different, given the fact that prisoners spent most of the time inside their cells. For the observations in this building, I was accompanied by the '*aktivitør*', who was responsible for the organization of leisure activities. Each day, she invited one or several prisoners of A1 or A2 for a walk in the courtyard or a visit to the library (with special attention for prisoners in complete isolation). Thus, I joined the walks, the library visits and the concerts, bingo and other activities that were organized during the observation period.

The aim was once more to establish the same kinds of relationships with prisoners as with staff members, but the practical organization of this prison made this challenging. I spent much more time hanging around in the living room and the kitchen talking to prisoners than in the staff office, which eventually resulted in a closer relationship with prisoners than with prison officers. In both Leira and Nermarka, I felt that my identity was very much defined by being 'non-Norwegian'. As a foreigner, I was made familiar with Norwegian eating habits and other customs. This became even more apparent in my contact with non-Norwegian prisoners, who seemed to consider this an important characteristic we had in common. With the words '*Belgians, Moroccans, same shit*', I was welcomed by the group of Moroccan-Palestinian prisoners, who always invited me for dinner, and even made me fries to make me feel at home. At the same time, I had good contacts with the group of Lithuanian and Estonian prisoners, who warned me about 'Norwegian racism'. Nevertheless, establishing trust required more effort and time than at Leira prison. Moreover, my credibility as prison researcher was explicitly challenged during the first few days. This came to the foreground when I first entered E1. One of the prisoners started questioning my research so harshly and loudly that all the other prisoners joined this conversation, as if they were the audience of our drama.

> After eating I sit down again with the people playing cards in the living room. The Lithuanian prisoner starts in about my research. He asks a few questions and then answers harshly and loudly, 'YOU KNOW NOTHING ABOUT THIS PRISON!', to which I answer just as loudly (because all the prisoners are suddenly looking at us and by now were standing around us), 'of course I know nothing yet, I've just started my observations!' [...]

> He continues: 'Why should I talk with you? What difference does it make if I talk or not? It's for you, not for me.' I tell him he has a point, indeed it won't change much for him. But what could change this system? I ask. Nothing, he answers, this system will never change. People write letters to journalists, but the staff never send them. ... Your research is just going to end up in a drawer somewhere... He says it's a pointless project, but his tone changes, and he says that it's a good project, and a good study, but it won't make much difference. (Field notes 26 March 2016, Nermarka prison, my translation)

Although this was an unpleasant situation at that moment, I wondered afterwards whether this man knew that he had done me a favour by giving me the chance to prove myself in front of all the prisoners in this unit. It seemed to work.

2.3 Conclusion

By shedding light on the four cases of this research, these descriptions showed that the material differences between the four prisons were immediately visible and the different atmospheres were tangible. Furthermore, entering these prisons gave a sense of how different living conditions inside are to those outside, and in many ways, Leira prison looked and felt far more 'normalized' than the other three prisons. It also became clear, however, that a thorough understanding of the role and meaning of normalization in each of these prisons required a more structured analysis, involving the aims, focus areas and results of the normalization process, as discussed in the first part of this chapter. Thus, the next chapters will use these three components of the normalization process to deepen our understanding of the different interpretations of normalization in Norwegian and Belgian prison policy and practice.

References

Beijersbergen, K. A., Dirkzwager, A. J. E., van der Laan, P. H., & Nieuwbeerta, P. (2016). A social building? Prison architecture and staff–prisoner relationships. *Crime & Delinquency, 62*(7), 843–874.

Bierie, D. M. (2012). Is tougher better? The impact of physical prison conditions on inmate violence. *International Journal of Offender Therapy and Comparative Criminology, 56*(3), 338–355.

Bosworth, M. (2007). Creating the responsible prisoner. *Punishment & Society, 9*(1), 67–85.

Breivik, S., & Thorisdottir, H. (2007). *Innsatt og utsatt. Håndbok for rustiltaket i Trondheim fengsel*. Stavne gård.

Crewe, B. (2011). Soft power in prison: Implications for staff–prisoner relationships, liberty and legitimacy. *European Journal of Criminology, 8*(6), 455–468.

Ducpétiaux, E. (1838). *Des progrès et de l'état actuel de la réforme pénitentiaire et des institutions préventives, aux États-Unis, en France, en Suisse, en Angleterre et en Belgique*. Hauman, Cattoir et Cie.

Dufaux, F. (2010). L'emploi des personnes incarcérées en prison: pénurie, flexibilité et précuriat. Une normalisation? *Déviance et Société, 34*(3), 299–324.

Engbo, H. J. (2017). Normalisation in Nordic prisons – From a prison governor's perspective. In T. Ugelvik & P. S. Smith (Eds.), *Scandinavian penal history, culture and prison practice: Embraced By the welfare state?* (pp. 327–352). Palgrave Macmillan.

Falkanger, A.T. (2015). *Besøksrapport Trondheim fengsel 17–19. mars 2015*. Oslo: Sivilombudsmannens forebyggingsenhet mot tortur og umenneskelig behandling ved frihetsberøvelse.

Feest, J. (1999). Imprisonment and prisoners' work: Normalization or less eligibility? *Punishment & Society, 1*(1), 99–107.

Fijnaut, F. (2014). *Criminologie en strafrechtsbedeling*. Intersentia.

Foucault, M. (1977). *Discipline and punish: The birth of the prison*. Pantheon Books.

Gobo, G. (2008). *Doing ethnography*. Sage.

Goffman, E. (1961). *Asylums. Essays on the social situation of mental patients and other inmates*. Penguin Books Ltd.

Hammerlin, Y. (2008). *Om fangebehandling, fange- og menneskesyn i norsk kriminalomsorg i anstalt 1970–2007*. University of Oslo, Faculty of Law.

Hammerlin, Y., & Larsen, E. (1997). Konsekvenspedagogikken. *KRUS Småskrift, 2*, 1–37.

Hancock, P., & Jewkes, Y. (2011). Architectures of incarceration: The spatial pains of imprisonment. *Punishment & Society, 13*(5), 611–629.

Holsvik Høyem, T. (2010). *Nytt forvaringsbygg Trondheim fengsel. Ferdigmelding nr. 692/2010*. Statsbygg.

Johnsen, B., & Granheim, P. K. (2012). Prison size and the quality of life in Norwegian closed prisons in late modernity. In T. Ugelvik & J. Dullum (Eds.), *Penal exceptionalism? Nordic prison policy and practice* (pp. 199–214). Routledge.

Kaminski, D. (2010). Droits des détenus, normalisation et moindre éligibilité. *Criminologie, 43*(1), 199–226.

Kelk, C. (2008). *Nederlands detentierecht*. Kluwer.

King, R. D., & Morgan, R. (1980). *The future of the prison system*. Gower Publishing Company Limited.

Knight, V. (2016). *Remote control: Television in prison* (1st ed. 2016). Palgrave Macmillan UK.

Kruttschnitt, C., & Dirkzwager, A. (2011). Are there still contrasts in tolerance? Imprisonment in the Netherlands and England 20 years later. *Punishment & Society, 13*(3), 283–306.

Liebling, A., assisted by Arnold, H. (2004). *Prisons and their moral performance. A study of values, quality and prison life*. Oxford University Press.

Liebling, A. (2011). Moral performance, inhuman and degrading treatment and prison pain. *Punishment & Society, 13*(5), 530–550.

Molleman, T., & van Ginneken, E. (2015). A multilevel analysis of the relationship between cell sharing, staff-prisoner relationships, and prisoners' perceptions of prison quality. *International Journal of Offender Therapy and Comparative Criminology, 59*(10), 1029–1046.

Morris, R. G., & Worral, J. L. (2014). Prison architecture and inmate misconduct: A multilevel assessment. *Crime & Delinquency, 60*(7), 1083–1109.

Rocheleau, A. M. (2013). An empirical exploration of the 'pains of imprisonment' and the level of prison misconduct and violence. *Criminal Justice Review, 38*(3), 354–374.

Rusche, G., & Kirchheimer, O. (1939). *Punishment and social structure*. Columbia University Press.

Shea, E. (2005). Les paradoxes de la normalisation du travail pénitentiaire en France et en Allemagne. *Déviance Et Société, 29*(3), 349–365.

Smith, P. S. (2012). Imprisonment and internet-access. Human rights, the principle of normalization and the question of prisoners access to digital communications technology. *Nordic Journal of Human Rights, 30*(4), 454–482.

Snacken, S. (2002). Normalisation en prison: concept et défis. In O. De Schutter & D. Kaminski (eds.), *L'institution du droit pénitentiaire. Enjeux de la reconnaissance de droits aux détenus* (pp. 133–152). Librairie Générale de Droit et de Jurisprudence et Bruylant.

Spradley, J. P. (2016). *Participant observation*. Waveland Press Inc.

Steiro, T. J., Andersen, B., Olsvik, L. S., & Johansen, P. (2013). Balancing structure and learning in an open prison. *International Journal of Management, Knowledge and Learning, 2*(1), 101–121.

Sykes, G. (2007). *The society of captives: A study of a maximum security prison* (First Princeton classic ed., Princeton classic editions). Princeton University Press.

Vander Laenen, F., Vander Beken T., & Bouverne-De Bie, M. (2012). Strafrecht en welzijnswerk. In R. Roose, F. Vander Laenen, I. Aertsen, & L. van Garsse (Eds.), *Handboek Forensische Welzijnswerk* (pp. 3–25). Academia Press.

van Zyl Smit, D., & Snacken, S. (2009). *Principles of European prison law and policy. Penology and human rights*. Oxford University Press.

Wener, R. E. (2012). *The environmental psychology of prisons and jails: Creating humane spaces in secure settings*. Cambridge University Press.

Yin, R.K. (2003). *Case study research: Design and methods* (3rd ed., Applied social research methods series 5). Sage.

3

Same Principle, Different Logics

The previous chapters already made it clear that the normalization principle plays an important role in Belgian and Norwegian prison policies. In both countries, the idea of normalizing the living conditions in prison builds on the acceptance that the deprivation of liberty should be the only intended punitive aspect of the prison sentence, and that it is the duration of this liberty deprivation that is to be proportional to the severity of the offence. Therefore, prisoners are to retain all their rights aside with the exception of the right to liberty, and their living conditions should resemble those outside prison as much as possible. Despite these similarities, however, the normalization principle seems to have a different impact on Belgian than on Norwegian prisons. Normalization has been associated with 'exceptionally' humane conditions in Norwegian prisons (Pratt, 2008), while such claims have never been made in the Belgian context. Contrary to what may seem the most obvious explanation, this different impact is not entirely due to differences in practical opportunities and limitations in the two countries. At a more fundamental level, there are also differences in the underlying philosophies, that is, the policy interpretation of normalization *in principle*. Therefore,

H. De Vos, *Beyond Scandinavian Exceptionalism*, Palgrave Studies in Prisons and Penology, https://doi.org/10.1007/978-3-031-28635-3_3

this chapter will first outline the underlying philosophies in both countries, before turning to the legislation and the prison practice in the next chapters.

In Belgium, the underlying philosophy is best reflected in the final report of the Prison Act Commission (2001) that covers the preparatory work on the Prison Act of 12 January 2005. At the time of its adoption, this Act was considered '*the monument for a decent, well-conceived prison policy in Belgium*' (Christiaensen, 2011: 9, my translation, emphasis in original). For the first time, prisoners were granted enforceable rights and the aims of the execution of the prison sentence were formally defined (Art. 9§2 of the Prison Act of 12 January 2005; Prison Act Commission, 2001; Smaers, 2005). Moreover, the Act enshrines the normalization principle as central to the philosophy underpinning Belgian prison policy. As one of its fundamental principles, normalization was intended to define the perspective from which the whole Prison Act was to be interpreted (Dupont, 1998: 142). In other words, the normalization principle reflects '*the spirit of the law*' that underpins '*the letter of the law*' (Snacken, 2015b: 179). Therefore, the final report of the Prison Act Commission elaborates in detail on the interpretation and the role of the normalization principle in Belgian prison policy. Nevertheless, two reservations should be kept in mind. First, the far-reaching idea of normalization, as it was articulated by this Commission, was toned down in the final text of the Prison Act. Second, some important articles of the Act had still not entered into force at the time of the observations, and other articles were amended before entering into force '*to keep the text more in line with the prison reality and the practical organization of the prisons*' (Parl. St. Kamer 2008–09, no. 2122/001: 3, as cited in Daems, 2010: 24, my translation).

Similarly, the Norwegian White Paper '*Stortingsmeldingen no. 37 (2007–2008) Punishment that Works: Less Crime—A Safer Society*' [*Straff som virker—mindre kriminalitet—tryggere samfunn* (St.meld. no.37)] elaborates in detail on the interpretation and the role of the normalization principle in Norwegian prisons. This White Paper reflects the views of socialist Jens Stoltenberg's Second Cabinet (2005–2013) on Norway's penal policy. Even though the succeeding centre-right government may not subscribe to all the policies in the paper, it still has a prominent place on the website of the Norwegian Correctional Service. Moreover, the normalization principle is the fifth of the five pillars on which the functioning of the Correctional Service is built, the others being (1) the legal aims of punishment, (2) a humanist approach to human beings, (3) the principles of due process and equal treatment and (4) the principle that convicted persons have paid their debt to society once the sentence has been served (website of the Correctional Service). Presenting these five pillars as the basis for the execution of sentences, the Norwegian Correctional Service still draws upon this White Paper, which is therefore used as a basis for understanding the underlying philosophy of the Norwegian normalization principle.

Of course, other policy documents could have complemented the analysis in this chapter. For the Belgian context, and more specifically for the Flemish context,[1] it is important to note that the normalization principle has also been incorporated and further developed in the policy documents of the Flemish Community regarding the social assistance and services to prisoners, which is a competence of the Flemish and not of the federal government. The same could be said for Norwegian policy documents that further develop the so-called import model.[2] Methodologically speaking, however, a valid comparison requires comparable data to start with. The final report of the Belgian Prison Act Commission and the Norwegian White Paper no. 37 (2007–2008) are comparable in the sense that both policy documents elaborate on the meaning and the role of normalization in their respective countries in a comprehensive way (not limited to a specific part of the prison conditions). Nevertheless, for this comparison, it is important to keep in mind that the two policy documents differ in their relationship to the prison legislation. While the Belgian document reflects the underlying views of the Prison Act, as understood *before* the implementation of the Act, the Norwegian document was built on an Act that had entered into force several years earlier.

[1] For practical reasons, only the Flemish Community will be considered, hence excluding the French Community and the German-speaking Community from this analysis.

[2] The import model entails that the services in prison, such as medical, educational, religious and library services, are delivered by providers from the local community.

3.1 An Intrinsic Versus an Instrumental Interpretation

A closer look at the underlying philosophies outlined in the two policy documents reveals different aims of imprisonment, different aims of normalization and differences in the relationship between both. The Norwegian normalization principle is interpreted in an instrumental way: it is intended to contribute to the aims of imprisonment. More specifically, normalizing the prison conditions is aimed to create the right conditions to encourage prisoners to change their way of life (rehabilitation) and to live a crime-free life after release (reintegration). This instrumental use is also linked to an evidence-based approach: normalization 'works', or is expected to work, to reduce recidivism. The Belgian approach is more ambiguous in this respect. On the one hand, the Belgian interpretation of normalization entails a clear intrinsic element, considering the protection of prisoners' rights as an aim in itself, but on the other hand, it also expects the normalization principle to 'work' in reducing the harmful effects of detention, or at least in not worsening them, which is considered a condition *sine qua non* for the aims of the execution of the sentence. This interpretation of normalization is both value-based (human dignity and prisoners' rights as valuable in themselves) and empirically inspired (normalization 'works' in reducing harmful effects). The following section will first elaborate on the Belgian views in this respect, and then on the Norwegian.

3.1.1 Prisoners' Rights and Harm Reduction in Belgium[3]

The Belgian Prison Act is based on two complementary ideas. First, the punishment should consist only of the deprivation of liberty, implying that prisoners remain *full legal citizens* [*rechtsburgers*] and retain all their rights except for the right to liberty (Prison Act Commission, 2001; Kelk, 1983, 2008). Second, imprisonment entails harmful effects both

[3] Parts of this section have been published in De Vos (2017).

for prisoners and for their social network that are largely caused by the total character of the prison, including the 'mortification process' and the 'role dispossession' described by Goffman (1961, cited by the Prison Act Commission, 2001: 66). The Prison Act Commission considered preventing or limiting these harmful effects a *precondition* for being able to work towards the aims of imprisonment, and thus a *priority objective* (Dupont, 1998: 138; Prison Act Commission, 2001). Based on these two ideas, the normalization principle is inextricably linked to both the protection of prisoners' rights and the prevention of the harmful effects of detention. More specifically, the Prison Act Commission defined normalization as '*a principle instrumental to operationalizing the harm reduction principle. The reduction of harmful effects of imprisonment requires at least an attempt to create living conditions in prison that resemble as much as possible living conditions in society, except for the fact that one is deprived of his liberty*' (Prison Act Commission, 2001: 8).

This starting point builds on the 'relative autonomy' between the sentencing aims and the aims of the execution of the prison sentence (Prison Act Commission, 2001: 61, see also van Zyl Smit & Snacken, 2009). This means that the sentencing aims are no longer decisive in the stage of the execution of the sentence, and that the aims of the execution of the sentence can be future-oriented, while the sentencing aims are past-oriented. Lieven Dupont, who was chairing the Prison Act Commission, explained this as follows:

> Whatever the objectives in imposing a prison sentence (retribution, general prevention, individual prevention, incapacitation, etc.), they cannot be considered objectives that must necessarily be met in the concrete execution of this sentence. (Dupont, 1998: 135, my translation)

As stipulated in article 9§2 of the Prison Act, the legal aims of the execution of the prison sentence are reintegration, rehabilitation and restoration. These three aims are interpreted in the light of the above-mentioned starting point and built on the concept of the prisoner as '*full legal citizen*' (Prison Act Commission, 2001: 81). Accordingly, the term of 'reintegration' was chosen over other conventional terms such as 'resocialization' or 're-education', because the latter two were considered to be too closely linked with '*individual (biological, psychological or social) disturbances or deficiencies that stereotype a convicted person as "the other"*' (Dupont, 1998: 143; Prison Act Commission, 2001: 73). With this conceptual shift, the Prison Act Commission takes explicit distance from the idea of therapy or treatment:

> The expressions listed are also typical of an ideology of treatment, that sets unrealistically high expectations of the possibilities for contributing to enduring behavioural changes in a forced situation that triggers numerous compensatory survival strategies and the façade of adaptation. (Dupont, 1998: 143; Prison Act Commission, 2001: 73–74)

Instead of therapy or treatment, reintegration is facilitated by limiting the harmful effects of the prison sentence '*especially in the degree to which they have negative repercussions on the future opportunities of the detainee to function normally in free society*' and by making available as '*differentiated as possible, but in no way mandatory selection of activities and services*' (Dupont, 1998: 144; Prison Act Commission, 2001: 74). In this view, effectively preparing prisoners' reintegration also requires a close link between prisoners' legal status in prison or 'intra muros' and prisoners' legal status 'extra muros', which among other things involves prison leave and conditional release (Prison Act Commission, 2001).

Along the same line, the Prison Act Commission's understanding of rehabilitation does not involve offender rehabilitation programmes based on some kind of therapy, but refers to the prisoner's readmission into society as '*someone deserving of the basic rights of active citizenship*' (Prison Act Commission, 2001: 81). The Commission argues that a prisoner must be enabled to '*bring about reconciliation with himself, with the victims, and with society with regard to the injustice caused by his crime*' (Prison Act Commission, 2001: 81). The third aim, restoration, is connected to the other two aims, and explicitly goes further than financial compensation to the civil party. In this context, restoration implies that the convicted prisoner can take responsibility for the consequences of his actions and that the needs of the victim are met (Prison Act Commission, 2001: 80; see also Dupont, 1998: 146). As already explained, however, the Prison Act Commission argues that these three aims cannot be achieved without first and foremost preventing or limiting the harmful effects of detention by normalizing the prison conditions.

3.1.2 Normalization with the View of Reducing Recidivism in Norway

In Norway, the normalization principle was introduced during the preparatory work on the previous Prison Act of 1958. The Norwegian policymakers at the time considered the normalization of living conditions in prison the natural consequence of the idea that the deprivation of liberty suffices as punishment: '*the deprivation of liberty should be implemented in such a way that the conditions correspond as much as possible to the conditions of life at liberty*' (*instilling* 1956: 61; cited in Schaanning, 2009: 123, my translation). Nevertheless, the present Act on the Execution of Sentences of 2001 refers only implicitly to the idea of normalization, while providing the general principles of the execution of sentences. Still, despite the absence of an explicit legal basis, the normalization principle is considered one of the guiding principles of Norwegian prison policy. Under the Correctional Service's policy, the normalization principle consists of three aspects (St. meld. no. 37; www.kriminalomsorgen.no/information-in-english.265199.no.html, original in English):

> *(1) The punishment is the restriction of liberty; no other rights have been removed by the sentencing court. Therefore the sentenced offender has all the same rights as all other* [sic] *who live in Norway.*
> *(2) No one shall serve their sentence under stricter circumstances than necessary for the security in the community. Therefore, offenders shall be placed in the lowest possible security regime.*
> *(3) During the Serving of a Sentence, Life Inside Will Resemble Life Outside as Much as Possible.*

When considering these three aspects, the similarities with the Belgian interpretation of normalization are striking: punishment consists only of the deprivation of liberty, which implies that prisoners should retain all other rights and that living conditions in prison should resemble those outside prison as much as possible. This also means that security measures should be as limited as possible. However, in contrast to the Belgian interpretation, the White Paper no. 37 (2007–2008) is clear about the instrumental use of the normalization principle in the pursuit of the punishment aims. This instrumental interpretation perfectly fits the philosophy underlying this White Paper that aspires 'punishment that works'.

This means that normalizing the prison conditions is intended to contribute to the punishment aims that are set out in article 2 of the 2001 Act on the Execution of Sentences. This article states that '*the sentence must be implemented in such a way that it takes into account the punishment aim, which includes reducing recidivism and reassuring society, and within this framework, ensuring satisfying conditions for the prisoners*'. From the preparatory works of the Act (ot.prp. no. 5) as well as from the White Paper, it is clear that the same punishment aims apply to both the sentencing itself and its execution. The White Paper relates the implementation of the prison sentence even more explicitly to the sentencing aims stipulated by the criminal law (*straffeloven* of 2005; Innst. O. no. 72 (2004–2005)), including (1) individual prevention by incapacitation, deterrence and rehabilitation; (2) general prevention by deterrence and 'attitude-shaping effects' in society and (3) prevention of social unrest (St. meld. no. 37: 19–20; see also Ugelvik, 2011). This is an important contrast with the 'relative autonomy' between these two stages in the Belgian prison policy.

While these punishment aims provide the framework for the interpretation and implementation of the normalization principle, only the aim of 'ensuring satisfying conditions for prisoners' can be understood as a reference to the normalization principle, albeit an implicit one. Since it is mentioned as a separate aim, it could even suggest an intrinsic approach to normalization. However, the instrumental approach emerges much more clearly in the explanation of this article in the 'Regulations relating to the Execution of Sentences': these satisfying conditions are aimed at giving the convicted prisoner the opportunity to change his way of life and to prevent recidivism. Additionally, the aim of 'reassuring society' implies that the 'public sense of justice' is always to be taken into account in the Correctional Service's decision-making process. This is explained as follows in the preparatory works of the Act of 2001:

> In some situations, the best interest of the person concerned will not be decisive when this is considered to conflict with the public sense of justice. This could be the case when the convicted person is immediately or quickly sent to a prison with a lower security level. (ot. prp. no. 5)

There is more to be found in the same article 2 of the Act. Its second and third paragraph stipulate two additional aims. The first aim is that convicted prisoners should be offered a restorative process and the second is that the harmful effects of pre-trial detention should be reduced. With regard to the latter aim, the Regulations relating to the Execution of Sentences explain that prisoners who are held in solitary confinement (remand *and* other prisoners) should get priority when it comes to activities and opportunities for contact with staff members, in order to reduce the harmful effects of isolation.

In addition to the punishment aims, the Act on the Execution of Sentences also defines the content of the sentence, which is set out in article 3. Three of the four sections (§§1–3-4) of this article, clearly show that all aspects of the implementation of the prison sentence are to contribute to prisoners' rehabilitation and reintegration, which should in turn lead to the prevention of recidivism. The first section explains that the implementation of the sentence is built on measures that promote prisoners' adaptation to society, and that prisoners should be enabled to make efforts to prevent new criminal offences. The third section provides for the obligation of convicted prisoners to carry out an activity in daytime, which is considered '*central to the content of the sentence*' (ot. prp. no. 5) and may involve employment, community service, education or another programme aimed at reducing recidivism. In the same spirit, the fourth section determines that the execution of the prison sentence will involve a stepwise transition from prison to freedom. In short, the instrumental approach is evident in these three sections of article 3.

Only the second section of article 3 seems to reflect a more intrinsic, human rights-based approach. This section seeks to protect the right of children to be together with their parents during the execution of the sentence. From a comparative perspective, it is remarkable that the most explicit expression of human rights in these 'general principles of the execution of sentences' does not concern the right of the prisoner but rather the right of his or her child. Building on the ideas underpinning the 1989 UN Convention on the Rights of the Child, 'the best interest of the child' has a prominent place in Norwegian penal policy. For example, special arrangements concerning child visits are not based on the right of the prisoner to have contact with his/her children but on the right of children to have contact with their mother or father (see e.g. *Rundskriv KDI 2/2017 barn på besøk I fengsel: besøksavdeling, besøkshus og—leilighet*).

Apart from this second section of article 3, it should be clear that the execution of the prison sentence is mainly focused on reassuring society and reducing recidivism. In line with these punishment aims, the main message throughout the White Paper no. 37 (2007–2008) is that reducing future crime and establishing a safer society requires effective punishment that builds on evidence-based rehabilitation and supervised, stepwise reintegration (St. meld. no. 37: 7–8). In elaborating on the safety of society, rehabilitation and reintegration, the White Paper also explains how normalizing the prison conditions contributes to each of these objectives.

The safety of society, firstly, is key to Norwegian penal policy. This means that due attention is given to the prevention of escapes and new offences, while it is at the same time acknowledged that a lower security level may facilitate prisoners' rehabilitation and reintegration. Considering both the advantages and the disadvantages of a high security level, the White Paper underlines the importance of the *right* security level for each prisoner. This is where the normalization principle comes into play: '*no convicted prisoner shall serve his sentence under stricter circumstances or with more restrictions than necessary*' (St. meld. no. 37: 8). Thus, limiting the security restrictions imposed on prisoners is considered a means to facilitate rehabilitation and reintegration. In addition, a lower security level is also expected to prevent the harmful effects of detention, and this should in turn create better opportunities for rehabilitation. In other words, in relation to the safety of society, normalization promotes the *right* security level for each prisoner in order to reduce recidivism after release.

Rehabilitation, secondly, is understood as enabling prisoners to change their way of life and to lead a crime-free life after release. Based on this philosophy, the Correctional Service's aim is that, after serving a prison sentence, every person '*is drug-free or has control over his drug use; has a suitable place to live; knows how to read, write and count; is able to find a job; is able to relate to family, friends and the rest of society; knows how to seek help for any problem he may encounter after release; and is able to live independently*' (St.meld. no. 37: 9). In this context, the White Paper points out the importance of normalizing the prison conditions, which includes prisoners' rights and duties. However, while it is stated that prisoners should have the same rights and duties as other citizens, and public services in prison should be of the same quality as those services in society, this statement is followed by a rather instrumental view on these rights:

> Important rights for the convicted prisoner are the right to education, the right to an individual plan and the right to social services. It could be important to give prisoners the right to measures that can prevent the harmful effects of the sentence and to enhance opportunities to live a crime-free life after release. (St.meld. no. 37: 109)

This connection between rehabilitation and prisoners' rights once again demonstrates how these rights are instrumentalized in order to serve the aims of punishment. The same is true for all activities and programmes offered in prison, such as work, education, health care, cultural activities and spiritual and other programmes, which are considered '*important and traditional tools for the rehabilitation of convicted prisoners*' (St. meld. no. 37: 9). This emerges clearly from the White Paper's example on 'music in prison', where it is explained that '*The main goal is to provide the prisoner with tools to manage his leisure time after release and by doing so to contribute to the prevention of relapse into drug use and crime*' (St. meld. no. 37: 116; as referred to by Schaanning, 2009: 142–143).

A gradual and supervised transition from prison to freedom, thirdly, is considered crucial for the prevention of recidivism, which is in line with the aims of the safety in society and rehabilitation. Thus, the aim of reintegration is linked to the ideas of 'progress during the execution of the sentence' and the 'assurance of reintegration'. The principle of progress is based on the idea that the gradual transition from a higher to a lower security level, e.g. by prison leave or a placement in a low-security prison or transition house, enhances the opportunities for rehabilitation and facilitates reintegration because there will be less differences from life at liberty (St. meld. no. 37: 10). The idea of 'assurance of reintegration' takes this even a step further by providing coordinated services during *and* after the prison sentence. Both principles will be discussed more in detail below (3.2.2 'Focus areas' and intended result of normalization in Norway).

In sum, the Norwegian prison policy is very transparent about the instrumental approach to normalization, even though it starts from the premise that the punishment consists of only the deprivation of liberty and for this reason, prisoners retain all their other rights. The fact that both the prevention of harmful effects of detention and the protection of prisoners' rights are seen (or presented in the White Paper) as 'tools' to enhance the opportunities to live a crime-free life after release is quite revealing. This brings us to the distinction made by Hammerlin between the two interpretations of normalization in Norwegian penal policy: first, '*the creation of prison conditions and initiatives resembling the surrounding world as much as possible*' and second, to '"*normalise*" *a person who is considered deviant or defined as having a deviant personality*' (Hammerlin, 2008: 565, as cited in Engbo, 2017: 332). Although Hammerlin is right that both interpretations are reflected in the White Paper no. 37 (2007–2008), the main conclusion here, based on the present analysis of the aims of normalization, is that Hammerlin's first interpretation of normalization is not considered an end in itself but rather a means to 'normalize the deviant person', in the sense that this person will be able to live a crime-free life after release.

3.2 Focus Areas and Intended Results of Normalization

In terms of 'focus areas' of normalization and the corresponding intended results of the normalization process, the scope of the Belgian normalization process is, *in principle*, almost unrestricted. The 'focus areas' are understood in a comprehensive manner, with a strong focus on the person's full legal status, including the enforceable rights to have contact with the outside world, to qualitative social assistance and services, and to prison leave or early release modalities. As already alluded to, however, normalization is much more restricted in the final text of the Prison Act. In the Norwegian White Paper no. 37 (2007–2008), by contrast, the accepted and even deliberate restrictions on normalization *as principle* are clearly stated, including the public sense of justice, the aim of deterrence, security reasons and practical limitations of the prison. The following section will first discuss the 'focus areas' and the corresponding intended results of the Belgian normalization process, and then the Norwegian.

3.2.1 'Focus Areas' and Intended Results of Normalization in Belgium

When it comes to the aspects of prison life that are to be normalized and the intended results of normalizing these aspects, article 6 of the Belgian Prison Act is crucial. Its first section stipulates that the prisoner '*shall be subjected to no other restrictions of his political, civil, social, economic or cultural rights than those arising from the sentence or the custodial measure, those that are inextricably connected to the deprivation of liberty and those that are determined by or under the law*' and the second section adds that '*avoidable harm from detention must be prevented*'. This article does not focus on the normalization of any particular aspects of the prison conditions, instead stipulating that the living conditions and legal position *in general* must be normalized. This reflects the underlying idea that *in principle,* the normalization principle is hardly ever limited in scope. Dupont (1998: 142, my translation) accordingly tried for a systematic implementation of the normalization principle '*inasmuch as the state of the custody permits it*' (which does not mean 'inasmuch as *prison practices* permit it'). Nevertheless, the limitations that are '*inextricably connected to the deprivation of liberty*' are elastic and thus vulnerable to a broader or more restrictive interpretation. The same applies to the concept of '*avoidable harm from detention*' mentioned in the second section of article 6. All the more so because the scope of this 'harm prevention' seems to have been reduced in the actual Prison Act. Whereas the Prison Act Commission spoke of 'harm from detention', article 6 mentions the 'avoidable harm from detention'.

The Prison Act Commission made this general rule more concrete by pointing out some specific aspects of prison life on which the normalization process should focus: e.g. the individual detention plan; the right to an individual accommodation; the right to wear one's own clothing; contact with the outside world; labour conditions, medical care, social assistance and services that correspond as much as possible with those in free society, and the right to complain (Dupont, 1998: 142–143; Prison Act Commission, 2001: 71–72). Additionally, the final report explained that the normalization principle also relates to the prisoner's legal position 'extra muros' (e.g. prison leave and conditional release) and to the working conditions of prison employees. Even though the translation of this underlying philosophy into legislation (i.e. into the definitive version of the Prison Act) and practice will be discussed in the following chapters, it is important to stress here that some of the provisions in the preliminary draft of the Prison Act that were considered especially valuable in the light of normalizing prison life, were either never incorporated in the definitive text of the Prison Act, or have only entered into force fifteen years after the publication of the Act. For example, the provisions regarding the maximum capacity of prisons and the right to individual accommodation, which was connected to the right to privacy, the equal wage regulation and social security never found their way into the definitive text of the law (Maes, 2009: 225–226; Prison Act Commission, 2001: 127). The implementation of these provisions was considered expensive and practically difficult, but there were also more substantive concerns. When the draft was discussed in the parliament two months before its publication, several Members of Parliament expressed their resistance against providing prisoners with rights and facilities that were equal to, or even better than, those of law-abiding citizens (Parl. St. Kamer 2004–05 of 2 December 2004; see also Daems, 2005, 2006). One of the MPs commented as follows on an earlier version of the Prison Act:

> He [the prisoner] also had the right to work and to a compensation if there was no work available. There surely must be a difference between a detainee and an honest citizen, who has lost his job beyond his control! (Parl. St. Kamer 2004-05 of 2 December 2004: 35, my translation)

In so doing, this MP argued against the far-reaching normalization efforts based on the *less eligibility* principle, which entails that prison conditions must always be worse than those in society (see also Daems, 2005, 2006; Sparks, 1996). This difficulty of implementing the far-reaching normalization principle is evident not only at the legislative level, where it was difficult to translate the underlying philosophy, but also from the prison practice, as will become clear in the next chapters.

3.2.2 'Focus Areas' and Intended Results of Normalization in Norway

The intended results of the Norwegian normalization process are reflected in the definition that we used as a starting point for this analysis: prisoners have the same rights as other Norwegian citizens; they shall be placed in the lowest possible security regime; and life inside prison shall resemble life outside as much as possible. However, the White Paper no. 37 (2007–2008) also mentions more specific 'focus areas' for the normalization process, together with the chosen reference points to represent the 'normal' living conditions (i.e. the intended results of normalizing the prison conditions). The five central focus areas that are discussed below—(1) duty of activity; (2) import model; (3) closeness principle; (4) principle of progression during the execution of the sentence; and (5) reintegration assurance—indicate that the 'normal' living conditions in Norwegian prisons are defined in such a way that they increase the chances for a crime-free life after release.

First, convicted prisoners are expected to participate in activities or programmes that contribute to their rehabilitation, such as work, education and psychological treatment (e.g. for drug abuse), cultural activities, religious services and other programmes. As already pointed out, all convicted prisoners have a *duty* to have a daytime activity, mostly involving work or education. The fact that these programmes are considered 'traditional tools for rehabilitation' (St. meld. no. 37: 9) also means that the reference point for what is considered 'normal' in this context has been carefully selected with a view to enabling a 'normal' law-abiding life after release. Also in the context of leisure activities, this means that activities in prison are normalized in such a way that they *prepare* prisoners for leisure activities as a law-abiding citizen.

Second, the provision of services is based on the *import model*. This means that the services in prison, such as medical, educational, religious and library services, are delivered by providers from the local community (St. meld. no. 37: 22 & 183). The import model builds on the idea that prisoners have the same rights, duties and responsibilities as other Norwegian citizens, including the right to services of the same quality, which entails the obligation for government agencies (other than the Correctional Service) to provide their services inside prison in the same way as they do outside prison (*Guidelines concerning the Act on the Execution of Sentences and the Regulations*; St. meld. no. 37: 109). The collaboration between the Correctional Service and other public agencies is considered one of the general principles of the execution of sentences (article 4 of the Act on the Execution of Sentences). Not only does this ensure the quality of the services, but it also allows for continuity, since prisoners are brought into contact with the agencies that will also provide these services after their release (see below: the 'assurance of reintegration'). In addition to public agencies, volunteer organizations also provide their services inside the prison (e.g. volunteers of the Red Cross). In doing so, society, and in the first place the local community, and its service providers become more involved during the execution of the sentence. The reverse is also possible: prisoners can be allowed to leave the prison in daytime to enjoy society's services in the community.

Third, the assignment to a particular prison is, or should be, based on the 'closeness principle'. This means that, if possible, prisoners are sent to a prison close to their homes in order to facilitate the contact with family and friends (St. meld. no. 37: 200). This is why the White Paper no. 37 (2007–2008) explicitly supports the policy of having many small prisons.[4] More recently, however, the importance of the closeness principle seems to have diminished in favour of the aspiration to greater efficiency: the prison of Halden has room for 250 prisoners, while smaller prisons are being closed.

Fourth, normalization is reflected in the principle that prisoners are encouraged to make 'progress during the execution of the sentence'. This principle implies a stepwise and structured plan towards reintegration that at the same time gradually provides more opportunities to 'test' new social skills in a controlled environment (St. meld. no. 37: 122). The gradual progression may involve placement in a lower-security prison or transition house as well as prison leave. The White Paper no. 37 (2007–2008) underlines that in this respect security considerations remain a priority, but that this progression is believed to reduce recidivism.

Finally, the 'assurance of reintegration' broadens the scope of normalization beyond the prison term. It entails the government's recognition of its duties regarding prisoners' reintegration and aims to strengthen the link between penal policy and social policy (St. meld. no. 37: 173–174).[5] This link was already clear from the White Paper no. 104 (1977–78), which pointed out that reintegration is a shared responsibility in the sense that all public agencies are responsible for providing their services to prisoners. The White Paper no. 37 (2007–2008: 173) takes this a step further by arguing that these services should be offered in a coordinated way, both during the prison sentence and after release from prison. This 'assurance' is not to be understood in the legal sense, but rather that it acknowledges that prisoners are still entitled to the same

[4] The distance between Oslo and Kirkenes (south and north of Norway) is about 2500 kilometres. To put this in comparative perspective: the distance between Arlon and Ostend (southeast and northwest of Belgium) is about 300 kilometres.

[5] As already mentioned, this concept was advocated by the former cabinet (2005–2013) and is not supported in the same way by the next governments. Nevertheless, supporting prisoners' reintegration and strengthening the cooperation between the *kriminalomsorgen* and other public agencies are still policy priorities, as explained in the recent policy document by the Ministry of Justice and Public Security: *'Reduced Recidivism to Crime. National Strategy for coordinated reintegration after served sentences 2017–2021'*.

services as Norwegian citizens, which involves an obligation for public agencies to provide their services in such a way that prisoners can make use of them. It is clearly stated, however, that this does not involve any special treatment of prisoners, '*but providing the services to which all citizens are entitled, such as housing, education, livelihood and health care*' (St. meld. no. 37: 174). The idea underpinning the 'assurance of reintegration' is that the progress made thanks to rehabilitation measures during imprisonment will be lost if the prisoners' fundamental needs are not also met after release (St. meld. no. 37: 174). Meeting these basic needs is considered crucial to reducing the risk of recidivism, which thus broadens the scope of the Norwegian normalization principle beyond the prison conditions as such. This requires collaboration between three actors: the Correctional Service, the other public agencies and the prisoner. The White Paper no. 37 (2007–2008) stresses the responsibility of the latter, arguing that he or she has the *choice* to live a crime-free life; this choice is considered decisive for a successful reintegration. Yet at the same time it also argues that there is 'room for (small) mistakes' without serious consequences and that '*the local community also has a shared responsibility in successfully reintegrating ex-prisoners who intend to quit their criminal lives*' (St. meld. no. 37: 174).

When it comes to the intended results of the normalization process, it should be noted that the Norwegian normalization principle is subject to at least four deliberate restrictions, already at the level of the underlying philosophy: (1) the public sense of justice; (2) the aim of deterrence; (3) security reasons and (4) practical limitations of the prison (ot. prp. no. 5; St. meld. no. 37; www.kriminalomsorgen.no/information-in-english.265199.no.html; see also Schaanning 2009). These deliberate restrictions largely stem from the sentencing aims that still play a role during the execution of the sentence. As already mentioned, the preparatory works of the Act on the Execution of Sentences explain that the public sense of justice is to be taken into account in decisions concerning the execution of the prison sentence, which might prevent convicted prisoners from being immediately sent to a low-security prison (ot. prp. no. 5). Moreover, from article 3 of the Act, it is clear that security reasons play a decisive role in the Correctional Service's policy. While defining the content of the prison sentence, this article refers first and foremost to the importance of security, which is explained as follows in the Guidelines to this Act: '*security inside and outside prisons will have the highest priority in all decisions*'. In addition to these deliberate restrictions on the scope of normalization, the Correctional Service's website ('Information in English') also mentions the practical limitations of the prison system as self-evident restrictions on the implementation of the normalization principle. However, despite their 'self-evidence', the Correctional Service states at the same time that all restrictions should be justified explicitly:

> The possibility to implement the principle of normality is of course limited by security reasons and the framework of the correctional management, the differences in the prisons and personnel, infrastructural and financial resources. Yet the basic principle is there, and deviation from it will need to be based on argumentation. You need a reason to deny a sentenced offender his rights, not to grant them. (www.kriminalomsorgen.no/information-in-english.265199.no.html, my emphasis)

3.3 Conclusion

Even though the philosophies underlying the Belgian and Norwegian normalization principle have been compared here rather in general terms, it can be concluded that the two comprehensive policy documents do reflect a different interpretation of the normalization principle in Belgium and Norway. These differences can be related to the two elements of the normalization principle distinguished by Engbo (2017). The Belgian approach is more defensive, focusing in the first place on avoiding unnecessary interventions in prisoners' opportunities to live a normal life, whereas the Norwegian approach is rather proactive, actively creating 'normal' living conditions. Whereas the Belgian idea is that the 'normal functioning' of prisoners is hampered by imprisonment, the Norwegian idea is that the 'normal functioning' can be improved during imprisonment. This seems to have implications for the interpretation of the reintegration aim as well. Whereas the Belgian aim of reintegration involves reintegration in society after the detention period, the Norwegian aim seems to suggest reintegration in society after a criminal life (which was of course followed by the detention period).

Such differences do not only emerge in relation to the reintegration aim but also in relation to both countries' punishment aims more in general. The Belgian Prison Act Commission has accepted the principle of relative autonomy between the sentencing aims and aims of the execution of the sentence. The legal aims of the execution of the prison sentence are therefore future-oriented: reintegration, rehabilitation and restoration. In Norway, by contrast, the sentencing aims of individual prevention, general prevention and prevention of social unrest still play a role in the decision-making process of the Correctional Service. This means that these sentencing aims have an impact on the interpretation of the aims of safety of society, rehabilitation and reintegration set out in the Norwegian White Paper no. 37 (2007–2008). As a result, the Norwegian interpretation of rehabilitation and reintegration is more occupied with shaping law-abiding citizens than the Belgian one. Nevertheless, it is worth noting that the Belgian understanding of rehabilitation is also reflected in one of the five pillars on which the Norwegian Correctional Service builds. More specifically, the fourth pillar entails '*the principle that convicted persons have paid their debt to society as soon as the sentence has been served*'. Moreover, restoration and the reduction of harmful effects of solitary detention are also mentioned in the White Paper no. 37 (2007–2008) as important aims during the execution of the sentence.

In fact, the analysis above shows that even though policies in both countries differ, and each do lean towards one more dominant interpretation, they do not completely fit the ideal-type. Take the question of whether normalization is used in an instrumental way or more intrinsically. The Belgian interpretation of normalization tends towards an intrinsic approach because of the focus on prisoners' rights, although the Prison Act Commission never completely distances itself from the instrumental approach. The intrinsic approach can be found in the fact that normalization is considered a *precondition* for achieving the punishment aims and thus not as a *means*. But the instrumental approach is still indirectly present in the aim of limiting harm from detention, which is needed to facilitate the prisoner's reintegration, rehabilitation and restoration. So the interpretation of the Belgian Prison Act Commission builds on both fundamental values and empirical evidence: the human dignity of the prisoners and their *full legal citizenship* are at the basis of the normalization principle, but at the same time normalization is expected to limit the empirically identified harm from detention (Dupont, 1998: 138–139, referring to harmful effects of detention identified by Goffman (1961), Goethals (1980) and Neys (1994)). Norway, on the other hand, seems to pursue a predominantly instrumental approach to normalization: the Norwegian White Paper clearly favours an empirical approach to normalization. And yet, the White Paper also acknowledges that '*it is a goal in itself to make life in prison worth living*' (St. meld. no. 37: 21), which highlights the intrinsic value of normalization in Norway.

Similarly, the Norwegian interpretation of normalization tends towards more of a disciplinary approach, whereas the final report of the Belgian Prison Act Commission assumes a more emancipatory view, as apparent from the concept of *full legal citizenship*. But this, too, needs to be nuanced. The question arises, for instance, whether normalization does not inevitably entail a disciplinary aspect. For instance, even if prisoners can choose whether or not to participate in certain activities organized in prison, the selected offer of these activities is in itself disciplinary. It conveys the message what citizens outside prison, or 'normal' citizens, 'normally' do or should do: they work or study in daytime, exercise in their spare time or do something creative, take language or cooking classes. And although the emphasis is on *voluntary* participation in a wide range of activities, the Belgian Prison Act Commission also stated that the harmful effects of detention must be limited '*especially in the degree to which they have negative repercussions on the future opportunities of the detainee to function normally in free society*' (Dupont, 1998: 144, my translation and emphasis), which does indeed sound quite disciplining even regardless of the exact understanding of 'functioning normally'. Additionally, it could be argued that the responsibilization of prisoners, which in both countries is indirectly related to normalization, always involves a certain degree of disciplinary emancipation or emancipating discipline, since prisoners are encouraged (more or less compelled) to take their responsibility, while lacking the personal/physical liberty that is often necessary to take real responsibility.

All of the above suggest that simply concluding that the normalization principle leads to more humane conditions in Norwegian prisons or that it is more far-reaching in Norway, as suggested by the concept of 'Scandinavian exceptionalism', would be too simplistic. From studying the underlying philosophies, it seems that the Belgian interpretation is actually more ambitious in this respect. But the underlying philosophy is not all there is to it, of course. The overall role and impact of normalization is determined by how this normalization principle is or is not reflected in legislation and practice. In other words: '*Humanistic values mean nothing if they are not translated into day to day practices*' (Liebling, 2006: 429). Since the abstract principle of normalization cannot be fully covered by legal provisions, the 'translation process' involves choices that inevitably narrow its scope. At the same time, however, parts of the underlying philosophy may re-emerge in practice, even if they were not covered by the legislation, for instance through the attitude of practitioners. This ongoing process is influenced by practical opportunities and difficulties, changes in political climate, security concerns, support or resistance by policymakers and practitioners and different views on what is to be considered 'normal' in a particular context. Normalization, in short, is an ongoing attempt rather than a fixed result, and a highly contextual process rather than a transferable product. This will become clear in the following chapters.

References

Christiaensen, S. (2011). Justitiële domeinen naar de gemeenschappen. Een nieuwe horizon voor gevangeniswezen, hulp- en dienstverlening en reclassering. *Panopticon: tijdschrift voor strafrecht, criminologie en forensisch welzijnswerk, 32* (2), 1–16.

Daems, T. (2005). Slachtoffers en evenwichtsdenken in het debat over de Basiswet Gevangeniswezen. *Fatik: Tijdschrift voor Strafbeleid & Gevangeniswezen, 106*, 5–9.

Daems, T. (2006). Wikken en wegen in de strafuitvoering. *Proces. Tijdschrift Voor Strafrechtspleging, 85*(1), 21–28.

Daems, T. (2010). Toeters noch bellen: Vijf jaar basiswet gevangeniswezen en rechtspositie van gedetineerden. *Fatik, Tijdschrift Voor Strafbeleid En Gevangeniswezen, 28*(125), 23–25.

Daems, T. (2015). Overzicht 2005–2015: een decennium Basiswet gevangeniswezen en rechtspositie van gedetineerden. In T. Daems, C. Hermans, F. Janssens, J. Millen, L. Robert, & V. Scheirs (Eds.), *Quo vadis?: Tien jaar basiswet gevangeniswezen en rechtspositie van gedetineerden* (pp. 13–30). Antwerpen/Apeldoorn: Maklu.

De Vos, H. (2017). Normalisering: een complex proces met subjectief karakter. Theoretisch kader voor de interpretatie en implementatie van het normaliseringsbeginsel. *Panopticon: Tijdschrift voor Strafrecht, Criminologie en Forensisch Welzijnswerk, 38* (3), 179–193.

Dupont, L. (1998). *Proeve van een voorontwerp van beginselenwet gevangeniswezen en tenuitvoerlegging van vrijheidsstraffen : Basisteksten, 30 september 1997*. K.U.Leuven.

Engbo, H. J. (2017). Normalisation in Nordic Prisons—From a Prison Governor's Perspective. In T. Ugelvik & P. S. Smith (Eds.), *Scandinavian penal history, culture and prison practice: Embraced by the welfare state?* (pp. 327–352). Palgrave Macmillan.

Goethals, J. (1980). *Psycho-sociale implicaties van de lange vrijheidsstraf*. Kluwer.

Goffman, E. (1961). *Asylums. Essays on the social situation of mental patients and other inmates.* penguin books ltd.

Hammerlin, Y. (2008). *Om fangebehandling, fange- og menneskesyn i norsk kriminalomsorg i anstalt 1970–2007*. University of Oslo, Faculty of Law.

Johnsen, B., & Granheim, P. K. (2012). Prison size and the quality of life in Norwegian closed prisons in late modernity. In T. Ugelvik & J. Dullum (Eds.), *Penal exceptionalism? nordic prison policy and practice* (pp. 199–214). Routledge.

Kelk, C. (1983). The humanity of the Dutch prison system and the prisoners' consciousness of their legal rights. *Contemporary Crises, 7*(2), 155–170.

Kelk, C. (2008). *Nederlands detentierecht*. Kluwer.

Liebling, A., assisted by Arnold, H. (2004). *Prisons and their moral performance. A study of values, quality and prison life*. Oxford University Press.

Liebling, A. (2006). Prisons in transition. *International Journal of Law and Psychiatry, 29*(5), 422–430.

Liebling, A. (2011). Moral performance, inhuman and degrading treatment and prison pain. *Punishment & Society, 13*(5), 530–550.

Maes, E. (2009). *Van gevangenisstraf naar vrijheidsstraf: 200 jaar Belgisch gevangeniswezen*. Antwerpen: Maklu.
Neys, A. (1994). Gevangenisstraf als doorleefde realiteit. In A. Neys, T. Peters, F. Pieters, & J. Vanacker (Eds.), *Tralies in de weg. Het Belgische gevangeniswezen: historiek, balans en perspectieven* (pp. 177–208). Leuven: Universitaire Pers.
Pratt, J. (2008). Scandinavian exceptionalism in an era of penal excess, part I: The nature and roots of scandinavian exceptionalism. *British Journal of Criminology, 48*(2), 119–137.
Prison Act Commission. (2001). Eindverslag van de commissie 'basiswet gevangeniswezen en rechtspositie van gedetineerden'. *Verslag namens de commissie voor de Justitie uitgebracht door de heren Vincent Decroly en Tony Van Parys, Parl.St. Kamer, 2000–2001*(1076), 001.
Rocheleau, A. M. (2013). An empirical exploration of the 'pains of imprisonment' and the level of prison misconduct and violence. *Criminal Justice Review, 38*(3), 354–374.
Schaaning, E. (2009). *Den tilsiktede smerten*. Oslo Academic Press.
Smaers, G. (2005). De basiswet in het licht van de internationale mensenrechten. In F. Verbruggen, R. Verstraeten, D. Van Daele, & B. Spriet (Eds.), *Strafrecht als roeping, Liber amicorum Lieven Dupont* (pp. 521–537). Universitaire Pers Leuven.
Snacken, S. (2015b). Tien jaar Basiswet - 'Back to Basics'. In T. Daems, C. Hermans, F. Janssens, J. Millen, L. Robert, & V. Scheirs. (Eds.), *Quo vadis?: Tien jaar basiswet gevangeniswezen en rechtspositie van gedetineerden* (pp. 179–203). Antwerpen-Apeldoorn: Maklu.
Sparks, R. (1996). Penal 'austerity': The doctrine of less eligibility reborn? In P. Francis & R. Matthews (Eds.), *Prisons 2000: An international perspective on the current state and future of imprisonment* (pp. 74–93). Palgrave Macmillan.
Ugelvik, T. (2011). Hva er et fengsel? : En analyse av manualen til en sosial teknologi. *Retfærd. Nordisk Juridisk Tidsskrift, 34*(1), 85–100.
van Zyl Smit, D., & Snacken, S. (2009). *Principles of European prison law and policy. Penology and human rights*. Oxford University Press.

4

Abnormal Kitchen Knives: Creating the Material Conditions for Normal Prison Life

If we are asked to think about living conditions in prisons, the material prison conditions are often the first that come to mind. It is therefore not surprising that most people have an implicit or explicit idea of what prisons 'usually look like' (see also Smith, 2014: 68; Smith & Ugelvik, 2017: 3). For example, the fact that many prison visitors are surprised to see the huge knives available in Norwegian prison kitchens (see e.g. Vander Beken, 2015) suggests that a prison is associated with certain seemingly inevitable and obvious material features. Any surprise about knives in a prison kitchen is based on the mental image of what a prison usually looks like rather than what a kitchen usually looks like. This imaginary 'usual' prison is often characterized by walls and fences, barbed wire, cameras and alarms. It is true that, in reality, the material prison conditions often do reflect the purpose of preventing escapes and ensuring security, in addition to the policy purposes that were dominant at the time of the prison's construction (see e.g. Wheeler & Cline, 2020), which in the case of Leuven and Hoogstraten prison is more than a hundred years ago. Yet, given that today's Belgian and Norwegian prison policies aim at normalizing the living conditions as much as possible, barbed wire should be at least as remarkable as kitchen knives. This

H. De Vos, *Beyond Scandinavian Exceptionalism*, Palgrave Studies in Prisons and Penology, https://doi.org/10.1007/978-3-031-28635-3_4

chapter will focus on the normalization of the material prison conditions, starting from the double premise that, first, material conditions are more than just the design, state or size of the prison buildings and that, second, materiality is only one part of and closely connected to other dimensions making up the prison experience as a whole.

4.1 Beyond 'Improving' the Material Environment

Most scholars will agree with Neumann (2012: 141) that '*Materiality is [...] only one aspect of imprisonment (and only one aspect of life in general), and good material conditions are [...] only one aspect of a respectful and humane institution*'. Moreover, research has pointed out that the quality of the social interaction between prisoners and staff is more relevant for the prison experience than the material conditions (Liebling, 2004). Without contradicting these insights, however, from a normalization point of view, it is not so much the hierarchy between the dimensions of imprisonment that is important, as the *intertwinement* of those dimensions, because the normalization of one dimension will arguably be facilitated by the normalization of other dimensions. This argument is supported by a growing body of literature that has established links between, on the one hand, the material prison conditions, and on the other hand, the social climate, the security level and incidents, and the use of time in prison, all of which impact the prison experience (Camp et al., 2003; Crewe, 2011b; Fransson et al., 2018; Goffman, 1961; Hancock & Jewkes, 2011; Huey Dye, 2010; Irwin & Owen, 2005; Johnsen, 2018; Johnsen & Granheim, 2012; Jones, 2007; Knight, 2016; Moore, 1981; Moran & Turner, 2019; Rocheleau, 2013; Sykes, 2007). For the same reason, material prison conditions are understood here in a broad sense and do not only refer to the architecture, the size and the state of the prison building, its individual spaces and its surroundings, but also to the furniture and equipment, practical arrangements with respect to hygiene, food, clothing, personal belongings and prisoners' access to health care and other services. The experience of this broadly defined material environment is where some of the direct and indirect 'pains' of imprisonment lie, setting prisons apart from the outside world and causing the need for normalization.

Since Sykes' (2007) identification of five 'pains of imprisonment', a whole series of such pains have been identified, including the pains of custody (Jones, 2007), spatial pains of imprisonment (Hancock & Jewkes, 2011), the pains of indeterminacy, the pains of psychological assessment, the pains of self-government (Crewe, 2011a), paternal pains of imprisonment (Ugelvik, 2014) and pains of freedom (Shammas, 2014). The prison experience is indeed associated with distress and frustrations, and these are partially due to or aggravated by the material conditions in prison. For instance, bad material conditions can exacerbate feelings of boredom or fear (Wener, 2012). Moreover, because prisoners are generally confined *to* and *within* the institution (Sykes, 2007), they are not only deprived of their liberty but also of their autonomy, self-determination and privacy to a greater or lesser degree (Crewe, 2011a; Goffman, 1961; Golash, 2005; Hancock & Jewkes, 2011; Sexton, 2015; Sykes, 2007; Wener, 2012). As a consequence, in addition to their material conditions, their feelings of control over these conditions also differ from those most people outside prison are used to. This includes perceived freedom of choice (van der Kaap-Deeder et al., 2017) and opportunities to withdraw from stressful situations (Goffman, 1961; Sykes, 2007; Wener, 2012). The reduced feeling of control over exposure to stressors exacerbates the experience of those stressors. Wener (2012: 197) pointed out that '*The level of control people feel they have over the noise is important in determining the amount of stress it causes*', a logic that he also applied to feelings of privacy:

> It is all too clear in corrections that being alone can be either the most positive condition or the most punitive. It depends on the level of choice and control experienced. (Wener, 2012: 256)

This gives us reason to believe that the way material conditions are experienced in relation to other 'pains' matters as much as the material environment itself, which is good to keep in mind when studying normalization.

If we then have a closer look at the material environment of various prisons, it is evident that, though sharing the deprivation of liberty as their reason for existence, prisons differ greatly in terms of material conditions and their impact on prisoners. For instance, prisoners experience views of greenery and access to nature in prison as calming and reducing stress (Moran & Turner, 2019; Wener, 2012). Furthermore, closed prisons in Norway with a capacity of less than 50 places are associated with a higher quality of life than those with more than 50 places (Johnsen & Granheim, 2012). One of the reasons is that smaller prisons are more likely to be located in city centres close to prisoners' homes and therefore more easily accessible for visitors (Johnsen & Granheim, 2012: 208). Another reason is that problems can be more easily detected and solved in small prisons (Baldursson, 2000). One of the most striking examples of a well-conceived modern prison design is the Norwegian prison of Halden. This prison became famous for allegedly being '*the most humane prison in the world*' (Benko [2015] in *The New York Times Magazine* and Gentlemen [2012] in *The Guardian*). It has been argued that '*every facet of Halden prison is purposefully designed to normalize the environment for those who live and work within its walls*' (Hancock & Jewkes, 2011: 622), including the colours deliberately used to create the desired atmosphere, daylight lamps to reduce aggression, IT facilities in the library, and the calming artwork and green views (Hancock & Jewkes, 2011; Moran & Turner, 2019). It was exactly this observation of remarkable differences in material prison conditions that made Pratt (2008) conclude that Nordic prisons, including Norwegian ones, have 'exceptionally' humane conditions.

However, in their exploration of the '*spatial pains*' in these '*new generation*' *prisons*, Hancock and Jewkes (2011: 623) found that while these new prison designs are more '*open, flexible and even playful*', they may produce their own distinctive pains of imprisonment. First, they note that even a well-conceived prison design and high-quality living conditions do not impact crucial '*external stressors*' (e.g. family problems or cancelled visits) or '*environmental stressors*' (e.g. boredom or lack of privacy). Second, Hancock and Jewkes (2011: 623) warn that although the '*deeper social relations which are produced and enabled by those buildings*' can result in more conversations and laughter, they can also engender more tensions and violence. Third, the provision of more comfortable living conditions than the neighbouring prisons goes hand in hand with the stimulation of a process of self-discipline: '*prisoners are encouraged to buy into authoritarian notions of "positive" outcomes for "good" behaviour knowing that the penalty for "bad" or unruly behaviour may be removal of privileges or expulsion from the pod*' (Hancock & Jewkes, 2011: 624). And finally, they also point out that the modern surveillance technologies in these prisons on the one hand enable a safer environment with more freedom of movement within the prison, but on the other hand, these technologies subject both prisoners and prison staff to '*near-constant surveillance*'. In short, while the authors do acknowledge that buildings that provide clean, humane and safe environments with daylight and access to outside space are '*unquestionably desirable for both prisoners and prison staff*' and alleviate certain pains of imprisonment, they question the assumption that *modern* always equates to *better* (Hancock & Jewkes, 2011: 611, 627).

It has been argued that the relatively high material standards in Nordic prisons resulted from the implementation of the normalization principle (Pratt, 2008). While this may be true, normalizing the material prison conditions is more complex than just 'modernizing' or 'improving' these conditions. Normalization can of course involve modernization when the material conditions in prison are less modern than those outside prison, as is often the case. But highly modern material conditions are not by definition more 'normal', or experienced as such. A more normalized prison environment also entails creating conditions that contribute to prisoners' dignity, safety, self-determination, privacy, and physical and psychosocial well-being in similar ways as outside prison, and that contribute to the mitigation of the institutionalization process. Whereas institutionalization implies a uniformity that may lead to depersonalization (Goffman, 1961), the normalization process aims at preventing these harmful effects by creating openness towards society, individual choices and personal belongings.

Another reason why the normalization of the material prison environment cannot simply be measured by the degree of modernity of its material conditions is the relative character of normalization. The understanding of normalization in policy and the practical implementation of this understanding will depend on what is seen as 'normal' conditions in a given context. This is a crucial point for comparative research because it means that even if the normalization principle were applied in the same way and to the same extent in, for instance, Belgian and Norwegian prisons, the prison conditions would still differ. Moreover, individual prisoners' expectations of prison life also play an important role when evaluating normalization (Sexton, 2015; Shammas, 2014). This element, too, has far-reaching implications in any comparative study. Since these expectations are shaped or affected by the norms and values of their society and by their idea of what prison looks like (or should look like) in this society, it is plausible that Norwegian citizens have higher expectations of, and thus more negative experiences with, living conditions in Norwegian prisons, even if the quality of life is better in Norwegian prisons than in prisons in other countries. Finally, the way in which the material prison conditions are normalized will also depend on the underlying views and aims of normalization. Whether the material conditions are normalized for intrinsic or for instrumental reasons will not only shape the normalization process, but will also determine whether or not prisoners' subjective experiences are relevant to assess the degree of normalization. When highly modern prison conditions cause additional or different pains, it is questionable if these conditions can be considered 'more normalized' when normalization aims at reducing 'pains'.

The same question arises in the context of very open prisons, where the liberty deprivation is less total and complete, and where 'freedom' is still within reach (Shammas, 2014). Using Crewe's (2011a, 2015, 2021) conceptualization of the '*depth of imprisonment*', these prisons can be characterized as '*shallow*'. The depth of imprisonment refers to the '*distance from freedom*' as experienced by prisoners, both in physical terms, i.e. '*being separated from free society and confined to a penal institution*', and in temporal terms, i.e. '*distance from release*' (Crewe, 2021: 4, 14). This concept also entails some areas of a prison, like the visitors' room, possibly being experienced as less 'deep' than others. Moreover, Crewe (2021: 18) underlines the subjective nature of '*depth*', arguing that prisoners' experiences will vary according to their personal life circumstances prior to imprisonment and the circumstances they will return to after release. While recognizing the complexities of this concept, it is safe to say that prisoners find themselves closer to freedom in very open prisons than in high-security prisons. Yet it is exactly this closeness that is associated with new pains. The frustrations caused by the relatively high degrees of freedom in open prisons are referred to by Shammas (2014) as five dimensions of the '*pains of freedom*': (1) confusion over conflicting roles (wage-earner in daytime and inmate after work); (2) anxiety and boundlessness; (3) ambiguity; (4) relative deprivation; and (5) individual responsibility for sentence outcomes. Along the same lines, Neumann (2012) draws attention to the impact of high-quality material conditions in combination with the requirement of self-discipline in Norwegian open prisons, pointing out the high demands and pains experienced by prisoners in such open prisons:

> The inmates would verbalize the extreme stress they experienced by the fact that they had the freedom to potentially leave the prison in the morning never to return. In order to return every day, they would have to build inner bars. (Neumann, 2012: 148)

Without minimizing the importance of any of the above-mentioned frustrations and painful experiences in prison, a study about normalization should also take into account that liberty deprivation in itself is frustrating and painful. The prison sentence is *intended* to be something negative. Defining which 'pains' or frustrations are directly linked to the intended punishment is challenging, and again related to the views and aims underlying the prison sentence and normalization. The question arises here to what extent the frustrations identified by Neumann and Shammas, for instance, are to be considered as unintended painful or harmful effects which are to be reduced by the application of normalization. Should they perhaps be considered as *intended* pains caused by the instrumental use of normalization in line with the recidivism-reducing aims of the prison sentence? How, then, does this relate to the intended and unintended pains of imprisonment and the intrinsic and instrumental approaches to normalization? Clues for answering this complex question are found in the way the normalization of material conditions is described in national legislation, the subject of the next section.

4.2 Legislative Translations of a Normalized Material Environment

While equally central to the prison policies of Belgium and Norway, the normalization of the material prison conditions is 'translated' into their respective legislation quite differently. The Belgian Prison Act of 2005 makes the intention of normalizing each individual aspect rather explicit. This is in line with the views of the Prison Act Commission (2001: 127): '*In elaborating the stipulations concerning the prisoners' material living conditions, [...] the normalization principle was applied as consistently as possible.*' In general terms, this view is reflected in articles 4 to 6 of the Belgian Prison Act. Article 4 stipulates that, in principle, the liberty deprivation takes place in a prison, and article 5 specifies that this prison must have '*psychosocial, physical, and material conditions that should respect human dignity, promote prisoners' self-respect, and appeal to their sense of individual and social responsibility*'. Along the same lines, article 6 protects prisoners' legal status and stipulates that the avoidable harmful effects of detention should be prevented. Pointing out these various aims, these general provisions reflect a combination of an intrinsic approach (e.g. respecting prisoners' human dignity) and an instrumental approach (e.g. appealing to their sense of responsibility). The intended results of this normalization process are in the first place prisoners' rights to decent material conditions.

The Norwegian Act on the Execution of Sentences of 2001 leaves this underlying philosophy rather implicit. The normalization principle is neither explicitly formulated in the Act nor does the Act systematically refer to the normalization of each aspect of the material environment or to prisoners' subjective rights in this context. It seems to be grounded in the general centrality of normalization in the Correctional Service's policy rather than in 'hard' legislation or enforceable rights. Nevertheless, the normalization of the material environment has been translated into the Act on the Execution of Sentences by enshrining several principles that are derived from the normalization principle or contribute to its implementation: the nearness principle, the principle of gradual transition from prison to freedom and the cooperation with other public agencies (the so-called import model).

The nearness principle holds that convicted prisoners should '*be placed near their home to the extent this is practically possible and suitable*' (art. 11 of the Act on the Execution of Sentences). This has resulted in the construction of many small prisons, spread all over the considerable length of the country. The principle of gradual transition from prison to freedom, covered by article 3 of the Act, implies a differentiation in security levels between prisons or units. Considering these two principles together, the Act supports small prisons with different security levels, thus shaping the material prison environment and supporting its normalization. It should be noted, however, that the Act also stipulates that, in principle, prisoners start their prison terms in a high-security prison (art. 11 of the same Act) and that the prison administration has the discretion to deviate from the principle of nearness for various reasons such as security, rehabilitation measures, the medical and psychological situation, the duration of the sentence and prison capacity (see art. 11.1 of the Guidelines concerning the Act). The principle of cooperation with other public agencies or import model (St. meld. no. 37: 22) is a more explicit translation of the normalization principle, and is enshrined in article 4 of this Act. The Guidelines concerning this article explain that

> Convicted persons and prisoners have, apart from the restrictions that result from the liberty deprivation, the same right to services and the same obligations and responsibilities as the rest of the population. The Correctional Service must therefore, as far as possible, arrange for other public agencies to provide their lawful services to convicted persons and prisoners, and arrange for convicted and remand prisoners to participate in these services. Health services, social services, education, labour market initiatives, and cultural services are provided by the public agencies that have this responsibility in society.

More clearly than in the Act on the Execution of Sentences itself, the underlying philosophy of normalization emerges from the Regulations relating to the Act on the Execution of Sentences and the related Guidelines. For example, the 2019 Guidelines for Self-Catering in Prison confirmed that '*The principle of normality is a guiding principle for the activities of the Correctional Service*' and followed to explain how self-catering for prisoners would '*strengthen the principle of normality, reduce the unintended harmful effects of the sentence and facilitate the reintegration to life outside prison.*'

When looking in more detail at the specific aspects typically associated with material prison conditions, it is striking that both countries' legislation cover the same aspects: accommodation, common areas, food, clothing, goods for purchase and personal belongings. In the Belgian Prison Act, most of these aspects have been formulated as subjective rights. The Norwegian Act, on the other hand, does not systematically refer to the normalization of these aspects, but does mention similar restrictions. This means that only the Belgian Act provides grounds on which prisoners can claim their right to each of these aspects, which is a significant difference between the Belgian and Norwegian legislative 'translations' of normalization. Despite its significance, however, it is fair to immediately qualify this difference. The degree of detail is both the strength and the weakness of the rights-based approach in Belgium. While abstract and broad provisions entail the risk of being interpreted more narrowly than specific provisions, very specific provisions entail the risk of overlooking important aspects, to which prisoners are consequently not entitled. This is all the more apparent when the sometimes vague formulations in the Belgian Act are specified, and thus often strongly restricted, in the internal rules of prisons, thereby undermining the normalizing value of these legal articles. Moreover, it is worth repeating that some of the relevant articles of the Act have only recently entered into force, which means, for instance, that the Belgian government has been struggling for almost fifteen years to define standards for compliance with health, fire safety and hygiene regulations, and to that end to establish rules that relate to the size of common areas, lighting, ventilation, sanitary facilities and maintenance.

When considering the material conditions in a broader sense, including the availability of health care, library services and other social services, both countries' prison systems are based on the import model, but the Norwegian legislation applies this principle much more consistently. In Norway, prisoners can claim the rights to health care, social or cultural services like other citizens on the basis of the Health Act [art. 3–9 of the *Lov om kommunale helse- og omsorgstjenester m.m*], the Education Act [art. 13-2a *Lov om grunnskolen og den vidaregåande opplæringa*] or the Social Services Act [*Lov om sosiale tjenester i arbeids- og velferdsforvaltningen*], which explicitly mention prisoners as target group, rather than on the basis of the Act on the Execution of Sentences. The intended result of this normalization process is that prisoners are provided with the same services as other citizens, with the aim of respecting prisoners' rights, facilitating their rehabilitation and reducing recidivism. In order to give effect to this principle, the Norwegian Correctional Service is responsible for establishing collaboration agreements with the other public agencies and to provide suitable spaces in prison for these public services to be properly implemented (as stipulated in the Guidelines concerning the Act). When it comes to financial social assistance, for example, Norwegian prisoners are not excluded from the regular social security system. This means that the Act on the Execution of Sentences does not need to repeat a list of prisoners' rights, since the relevant legislation concerning health care, social assistance and education still applies to prisoners. In Belgium, on the other hand, the Prison Act explicitly protects prisoners' rights to health care, library services and other social services, and in doing so, it provides a parallel system for prisoners that is supposed to be *as similar as possible* to that outside prison. Only the Flemish Decree of 31 April 2007 on Adult Education explicitly mentions prisoners as part of its target group (as does the Decree of 8 March 2013 concerning the Organisation of Social Assistance and Services for Detainees, of course, but this Decree focuses *exclusively* on prisoners). As a consequence, the Belgian Act seems to implement the normalization principle much more systematically, but such a conclusion overlooks the fact that the normalization principle is considered inherent to the Norwegian prison policy *and* social policy, even without being repeated for every single aspect.

The rights-based approach of the Belgian Prison Act was inspired by Kelk's notion of 'full legal citizen'. The Prison Act Commission (2001: 67–68) followed Kelk in arguing that it is characteristic of total institutions to define the duties of inmates clearly but their rights only vaguely or as privileges. With a view to reducing the 'total character' and the harmful effects caused by the lack of enforceable rights, the Prison Act Commission (2001: 68) advocated clearly defined rights so that they could be enforced by prisoners. Prisoners should thus be able to know their rights and exercise them. The initial objective of reducing the 'total character' and the institutionalization process is jeopardized, however, when prisoners' rights are stipulated too specifically or narrowly. This tension is reflected in the opposing views of van Zyl Smit and Snacken (2009) versus Engbo (2017). Together with van Zyl Smit, Snacken, who acted as independent expert for the Prison Act Commission, argued that normalization means '*guaranteeing all prisoners a good "average" standard of living rather than accepting extreme differences between prisoners*' (van Zyl Smit & Snacken, 2009: 105). While this seems a fair starting point in abstract terms, it risks losing its value when translating this 'good average standard of living' into concrete, detailed legal provisions. This is for instance the case for the normalization of food: '*The prisoner shall be given sufficient food meeting the standards of modern hygiene*' (art. 42 of the Belgian Prison Act). While providing a good average standard, this provision is reminiscent of Sykes' concerns (2007: 68) in the context of prisoners' deprivation of goods and services:

> Now it is true that the prisoner's basic material needs are met – in the sense that he does not go hungry, cold, or wet. He receives adequate medical care and he has the opportunity for exercise. But a standard of living constructed in terms of so many calories per day, so many hours of recreation, so many cubic yards of space per individual, and so on, misses the central point when we are discussing the individual's feeling of deprivation.

For this reason, Engbo (2017: 345, see also Chapter 2) advocates the opposite: '*a forced order of social equality deviating from the social order in the free society would involve a violation of the requirement of normality*'. In his view, authorities should develop a framework that enables prisoners to create their own lives, instead of normalizing concrete aspects in a predetermined manner. This framework must not be too stringent, since that would result in institutionalization rather than normalization. This seems an equally fair starting point in abstract terms, but it may result in inequalities between prisoners, which van Zyl Smit and Snacken (2009: 105) consider among the *negative* aspects of life outside prison that are to be avoided inside prison.

These opposing lines of argument suggest differences in the authors' frame of reference. They may have had different prison practices in mind when making their respective points about normalization. Even theoretical and legal thinking about normalization usually starts from the observation that the prison practice is in many ways 'abnormal' when compared to society outside prison. While Snacken is most familiar with the 'abnormality' of Belgian prison practice, Engbo is most familiar with it in Danish prisons. These different starting points may have led them to conclude that a 'good average standard' is a satisfying result of normalization for Belgian prisons but not for Danish ones. Their differences in reasoning may also result from cultural differences in valuing enforceable rights. In the context of the Swedish welfare state, Barker (2013) has argued that: '*In Sweden then, individual freedom is constructed through the State rather than conceived as freedom from the State*' (Barker, 2013: 11, emphasis in original). This has resulted in a weak legal tradition of individual rights and greater possibilities for state intrusion '*for the public good*'. The latter has also been argued for Norway (Smith & Ugelvik, 2017) and is in line with the finding that Scandinavians generally have more trust in the authorities of their countries than other Europeans (Lappi-Seppälä, 2008). Belgium, on the other hand, has a strong tradition of individual rights that protect citizens *against* state intrusion. Historically, Belgium became part of France only a few years after the start of the French Revolution (in 1795), which has strongly impacted the Belgian legal tradition (Stevens, 1988). Considering these legal-cultural differences, it makes more sense to argue for a framework within which prisoners can create their own lives in a country with higher levels of trust in the authorities. In a culture with higher levels of scepticism about these authorities, it is more appropriate to protect very specific rights, so that at least these rights can be enforced.

The downside of a detailed list of prisoners' rights is that it risks overlooking other important rights or aspects to which prisoners are consequently not entitled. Some aspects of the material prison environment have been implicitly or explicitly excluded from the normalization process (e.g. the income from labour), but other aspects are simply not mentioned at all. This is the case in both countries for the normalization of the prison architecture, its interior design and its surroundings, despite literally being the framework for the normalization of the living conditions inside the prison. In Norway, article 17 of the Act on the Execution of Sentences contains a principled choice for a communal regime, suggesting that there should be common spaces in prison suitable for labour, education and other programmes, as well as for eating together and spending free time in group (Guidelines concerning the Act). As for prisoners' individual rooms, it is stipulated that these should be provided with adequate furniture and equipment, and that prisoners should keep their rooms clean and not cause any damage (art. 3-22 Regulations). Even though these Regulations and Guidelines suggest that prison design is an important factor in implementing the normalization of daily life in prison, this does not appear anywhere explicitly in legislation. In Belgium, the final report of the Prison Act Commission (2001) only briefly mentioned the architecture in the context of static security. These concise considerations, however, have only been vaguely reflected in the Prison Act (art. 41§2), thus leaving the normalization of the architecture unconsidered and passing the actual decisions in these matters on to the government. The interior design, on the other hand, seemed central to the Prison Act Commission, but the actual Prison Act did not include the right to an individual cell in the end, thus avoiding the long-lasting problem of prison overcrowding in Belgium. Instead, the original intention was watered down to the protection of prisoners' right to '*arrange the accommodation assigned to him at his discretion, subject to stipulations in the internal rules in the interest of order or safety*' (art. 41§1 of the Belgian Prison Act). The scope of this right was even further restricted by the internal rules of the prison.

Equally absent in both countries' legislation is the access to internet. Article 65 of the Belgian Prison Act *forbids* all telecommunications that are not provided by the prison, and article 30 of the Norwegian Act on the Execution of Sentences reads as follows: '*the Correctional Service may grant prisoners access to electronic communication with text, sound and images, if there are no security concerns or concerns regarding the management of resources*' (my emphasis). Since the Belgian and Norwegian Prison Acts were written about twenty years ago, it is not surprising that they do not highlight the importance of internet access as part of normalized material conditions, or even as a human right. It is only more recently that the Human Rights Council of the United Nations has underlined '*the importance of applying a comprehensive human rights-based approach in providing and in expanding access to Internet*' (UN Resolution of 1 July 2016 on The Promotion, Protection and Enjoyment of Human Rights on the Internet). However, the relative character of normalization entails the degree of normalization remaining the same when prison conditions evolve at the same pace as the living conditions outside prisons. Otherwise, the degree of normalization decreases, even if the prison conditions are slowly but surely being 'modernized' (Engbo, 2017; Smith, 2012). The risk that the relevant legislation evolves more slowly in prison than outside prison can be mitigated by including prisoners' rights in the legislation that applies to all citizens, instead of in specific legislation that only applies to prisoners, as is done in Norway for various social services.

In sum, the normalization of the material conditions is reflected in the Belgian Prison Act as subjective rights for prisoners, even though there are many exceptions and many restrictions to these rights. This rights-based approach suits the Belgian socio-legal context but has its pitfalls when it comes to normalization. The Norwegian normalization principle is more implicitly but at the same time more deeply embedded in prison and social policies. The material environment, including the prison architecture, can therefore be expected to be more normalized in the Norwegian practice than a narrow interpretation of the Norwegian Act on the Execution of Sentences would suggest. This will become clear in the next section.

4.3 The Material Prison Environment in Practice

The four prisons in this study have their own distinctive material features. Hoogstraten prison was originally a castle, built in the mediaeval period. Leuven prison was constructed in the nineteenth century in accordance with the then-innovative radial design; Leira prison was built in the 1930s as a boarding school for girls[1]; and Nermarka prison consists of ten separate buildings constructed between 1968 and 2010[2] and all surrounded by an enormous wall. While Leira prison is rather small with capacity for 29 prisoners, the other three are much larger: Nermarka has capacity for 154 prisoners, Leuven for 149 (but often overcrowded in practice) and Hoogstraten for 170. Despite their comparable size, however, Leuven and Hoogstraten are relatively small prisons by Belgian standards, while Nermarka is large by Norwegian standards. In what follows, the normalization of the material environment will be discussed as it emerged from the observations, informal conversations and semi-structured interviews conducted in these four prisons. The interviews and conversations with staff and prisoners are key to a better understanding of their perception of the material prison conditions in relation to what they consider 'normal' in this respect. It is worth repeating though that prisoners' complaints about a lack of privacy, unappetizing food or excessive bureaucracy are *in themselves* no indicators of any differences between the living conditions inside and outside prison. The focus is not on the experiences as such, but on what these experiences tell us about the normalization of these conditions.

4.3.1 Mediaeval but Normalized: Inside the Old Stone Castle

In his influential work on '*limits to pain*', Nils Christie (1982: 9) argued that the material prison conditions, and their 'harshness', are to be assessed in the light of the societal standards of the time. In his view, assessing prison conditions from earlier times by today's standards would be biased by anachronism:

> Those who look at penal history as stages in progress might argue that I refrain too fast. They would see developments, a gradual decrease in pain,

[1] http://www.regjeringen.no/contentassets/a5383153c8d04effbd328a6a3750e6c0/trondheim_fengsel_leira.pdf (last accessed on 29 April 2020).

[2] www.statsbygg.no/Prosjekter-og-eiendommer/Eiendommer/Justissektor/02598-Trondheim-Fengsel-Tunga/ (last accessed on 29 April 2020); www.regjeringen.no/contentassets/a5383153c8d04effbd328a6a3750e6c0/trondheim_fengsel.pdf (last accessed on 2 May 2020).

> which would make ranking possible. [...] From slaveries and workhouses with their uncontrolled abuses, to well-ordered penitentiaries, is that not progress? From whipping for disobedience to loss of privileges? From the old smelling stone castles to single rooms with hot and cold water, - does that not exemplify reduction in pain?
>
> I just do not know. Each form would have to be evaluated according to its own time, by those receiving the pain, in the framework of their usual life and other people's usual life, and in the light of what they saw as their sins. (Christie, 1982: 9, my emphasis)

Ironically enough, the prison of Hoogstraten is still a stone castle in which the rooms have only cold water, and toilet buckets are used at night, resulting in a smelly morning routine of emptying these buckets at 6:30. In line with Christie's argument and with the relative dimension of normalization, these material prison conditions should be assessed in relation to today's living standards in Belgium. However, because the castle is protected heritage, it cannot be adapted to modern living standards. As a result, it is poorly insulated and its electrical system cannot support the use of electric kettles or microwave ovens in the individual cells, leaving prisoners dependent on the hot water that is distributed together with the coffee or food. Nevertheless, most prisoners experienced the living conditions in this old castle as *more* normalized than those in most other Belgian prisons. This paradoxical finding is related to three general observations regarding the normalization of this material environment, which together confirm the need for a holistic approach to normalization.

First, the fact that the material conditions in this old castle were experienced as relatively normalized in comparison to other Belgian prisons indicates that the normalization of the material environment was not understood in terms of material comfort, but in relation to the other dimensions, i.e. as the material framework for a more normalized social environment and a more normal way to spend time. This is why the mediaeval castle with its green surroundings, large courtyard with grass and flowers, many workshops and old-fashioned manually opened and closed doors and gates (which increases personal contact), was considered more normalized than other prisons, despite the undeniable gap between the material living conditions inside and outside prison. Lorenzo, a 40-year-old prisoner, explained this ambivalence as follows:

> *Lorenzo*: Well there are good sides to these bad things, Helene… In other prisons, you have… at least that's how I experience this, in other prisons you can get a PlayStation 2 and stuff, but when you leave your cell, it's all grey, you're sitting in a grey building, so yeah, that does not outweigh what I see here … . (Interview Lorenzo, Hoogstraten prison)

Prison officers also generally preferred the material environment of Hoogstraten over that of more modern prisons:

> *Prison officer Bob*: It's old and creaky, but has its own charm. I like working here and wouldn't want to work in any of these new prisons. (Field notes 27 November 2014, Hoogstraten prison)

Crucial to note here is that being *more* normalized does not mean that something is also considered to resemble the conditions outside prison. By using the living conditions in other Belgian prisons as a common reference point for their assessment of the degree of normalization in this prison, prisoners and prison officers made it implicitly clear that the material conditions in Hoogstraten still differed from those outside prison to such an extent that it was hard to even compare them. For example, during the daily two-hour 'walk', prisoners were allowed to move *independently* from the courtyard to the large room with television, telephones, and pool table and back. This is impossible in other prisons, but this does not mean that the 'walk' in Hoogstraten prison resembles the way in which people usually take a walk outside prison.

Second, it is hard to implement a rights-based normalization process in a material context that is not designed for that purpose. It is true that prisoners' most basic material needs are met by providing them with an individual cell, access to sanitation and basic toiletries, bed linen and towels, three meals a day and clothes (i.e. prison uniforms at the time of the observations). There are toilets in the corridors and showers on the ground floor of the castle. The standard equipment of the cells includes a toilet bucket (or toilet in section A), a table, chair, bed with mattress and pillow, sink, closet, coat rack, bulletin board, mirror, floor squeegee, mop and bucket, a dustpan and brush, a plastic dish bowl, a refrigerator and a television. Prisoners who want to use this television must pay a monthly rent. Furthermore, prisoners' rights to health care, social services, education and work are materially reflected in the availability of a doctor's office, several conversation rooms, classrooms, workshops, an industrial kitchen and bakery, and a farm. Similarly, prisoners' rights to library services, religious services, socio-cultural and other leisure activities are materially supported by the availability of a library, in collaboration with the municipal library of Turnhout, Catholic and Protestant chapels (i.e. the former armoury and a meeting room), the 'cinema room' where films are screened once a month in the winter but which is also used for other activities, and the large room with a television, telephones and a pool table. The gym and sports fields provide opportunities for indoor and outdoor exercise; the telephones in the corridors enable daily phone calls and the visitor's rooms enable visits, to which prisoners are legally entitled. Finally, the right to spend at least one hour a day outdoors is reflected in the large courtyard of the castle and the smaller separate courtyard for the prisoners of section A.

This material reflection of the rights-based approach to normalization has two main pitfalls in this prison. The first one was already mentioned in the context of the 'legislative translation', and entails the above-mentioned rights covering only part of the material environment, leaving important aspects out of the normalization process: kitchens, living rooms or dining rooms for common use, despite Hoogstraten officially being a prison with an '*open communal regime*'. The second pitfall is that prisoners in Hoogstraten largely lack the autonomy that is needed for a normalized use of the material facilities available in the prison. The fact that they are locked inside their cells when not participating in organized activities and cannot walk around the prison or section determines the ways in which they can exercise these rights in practice. Their cell doors must be opened by a prison officer for them to participate in any activity, as well as to receive food, go to the toilet or make a phone call. It means that prisoners are extremely dependent on prison officers. A further consequence of the limited autonomy over the use of the material facilities in this prison is that the normalization process is largely given shape from the perspective of the prison, meaning that it is the prison that defines what normal conditions are, with few opportunities for prisoners to individualize their conditions (e.g. prisoners' choice between three menu types and opportunity to buy additional food, drinks and toiletries from the prison canteen). In so doing, the differences between the material living conditions inside and outside prison can be reduced in ways that are not *experienced* as reduced by all individual prisoners.

This was most apparent in for the normalization of the meals. Given the lack of material opportunities for prisoners to prepare their own meals (except during organized activities), the prison had normalized the meals as follows. Prisoners received three meals a day: a hot dish around noon, and soup with bread in the evening, along with the bread for the next day's breakfast. On Thursdays they also received 'breakfast fruit' and on Sundays usually fries or croquettes. Upon their arrival in this prison, prisoners were asked to choose the regular, pork-free or vegetarian menu, but they could change this afterwards by writing a 'report letter' to the prison governor. These different menus reflect the intention to normalize the meals with respect for individual preferences and cultural differences, while the Sunday fries and daily soup are a traditional Belgian choice. The food was delivered to the cells by the prisoners in charge of this task, together with the prison officer of the section, and consumed individually behind the locked cell doors. Despite the normalization efforts on the part of the prison, with a limited budget (between €3 and €4 per prisoner per day), the food was one of the aspects most commonly complained about by prisoners.

> I'm talking with several prisoners about the food. While they are complaining, I notice that the food looked actually really good today. Today's menu was steak with pepper cream sauce, croquettes and chicory, and a pastry for dessert. 'Yeah but it sounds much better than it was though, and we only got eight croquettes'. (Field notes 26 October 2014, Hoogstraten prison)

When defining the menu for 170 prisoners, it is not surprising that these meals are not considered 'normal' by all of them. But the relationship between normalization and such complaints is more complex. On the one hand, prisoners' negative comments, especially when expressed in group as in the quote above, do not necessarily reflect their actual opinions. Complaining about material conditions can be a way for prisoners to complain about their incarceration situation without showing personal weaknesses, which seems to be the case when prisoners complain about getting 'only eight croquettes' for dinner. On the other hand, sometimes the food was disliked because of its *high* quality. Prison officer Martine explained this in the context of the festive meal that prisoners receive on Christmas day:

> *Martine*: The food during the holidays is really delicious. Really good game, for instance. But many prisoners don't eat this wild game meat because they don't know it. They would rather have deep-fried sausages with chips on Christmas and New Year. (Field notes 21 October 2014, Hoogstraten prison)

Whether or not this normalization process, which is largely given shape from the perspective of the prison, still contributes to its aims is to be assessed in the light of these aims. According to the Belgian Prison Act, these are first and foremost to reduce the harmful effects of detention and to ensure prisoners' rights. While unlikely to cause harmful effects in itself, disagreeable or unhealthy food can be experienced as a frustrating difference between the living conditions inside and outside prison, which can worsen the distress caused by other stressors such as boredom or the lack of privacy (Wener, 2012). The same goes for other aspects of the material environment of Hoogstraten prison, such as the shower water being too hot or too cold at times, the toilet buckets inside the cells and the threadbare prison uniforms.

Third, and related to the second observation, is that normalizing specific aspects of the living conditions without taking into account the 'abnormality' of the context can cause unwanted side effects. The assessment of the degree of normalization does not only depend on the individual or socio-cultural reference points used to define 'normal' living conditions in prison, but also on the way in which the other conditions have been normalized. For instance, prisoners' assessment of whether it is more normal to have private toilets inside the cell rather than shared toilets in the corridors will depend on, first, whether they can independently walk to the toilet in the corridor or not; second, whether there are other opportunities to leave their cell or not; and third, whether these toilets inside the cells are actually private. While the cells in section A were all equipped with a toilet, in practice these toilets were less private than those in the corridor, since these cells were temporarily being used as double cells (and the toilets were not separate space). For Lorenzo, who had quite some prison experience and for whom privacy was no major concern, going to the toilet in the corridor came with a feeling of freedom. He acknowledged that having a toilet inside the cell is preferable for reasons of privacy and hygiene, but having a reason or excuse for leaving the cell was even more valuable to him:

> *Lorenzo*: Well in [a newly built Belgian prison] … you see the difference… how prisoners can walk around or not… Here you still have the toilets… so if you go to the toilet, you can leave your cell… so that's a start. Of course, you prefer your own toilet, but on the other hand… it makes me feel free in my head, being able to press that bell for going to the toilet. And that's a good thing, you're gone, you go to the toilet, and meanwhile you can have a chat here and there … . (Interview Lorenzo, Hoogstraten prison)

Another example of how the normalization of one aspect is influenced by the normalization of its context was the screening of an erotic film on prisoners' televisions. This film was chosen with the intention to normalize the prison conditions in some way, and prisoners had voted for this film over another one. In practice, however, instead of each prisoner having a private experience, it resulted in a large group of prisoners watching the same porn at the same moment, while also being visually checked on a regular basis by the prison officers of their section. Some prisoners and prison officers questioned the normalizing value of this kind of film screening (Field notes 26 October 2014, Hoogstraten prison). Such an attempt to normalize *one* aspect of the material living conditions without normalizing its context can have unintended side effects and even result in an unintended form of institutionalization. This also explains why many prisoners explicitly accepted and even supported certain differences between the material living conditions inside and outside prison, and referred to these differences as being 'normal in prison'. Having to shower during the shower routine after work, for instance, was considered 'normal' given the fact that the castle houses more than a hundred prisoners, who all need to shower on the ground floor of the castle:

> *Lorenzo*: Yeah, of course, that makes sense... right? How crazy would it be if 400 men can all freely choose when to take a shower? That's not possible! That doesn't make sense at all ... . (Interview Lorenzo, Hoogstraten prison)

Applying a holistic approach to normalization, this observation should not be interpreted as if a standardized shower routine is experienced as more normal than having some freedom to choose when to take a shower, in the same way that the more normalized experience in this former castle with toilet buckets and no hot water in the cells is not a plea against modern prison buildings or modern sanitary facilities. It does mean, however, that a further normalization of this aspect depends on the fulfilment of certain preconditions, for instance smaller units with toilets and showers, in which prisoners have some freedom of movement.

4.3.2 Normalizing Life in a Nineteenth-Century Prison

Designed in the nineteenth century, Leuven prison was not aimed to normalize the material living conditions inside its walls. On the contrary, its radial design, featuring a central control point connecting the three prison wings, reflects the nineteenth-century penological philosophy of solitary confinement combined with religious education for the purpose of moral improvement (Ducpétiaux, 1854). Two of these wings, which consist of three landings each, are used to house the prisoners in one-person cells, and the third wing accommodates the punishment cells, the prison kitchen, the staff refectory and the offices for the psychosocial service. The central control point enabled an overview of the wings, landings and cell doors, and thus, of all prisoners who are physically outside their cells. This function, however, has been replaced by camera surveillance, since this central point of the prison is dilapidated and needs renovation. Prison officers are nevertheless still able to oversee the wings in their entirety, while also regularly checking what happens inside the cells through the small window in each cell door. Aside from its panoptic design, however, this material environment also provides the facilities to which prisoners are legally entitled. Very similar to Hoogstraten prison, these material facilities include a 'chapel' (used for religious and humanist services), 'cinema room' (used for various group activities), a gym, two classrooms, one of which has computers, several conversation rooms, a visitors' room, an infirmary, a library in collaboration with the municipal library of Leuven, some workshops and the prison kitchen. On each landing, there are several showers and telephones available, in addition to a staff office and the cells. Every cell has its own toilet and sink, chair, bed, small and large closet, and TV. Leuven also has an outdoor courtyard with two ping-pong tables and a football/basketball court. Still similarly to Hoogstraten, the prisoners were locked in their cells when not participating in the organized activities, and therefore were also dependent on prison officers opening their cell doors to receive food, make a phone call or participate in activities. Unlike Hoogstraten, however, prisoners in Leuven were allowed to have a toaster and electric kettle in their cell, which some of them used creatively to prepare their own meals.

The intention to normalize this material environment within the limits of this old building has the paradoxical result that while prisoners have some high-level material comforts (e.g. they can buy or rent a PlayStation or DVD player, and they can borrow all books available in the municipal library), the material environment still has limitations in terms of basic needs, such as hygiene, ventilation and natural light, and with almost no opportunities for prisoners to leave their cells. Prison officer Vincent described this as follows:

> *Vincent*: 'They just lie in their beds all day, doing nothing at all. It's not too bad in here: they have a TV, and they can rent or buy a PlayStation and Wii, which are things not everyone outside can afford.' Then his tone changes as he admits that he would

> not want to be in their situation, being locked up without even having a door handle on the inside of the room, only able to leave if someone else makes this possible. He assumes that he would go crazy in such a small room. 'But the men are doing this quite well', he says... 'even with two people in a cell ... there is surprisingly little aggression in this prison.' (Field notes 2 November 2015, Leuven prison)

Despite the similarities between the material environments of Leuven and Hoogstraten prison, the following four differences caused the life inside these two prisons to differ significantly, and the prison conditions in Leuven to be experienced as much more painful, and potentially harmful, than those in Hoogstraten. First, Leuven does not have the green surroundings that were valued by prisoners and prison officers in Hoogstraten. The only greenery accessible to prisoners is the tiny bit of grass at the edge of the courtyard. Moreover, prisoners do not leave this building when moving from their cell to the visitors' room, the library, gym or workshops. The only occasion for prisoners to leave the building and to get fresh air is therefore the daily 'walk' on the stone courtyard. Second, the workshops of Leuven prison are located in the basement of this nineteenth-century building. The lack of natural light and fresh air impacts not only the working conditions, but also the type of work that can be carried out in these workshops. The limited work that was available mainly consisted of counting then packing or wrapping a specific number of items in a box or a bag.

> Eddy shows me around the parts of the prison that I haven't seen before. We first go to the basement. Arriving downstairs, we see several prisoners and prison officers building a new bed. This dark workshop smells like wood and metal, and there seems to be little fresh air. We continue our tour and pass a long dark corridor that smells like sewage. We then walk to the workshops, where prison officer Wim is working at his desk. In the large room behind him, two prisoners are sitting on a table, watching the third one who seems to be working. (Field notes 5 November 2015, Leuven prison)

As a consequence, most prisoners spent the majority of their time inside their cells, and had little opportunity to earn money with prison labour. Two other material differences between Leuven and Hoogstraten prison exacerbate the impact of spending so much time inside the cell. As Leuven prison is often overcrowded, one-person cells are commonly shared with one or sometimes two other prisoners, who then sleep on a mattress on the floor. Finally, the cells in Leuven do have toilets inside. This means on the one hand that prisoners do not depend on prison officers to go to the toilet, but on the other hand that going to the toilet does not afford them the chance to leave their cell.

When explicitly asked to compare the living conditions inside this prison with those outside, prisoners pointed out the great deal of time spent inside the cell, caused by the lack of work, as the most disturbing difference, which was generally considered painful and harmful, i.e. feared to cause long-lasting negative effects on prisoners' well-being (this will be discussed in more detail in Chapter 7). Most material differences, however, were expressed in terms of frustrations rather than aspects that would cause serious psychological damage, such as distasteful food, poor hygiene, mice in the corridors or limited access to the fitness room (once a week). Other material differences were left remarkably unmentioned during the interviews. None of the prisoners interviewed mentioned having to wear prison uniforms, or the absence of smartphones or computers with internet connection. Some of them may have had access to a smuggled phone, but they certainly did not have the same freedom to use it inside as they had outside. Neither did they mention the differences between the classrooms and workshops inside and outside prison, despite the fact that these differences did hamper the normalization of the activities that took place there. This was explained by the teacher of 'Dutch for non-native speakers'. She could not use video fragments or a touch screen, as she would do in her classes outside prison. Moreover, although the participants have very different cognitive levels, they all take part in the same class, which makes teaching more challenging. Outside prison she teaches several language classes, grouped by language level and cognitive level. All participants are male, wear the same uniform, and sometimes she senses tensions among her students in prison that she does not notice among her students outside the prison

(Field notes 19 November 2015, Leuven prison). The circus techniques instructor also observed that the prison's 'cinema room' was not an ideal place to teach a group of people how to juggle.

The fact that these differences in material conditions seemed to be more noteworthy to the instructors than to the prisoners can be explained in three ways. First, since these teachers only come to the prison once or twice a week, and are used to teaching outside prison, their reference point for 'normal' material conditions is those outside prison. Many prisoners, on the other hand, have become used to the restrictions of this material environment. The absence of smartphones or smartboards, then, may have been so obvious to them that it was not worth mentioning. Moreover, some prisoners' reference point for 'normal' living conditions was affected even more strongly by having spent large parts of their lives in foster care, psychiatric institutions and rehabilitation centres. As positively voiced by Marc, this made it easier for them to put the prison conditions into perspective:

> *Marc*: I have always lived in institutions, so I have, uhm I have always experienced these things. I am not familiar with anything else. I have always been in institutions, psychiatry, prisons,...so I can put things more easily into perspective than someone who has always lived at home and lived alone. I think it is more difficult for them to put this into perspective. (Interview Marc, Leuven prison)

Second, but related to the first explanation, prisoners who have never taken language classes or circus courses before they came to prison cannot notice these differences. This explanation is supported by the fact that almost all courses in Leuven prison are at beginners' level, which indicates that the normalization process in this context is understood not as ensuring the continuation of any courses that these individuals were taking outside prison, but rather as providing certain courses that are considered 'normal' from a policy perspective. This is in line with a rights-based approach to normalization that provides prisoners with access to the same services as outside prison regardless of whether they made use of these rights or services before their incarceration.

The third explanation for why some obvious differences between the material living conditions inside and outside prison were not mentioned by the interviewed prisoners is that other differences were considered more significant. While many of the differences in material living conditions were experienced as frustrating or 'painful', as mentioned above, prisoners were more concerned with the aspects of prison life that they feared would have long-lasting negative effects. Since boredom, unhealthy or insufficient food, the lack of physical movement, and long waiting lists for psychological help and dental care were feared to cause harmful effects, it is not surprising that prisoners did not mention the absence of video and audio support for the language classes in prison when they were asked to compare the conditions inside and outside prison. Maarten, for instance, was concerned about prisoners who could not afford to buy additional food from the canteen, and would sometimes go hungry.

> *Maarten*: I know that they have a limited budget of three euros and something for everything, but …it's still a basic need, and there are people in here who go around hungry, that's just so… I know… I have experienced it myself the first two weeks in here. That's just wrong… . (Interview Maarten, Leuven prison)

Instead of comparing the material conditions inside and outside prison, prisoners found it easier to compare the material conditions in Leuven prison to those in other Belgian prisons. Using this comparison, prisoners tend to prefer the prisons with more opportunities for activities: more work available, more variation in educational and social activities, and more access to the fitness room.

> *Senne*: Yes, I've also been to [a newer closed prison]. And it's really strict over there. Really strict. But you have much more opportunities, of course. You can buy more things from the canteen. Uhm ... the walks are better. The fitness room is better… (Interview Senne, Leuven prison)

As already explained for Hoogstraten prison, one of the reasons why it is hard to compare material conditions inside and outside prison is because it does not make sense to assess the degree of normalization of specific aspects in an 'abnormal' context. Normalizing particular aspects of the material environment is no guarantee of a more normalized *experience* of this environment, or thus for reducing the frustrations or painful effects associated with this environment. A more comprehensive implementation of this normalization process was found in the two Norwegian prisons.

4.3.3 Window Dressing in Norway?

In general terms, the material conditions and facilities in Nermarka prison seem to be normalized in similar ways to those in the two Belgian prisons. There are classrooms, workshops, conversation and meeting rooms, offices for prison administration, a visitors' room, an exercise room, a shop, a library and a multifunctional room, which is used for sports, religious services, child visits, information meetings and leisure activities. The individual cells are furnished with a bed, table, chair, closet and sink, and many prisoners also have their own TV and radio. Like in Belgium, prisoners are allowed to have a limited number of books, CDs and some personal belongings and clothes in their cell. The lawns and trees between the buildings provide some greenery within the prison walls, which is also the case for the remarkably large outdoor area where the prisoners of the E and M buildings get their daily doses of fresh air (the A and F buildings have their own, smaller courtyards). Based on the import model, health, educational and social services are organized by service providers from outside prison, such as the medical doctors and nurses from Trondheim municipality and psychologists from Trondheim's hospital, NAV counsellors, teachers from the neighbouring high school and priests of the Church of Norway. The prison library is a branch of Trondheim's municipal library, and the school is a branch of a neighbouring high school. This means that prisoners can borrow the same books as citizens outside prison, and that they participate in similar educational programmes as the other students at this school, while the jobs in the workshops and the kitchen are recognized as apprenticeships.

A closer look, however, shows that the gap between the material conditions inside and outside prison was smaller for Nermarka prison than for the two Belgian prisons. This prison's material environment provides more opportunities for normalized social interactions and a higher degree of autonomy and freedom of movement, which enables a more normalized use of the prison facilities. It thus seems to address the material restrictions that caused many of the frustrations in the two Belgian prisons. A logical assumption then, which is in line with the Scandinavian exceptionalism thesis, would be that staying in Nermarka prison is experienced as less painful or frustrating than staying in the Belgian prisons. But this assumption does not hold. On the contrary, the frustrations expressed by prisoners in the E building of Nermarka prison were remarkably similar to those expressed in the two Belgian prisons. The material environment of *Modulen*, by contrast, was experienced as much more normalized. Prisoners in *Modulen* did not only have more personal space and privacy, but would also regularly leave the prison premises. The following paragraphs will first discuss four striking differences with the Belgian prisons, together with prisoners' perspectives in this respect, and then turn to the *Modulen* building.

The first difference was the living units for about twenty prisoners each. These units have their own kitchen, living room and corridor with cells on both sides, showers and two toilets. The living room has couches, a small table, a television, board games and a ping-pong table. The kitchen is furnished with wooden tables and chairs, and with a stove, an oven, a microwave, an electric kettle, a dishwasher, refrigerators with freezers, crockery and cutlery, and kitchen knives which are securely chained to the wall. After the working day, when prisoners have returned to their own unit, they can choose to eat together, or eat alone if they prefer to eat in their cell, and to prepare their own meals. The living room allows them to spend leisure time in group, while the individual cells, to which they have their own key, provide the opportunity to be alone. The showers and toilets in the corridor can be used independently when prisoners are using this common area.

These material conditions are designed to normalize the daily-life activities that take place before and after the working day, to increase prisoners' autonomy and freedom of movement, and are a material reflection of the communal regime as an arena to develop social skills. These 'cosy' living units greatly contrast with the bare corridors in Leuven and Hoogstraten, but this material context in which twenty prisoners live very closely together still differs from the living conditions outside and comes with its own its own challenges. In terms of material conditions, it suffices to say that the common area is crowded and noisy, especially when some prisoners are playing ping-pong and others are watching TV a few metres from each other, and the kitchen is to be shared with more than ten people who all want to use the cooking facilities more or less at the same time.

> *Olav*: it is chaotic, there's so many people to use one little oven. It's absolutely chaotic. [...] Everyone rushes in three hours cooking. Everyone wants to cook. It's like, oh man... [laughs] that's very bad. (Interview Olav, Nermarka prison)

Comparing observations in Nermarka with those in Belgium, at this point, would suggest that these living units could mitigate many frustrations regarding the lack of independency experienced by the Belgian prisoners. It was therefore remarkable from a comparative perspective that one of the most decisive differences between life inside and outside prison experienced by prisoners in the E building was precisely this dependency on the system and the low level of autonomy.

> *Fredrik*: The biggest difference, actually from my point of view, is the ability to do what you ... free choice of what you can do. They take away this freedom to be able to judge for yourself. (Interview Fredrik, Nermarka prison)

***

> *Arne*: But inside here we must do what the guards say you got to do. You must go in your room, stay there, and you must do everything the guards say... (Interview Arne, Nermarka prison)

The living units were clearly not sufficient to solve the lack of autonomy caused by the general operation of the prison, for instance the prison routines (as discussed in Chapter 7) and having to ask prison officers for permission to leave their cells for all kinds of things, including going to the toilet.

The second difference was that the material conditions and facilities were more modern in Nermarka prison than those in Hoogstraten and Leuven. This is of course not a difficult feat in itself, given the fact that the two Belgian prisons were built more than 150 years ago. Both prisoners and prison officers in Nermarka did, however, complain about the obsolescence of this building and its facilities, of which the oldest parts have been in use since 1971. The multifunctional room, for instance, was considered unsuitable for large group activities such as film screenings, and the gym was not satisfying:

> *Farid*: We have one training room with uh… three machines… sharing… how many people? One hundred… (Interview Farid, Nermarka prison)

***

> *Olav*: I've been to the gym a couple of times, but also there's only like five different types of machines you can do. It's not very… it's very few muscles groups you can train. And also there is the same problem that you are getting stuffed by other people that … many of them is just interested in coming there to talk. … But then again, you can't of course, you can't send one and one people down, because it's too small and too many prisoners. (Interview Olav, Nermarka prison)

In contrast to the Belgian prisoners, however, prisoners in the E building could not clearly identify the aspects of the material environment that caused the distress they were experiencing. In Hoogstraten prison, the toilet buckets and the holes in their uniforms were almost symbolic of their difficult situation, and made it easy to explain to an observer like me what was wrong with these conditions. Prisoners in the E building would complain about the food, echoing the Belgian prisoners about getting too many potatoes and too few vegetables, unappetizing or unhealthy food, which, like in the Belgian prisons, could be explained by the limited budget, about 40 NOK per prisoner per day

(Field notes 26 March 2016, Nermarka prison). But in addition to the regular meals provided by the prison, prisoners also had the opportunity to prepare their own meals, using the kitchen facilities and with ingredients they could buy in the shop. Many prisoners prepared their own food several days a week, mostly with a small group of other prisoners (to share the cost of the ingredients). This way, they could prepare food according to their own personal and cultural preferences. The complaints about the food became therefore less legitimate than in the Belgian prisons, both for me as an observer and for them. Trying to convey the hardships of this prison context, which they clearly experienced, was less straightforward in the E building.

> Everyone likes the food today. In fact, the Syrian man thinks it is so good at times that he feels he doesn't deserve it. In prison you should feel that you are in a prison, he says, sometimes you get better food here than outside. (Field notes 22 March 2016, Nermarka prison)

With regard to health care as well, many prisoners acknowledged that the care some people receive in prison is better and more accessible than the care they had outside, despite the many frustrations caused by long waiting lists.

> *Farid*: this is one of the best aspects of the prison. [...] I went to the doctor, I went to chiropractor, I went to dentist, ...I took blood samples, you know, and uh everything. ... they found out that I'm intolerant against this milk, so I get my own special milk. ... the dentist took my tooth, here, first time in my life I lose my tooth, but I don't regret it, because it was a bad tooth and I have no more pain. So they fixed me! [he laughs] (Interview Farid, Nermarka prison)

Frustrations in the E building were rather vague, which seemed to be frustrating in itself. When asked about their experiences with these material conditions, prisoners answered that they missed full internet access (internet access is restricted to certain websites and educational purposes), a DVD player (while they can borrow DVDs from the library, some had been waiting for months to get the chance to buy a DVD player) or an Xbox (which had been promised and therefore frustrating), but at the same time they had to acknowledge that for a prison these were good material conditions. Not being able to point out the painful aspects of the material conditions was even more frustrating due to the knowledge that Norwegian prison conditions are generally considered to be humane and comfortable, and the awareness that the public *thinks* that they live in hotel-like material conditions.

> Emil finds it very frustrating that prisons are often compared to retirement homes by Norwegian media. The frustrating thing, he says, is that they take the worst room in the retirement home, then say they only get washed once a week, and they compare that to a brand new room in Halden. Of course that's a good sales trick, but it's not a fair comparison. Because actually, given how Norway perceives itself, how proud Norway is, they should be ashamed of their prisons, because this is embarrassing for Norway. (Field notes 27 April 2016, Nermarka prison)

The painful experiences were not due to the material conditions themselves, but due to the way in which they could be used: the social context and the dependency, or feelings of dependency, on the system, and limited opportunities to meaningfully spend their time.

The third difference was the remarkable large and green yard of Nermarka prison. The area consists of grass fields with picnic tables, benches and football, basketball, volleyball and tennis courts, and is surrounded by a walking trail of about 400 metres. From certain parts of this yard, one can look over the outer prison wall and see the mountains and the sea. This outside area is used to give prisoners of buildings E and M their daily dose of 'fresh air' as well as for organized activities, e.g. a volleyball game for *Modulen* prisoners or a kubb game for prisoners of the A building. At the far left is a much smaller section, with several benches, but completely fenced in, like a cage, for the *forvaring* prisoners who do not have permission to go outside with the others. This yard was much larger and provided many more opportunities for sports and leisure activities than the courtyards in the two Belgian prisons, especially Leuven. Yet again, prisoners experienced it as frustrating that they were only allowed to spend time in the yard between 17:15 and 18:15. This was especially the case if it was sunny at 16:00 but cloudy an hour later; after the long dark winter, the sunlight in April and May is highly valued in Trondheim (inside and outside prison). This makes it more painful for Trondheim prisoners than for Belgian prisoners to be shut inside when they can see that it is sunny outside. Even though this yard probably mitigated many prisoners' frustrations, compared to prisons without such a yard, it nevertheless shows that the way in which the material conditions can be used, and especially the feeling of dependency on the system, is important for prisoners' subjective assessment of normalization. More substantially, however, it again indicates the more general feeling that their situation was still painful, even though to an observer the material conditions may *look* comfortable.

The fourth difference that indicates a more normalized material environment in Nermarka than in the two Belgian prisons was the shop, which was conceived as an actual shop. Prisoners could visit the shop once a week at fixed times to buy toiletries, drinks, cigarettes, food and ingredients to prepare their own meals. Resembling a Belgian 'night shop' (convenience store) without alcohol and with more vegetables, although its range of products is still limited, the shopping experience is much more normalized than the 'canteen system' in Leuven and Hoogstraten, with forms to be filled out and goods delivered to prisoners' cell doors. Prisoners' income from work was as low as in Belgium (65 NOK/day), which limited some prisoners' opportunities to buy these additional goods and even to prepare their own food, and led to exactly the same complaints as heard in the two Belgian prisons. Nevertheless, all Nermarka prisoners were given partial compensation for the low income in the form of a selection of free food or drinks of their choice, to a value of 120 NOK a week, which was not the case in Leuven or Hoogstraten. Small groups of three or four prisoners tended to cook together so that they could combine their 120 NOK in order to buy all the ingredients they needed. Despite these differences, the prisoners in Nermarka had exactly (even literally) the same complaints in this respect as the Belgian prisoners. Most would argue that the income from prison labour is not enough to buy the additional food from the shop. Some of them explained that if they did not have enough of their own money, they needed financial support from family:

> *Samir*: The work… it's not hard work, but it's not money. Because 65 kr. they give per day. It's not enough to buy cigarettes because cigarettes in here cost too much. One packet costs 105 kr. you have to work two days almost for one packet. […]
> *Me*: So how do you pay for these things?
> *Samir*: Somebody from my family helps me, and I don't buy too much food, I don't talk too much in telephone… and I don't smoke too much… (Interview Samir, Nermarka prison)

In sum, the material conditions of prisoners in the E building look much more normalized than those in the Belgian prisons, but prisoners' experiences with these conditions resembled those of the Belgian prisoners, even though prisoners in the E building could not easily identify the aspects of the material environment that caused their hardships. An explanation could be that Norwegian prisoners have unrealistically high expectations of prisons. It is true that Norwegian prisoners generally did have high expectations, which was clear from the fact that non-Norwegian prisoners were generally much more satisfied with the material conditions. However, the comparison with *Modulen* showed that this was not the reason for their negative experiences. When prisons are compared to hotels, the attention is drawn to the material conditions, but the hardships experienced by these prisoners did not stem from the material conditions as such, but from how the material facilities could be used, which is affected by social interactions and the prison routines (discussed in Chapters 6 and 7).

The *harmful* effects of staying in the E building only became clear from the comparison with *Modulen*. Since these prisoners had first stayed in the E building before being transferred to *Modulen*, the first building was the common reference point for assessing their new material conditions. In comparison with the E building, the material environment in *Modulen* was more normalized in two ways. First, there was more material comfort, resulting in more privacy (each cell had its own toilet and shower) and more personal space (more square metres per person). This was meant to 'reward' these prisoners' commitment to their rehabilitation. Even though the differences in material conditions were subtle and, from an observer's perspective, seemed less relevant than those between the E building and the Belgian prisons, prisoners' experiences with these material conditions were completely different.

> Andre showed me his cell. He was very satisfied with it. Much larger. Nicer view: he can see the sea from his cell, and see cars driving. Lighting is better, he coughs much less than in the E building, and he has a private shower and toilet, so more privacy. (Field notes 24 May 2016, Nermarka prison)

The common areas are more spacious and shared by fifteen instead of twenty prisoners. Next to the kitchen with a dining table, there are two living rooms, one with a pool table and a couch and one with several couches and a television, an exercise room and toilets. *Modulen* also has a staff office, a room for urine tests, conversation rooms and storage rooms. As was the case in the E building, these facilities can be used freely in the afternoons and at weekends. Additionally, this building is surrounded by a lawn with a picnic table and volleyball net, which is separated from the main prison area by a fence. On a sunny day, the staff members could decide to open the outside door so that *Modulen* prisoners could spend their leisure time outside.

> I could see from afar that they were outside… Four men were lying in the sun, on towels or blankets. Andre and Emil were playing chess at a picnic table and the rest were playing cards or chatting at the other picnic table. The sunbathers were smearing themselves with baby oil to tan more quickly. Pål calls out to me: 'Yes, this is normal in Norwegian prison, we are normal!' (Field notes 5 June 2016, Nermarka prison)

Second, for prisoners in *Modulen* the material environment extended beyond the prison walls, since activities regularly took place outside of the prison premises. This was the most significant difference between the E building and *Modulen*. These activities, plus the time spent preparing and 're-entering' prison life, were an intense experience: most prisoners felt excited about leaving the prison, but the activities also caused distress. The activities always entail a physical and mental transition from the high-security prison to freedom and back to high security, which each time involved security checks, very often strip searches. Sometimes this re-entry caused a shock afterwards, especially after a multi-day activity outside of the prison.

During my observation period, the group went on a three-day trip somewhere outside Trondheim. The preparation for this trip also involved activities outside of the prison: three prisoners went to buy some sports clothes in a store in the neighbourhood, and all prisoners needed some information and practical training for the orienteering exercise that would be held on this trip (Field notes 24 May 2016, Nermarka prison). I joined them on the practice run, thereby observing both the excitement about being outside the prison walls and the security checks upon our return to prison.

> When we arrive at the parking lot, we divide ourselves into three groups. Each group is given two maps and two compasses, and a member of staff joins each group. … It's a nice walk, in nature, with beautiful views over the city and the sea, and we were lucky with the weather. The atmosphere is relaxed. At one point, Asgeir walks back to see if we've missed an orientation point. The four of us are waiting. Nils jokes: we better just leave the guard behind … We walk on, and Asgeir rejoins us after a while.
>
> When returning to prison, they joke: 'glad to be home'. The prison officers re-enter through the staff entrance. The prisoners have to go through another door, one by one. I ask what's happening now. Andre does not know himself, because it is also his first time. Someone else answers: 'It could be strip searches, they used to be much more relaxed about this, but nowadays they are much stricter. Last time I was here, I could have had to do strip searches eight times a week.' I join the queue and notice that there are no prison officers around. For a moment, I am not entirely sure that they are just going to let me walk through… When a staff member sees me in line, he laughs with me, and lets me walk through. (Field notes 25 May 2016, Nermarka prison)

The downside of the activities outside prison is the re-entry. After the three-day trip, the liberty deprivation was much more tangible. They had experienced freedom again, which caused new frustrations afterwards that they had not felt before their trip. Some of them were experiencing physical pains after three days of 'normal life', which caused new concerns about the impact of prison life on their bodies and minds.

> After the three-day trip, I ask how it has been. They react very enthusiastically, even Nils, who had been sceptical because he doesn't like mountains at all. Now, he has to admit that he liked it very much and now loves mountains more than before: fishing, soccer, orientation, campfire and baked fish. [...] They had had very nice weather, everyone was enthusiastic about it. And some did have the feeling: am I still in prison? [...] Back in prison, they feel very tired. Several men complain that their bodies are so tired because they are not used to being so active for three days, with so many impressions. Emil finds it alarming that your body can be so tired and hurt after three days of 'normal life'. That says a lot about the way our bodies work in prison. (Field notes 4 June 2016, Nermarka prison)
>
> ***
>
> Nils and Emil complain that it is hard to get used to prison life after the three days trip outside. 'It has been three years that I haven't felt this way', says Bjorn. 'When I arrived here, I prepared myself that I would have to stay here for a long time. So, I didn't really have the feeling of "I want to go outside", but now I want to go outside, especially when the weather is nice.' Emil has the same feeling: it is not that easy to get used to the regime without freedom again. (Field notes 7 June 2016, Nermarka prison)

The distinction between painful and harmful effects of imprisonment is particularly relevant here. The more visible the freedom, the more tangible the liberty deprivation. These confrontations with freedom are painful in many ways, but not harmful. On the contrary, prisoners expected this to contribute to their reintegration by reminding them how different the living conditions in prison are when compared to those outside, even if they were already in the most normalized unit of this prison. These confrontations with freedom, caused by less-restrictive material conditions, play an even more prominent role in Leira prison.

4.3.4 Normal Material Conditions for a Normal Drug-Free, Crime-Free and Responsible Life

'*This is heaven, Tunga is hell.*' These were the words that Kjetil, a prisoner in his fifties, used to summarize the differences between Leira and Nermarka prisons on my first observation day in Leira. The man sitting at the table next to us pointed out the role of people's reference points when assessing these living conditions, and added that the only prisoners who tend to complain about these conditions are those who come to Leira prison without first having experienced a closed prison. For that reason, Kjetil argued that all prisoners should start their sentence in another prison, as he did. When I asked the other man if he had started in another prison, he answered that he started in Leira and that he has been here for ten years now. He must have noticed the confused look on my face, when he clarified: '*I have been working here for ten years now*' (Field notes 2 June 2015, Leira prison).

Unlike the three other prisons in this study, the material conditions of Leira prison have not been instrumentalized for the purpose of liberty deprivation. Instead, the building was conceived as a place for living and working, with a homey design and green surroundings. The homey impression results from the small scale (with 29 bedrooms in total), the layout with living rooms, kitchen and dining room, the wooden floor, and the smell of coffee and home-baked bread. The near absence of static security measures and the total absence of prison uniforms contribute to this impression. As described in Chapter 2, there are four living rooms. The first one connects the entrance hall with the three other living rooms and is furnished with several couches and a small table with board games. The other living rooms are furnished with couches and a television, and the largest one also has a pool table. The kitchen with dining area is equipped with modern cooking facilities, refrigerators, an industrial dishwasher, coffee and tea facilities, a milk dispenser and several round tables. On the first floor, there are 21 individual rooms, a room for urine tests and several conversation rooms. The bedrooms are smaller than those in the other prisons, but prisoners are allowed and encouraged to use the common areas as much as possible. The toilets are in the corridor and the showers are on the basement floor, next to the fitness room. The main building is surrounded by a garden-like lawn with a small playground and several separate buildings, including the garden centre with shop and greenhouses, the classroom, the horse stable, the car repair shop, an apartment for the four female prisoners, one for four male prisoners and two for visitors (close family members who have to travel a long distance). Each apartment has its own living room, kitchen, bedrooms and bathroom.

These material conditions approximate those outside prison in three ways. First, the material standards in this prison are as high as those outside prison. When prisoners were specifically asked to point out the differences with living conditions outside, they mentioned the low wages, which were around 70 NOK a day, and the fact that they did not have access to their smartphone and laptop: '*Yeah….of course I could use a phone and a computer, but we're not allowed so…*' (Interview Jonas, Leira prison). However, these differences were considered inherent to any prison system, and did not cause additional frustrations. Some aspects, such as eating practices and hygiene, were even considered to be more comfortable in Leira than what some prisoners were used to outside prison, especially if their life outside was heavily affected by their drug use.

> *Petter*: Yes, so, I think the food is good. But the people who is making much noise about the food here, 'oh, it's so bad', then I'm thinking what they have on the outside. So, the people who is complaining much, these are the people who have nothing outside, I think. (Interview Petter, Leira prison)

Second, the material environment of Leira prison supports the normalization of the other dimensions, including the social environment and the activities, for instance by providing professional workshops and a garden centre, and cosy living rooms, kitchen and bedrooms. Indeed, rather than focusing on the similarities and differences between the prison conditions and individuals' living conditions outside prison per se, the normalization of this material environment has been instrumentalized for its function as a drug-management unit and for the implementation of the 'consequence pedagogy method' (see also Chapter 2).

As a drug-management unit, this prison aims at preparing prisoners for a drug-free life after release. This aim is materially supported by the spaces designed for activities that contribute directly and indirectly to drug rehabilitation, such as urine tests, therapeutic conversations, education, work, physical exercise, daily-life activities and other social activities. The implementation of the consequence pedagogy method requires material conditions that enable group activities that strengthen prisoners' capacities to make their own choices in life and to live a crime-free life after release. Following this philosophy, the garden centre allows prisoners and prison staff to work together, the dining room enables them to eat together and they can and do exercise together in Leira's gym. In the same light, the culture of consultation and dialogue is supported by the small scale of this prison, the shared living rooms and kitchen, the white board in the dining room which is used to share practical information (e.g. organized activities, bus schedules or general meetings) and by the location of the staff offices. The administrative office is easily accessible for prisoners since it is located next to the kitchen, and the manager's office is right next to this first office, which facilitates the communication between the manager and the other staff members.

The way in which these material conditions are used in practice, is greatly impacted by prisoners' freedom of movement on the prison premises. After the working day, they are free to use the kitchen, the exercise room, the living rooms and the garden, as well as their own bedrooms. This physical independence allows them to use these material facilities in ways that they consider 'normal' at that moment, which prevents or reduces many of the frustrations or 'pains' heard about in the other three prisons. For instance, they can just go and sit outside on a sunny afternoon, or go exercise when they notice that the gym is available. The autonomy that prisoners have to prepare their own food resembles the autonomy of people outside prison in this respect, including the fact that they buy their ingredients in a regular supermarket and do not depend on the prison's selection, as was the case in the three other prisons. It is fair to say, however, that while prisoners can choose to make their own food, they always have a backup in the form of the food provided by the prison, which is not common practice outside prison. The two prisoners who work in the kitchen are responsible for preparing a buffet for lunch, which was highly valued by prisoners, with freshly baked bread, vegetables, eggs, ham, cheese and leftovers from the previous dinner, and for serving the dinner that was prepared at Nermarka prison. Adrian, a prisoner in his twenties, explained this as follows:

> *Adrian*: The dinner could be better, it's not good food.
> *Me*: It's not tasty, or not healthy, or not…?
> *Adrian*: Maybe it's healthy, but it's not tasty. No, it's very disgusting food.
> *Me*: And is that important to you?
> *Adrian*: No [laughs] because we can make our own food, so it's no problem. Maybe, in one week, maybe I eat dinner two times.
> *Me*: And the other days, you cook yourself?
> *Adrian*: Or… we order pizza or something. No, the food is not good here. […] Because Tunga is…. Not good. (Interview Adrian, Leira prison)

The high degree of physical freedom not only reduces frustrations faced by prisoners in the other prison, it also stimulates prisoners' sense of responsibility. Giving prisoners the opportunity to prepare their own meals is one way to do so, even if some individual prisoners were not used to preparing their own meals before their prison sentence.

> *Petter*: So, if you put people in prison, in closed prison, you lock them in, and when you let them out, lots of them have problems. Because it's too different life. When you are in prison, you are not shopping, you are not…yeah everything, you are like a little child. They say 'go to bed', nine o'clock they close you in, they are giving you food. So you can, if you want, you can just sit and they give you food with a spoon in your mouth. And many people, after living like that, they can't go back to normal. So open prison is good for, so it's not so hard to get back to normal life. (Interview Petter, Leira prison)

The third way in which these material conditions approximate those outside prison is through the stimulation of ongoing interaction with society. The most visible example of this interaction is Leira's garden centre, which is freely accessible for customers, to whom this is a *regular* garden centre. In other words, this garden centre does not *approximate* but *is* a garden centre in society. The same logic applies to the social and other services. Based on the 'import model', most social services are provided by external service providers. This was also the case in Nermarka prison (and in the Belgian prisons) but in the prisoners' experience, this provision was much more effective in Leira. In practice, the import model entails, on the one hand, Leira prison being regularly visited by the psychologist, two drug therapists, the teacher and NAV consultants, and, on the other hand, prisoners regularly leaving the prison for a visit to the municipal library, the local supermarket or the football stadium. These services do therefore not just *approximate* those used by other citizens, but are exactly the same. For instance, a group of eight prisoners, based on a rotation system, leave for the supermarket on Mondays, Wednesdays and Fridays at 16:00. They are accompanied by a staff member who gives them a ride in Leira's black minivan, which is also used for going to the library, football trainings and other social activities. The only 'in-house' medical services in Nermarka prison are provided by a general practitioner and dentist, but prisoners are also granted leave to visit a medical specialist outside of the prison.

> *Issam*: I can go to the centre if there is something I need. I can write [to get] a permission [prison leave] and I get it very very quickly. But in another prison, there is no chance. … But here, I can get, if I have a reason, I go to [a doctor to] check my eyes or I go to buy something for myself... (Interview Issam, Leira prison)

Although the relatively high degree of physical freedom and ongoing interactions with the outside world reduced the painful effects that were associated with the material conditions in the other prisons, they also caused some new frustrations and challenges. In line with the findings of Shammas (2014) and Neumann (2012), prisoners experienced the need for self-discipline in this prison in order to compensate for the lack of material restrictions, while still being very conscious of all restrictions associated with the liberty deprivation. For prisoners, the boundaries between the prison and the 'outside world', or between what was allowed and what was not (which could cause them to be sent back to a closed prison) were very clear:

> *Jonas*: Even if you are outside prison walls... we are here, but there are still walls, you know. You can't see the walls, but they are there. (Interview Jonas, Leira prison)

The requirement of self-discipline emerged for instance during a walk with Andreas. As already mentioned, prisoners can go for a walk of 4 or 8 kilometres (and must do so at least on Tuesdays and Thursdays), which extends their freedom of movement beyond the prison premises. At the same time, it increases the need for self-discipline since they must stick to the marked route, inform the prison staff when they leave and check in again within 40 or 90 minutes.

> When I ask if we should walk fast so we can return on time, he reassures me that 40 minutes is enough to walk calmly. [...] When we arrive back at the prison, I'm about to take the shortest route and walk directly to the back entrance of the main building via the garden centre, but Andreas would not follow me, explaining that he is not allowed to take that route. The walk starts and ends at the main entrance of the prison and they are not allowed to take shortcuts or to choose another route. So we walk a bit further, around the building, and use the main entrance to go inside. He enters the staff office for a second to tell them that we are back. (Field notes 5 June 2015, Leira prison)

While any observer would consider this walk as a *normal* and lovely walk, it is one of the many occasions where the liberty deprivation becomes *more* tangible to prisoners. This is not only because prisoners have to show some self-discipline and stick to the fixed route, but also because they *see* the liberty they are deprived of. This was pointed out by Kjetil, when he compared Leira and Nermarka prisons. After having described Leira as '*heaven*' compared to Nermarka prison, he also pointed out the difficulties in Leira.

> Because you are much closer to freedom, you also think much more about freedom and you feel more strongly what you are missing. Moreover, you come much more often in contact with those things you are missing. For example, during your walk, you may encounter people who are drinking alcohol. That makes it more difficult. In Tunga, you can easily switch off your thinking, you just follow the regime. (Field notes 2 June 2015, Leira prison)

In other words, the liberty deprivation seems to be felt *more* strongly in this prison, precisely because the freedom they are deprived of remains clearly visible as a consequence of the lesser degree of liberty restriction (see also De Vos & Gilbert, 2017). This is a challenging aspect of the very open character of this prison that is largely absent in any closed prison (with the exception of *Modulen*). Petter's and Jonas' experiences were very similar to what Kjetil described earlier. The open character makes it harder or impossible for prisoners to deliberately isolate themselves from the outside world, in contrast to what many prisoners tend to do in a closed prison.

> *Petter*: You can see the cars pass but you can't drive it. So when you are in a closed prison, your thought[s]… they are stopping in the wall. When you're here, your thoughts go further, further, they don't stop.
>
> *Me*: And is that positive or negative?
>
> *Petter*: It is harder. Harder to be in open, because, you're thinking longer, you can see the life outside but you can't do it. When you are in a closed one, you are locked, you can close you in. You can close you in in open prison, but it's not the same: you see the cars, you see people come. (Interview Petter, Leira prison)

***

> *Jonas*: in closed prison, your brain is just like turned off: you don't think, you don't do, you just…
>
> *Me*: And what makes that you don't do that here?
>
> *Jonas*: Because, I'm much closer to freedom, I don't have the same ability to close my mind, because I'm out doing things all the time. (Interview Jonas, Leira prison)

Even though these confrontations with freedom were challenging and painful in some way, prisoners expected them to positively impact their reintegration, and therefore felt they were beneficial rather than harmful. Moreover, the feelings of self-discipline and responsibility, which resulted from the increased level of freedom and were certainly frustrating at times, are in line with Leira's philosophy and with the policy aims attributed to the normalization process. These frustrations can therefore not be considered *unintended* painful or harmful effects that are to be prevented or reduced by normalizing the prison conditions, but rather as *intended* results of this normalization process, which itself aims to contribute to a crime- and drug-free life after release.

Does this mean, then, that the material environment of Leira prison is perfectly normalized? The answer depends on one's perspective. The differences between the material conditions inside and outside are effectively reduced in a way that contributes to the implementation of Leira's philosophy: it does stimulate a constructive social climate and meaningful activities that increase prisoners' responsibility and promote a sense of responsibility. From this policy perspective, it can be concluded that this normalization is being implemented effectively. Prison visitors who are surprised to see kitchen knives in a prison kitchen, as mentioned in the introduction to this chapter, would be very surprised to see how much normalization is possible in a prison, yet that it *is* still a prison *and* it is experienced as such by prisoners. From the prisoners' perspective, almost all aspects of the material environment are experienced as more normalized when compared to Nermarka, or another closed prison, but that does not mean that living closely together with 28 other prisoners is experienced as 'normal' living conditions. The situation of living closely together with a group of prisoners requires adaptations to the material environment that are not common outside prison to give prisoners a similar sense of privacy to what they have outside. Moreover, despite the openness towards society, some prisoners still considered a stay in Leira prison like living in a 'bubble' outside of society. They explained that it is fairly easy to stay drug-free, make constructive plans for the future and do what you are expected to do in this prison, but the real challenges are only faced *after* release. Thus, life in Leira prison requires a high level of self-discipline, when compared to staying in a closed prison, but living a crime-free life outside prison requires even more self-discipline for people who were used to a criminal lifestyle before their incarceration, which is the target group of Leira prison.

4.4 Conclusion

There is no doubt that the material environment is only one dimension of prison life, but it provides a framework that enables or hampers the normalization of the other dimensions. Some material conditions are particularly important for normalizing the other dimensions: relatively free access to fresh air and green surroundings; the space available for leisure and work activities; and the size of the living units. At the same time, the normalization of the other dimensions (i.e. security, social environment and the use of time) determines how the material environment can be used. For instance, greenery around the prison building can increase the perceived quality of life, if prisoners are free to go outside and enjoy the nice weather; it can also become a source of frustration if prison policy limits the airing of prisoners to a restricted time window when the sun no longer shines. When research shows that modern does not equal better (e.g. Hancock & Jewkes, 2011) or does not equal 'normalized' if you will, it does not question the material standards as such, but their impact on the other dimensions of prison life. Given this interdependency, it is key for a normalized experience that the normalization of the material prison context is approached holistically.

This holistic perspective is more in line with the Norwegian than with the Belgian approach to normalization. The Norwegian normalization principle is more deeply embedded in the prison and social policy, despite its implicit reflections in the Norwegian Act on the Execution of Sentences, and is interpreted instrumentally, which makes it more important to create the individual and common spaces necessary for rehabilitation activities. The Belgian Prison Act, by contrast, guarantees basic material conditions as subjective rights for prisoners (albeit with many exceptions and restrictions). As mentioned, some minimum material standards were still not being met in practice, like the toilet buckets, prison uniforms with holes in them or one-person cells shared by two or three prisoners, which confirms the need for such a rights-based approach. At the same time, however, this rights-based approach gives the illusion that the material conditions can be normalized independently of their context. This leads to paradoxical situations where prisoners can have a PlayStation inside their cell but no physical exercise. Moreover, it was mainly the aspects of the material environment not covered by the Prison Act that contributed to a more normalized experience in Hoogstraten: nature, sports fields and the character of the building. The individual rights can therefore be understood as minimum requirement for a normalized material context, but the normalization of the material environment must always be seen as instrumental to the normalization of the other dimensions, even when the normalization is in principle understood intrinsically.

Since normalizing is about reducing differences between living conditions inside and outside prison, this comparison is about the gap between the material living conditions inside and outside prison. This gap was wider in Belgium than in Norway. From an observer's perspective, the material conditions in the Norwegian prisons *looked* without any doubt more normalized than those in the Belgian prisons, even when bearing in mind that material living standards are generally higher in Norway than in Belgium. However, this was not reflected in prisoners' experiences, not simply because the Norwegian prisoners had higher expectations, but because normalized conditions do not guarantee a normalized use of those conditions. In line with the findings of Wener (2012) and van der Kaap-Deeder et al. (2017), the sense of autonomy and freedom of movement mattered more than the objective material standards. If prisoners are free to use the kitchen, the exercise room, the living rooms, the garden, as well as their own bedrooms after working hours, they can use these material facilities in ways that they consider 'normal' at that moment. The less autonomy prisoners have over their material conditions and how to use them, the more the prison imposes a particular implementation of the normalization process. These 'normal' material conditions are then defined and provided in detail, tending towards institutionalization rather than individualization or freedom of choice. Whether this institutionalization is experienced as painful will depend on the subjective experience of a prisoner. Whether it is harmful will also depend on how it interacts with the other dimensions of normalization. It should be noted, however, that prisoners are aware of and accept the limitations of the prison context. This is even more so when they take other prisons as reference points to assess the degree of normalization, rather than the living conditions outside prison. Therefore not all differences with the material conditions from outside prison cause additional frustrations. What prisoners are much more concerned about are differences that were feared to have long-lasting negative effects (after release). In this respect, the most meaningful differences between the four prisons were the relatively high levels of physical freedom and of discretion to use the material facilities in an autonomous way, and the ongoing confrontations with freedom in Leira and Modulen.

Leira prison demonstrates that the allegedly standard prison features of high walls and fences are not imperative. Imprisonment in Leira is '*shallow*' (Crewe, 2011a, 2021), since freedom remains visible and tangible. When the depth of imprisonment is understood as '*the distance to freedom*' or the '*difference from the outside world*', it makes sense to argue that the more '*shallow*' the imprisonment, and the closer to freedom, the more normalized the prison conditions. In practice, the shallowness or openness in Leira means that, objectively speaking, some aspects of the living conditions of the prisoners concerned do not just approximate those of other citizens but are exactly the same (e.g. the garden centre, shop, library, sports fields). Moreover, some aspects, such as food and hygiene, were experienced by some prisoners as better inside than outside prison.

One may ask, then, as Shammas (2014) did in his well-known article on '*the pains of freedom*': '*Where is the pain in exceptional prisons?*' Or: is it still punishment if some conditions in prison are experienced as beneficial? The answer to this question is positive because it is the liberty deprivation that is the intended pain. It is not because prisoners positively value the food or hygiene in prison that they do not experience their liberty deprivation as pain. Prisoners in Leira were not free, and did not feel free. On the contrary, because freedom remained visible, the liberty deprivation was felt more strongly here than in closed prisons. Indeed, in line with findings of Shammas (2014) and Neumann (2012), the ongoing confrontations with freedom caused some new frustrations and challenges. Prisoners require higher levels of self-discipline in such prison regimes to compensate for the lack of material restrictions and are continuously reminded of what they are deprived of. Most of the frustrations related to the confrontations with freedom or relative deprivation are, however painful, not harmful in the longer term. On the contrary, prisoners in Leira and *Modulen* expected these frustrating and demanding aspects of the openness to be beneficial for their reintegration. Shammas (2014: 120) concluded his analysis by arguing that our insights into these 'pains of freedom' '*can strengthen the political legitimacy of "soft" incarceration, showing that this imprisonment form is sufficiently painful...*'. But there is even more to these pains: insofar as they emerge directly from the liberty deprivation itself, in this case from its less total application, they could be said to be the *intended* pains of liberty deprivation. After all, normalization is not intended to reduce the pains caused by the 'pure' liberty deprivation, which is still an '*evil that the state imposes on an offender because of the offense, with the intention to be experienced as an evil*' (Andenæs, 1962 cited in Fredwall, 2017, my translation). If it is true that the more open the prison, the 'purer' the liberty deprivation, and thus the more normalized the conditions, are normalization and security then to be considered mutually limiting? This question is addressed in Chapter 5.

References

Baldursson, E. (2000). Prisoners, prisons and punishment in small societies. *Journal of Scandinavian Studies in Criminology and Crime Prevention, 1*(1), 6–15.

Barker, V. (2013). Nordic exceptionalism revisited: Explaining the paradox of a Janus-faced penal regime. *Theoretical Criminology, 17*(1), 5–25.

Benko, J. (2015, May 26). *The New York Times Magazine*. https://www.nytimes.com/2015/03/29/magazine/the-radical-humaneness-of-norways-halden-prison.html. Last accessed on 11 February 2019.

Camp, S. D., Gaes, G. G., Langan, N. P., & Saylor, W. G. (2003). The influence of prisons on inmate misconduct: A multilevel investigation. *Justice Quarterly, 20*(3), 501–533.

Christie, N. (1982). *Limits to pain*. Robertson.

Crewe, B. (2011a). Depth, weight, tightness: Revisiting the pains of imprisonment. *Punishment & Society, 13*(5), 509–529.

Crewe, B. (2011b). Soft power in prison: Implications for staff–prisoner relationships, liberty and legitimacy. *European Journal of Criminology, 8*(6), 455–468.

Crewe, B. (2015). Inside the belly of the penal beast: Understanding the experience of imprisonment. *International Journal for Crime, Justice and Social Democracy, 4*(1), 50–65.

Crewe, B. (2021). The depth of imprisonment. *Punishment & Society, 23*(3), 335–354. https://doi.org/10.1177/1462474520952153

De Vos, H., & Gilbert, E. (2017). Freedom, so close but yet so far: The impact of the ongoing confrontation with freedom on the perceived severity of punishment. *European Journal of Probation, 9*(2), 132–148.

Ducpétiaux, E. (1854). *Avant projet de loi sur le régime des prisons, soumis à la Commission chargée par l'arrêté royal du 25 juin 1853 de préparer la révision de la législation pénitentiaire. Exposé des motifs, projet de loi et appendice*. M. Weissenbruch.

Engbo, H. J. (2017). Normalisation in Nordic prisons—From a prison governor's perspective. In T. Ugelvik & P. S. Smith (Eds.), *Scandinavian penal history, culture and prison practice: Embraced by the welfare state?* (pp. 327–352). Palgrave Macmillan.

Fransson, E., Giofrè, F., & Johnsen, B. (2018). *Prison, architecture and humans*. Cappelen Damm Akademisk/NOASP (Nordic Open Access Scholarly Publishing).

Fredwall, T. E. (2017). Straff som pine. *Retfærd: Nordisk juridisk tidsskrift, 40*(3–4), 24–37.

Gentlemen, A. (2012, May 18). *The Guardian*. www.theguardian.com/society/2012/may/18/halden-most-humane-prison-in-world. Last accessed on 11 February 2019.

Goffman, E. (1961). *Asylums. Essays on the social situation of mental patients and other inmates*. Penguin Books Ltd.

Golash, D. (2005). *The case against punishment: Retribution, crime prevention and the law*. New York University Press.

Hancock, P., & Jewkes, Y. (2011). Architectures of incarceration: The spatial pains of imprisonment. *Punishment & Society, 13*(5), 611–629.

Huey Dye, M. (2010). Deprivation, importation, and prison suicide: Combined effects of institutional conditions and inmate composition. *Journal of Criminal Justice, 38*(4), 796–806.

Irwin, J., & Owen, B. (2005). Harm and the contemporary prison. In A. Liebling & S. Maruna (Eds.), *The effects of imprisonment* (pp. 94–117). Willan Publishing.

Johnsen, B. (2018). Movement in the prison landscape: Leisure activities—Inside, outside and in-between. In E. Fransson, F. Giofrè, & B. Johnsen (Eds.), *Prison, architecture and humans* (pp. 65–85). Cappelen Damm Akademisk/NOASP (Nordic Open Access Scholarly Publishing).

Johnsen, B., & Granheim, P. K. (2012). Prison size and the quality of life in Norwegian closed prisons in late modernity. In T. Ugelvik & J. Dullum (Eds.), *Penal exceptionalism? Nordic prison policy and practice* (pp. 199–214). Routledge.

Jones, H. L. (2007). *The pains of custody: How young men cope through the criminal justice system.* Thesis submitted for the Degree of Doctor of Philosophy in the University of Hull, UK.

Knight, V. (2016). *Remote control: Television in prison* (1st ed.). Palgrave Macmillan.

Lappi-Seppälä, T. (2008). Trust, welfare, and political culture: Explaining differences in national penal policies. *Crime and Justice, 37*(1), 313–387.

Liebling, A., assisted by Arnold, H. (2004). *Prisons and their moral performance. A study of values, quality and prison life.* Oxford University Press.

Moore, E. (1981). A prison environment's effect on health care service demands. *Journal of Environmental Systems, 11*(1), 17–34.

Moran, D., & Turner, J. (2019). Turning over a new leaf: The health-enabling capacities of nature contact in prison. *Social Science & Medicine, 231*, 62–69.

Neumann, C. B. (2012). Imprisoning the soul. In T. Ugelvik & J. Dullum (Eds.), *Penal exceptionalism? Nordic prison policy and practice* (pp. 139–155). Routledge.

Pratt, J. (2008). Scandinavian exceptionalism in an era of penal excess, part I: The nature and roots of Scandinavian exceptionalism. *British Journal of Criminology, 48*(2), 119–137.

Prison Act Commission. (2001). Eindverslag van de commissie 'basiswet gevangeniswezen en rechtspositie van gedetineerden'. *Verslag namens de commissie voor de Justitie uitgebracht door de heren Vincent Decroly en Tony Van Parys, Parl.St. Kamer, 1076*(2000–2001), 001.

Rocheleau, A. M. (2013). An empirical exploration of the 'pains of imprisonment' and the level of prison misconduct and violence. *Criminal Justice Review, 38*(3), 354–374.

Sexton, L. (2015). Penal subjectivities: Developing a theoretical framework for penal consciousness. *Punishment & Society, 17*(1), 114–136.

Shammas, V. L. (2014). The pains of freedom: Assessing the ambiguity of Scandinavian penal exceptionalism on Norway's Prison Island. *Punishment & Society, 16*(1), 104–123.

Smith, P. S. (2012). Imprisonment and internet-access. Human rights, the principle of normalization and the question of prisoners access to digital communications technology. *Nordic Journal of Human Rights, 30*(4), 454–482.

Smith, P. S. (2014). *When the innocent are punished: The children of imprisoned parents* (Palgrave Studies in Prisons and Penology). Palgrave Macmillan.

Smith, P. S., & Ugelvik, T. (2017). *Embraced by the welfare state? Scandinavian penal history, culture and prison practice* (Palgrave Studies in Prisons and Penology). Palgrave Macmillan.

Stevens, F. (1988). L'introduction de la législation révolutionnaire en Belgique. In *La Révolution et l'ordre juridique privé. Rationalité ou scandale?* (pp. 472–493). PUF.

Sykes, G. (2007). *The society of captives: A study of a maximum security prison* (First Princeton classic ed.). Princeton University Press.

Ugelvik, T. (2014). Paternal pains of imprisonment: Incarcerated fathers, ethnic minority masculinity and resistance narratives. *Punishment & Society, 16*(2), 152–168.

Vander Beken, T. (2015). *Howardreizen. De rol van de gevangenis in Europa.* Maklu.

van der Kaap-Deeder, J., Audenaert, E., Vandevelde, S., Soenens, B., Van Mastrigt, S., Mabbe, E., & Vansteenkiste, M. (2017). Choosing when choices are limited: The role of perceived afforded choice and autonomy in prisoners' well-being. *Law and Human Behavior, 41*(6), 567–578.

van Zyl Smit, D., & Snacken, S. (2009). *Principles of European prison law and policy. Penology and human rights.* Oxford University Press.

Wener, R. E. (2012). *The environmental psychology of prisons and jails: Creating humane spaces in secure settings.* Cambridge University Press.

Wheeler, S., & Cline H. J. (2020). *The Scandinavian prison study* (Palgrave Studies in Prisons and Penology). Palgrave Macmillan.

5
Security and Normalization: A Double Balancing Act

Heightened security is the single most characteristic feature of prisons, not only for outsiders but arguably also for prisoners and personnel. The need for security measures is a consequence of the liberty deprivation that is at the centre of a prison sentence. It makes the lack of freedom visible and tangible. Without liberty deprivation, no need for security measures, and consequently, no need for normalizing the living conditions in prison. '*Because in the nature of things security necessarily leads to constraints which exaggerate the differences between life inside and life outside of prisons*' (King & Morgan, 1980: 36), one might assume that normalization and security are communicating vessels. Following this reasoning, the normalization of living conditions in prison requires a minimum use of security, or, put more simply, the more normalization, the less security. But as already hinted at in the previous chapter, such an assumption must be qualified. It is true that security considerations are often used to legally justify restrictions to the normalization process, but at the same time, security or the feeling of security, is in itself also a crucial aspect of normal, or at least desirable, living conditions. As Sykes (2007/1958: 76–77) has argued for prisoners of the New Jersey State Prison, the deprivation of security often results from being

H. De Vos, *Beyond Scandinavian Exceptionalism*, Palgrave Studies in Prisons and Penology, https://doi.org/10.1007/978-3-031-28635-3_5

forced to associate with the other prisoners. Hence, many prisoners and prison staff consider security measures 'normal' in prison, even if these measures differ from what they consider 'normal' outside prison. Therefore, this chapter will not only be concerned with the ways in which the different sorts of security measures are normalized, but also with the ways in which all these sorts of security measures limit, expand or influence the scope of normalization in practice.

5.1 The Ambiguous Relationship Between Normalization and Security

Official mission statements of correctional services generally include the security and safety in prison as well as in society, by aiming to prevent escapes, reduce or manage risks, and reduce recidivism (O'Donnell, 2016: 42–43). The correctional services are not alone in prioritizing security, since this is also a central concern for prisoners and prison staff. This was already pointed out by Sykes in 1958, but also Liebling (2004: 432–434) has identified the lack of order and organization, and the presence of drugs in prison as aspects of prison life that '*really mattered*' to prisoners. Given the particular characteristics of the prison context, however, it is not surprising that measures aimed at enhancing security and safety entail their own risks to prisoners' privacy, feelings of fairness, integrity and well-being, and indirectly to the safety in prison and in society. Most obvious in this context are the strip searches, cell searches and the monitoring of communication with family and friends, all of which contribute to prisoners' mortification process (Goffman, 1961: 35–36) and hardships (see, e.g., Schaanning, 2009). Snacken (2005 cited in van Zyl Smit & Snacken, 2009: 43) found that prisoners experience a level of *institutional violence*, which is '*the pressure exercised by the institution on its inmates through its mere existence*'. King and Morgan (1980: 37) therefore advocate the 'minimum use of security', which is based on the principles of proportionality and subsidiarity: '*prisoners should be subject to only that degree of security necessary to safeguard the public against any realistic threat, and to ensure that prisoners complete their sentences in the prisons to which they are allocated*'. From this quote, however, it is clear that King and Morgan mainly focused on public safety and avoiding escapes, and not on the security *inside* prison.

The promotion of security inside prison can be done through the material as well as the social dimension of the prison environment. Whereas static security relates to the material aspects that are expected to contribute to a safer environment, such as cameras, fences, and alarms and dynamic security relates to the interpersonal relationships between prisoners and prison staff that allow prison staff to sense unrest and intervene preventively. Although static security is certainly valuable in some respects, research has shown that the role of dynamic security is at least equally important (van Zyl Smit & Snacken, 2009). Stressing the importance of interpersonal relationships even further, Liebling (2011) points out that staff-prisoner relationships, and the way in which prison staff uses its authority, do not only relate to order in prison, but also contribute disproportionately to prisoners' evaluation of fairness and ultimately to their well-being.

> What made one prison different from another was the manner in which prisoners were treated by staff, how safe the prison felt and how trust and power flowed through the institution. Prisoners' well-being was to a large extent a consequence of their perceived treatment. (Liebling, 2011: 534)

Likewise, both the material environment and the interpersonal relationships can provide safety for society. Physical features of the prison can prevent escapes, and interpersonal contacts allow for social assistance, risk assessment and rehabilitation. Pollock et al. (2012) found that effective treatment requires that prisoners feel physically, socially, psychologically and morally/ethically safe, hereby referring to Bloom's '*sanctuary model*' (1997). This means that providing effective treatment is difficult or impossible in prison environments in which prisoners have to concentrate on survival in the first place (Pollock et al., 2012). This was confirmed by Crewe et al. (2014: 400):

> This lack of safety, and the absence of staff support, denied prisoners the 'headspace' and assistance required for their own personal development.

> Attention was focused on surviving the present rather than planning for the future.

Despite the importance attached to prison officers' role to provide security in prison, research shows that not only the use of 'hard', authoritarian power but also the use of 'soft power' gives rise to pains and frustration for prisoners (Crewe, 2011b). While 'hard power' causes physical victimization and fear of victimization, 'soft power' causes psychological distress by placing high, and sometimes unrealistically high, demands on prisoners in terms of self-regulation. Crewe (2011a) identified new 'pains of imprisonment' caused by the modern and seemingly softer English and Welsh prison system, including the pains of indeterminacy, psychological assessment and self-government. Processes of risk assessment and psychological assessment in these prisons tend to reduce prisoners' personality to a number of risk factors and even trap them in '*the carceral net*', which is explained as follows:

> Those who dispute the prevailing institutional discourse may be considered 'in denial'; those who adopt it with too much enthusiasm may be suspected of insincerity and 'people-pleasing behaviour'. (Crewe, 2011a: 515–516)

As Neumann (2012) and Shammas (2014) have pointed out for open prisons, imposed responsibility or self-discipline also provokes distress and anxiety in prisoners, as they are aware, and constantly remind themselves, of the fact that '*beyond the core of soft power and self-regulation, the penal perimeter remains firm and coercive*' (Crewe, 2011a: 523). It could therefore be argued that *normalizing* the use of power involves *reducing* the power exercised by prison officers. But this conclusion would disregard the unintended side effects of reducing prison officers' power, which involve increased feelings of insecurity. In this context, Crewe et al. (2014: 397) found that the power of prison officers is applied most legitimately when it is '*light*', i.e. relaxed, cooperative and approachable, but at the same time '*present*', i.e. visible/available, interventionist and confident/authoritative. When prison officers' power is invisible or weak (i.e. '*absent*'), violent incidents and feelings of insecurity tend to increase, which is undesirable for both prison officers and prisoners (Crewe et al., 2014). This confirms earlier findings that prisoners accept the power and authority of prison staff, as long as it is used fairly and with respect (Liebling, 2004: 346; see also Irwin & Owen, 2005: 105–107). The following paragraphs will outline how this complex relationship between normalization and security is given shape in the legislation of Belgium and Norway.

5.2 Security in Relation to Normalization: A Legislative Perspective

Belgian and Norwegian penal policies both strive for a balance between security measures and normalization, albeit officially for different reasons. The rather intrinsic approach to normalization underlying the Belgian Prison Act entails the following inherently conflicted relationship between the two concepts: on the one hand, security in prison is considered an important aspect of 'normalized' living conditions, but on the other hand, security considerations are explicitly considered legitimate limitations to the normalization process, implying that the concepts are also considered opposites. In line with the rights-based approach in Belgium, the security of prisoners, prison staff and society is to be ensured without compromising prisoners' dignity, privacy and other rights any more than necessary. A similarly balanced relationship between security and normalization is expressed in Norwegian penal policy, but here it is understood in a more instrumental way: more normalized living conditions entail fewer or less stringent security measures, leading eventually to more security in prison and in society. Thus, security and normalization are presented as opposites: the more normalized the living conditions, the lower the security level, and the other way around. At the same time, however, normalization is also in line with the security objective of Norwegian penal policy, since it is instrumental to achieving more security in prison and in society.

The available security measures *inside* prisons in Belgium and Norway show clear similarities. In Belgium, the general rule concerning order and security in prisons is stipulated in article 5§2 of the Belgian Prison

Act: '*In executing the prison sentence or detention, order and safety shall be ensured*'. Many articles explicitly restrict or may restrict prisoners' rights for reasons of 'order or safety' (e.g. articles 13, 41, 43, 45, 47, 55, 56, 59, 64, 77, 85), while maintaining order and safety in the prison is at the same time seen as benefitting the '*living conditions to which the prisoner has a right in this forced society*' (Prison Act Commission, 2001: 60). Along the same lines, the Belgian Prison Act defines 'order' as '*a condition in which the rules for behaviour are obeyed that are necessary for creating or maintaining a humane social climate in the prison*' (art. 2, 7° Prison Act). Order and security are thus considered aspects of normalized living conditions. However, the hot topics of prison overcrowding, radicalization, prison officers' strikes and cost-cutting measures have led to security considerations gaining even more prominence in more recent policy documents. So much so that the then minister of Justice saw no alternative than '*to use military staff in the prisons to maintain decent living conditions for the prisoners*' (Geens, 2017: 1).

Security in Belgian prisons is ensured by a combination of static and dynamic security measures and a series of control and security measures that may be taken in specific circumstances. The general principles that are enshrined in article 105 of the Prison Act imply '*a dynamic interaction between prison staff and prisoners on the one hand, and a balanced relationship between the technological means used and a constructive detention regime, on the other*', with security measures that are '*in proportion to these objectives, both in their nature and their duration*'. The underlying principles of proportionality and subsidiarity are obvious: security measures must always be *necessary* for order and safety and must always involve the *least invasive measure* for achieving their intended purpose. In the subsequent articles of the Prison Act (art. 107–121), which list control measures (e.g. identification, search of clothing, body searches and cell checks) and exceptional security measures (e.g. taking away or withholding objects; exclusion from participation in certain group or individual activities; observation day and night, but with maximum respect for sleeping hours; mandatory stays in the prisoner's own cell; and accommodation in a secure cell, with no objects whose use could be dangerous) in more detail, security and normalization are presented primarily as opposites, with safety and security concerns imposing restrictions on the normalization process and, in turn, the normalization imposing restrictions on the use of these measures. Each control and/or security measure is individually subjected to the principles of subsidiarity and proportionality, and the prisoner on whom a particular measure is imposed explicitly keeps his/her other rights (see, for example, art. 113 and art. 117 §2). The more far-reaching the measure is, the more guarantees are attached to it. For the 'clothing check', for example, the law only provides a few vague guarantees (art. 108 §1–3), while the 'placement in an individual security regime' requires a much more strict procedure (art. 116, 117 and 118).

In Norway, like in Belgium, security is a decisive consideration in prison policy, reflected in articles 2 and 3 of the Act on the Execution of Sentences, which define the aims and the content of the sentence, and in the mission statement of the Correctional Service:

> The Correctional Service shall organize the sentences and pre-trial detention in such a way that it ensures public safety and prevents recidivism, by enabling offenders to change their criminal behaviour. (website of the Norwegian Correctional Service, www.kriminalomsorgen.no/om-kriminalomsorgen.237840.no.html)

The relationship between normalization and security emerges from the definition of the normalization principle itself, which includes that '*No-one shall serve their sentence under stricter circumstances than necessary for the security in the community. Therefore offenders shall be placed in the lowest possible security regime*' (website of the Norwegian Correctional Service, original in English). Normalization and security measures are thus presented as opposites, meaning that living conditions in lower-security regimes are by definition more normalized than those in higher-security regimes, and that security measures in higher-security regimes are by definition legitimate restrictions to the normalization process. Following this reasoning, prisoners are supposed to be brought to a lower-security prison when these restrictions are not necessary (or not any longer), but in reality all prisoners are first sent to a high-security prison (art. 11 and 15 of the Act on the Execution of Sentences).

Like in Belgium, the Norwegian Correctional Service explains that the concept of security entails static security measures (such as cameras and locks), organizational security (e.g. 'good' routines) and dynamic security (respectful relations between prisoners and prison staff with clear expectations) (www.kriminalomsorgen.no/type-fengsel-og-sikkerhet.237877.no.html). At a more concrete level, it is the Act on the Execution of Sentences together with the corresponding Regulations relating to the Execution of Sentences, and Guidelines concerning the Act and the Regulations that formulate the preventive security measures (art. 14, 27–29, 37–38, e.g. transfers to other prisons, inspections, exclusion from association with other prisoners) and reactive security measures (art. 39–40, disciplinary actions if internal rules are violated) that can be applied in prison. Especially in the context of inspections (art. 28) and drug prevention measures (art. 29), security concerns seem to overshadow normalization considerations. For example, the inspection of the prisoner upon entry and before and after prison leave can only be *omitted* if this can be justified on security grounds, while drug tests may be carried out randomly, by any means (blood, urine, saliva, sweat, breath), and without cause, i.e. concrete indications of drug use. Only the Guidelines state that '*the examination shall not be more invasive than necessary*' and that the '*urine tests should happen in a way that is least painful or humiliating for prisoners*' (Guidelines 29.1 and 29.2). The principles of proportionality and subsidiarity emerge more clearly in the context of the exclusion of prisoners from association with other prisoners (art. 37) and the use of coercion (security cell, restraining bed or other approved coercive measure) (art. 38). These preventive measures may only be used if they are strictly necessary for the aims listed[1]; if other measures are insufficient; and for the shortest possible time. Unlike in the case of preventive

1

Art. 37: The Correctional Service can decide that a prisoner is to be excluded completely or partly from association with other prisoners if this is necessary in order to a) prevent prisoners from continuing to particularly negatively influence the prison environment; b) prevent prisoners from injuring themselves, acting violently or threatening others; c) security measures, prisoners' legal guarantees are clearly described in the context of these disciplinary sanctions (art. 3-37 to 3-39 Regulations). Here, too, the Guidelines underline the principles of proportionality and subsidiarity, stating that '*the sanctions shall not be more invasive than necessary to reach the goal of the measure, and the chances of potential unintended consequences should be reduced as much as possible*' (art. 40.1 Guidelines). As for the disciplinary sanctions, it is the '*loss of privileges*' (exhaustively described in art. 3-37 Regulations) that is particularly interesting in the light of the normalization principle. In principle, prisoners have, or should have, the same *rights* as other citizens, which opposes the idea of *privileges* that can be taken away.

So all in all, security inside prisons is built in the legislation along the same lines in Belgium and in Norway. Only the Norwegian preventive security measures on inspection and drug prevention, respectively, have no counterparts in the Belgian Prison Act. In contrast to the relevant articles of the Belgian Prison Act, however, the articles of the Norwegian Act (and their explanation in the Ot.prp. no. 5 (2000–2001)) are not systematic reminders of the conflict between these security measures and the normalization principle, nor do they present security measures as facilitators to normalize the prison conditions. The principles of subsidiarity and proportionality and prisoners' procedural rights in this context, consistently underlined in the Belgian Prison Act, also appear in the Norwegian Act but in a less systematic way. Moreover, in Norway, prisoners' legal safeguards are formulated more as instructions to prison officers than as enforceable rights of prisoners. From a comparative perspective, it is also remarkable that Norwegian prison

prevent considerable material damage; d) prevent criminal acts; e) ensure peace, order and security [...]

Art. 38: The Correctional Service can use a security cell, restraining bed or another approved coercive measure, in order to a) prevent a serious attack on or injury to a person, b) prevent the execution of serious threats or considerable damage to property, c) prevent serious riots or unrest, d) prevent escape from prison, during transportation or at the place of destination, e) prevent unlawful intrusion into prison, f) ensure access to a closed or barricaded room [...]

policy requires a justification for *not* searching prisoners (art. 3-25 Regulations), whereas the Belgian prison policy requires a justification for each search.

When we now turn to the relationship between normalization and *public safety*, it is clear that it is equally tense in both countries: normalization can contribute to security *if* it does not imply security risks. Indeed, normalized living conditions (including prison leave) are considered to directly or indirectly contribute to more societal security, but they are only allowed when security can be assured to a greater or lesser extent. However, this tense relationship is reflected differently in the two countries. In Belgium, short and regular prison leave must *in principle* be granted if there are no contraindications. In Norway, on the other hand, the focus is more explicitly on security. Nevertheless, it is fair to note that various types of prison leave are more often granted in Norway than in Belgium[2] (DG EPI, 2016; Kriminalomsorgen, 2016).

In Belgium, this is primarily expressed in the context of the modalities for executing the sentence laid down in the Act of 17 May 2006 regarding the *Extra Muros* Legal Status of Convicted Prisoners and the Rights of Victims in the Context of the Execution of the Prison Sentence, shortened to: Act concerning the *Extra Muros* Legal Status (hereafter: WERP). The various ways of executing the prison sentence that give prisoners more freedom in a controlled manner, step by step, are seen as a good way to prepare them for reintegration. These modalities are only assigned, however, if there are no contraindications, including the absence of prospects of social reintegration and the risk of their committing new serious offences. In other words, the modalities for executing the sentence are seen as an instrumental form of normalization, with the aim of promoting reintegration and thus public safety, but can only be used when public safety can be guaranteed (in advance) to a certain

[2] In 2015, prison leave was granted 33,086 times in Norway (Kriminalomsorgen, 2016: 57). In Belgium, 1,646 prisoners were granted prison leave for a maximum of three times 36 hours per trimester, and 3,586 prisoners were granted short prison leave (DG EPI, 2016: 43). These numbers are hard to compare since Belgian prisoners may have been granted such regular and short prison leave several times that year, which is not reflected in the Belgian numbers. Nevertheless, based on these numbers, it is safe to conclude that prison leave is more often granted in Norway, especially given the significant difference in average prison population, which was in 2015 3,746 prisoners in Norway and 11,040 in Belgium.

extent. More in specific, the Act concerning the *Extra Muros* Legal Status provides for (1) short prison leave; (2) regular prison leave; (3) placement in a transition house; (4) interruption of the sentence; (5) limited detention; (6) electronic monitoring; and (7) various types of early release (conditional release, early release for medical reasons and early release in the context of removal from the Belgian territory). Prison leave is granted for several reasons (art. 4–7 WERP), but it suffices to say here that is a right and not a privilege for convicted prisoners, since it does not have to be 'earned' (art. 5 WERP). If there are no contraindications related to escape, to new *serious* offences or to the harassment of the victims and if the prisoner accepts the condition to not commit any new offences, prison leave is granted. The same reasoning holds true for the alternative ways to execute the prison sentence as well as for conditional release. In both cases, the prisoner is expected to comply with specific conditions in order to avoid new offences (art. 9/3, 21–23, 25, 28§1, 47§1 and 48 WERP). These conditions again reflect the tension between security considerations and normalization with a view to reintegration. These alternative forms of execution of the sentence are seen as a means to promote reintegration and thus public safety as well. However, they can only be used if public safety can already be guaranteed to a certain extent.

In Norway, compared to their security measures inside prisons, normalization plays a more significant role when it comes to *public safety*. The Norwegian Act on the Execution of provides for a variety of ways to implement the sentence: (1) a prison with a high security level (art. 10); (2) a prison with a low security level (art. 10 and 11); (3) a transition house (art. 11 and 15); (4) a rehabilitation institution (art. 12); (5) a hospital (art. 13); (6) outside prison, in compliance with the conditions imposed, which can include electronic monitoring (art. 16); or (7) by way of conditional release (art. 43). Although article 14 stipulates that '*convicted prisoners shall not be transferred to a more restrictive prison than necessary*', the same article also contains an exhaustive list of the reasons to send a prisoner to a higher security level, such as in order to maintain order and safety. Moreover, contrary to what is suggested by the Correctional Service's definition of the normalization principle, prisoners are not automatically transferred to a lower-security regime as soon as security considerations allow it. In exceptional cases, the material state of the building and the lack of adequate staff or space can even justify a transfer to a more restrictive prison (art. 3-7 Regulations). Thus, security and organizational reasons are formally accepted restrictions to the normalization process. Additionally, as already pointed out in Chapter 3, the fact that '*the aims of the sentence*', including the '*public sense of justice*', are mentioned as possible objections to transferring a prisoner to a lower security level fundamentally narrows the scope of the implementation of the normalization principle in Norway. But it also reflects the paradox inherent to this interpretation of normalization, in which normalization is seen both as a tool to achieve security and as a security risk. This indicates again the troubled relationship between normalization and security: normalization can contribute to security *if* it does not involve security risks.

The instrumental approach that at least in theory favours the lowest possible security regime also applies to the different types of prison leave, which are considered '*important tools in the rehabilitation and normalization process towards prisoners' release*' and '*help to reduce the harmful effects of detention*' (Ot.prp. no. 5 (2000–2001): 140). However, not all prisoners are eligible for this stepwise progression to freedom. The decisions made in this respect are based on a holistic security assessment, including information about the crime, the prisoner's functioning in prison (in association with other prisoners and at work or school) and about his or her social network (see Guidelines: '*Alminnelige prinsipper for sikkerhetsvurdering*'). Various security measures, such as urine tests, police involvement or supervision by prison officers, can apply as conditions to these forms of leave. The Act on the Execution of Sentences further defines the possible forms that prisoners can be allowed for a given period of time: (1) day release (art. 20; for more detail see art. 3-14 Regulations and Guidelines 20.1–20.8); (2) leave of absence (art. 33 Act; art. 3-30 and 3-21 Regulations; Guidelines 33.6), which comes in three types (regular, short or welfare leave of absence); (3) supervised leave from prison (art. 34 Act; Guidelines 33.4 and 34.1–34.6); (4) interruption of the sentence, for example in case of serious health problems; and (5) early release after serving at least 60 days and two-thirds of the sentence (art. 42–43 Act). Like in Belgium, these various forms of prison leave and early release are intended to facilitate prisoners' rehabilitation and reintegration, and thus to protect public safety in the long term, by lowering the level of security and increasing the level of normalization. One provision that deserves special attention in the context of normalization is that prisoners who take leave in order to work outside prison and consequently earn a normal wage have to pay a certain amount for the food and the lodging that they receive in prison (Guidelines 20.8). Prisoners who go to school, on the other hand, receive the same daily pay as prisoners who work or go to school inside prison, and additionally, their food expenses outside prison are covered by the prison (Guidelines 20.8).

5.3 Striking the Right Balance Between Security and Normalization in Prison Practice

The prisons of Hoogstraten and Leira are low-security or open prisons, while the prisons of Leuven and Nermarka are high-security or closed prisons. As explained before, the selection of a low- and a high-security prison in both countries was based on the assumption that the security level would impact the normalization of the living conditions in these prisons. One indication of the different security levels in practice was the number of locked doors or gates that prisoners would have to pass from their cell to the street: in Leira prison there were no locked doors, in Hoogstraten there were three, in Leuven seven and in Nermarka nine (and even more in the *forvaring* building). However, despite the differences in formal security levels and in the number of locked doors, the prisons of Hoogstraten, Leuven and Nermarka are relatively similar in terms of their static, dynamic and organizational security. Leira prison, on the other hand, differs strongly in these three forms of security and in the way in which security relates to normalization.

5.3.1 Openness as a Security Risk

Hoogstraten prison is formally categorized as an open prison. This means that the security measures in this prison are supposed to be less strict than those in other Belgian prisons (except for the three other open prisons in Belgium). Prisoners are transferred to Hoogstraten to prepare their reintegration during the last stage of their sentence. In practice, however, balancing between normalization and security remains an ongoing struggle in this prison in at least two ways. First, the prison regime aims at facilitating prisoners' reintegration through its open character, but this openness is at the same time considered a security risk which needs to be controlled at all times. Therefore, the lower static security is compensated by increased organizational security, consisting of strict security routines. Second, the more personal contact between prisoners and prison staff contributes to more dynamic security, but involves at the same time a 'grey zone' of unclear rules that in effect give staff members more power of discretion. The following paragraphs will discuss these tensions in Hoogstraten prison, focusing in order on static, organizational and dynamic security.

Regarding static security, the outer gate is permanently staffed by two prison officers; all gates and doors, exterior and interior, are locked, making it impossible to move around the prison site without a key; and prisoners are locked inside their cells whenever they are not participating in organized activities. Unlike most closed prisons in Belgium, there is no camera surveillance inside the prison, and the oval castle's rounded corridors are impossible to completely oversee. In addition, the prison site is not entirely surrounded by walls, which means that it is possible for a prisoner to escape without climbing over a wall—something many prison officers considered the essence of the open character of this prison. Moreover, some prisoners who have earned a certain amount of trust have keys and can move independently from one place to another, when this is needed for their daily tasks, and some of them, for example those who work on the prison farm, are not closely supervised. Due to the lower level of static security, Hoogstraten prison is seen by prisoners and prison officers as a prison in which security is taken less seriously than in other

Belgian prisons. The observed 'security flaws' are mockingly described as 'typical' of this prison.

> Rudy [prison officer] asks me what is odd about this courtyard. I look around and see two sets of scaffolding in front of the renovation work on section D. One of these is close by the roof of section A, so that prisoners could actually get up on the roof easily, and the other is right by the wall, so that prisoners could crawl over the wall. Rudy explains with a laugh that this is all typical of Hoogstraten. When the 'walk' is over, Frans and a few prisoners jokingly suggest that they should put a sign with an arrow saying 'exit this way'. (Field notes 17 October 2014, Hoogstraten prison)

The organizational security, however, seems to compensate for the reduced static security. A head count is taken at least seven times a day (between 6:10 and 22:00) and regular visual checks of all prisoners are also done at night. Counting prisoners was commonly mentioned by prison officers as their main task. This means that prison officers always have an overview of the location of each individual prisoner. Additionally, before and after visits, prisoners are superficially frisked and their fingerprints are taken before they enter and leave the visitors' room (in order to avoid a prisoner leaving the prison with the visitors or instead of a visitor). Moreover, all 'movements' are strictly monitored and supervised, while all possible escape routes are guarded by one or more prison officers. For example, the 'movements' from section A to the workshops proceed as follows:

> The cells doors of the prisoners going to work are opened again. They are allowed to leave their cells and are superficially frisked. They wait at the grille separating their corridor from the exit of section A. The grille is opened and the prisoners walk through, and are counted again. At the outer door of section A they wait for the signal that the 'work movement' may start. After this signal, the door of section A is opened and Rudy, the guard, goes first outside about 50 meters further. From there, the prisoners must line up in rows of three across and are counted again. Then they must follow Rudy to the castle. Meanwhile Rudy explains to me that in other prisons you would never walk with your back to a group of prisoners, as it is considered too dangerous. Other guards stand

> on both sides of the path to the bridge leading to the castle to supervise this 'work movement'. The prisoners must assemble by work house in the castle courtyard. Next each work-house group goes off separately to their work house, led by the 'work house chief'. Only once each group has passed do several more guards join and follow the prisoners until they reach the work house. Then Rudy and I walk back to section A. (Field notes 17 October 2014, Hoogstraten prison)

Because these routines take place several times a day, security is a highly visible aspect of prison life. As already mentioned, this indicates one of the tensions inherent to the open character of Hoogstraten prison: the openness is aimed at facilitating prisoners' reintegration and thus at ensuring security in society, but at the same time it is considered a risk to societal security.

In addition to the security routines intended to prevent escapes, prisoners are also searched regularly (albeit in such a superficial way that it is unlikely anything would be found, unless prisoners were so careless as to put drugs or weapons in their pockets or in their sweatshirt hoods), prisoners of section A can be asked to pass through a metal detector when entering or leaving their section, and strip searches are performed, for example, after conjugal visits. Furthermore, several randomly selected cells are searched on a daily basis and the presence of mobile phones is occasionally checked by technical means. However, the external team performing those checks rarely finds any phones, presumably because the team's arrival is quickly noticed by the prisoners of section A. Another sign of the ineffectiveness of these kinds of security measures is the unmistakeable smell of cannabis in this prison. Again, this leads both prisoners and prison officers to conclude that security is not taken too seriously in Hoogstraten prison.

In terms of dynamic security, Hoogstraten prison differs from most other Belgian prisons. This was explained by prisoners and prison staff who had experienced other prisons. More specifically, the social climate in Hoogstraten prison is experienced as more relaxed than in most other Belgian prisons, involving less tension and less aggression between prisoners, and between prisoners and prison officers. Prisoners and prison officers are commonly addressed by their first names, and prison officers are physically present on the courtyard when supervising the 'walk' (in most other Belgian prisons this is done from behind glass or by cameras). For these reasons, many prison officers appreciate working here and many prisoners are grateful being transferred to this prison. Again, the reference for their appreciation is the living conditions in other Belgian prisons, rather than those in society. Almost all of them, prisoners and staff alike, had experienced more stressful and violent living or working conditions in other prisons. Stories about violence and inhumane treatment by prison staff in other prisons were regularly shared by prisoners as well prison officers to express their disapproval of those conditions. However, this relatively relaxed and arguably more normalized climate is related to another tension between normalization and security: the so-called 'grey zone' of unclear rules about what is allowed and what is not, the wide discretionary power of prison officers and inconsistent decision making. According to some prison officers, this 'grey zone' makes working in Hoogstraten prison more difficult. Many prison officers refer to this 'grey zone' to explain that some things are strictly speaking not allowed, but *in this case* he or she thinks that it is all right to allow it. Others are stricter and disapprove of this attitude of their colleagues.

> Sarah walks up and down the corridor to see that everything is in order. Some prisoners are in the corridors talking. Sarah says that in principle this isn't allowed, but that it doesn't bother her if it's only for a few minutes. (Field notes 16 October 2014, Hoogstraten prison)

* * *

> A prisoner asks Wendy if another man can give him some milk, and Wendy agrees. She explains to me that prisoners are actually not allowed to exchange anything with each other, but that they usually allow small things like a serving of milk. However, she adds that of course, you can't always be sure that it's really milk. (Field notes 27 November 2014, Hoogstraten prison)

The same 'grey zone' is mentioned by prisoners too. Some use it to gain more freedom inside the prison, while others considered the inconsistencies a characteristic and negative aspect of the regime in Hoogstraten prison. Again, the reference point for this assessment is other Belgian prisons, in which the rules are applied more strictly, and not Belgian society in general.

> The prisoner who cleans the halls and toilets, walks freely around section B, giving me the opportunity to chat with him. He thinks the regime in [closed prison A] is actually better. Another prisoner had told me earlier that he thought the regime in [closed prison C] was better. They both gave the same reason: in other prisons, you know where you stand, you know the rules and everyone follows the same rules. But in Hoogstraten there is a huge grey area: if you ask a guard if you can do something and he/she refuses, then you just ask a different one and they might allow it. And something that is allowed one day may be forbidden the next. (Field notes 23 October 2014, Hoogstraten prison)

Indeed, the more relaxed and arguably more 'normalized' prisoner-staff relationships in this prison are associated with a decrease in the level of aggression, but not necessarily with an increase in perceived fairness of the regime. Additionally, the dynamic security that is linked to these prisoner-staff relationships is not considered to effectively ensure the public safety. Instead, the open character of this prison is compensated by frequent and strict security routines. This means that balancing between normalization and security remains an ongoing endeavour in this prison.

5.3.2 The Panopticon in Action

Leuven prison is officially a remand prison. This means that the regime is largely focused on, on the one hand, security and preventing escapes, and on the other, on presuming innocence by safeguarding prisoners' rights as far as possible. In this context, security and normalization are seen as conflicting: prison conditions, including prisoners' rights, are normalized to the extent that security considerations allow. In daily practice, this means that security considerations tend to outweigh the normalization efforts. As explained in the previous chapter, the prison is constructed in such a way that the wings and the cell doors can be easily surveyed, which is done at all times by several prison officers and by cameras. Prisoners spend most of the time behind the locked doors of their cells, they are closely supervised when they leave their cells, and they are counted several times a day. The beginning and the end of each activity are announced over loudspeakers by the prison officers in the 'centre of the prison' who coordinate all activities, so that the right prisoners are unlocked at the right times and, right after the activity, are locked back up inside their cells. The 'walks' are the only occasion on which a large group of prisoners leave the cells and come together in the courtyard. All prison officers coordinate their efforts to ensure security during these walks. The courtyard is checked beforehand for drugs or other things that could be dropped here, two prison officers take their places in the two booths on opposite sides of the courtyard in order to supervise the prisoners through the windows, prisoners' cells are unlocked by their section's prison officer and sent to the entrance door of the courtyard, where they are superficially searched by other prison officers. Prisoners are counted when they enter the courtyard, in case police would have to intervene in a serious incident and would need to know the size of group. Once all prisoners have entered the courtyard, the door is locked behind them. At the end of the walk, prisoners leave again section by section and are locked up inside their cells.

In addition to the static and organizational security, some prison officers spontaneously mentioned the importance of dynamic security. Both prisoners and prison officers mentioned the 'relaxed atmosphere' in this prison, especially those who had been to other Belgian prisons with more tense and violent atmospheres. However, similarly to Hoogstraten prison, this more relaxed atmosphere was associated with inconsistencies in prison officers' decision making and the alleged ineffectiveness of security measures.

> Prison officer Jef has also worked in [closed prison A] and when I ask him if it's very different there, he answers that it's like 'day and night'. The atmosphere is much warmer here. I ask him if he means towards prisoners or between staff members. He answers 'among the staff', it's much friendlier here, there's good communication between colleagues. He is very happy to be working here. He does think, however, that his

> colleagues do not all form a unified front towards prisoners, and that often a colleague will tell a prisoner 'just ask another guard'. The attitude towards prisoners has become less 'firm but fair'. In his opinion, it should be clear whether something is allowed or not. You have to be strict, but if you make a promise you have to keep it, otherwise you lose all your credibility. (Field notes 13 November 2015, Leuven prison)

While the more 'relaxed' atmosphere was experienced positively by prisoners and prison officers, the less consistent application of the prison rules was not.

> *Marc*: It can't always be too loose, can it…I mean, it's prison of course, you're put here, you're being punished and like that, there have to be times when it's 'like this and not like that' because otherwise things get completely screwed up … I also notice this with clothing exchanges, if we allow too much it's like you give them an inch and they take a yard.
> *Me*: Right… so you have to be strict as well?
> *Marc*: Yes, I do, but I think above all you have to be consistent… if you allow one person something, you have to allow it with the other… that's what I think and that's also what my bosses in the laundry say: if you give one guy something, you have to give it to the other guy if he asks for it. (Interview Marc, Leuven prison)

Once again, when prisoners were reflecting on the security measures, their reference point was not 'living conditions in society' but rather 'living conditions in other prisons' or 'expected living conditions in prison'. Indeed, in Marc's view, the consistent application of the rules is necessary to manage prison life in an organized way. Following his reasoning, normalization of security measures is not desirable if the other living conditions are not normalized as well. The same logic can be found in some prisoners' opinions about the use of security measures. These prisoners consider the superficial searches to be a problematic aspect of this prison, because it may lead to dangerous situations. Others value the moderate use of security measures such as strip searches and cell searches. Thus, the mutually limiting relationship between normalization and security also emerges from different prisoners' perspectives. Both

Senne and Karim argue that the security measures in Leuven prison are insufficient to ensure security in this prison, but while Karim experienced this negatively, Senne did not.

> *Senne*: I actually don't have a problem with that. Yeah, no, the frisking and all that, the cell checks... that's all ... really pretty useless. [...] Places for a prisoner to hide stuff ... they're in their cells 22-23 hours a day, they know everything about their cell. Then they [guards] want to come do a cell check. Dumb guys, OK, they get caught. But if you...know a bit, then you don't. (Interview Senne, Leuven prison)

***

> *Karim*: If somebody wants to get something in, then they'll do it. Then they can frisk you as much as they want. These guys swallow it or stick it up their....it always gets in here. Or it gets thrown over the wall. It gets in. They can't stop it. And that frisking, that's just for show, yeah. If you want to get a knife out, then you'll get it out, you just put it in your shoe, it's flat, right? And you...So the frisking, what good does it do... like someone's going to put a knife in his pocket. Or here [touches his collar], sometimes they really feel you here, what are you going to put there? Come on...And they really frisk you like this [shows it superficially on arms and legs], but here they don't frisk you [belly and waist]. They aren't stupid, these guys [...] But we live with it, we're in prison and we take it, sometimes we laugh about it. Like 'yeah, I got it in. They frisked me but they didn't find anything, just air. (Interview Karim, Leuven prison)

Maarten, on the other hand, appreciates the moderate security measures in Leuven prison. But he acknowledges that this appreciation may result from his considerable prison experience and that prisoners who enter the prison for the first time might experience the security measures as much more intrusive, especially the strip searches.

> *Maarten*: I'm just so used to it, aren't I, standing there in the altogether, that it doesn't affect me anymore. I know that for a lot of people, people who come in for the first time and sometimes

> haven't even done anything wrong, and then suddenly have to undergo a strip search, that can be really heavy. Personally I'm not bothered. I'm not embarrassed easily, so it doesn't matter much either [laughs]. (Interview Maarten, Leuven prison)

Ali is the only prisoner interviewed who thinks that the searches are effective. Moreover, he is convinced that it is the prison officers' duty to ensure security in prison by performing actions such as cell searches.

> *Ali*: It's good, because it protects people. What if somebody brings something to harm people? So, it's better for them to search everything, to be one step ahead because it protects ourselves. There are people who have a psycho problem here and they can do anything to harm anybody. Maybe they say, I wanna do something to finish my life… How are we gonna protect ourselves, we need someone to protect [sic], the protection is our 'chief' [prison officer]. To do that I think, even if they want to put more search is better, because it protects us, while sitting with other people. So, I think it's the best thing to do. Because if we cannot be sure of our protection, then we live in a situation of fear. (Interview Ali, Leuven prison)

Similar views emerged in the context of the disciplinary sanctions. The prisoners interviewed believed that disciplinary sanctions are necessary in a prison and acceptable as long as they are applied consistently. This relationship between normalization and security did not only stem from the way security was organized in these two Belgian prisons, but also from the way normalization was understood and implemented: in a rather intrinsic and rights-based way. Yet the nature of the relationship between normalization and security changes when both security and normalization are understood and implemented differently, as is the case in Leira prison.

5.3.3 Synergies Between Security and Normalization

Leira prison has the lowest security level of the four prisons observed, while it is one of Norway's most secure prisons, in the experience of Leira's prisoners and staff. The low security level refers to the static security, which is almost non-existent in this prison. There are no walls or fences around the prison, no cameras and no alarms, and the interior and exterior doors remain unlocked during the daytime, which means that prisoners can walk around and can easily leave the prison site (although the latter is not allowed without explicit permission). In addition, visitors can enter and leave the building by themselves, and the garden centre is easily accessible for customers without them noticing that this garden centre is part of the prison. Moreover, prisoners regularly leave the prison, individually or in groups and with or without staff members. The weekly visits to the store and the library are supervised by the staff member who is also driving, the walks on Tuesdays and Thursdays *can* be supervised, but also unsupervised prison leave of five hours or several days is regularly granted to individual prisoners. Thus, the low security level in this prison involves a high degree of physical freedom. Nevertheless, as already pointed out, prisoners were clear about the fact that this is still a prison. As Petter aptly expressed, '*In an open prison, there is an invisible fence around*' (Interview Petter, Leira prison). Additionally, he described the security measures in Leira prison as follows:

> *Petter*: You are not allowed to just go out and do things, you must remember that you are in prison. [...] So, I think they control if you are working... There is control of your money. And they control for drugs. You are not allowed to have too much money here... They control you stand up, they control you go to work, and they control you are inside in the night, they check you in your room, they open your door and see if you are in your bed and they lock again and go to the next. [...] Yeah, that's all I think they control. (Interview Petter, Leira prison)

As illustrated by the above quote, only the level of static security is low in this prison, while the levels of dynamic and organizational security are high. This is in line with the instrumental and rather disciplinary interpretation of normalization: the open character of the prison prevents the harmful effects of detention and facilitates prisoners' rehabilitation and reintegration, but it also requires discipline from them: prisoners have to comply with prison rules that are stricter than those in other prisons, and receive close but personalized and cordial supervision. In this sense, normalization and the static security can be considered mutually limiting, at the same time that normalization and the dynamic and organizational security are mutually reinforcing.

The small scale of Leira prison and its underlying philosophy, the 'consequence pedagogy method' (see Chapter 2), are important facilitators for dynamic and organizational security. Being based on the consequence pedagogy method means that this prison regime involves dialogue, respect and participation in social activities. It also involves that all prisoners sign a contract in advance confirming that they will comply with the prison rules and understand the consequences of non-compliance. The small scale ensures that prisoners and prison officers know each other, which reduces anonymity and increases respect for each other and for each other's work (this is the case among prisoners, between prisoners and staff members, and among staff members). The result is not only a more relaxed prison climate but also a more efficient use of security measures. The small number of prisoners makes it easier to count them (three times a day) and to oversee all prisoners' activities. In addition, visitors are immediately recognized and guided to the staff office. Moreover, all staff members are informed of activities, incidents and decisions concerning individual prisoners, such as whether prison leave was granted or declined, and the small number of prisoners enables more individualized security assessments. According to Adrian, for example, prison staff assess conscientiously whether drug tests are necessary or whether a prisoner is to be trusted.

> *Adrian*: So someone gets a urine sample very often, but other people they trust more. But it is like if you show them you can be trusted, they trust you, so I think it's good.

Me: And do you have to do it often?
Adrian: Of course not! [laughs] (Interview Adrian, Leira prison)

This strict policy is acknowledged by staff members, and prisoners are informed of it in advance. As a consequence, the security measures are seen as legitimate by many prisoners. Being considered legitimate does not mean, however, that the urine tests as such are not experienced as intrusive and disturbing. Jonas explains that even with considerable prison experience, it is still demeaning when someone can ask you at any time to urinate and then watch you.

Jonas: There are urine tests and alcohol tests.
Me: Often?
Jonas: Sometimes. But you don't know when they are coming. It's like [makes a whip sound] come here.
Me: And what is it like?
Jonas: Uhm…it's annoying, irritating…because, they just pick you up, you have to go into a room and they have to watch you pee. It is…. […] you feel small, you know. You don't feel like…. You feel…small, because somebody's got all the power over you. (Interview Jonas, Leira prison)

The result of Leira's strict drug policy is that it is a drug-free prison. This is very much appreciated by the prisoners for at least three reasons: a drug-free environment facilitates their own drug rehabilitation; it also means that there is no drug-related violence or theft; and this in turn allows prisoners to focus on their reintegration rather than on avoiding being victimized. Again, this means that Leira's security policy, or at least its drug policy, is consistent with the way in which the living conditions are 'normalized' in this prison.

Petter: they are taking urine tests. … When I know people take the test, they don't cheat. I like [to be] in a place where people are not using drugs, because when people are using drugs, it's … bringing some other problems. People steal, … when you start using drugs, you get this…. you are changing your personality. So, so, I like when the people are free of drugs…so… I like these urine tests…

> and they are taking alcohol tests... I think they take maybe one to three persons every day. (Interview Petter, Leira prison, original in English)

The small scale, the prison's philosophy and the drug tests are not the only reasons for this relaxed prison climate. The dynamic and organizational security aspects are enhanced by the fact that prisoners risk being sent back to a closed prison if they violate the prison rules. In other words, the prison's security is largely based on its prisoners' self-discipline. The liberties that prisoners enjoy thanks to the open character of the prison are at the same time the reason why prisoners comply with the rules and thus how security in this prison is ensured. This aspect was not often mentioned by prison staff, but it was prominent in prisoners' stories. Jonas and Issam explained this clearly:

> *Jonas*: Yeah, they can come and say we want a urine test from you. But, you are already in a closed prison, so... fuck off, what are they gonna do? They can't send you to an even more closed one. But if you deny here, you'll have to go to Tunga [Nermarka]. (Interview Jonas, Leira prison)

***

> *Issam*: But you cannot fight or do something wrong, you know, because you know: wrong here [snaps his fingers] to Tunga [Nermarka]. ... I don't want to go to hell again. I want to stay here, I want to do everything they need from me. This is a big reason for people to keep it quiet. Be quiet, be gentleman.... (Interview Issam, Leira prison)

Issam even tends to warn other prisoners to behave calmly, especially those for whom Leira is their first prison, who have not experienced the conditions in closed prisons.

> *Issam*: They are not normal, because here it is very okay to stay... but too many of them, they come directly here, they don't know what it's like... I say always 'shut up, just shut up and keep move on, be quiet, be gentleman, because you don't know how it's going

on there, how tough it is there'. (Interview Issam, Leira prison, English in original)

Although this self-discipline is considered one of the aspects that makes detention in Leira prison more demanding, it is not experienced negatively. One reason for this is that the *other* prisoners also have to discipline themselves, and there is some social pressure among prisoners to comply with certain rules, in the sense that it is not acceptable for some prisoners to not perform their part of the tasks.

Me: Do you think that this kind of prison can only exist if there are also closed prisons, so that you can be sent back?
Adrian: If uhm … yeah, it's like if someone does something wrong they get sent back. For some people. Because this is also a prison, but it's like I say, if they trust you, they give you a chance. But if you fuck that up, you go back. So, you want to do your prison time and be done with it. So, it's easier to don't do anything wrong here than in closed prisons…. But for some people it's important that there is also closed prison, because then they must be good when they are here…
Me: But… even if you could not be sent back, would you walk the walk and follow the rules?
Adrian: Yeah, of course, because, it's how you act and …. this is a very small prison, so if two or three people don't do anything and they just …uhm… don't give a fuck, they won't be liked by the other prisoners. Because, if you go upstairs and sleep [when you are supposed to be working], why can't the others not go up and sleep, you know?
Me: Yeah, so you follow the rules because…
Adrian: Everyone does it, so, yeah. (Interview Adrian, Leira prison)

In sum, security and normalization are mutually reinforcing in Leira prison and together contribute to feelings of safety. The low level of static security in combination with the high levels of dynamic and organizational security goes hand in hand with the instrumental and rather disciplinary interpretation of normalization, in which self-discipline plays an important role. Moreover, the ways in which the material environment (see Chapter 4) and the social environment (see Chapter 6) are normalized contribute to this approach to security. This means that the Norwegian policy in terms of security and normalization has been effectively and holistically implemented in Leira prison.

5.3.4 Security as a Means to Normalize or Discipline?

Nermarka prison has a high security level. Its large perimeter is secured with a high wall surrounded by fences with barbed wire and there is camera surveillance. The external and internal gates and doors are locked, prison officers and visitors wear an alarm system, and prisoners systematically pass through a metal detector when they go to or return from the workshops. In terms of organizational security, prisoners are counted several times a day, they are closely supervised when they move from one place to another and prison officers always know the location of all prisoners of their unit. In addition, there are regular urine tests and searches, including strip searches and cell searches, which can be done with sniffer dogs. Despite being a high-security prison, however, the four prison buildings differ in their security levels. The *forvaring* building has the highest security level but will not be discussed here, since there were no observations conducted in this building. In the A building, prisoners spend most of the time in their cells and are closely supervised when they leave them, and they eat with plastic cutlery (in A1). In the E building, prisoners have more liberties than in the A building, they work or go to school in the daytime and spend a large part of the afternoon in their unit, together with other prisoners. The *Modulen* (M) building has the most liberal regime, with regular activities outside the prison walls, during which prisoners are not always closely supervised by prison staff.

From the prison's perspective, the relationship between security and normalization is reflected in the way in which prisoners can gradually move to a lower-security regime if they show motivation to work on their problems, including drug-related problems: from A to E to M or to an open prison, and back to A if they violate the prison rules. This principle reflects the instrumental approach to normalization. The prisoners recognized that this gradual progression was the way to freedom, but with mixed feelings. Since the M building only has room for 15 prisoners, many prisoners never get the opportunity to be transferred to this building, while they can clearly see the privileges of those prisoners, and while many of them also feel the need for drug and other rehabilitation. The same discontent was expressed in the context of prison leave. Whereas prisoners in the M building were regularly granted prison leave, prisoners in the E building had the feeling that their leave was always rejected without clear justification. Indeed, the downside of this system of progression for a selected group of prisoners seems to be that other prisoners feel unfairly disadvantaged and stigmatized as 'dangerous'. Steinar expresses the frustration shared by many prisoners in the E building:

> *Steinar*: It's only people from Modulen that's getting permission, it seems like. Nobody from this building.
> *Me*: And do you know why that is?
> *Steinar*: I don't know. I don't have any idea. I think the management here should have changed to some people that really understand the inmates and don't put a label on them just because they're inmates. They are people, you know, ordinary people, with family and kids and everything. (Interview Steinar, Nermarka prison)

From the prisoners' perspective, the relationship between security and normalization is in the first place reflected in their need for safety. In this respect, normalization means ensuring safe living conditions, and in this sense, normalization and security are mutually reinforcing. Indeed, many prisoners stated that security measures are 'normal' in prison. Since threats to their security are commonly from other prisoners, most were in favour of security measures that control their fellow prisoners. Some argued even that there should be camera surveillance on the units and that prison officers should be physically present on the units more often. Fredrik, for example, was in favour of more camera surveillance.

> *Fredrik*: There are no surveillance cameras in here. So… there are many things they don't see. … 2-3 weeks ago, there was someone

fighting here, and they just opened a refrigerator door, so they [prison officers] cannot see that they [prisoners] fight. But both of them were send to …

Me: To the A-building?

Fredrik: Yeah. This is actually the first prison where I've been to where there is no surveillance in this area.

Me: And what do you think of it?

Fredrik: Yeah…. I don't think so much about it. I think someone may be concerned about it, but that depends on the person I think… From my point of view, there should be one. (Interview Fredrik, Nermarka prison)

Like Fredrik, Farid and Arne also pointed out that security threats mainly come from other prisoners. Since prisoners do not want or do not dare to snitch on other prisoners, they consider it crucial for their own safety that prison officers observe these threats themselves and prevent violence.

Farid: I don't think they would be able to… react that fast, if something happens. So, it's not too good, it's alright. Because … guards have an alarm, but if something happens in one of the rooms, how long will it take to fix the problem? This is the discussion, you know. Because you can do a lot of things in 30 seconds and I think they can't react in any way in 30 seconds. […] And when it happens, they never, never avoid people hitting people. They [prisoners] always fight and then they [prison officers] take action. (Interview Farid, Nermarka prison)

***

Arne: They [prison officers] search for something to kill someone and for drugs, they search all the rooms. […] They can come every day and say 'take off your clothes', if they want. And if I say no, I don't want, they take a report on me, and I don't want that, so I take my clothes off and they check me. (Interview Arne, Nermarka prison)

Despite this plea for efficient security measures, however, prisoners consider some measures disproportionate or humiliating and therefore illegitimate, such as the random use of strip searches, described in the quote above, or sniffer dogs inside the cells. In these cases, the balance between security and normalization seems to be lost in the prisoners' view. Steinar expresses a commonly heard opinion on strip searches:

> *Me*: What do you think of the security measures?
>
> *Steinar*: I think it's ok, but I don't like, you know, when you're going to get stripped and get nude and… you know, I don't like that kind of behaviour. You know, when you have to take all your clothes off and…
>
> *Me*: Does it happen often?
>
> *Steinar*: No.. no… sometimes, but it happens and it's not cool, you know. Your self-esteem is like shit after…[…] If you are inside the cell and they want to, they just ask you: take off all your clothes. Some people do, but not all the guards, some guards are crazy and ask you to do it. And that's not funny. (Interview Steinar, Nermarka prison)

In the context of disciplinary sanctions as well, the right balance between normalization and security seems difficult to achieve in practice. Prisoners agreed that violations of the prison rules should be punished, but while some argue that being sent to the A building is not a real punishment, others think this is far too punitive and illegitimate. Farid is one of the men who argues that this punishment is too lenient to deter prisoners and therefore does not ensure their safety.

> *Farid*: It doesn't work… you know when I came to prison, the first one and a half months I was in this strict area. Everybody has to go through this strict area. So, imagine, when you first come to prison, you get the punishment, so how come it's gonna work as punishment later?… What if I do something really wrong?! (Interview Farid, Nermarka prison)

In addition to the static and organizational security, prison officers also stress the importance of dynamic security, stating that good relationships between prisoners and prison officers prevent conflicts and aggression in this prison. However, although most prison officers acknowledge this, the way in which they interact with prisoners differs strongly. While some of them spend a lot of time on the section, having conversations, playing board games or eating with prisoners of the E building, others spend only a minimum of time on the section and stay in the staff office for most of the time. This is different in *Modulen*, where all prison officers eat with prisoners and participate in activities. Prisoners, on their part, did not question the prison officers' intentions to prevent aggression, but did question the impact of their 'good relations' with prisoners. Whereas prison officers suggest that the low level of aggression in this prison results from their personal interactions with prisoners, prisoners argue that the good relations with prison officers result from everyone's sense of discipline. The reasons given by prisoners for avoiding fighting and even arguing with prison officers include the fear of losing the chance of release after serving two-thirds of the sentence or of being transferred to *Modulen* or Leira prison. Boriss, for example, is convinced that the main reason is prisoners' fear of losing their option for early release.

> *Boriss*: Everyone is about friendly…But this is, you know, I speak with lot of people, nothing is happening here because everyone is scared about this 'two third'. … But… Norwegians very often, don't get this two third. (Interview Boriss, Nermarka prison)

Arne is even worried that he will have to stay longer in prison than his full sentence if he violates the prison rules. For him, this is a reason to behave as well as he can.

> *Arne*: If I fight inside here, they can… I can get 1 year, 2 years more…
> *Me*: So that's why you keep calm?
> *Arne*: Yeah, I try to be nice to everyone, to everybody. I don't want to stay inside here all my life… (Interview Arne, Nermarka prison)

In *Modulen*, the disciplinary and self-disciplinary processes are similar to those in Leira prison. Prisoners in *Modulen* know very well that they receive more privileges than the other prisoners, and do not want to lose them. They 'voluntarily' comply with regular drug tests, with group and individual conversations and other activities, and in return, they get a more liberal arrangement. During the observation period, they had been on a three-day trip somewhere outside of Trondheim. Upon their return, some prisoners explained that the return to prison was very hard. It is hard to be locked up again, after having been outside of prison for three days without any security problems.

> Nils is convinced that even if the prison wall was only a meter high, only a few prisoners would escape. Emil adds that no one would escape from the Modulen, because they have already advanced quite far. They could have easily escaped in [place outside Trondheim] but no one did, and then it felt strange to have to come back inside these high walls, looking out at barbed wire. (Field notes 7 June 2016, Nermarka prison)

Nils and Emil explained that the original idea was to build this *Modulen* building outside of the prison walls. According to them, this would make much more sense, since this is an open unit in a closed prison, meaning that they are constantly switching from the lowest security level (where they can walk around in nature without prison officers), to this high security level with walls and barbed wire. This is psychologically very difficult and involves a lot of strip searches. On the other hand, Nils and Emil realize that given the seriousness of their crimes, it is unlikely that they personally would have gotten a chance in *Modulen* if it was considered an open prison.

5.4 Conclusion

As outlined in the introduction of this chapter, King and Morgan (1980: 36) have influentially argued that the normalization of living conditions in prison requires a minimum use of security. While this is true from a certain perspective on security and on normalization, the analysis of the four prisons shows that some nuance should be brought to the idea that security measures and normalization are by definition mutually limiting. Firstly, security and normalization are also mutually reinforcing in the sense that feeling safe and secure is also part of normal, or at least desirable, living conditions. As many prisoners distrust or even fear fellow prisoners, and thus feel a need for security, they rely on the prison's security measures to guarantee their own safety. In that sense, to experience the same feeling of safety as any other citizen outside of prison, prisoners seem to expect heightened rather than lowered security levels. This was certainly the case in the high-security prisons in both countries, where it was considered a prison officer's task to supervise prisoners and prevent violence by applying effective security measures. Nevertheless, prisoners in all four prisons agreed with King and Morgan that principles of subsidiarity and proportionality are to be respected, and that they indeed experienced some security measures as disturbing or humiliating. This is in line with the findings of Crewe et al. (2014) that the power of prison officers is applied most legitimately when it is '*light*', and at the same time '*present*'. The point here is not that a higher security level is experienced as more normalized, but that reducing security measures without normalizing the rest of the prison environment will not necessarily lead to a more normalized experience. This may require smaller units or prisons, and more satisfying activities. A second point, but related to the first, is that security measures and risk management are increasingly present in society and have thus become part of the 'normal' living conditions outside prison. In this sense, security measures and normalization cannot be considered opposites (see also Engbo, 2017).

Thirdly and most relevant for this comparative research, the meaning of any statement about security in relation to normalization differs according to whether the static, organizational and/or dynamic aspects of security are taken into account; and whether normalization is understood as an intrinsic or an instrumental process. Hence a 'double balancing act': even when considering only one form of security and normalization, both concepts are mutually limiting in some ways, and mutually reinforcing in other, but the various forms of security and the different interpretations of normalization add another dimension to this relationship. Indeed, from the observations in the four prisons, it is clear that the different forms of security relate to normalization in different ways. When security and normalization are presented as opposites, this is in the first place with static security in mind, certainly when the primary aim of security is to prevent escapes. In this sense, it can be argued that the high-security prisons of Leuven and Nermarka, being entirely surrounded by walls and equipped with cameras, are less 'normalized' than the low-security prisons of Hoogstraten and Leira, which were not, or not entirely, surrounded by walls or fences. This is of course only one aspect of the prison conditions; one can still wonder whether it can be considered more 'normal' to live in a former castle with relatively easy escape routes than to live in a former castle with more difficult escape routes. Leira prison, which has almost no static security, was indeed experienced by prisoners and prison staff as highly normalized.

Despite its low level of static security, the levels of dynamic and organizational security were high in Leira prison. However, the latter two should not be seen as limiting the normalization process but rather a result of the instrumental way of normalizing the living conditions in this prison. Thus, in Leira prison, normalization leads to *low* static security and *high* dynamic and organizational security. Its open character, involving the responsibilization of prisoners and close and personal supervision by staff members, is central to the operation of this prison. All these aspects contribute to Leira's mission to facilitate prisoners' rehabilitation and reintegration. The open character in Hoogstraten prison was also intended to aid prisoners' reintegration, but led to an inherent paradox in its functioning: although it was an open prison, there was a continuous endeavour to prevent escapes through strict security routines.

It is true that the importance of dynamic security was also stressed in Hoogstraten prison, but the following three differences between Leira and Hoogstraten prison may explain why the dynamic security was less effective in Hoogstraten. First, the difference in scale: 29 prisoners in Leira versus 170 in Hoogstraten. Leira's small scale enabled close and personal supervision, in ways that were not possible in Hoogstraten. Second, the more relaxed climate in Hoogstraten was associated with a less-consistent enforcement of the rules, while Leira's functioning explicitly involved clear rules as well as clear consequences in the event of non-compliance. Previous research has explained that prisoner-staff relationships are in themselves not sufficient to provide dynamic security and that the role of the perceived fairness in regime delivery should not be underestimated in this respect (Bottoms et al., 1990). Third, the explicit instrumental use of normalization in Leira leads to and builds on effective self-discipline of and by prisoners. Indeed, prisoners in Leira were well aware that they would be sent back to a high-security prison if they violated the prison rules. This played a less important role in Hoogstraten since this prison did not differ as much from the closed prisons as Leira prison did. As already discussed in the previous chapter, this phenomenon of self-discipline has been described as a 'pain of imprisonment' in open prisons that has too often been underestimated. Imposed responsibilization or self-discipline may provoke distress and anxiety in prisoners, since they have to constantly remind themselves of the fact that they risk being sent back to a worse situation if they do something wrong (Neumann, 2012; Shammas, 2014). This kind of self-discipline was most apparent in Leira prison, but also in Nermarka's *Modulen*, where prisoners were most preoccupied with losing their 'privileges'. However, the prisoners interviewed did not express any negative feelings in this respect. They acknowledged that this aspect of discipline made life in some ways more demanding than 'doing time' in a closed prison, but at the same time it was linked to positive feelings of 'being trusted' by staff members and spending their prison sentence in a violence- and drug-free environment. Of course prisoners' reference point may have played a significant role in this positive assessment, since all prisoners interviewed spontaneously compared their stay in Leira to their previous experiences in a high-security prison.

In sum, an intrinsic approach to normalization requires the minimum use of security measures needed to ensure public safety as well as prisoners' and prison staff's right to personal safety. It can be argued that security is part of the normalization process in prison, if the principles of proportionality and subsidiarity are respected, if the rules are transparent and applied consistently, and if security controls are conducted in a respectful and professional way. Following an instrumental and rather disciplinary approach to normalization, lower static security goes hand in hand with an effective use of dynamic and organizational security, which relies on the self-discipline of prisoners to safeguard security in prison and in society. Elements of both approaches can be found in Belgian and Norwegian prison policy and practice. While the Belgian approach tends to be more intrinsic than the Norwegian and the other way around, respecting prisoners' right to security is important in both countries. The same is true for dynamic security, which always involves an instrumental approach to normalization, in the sense that the normalization of the social interaction between prisoners and prison staff is instrumental to the security in prison. The dynamic security and the 'soft power' used by prisoners officers, but also self-discipline expected of prisoners, relate to the way in which the social environment is normalized. This will be addressed in the next chapter.

References

Bloom, S. L. (1997). *Sanctuary: Toward the evolution of sane societies*. Routledge.

Bottoms, A. E., Hay, W., & Sparks, J. R. (1990). Situational and social approaches to the prevention of disorder in long-term prisons. *The Prison Journal, 70*(1), 83–95.

Crewe, B. (2011a). Depth, weight, tightness: Revisiting the pains of imprisonment. *Punishment & Society, 13*(5), 509–529.

Crewe, B. (2011b). Soft power in prison: Implications for staff–prisoner relationships, liberty and legitimacy. *European Journal of Criminology, 8*(6), 455–468.

Crewe, B., Liebling, A., & Hulley, S. (2014). Heavy-light, absent-present: Rethinking the 'weight' of imprisonment. *The British Journal of Sociology, 65*(3), 387–410.

DG EPI. (2016). *Jaarverslag Directoraat-generaal Penitentiaire Inrichtingen 2015*. FOD Justitie.

Engbo, H. J. (2017). Normalisation in Nordic prisons—From a prison governor's perspective. In T. Ugelvik & P. S. Smith (Eds.), *Scandinavian penal history, culture and prison practice: Embraced by the welfare state?* (pp. 327–352). Palgrave Macmillan.

Geens, K. (2017). Woord van de Minister. In Directoraatgeneraal Penitentiaire Inrichtingen. *Jaarverslag Directoraat-generaal Penitentiaire Inrichtingen 2016*. FOD Justitie.

Goffman, E. (1961). *Asylums. Essays on the social situation of mental patients and other inmates*. Penguin Books Ltd.

Irwin, J., & Owen, B. (2005). Harm and the contemporary prison. In A. Liebling & S. Maruna (Eds.), *The effects of imprisonment* (pp. 94–117). Willan Publishing.

King, R. D., & Morgan, R. (1980). *The future of the prison system.* Gower Publishing Company Limited.

Kriminalomsorgen. (2016). *Kriminalomsorgens årsstatistikk 2015*. Kriminalomsorgen sentrale forvaltning.

Liebling, A. (2011). Moral performance, inhuman and degrading treatment and prison pain. *Punishment & Society, 13*(5), 530–550.

Liebling, A., assisted by Arnold, H. (2004). *Prisons and their moral performance. A study of values, quality and prison life*. Oxford University Press.

Neumann, C. B. (2012). Imprisoning the soul. In T. Ugelvik & J. Dullum (Eds.), *Penal exceptionalism? Nordic prison policy and practice* (pp. 139–155). Routledge.

O'Donnell, I. (2016). The aims of imprisonment. In Y. Jewkes, J. Bennett, & B. Crewe (Eds.), *Handbook on prisons* (2nd ed., pp. 39–54). Routledge.

Pollock, J. M., Hogan, N. L., Lambert, E. G., Ross, J. I., & Sundt, J. L. (2012). A utopian prison, contradiction in terms? *Journal of Contemporary Criminal Justice, 28*(1), 60–76.

Prison Act Commission. (2001). Eindverslag van de commissie 'basiswet gevangeniswezen en rechtspositie van gedetineerden'. *Verslag namens de commissie voor de Justitie uitgebracht door de heren Vincent Decroly en Tony Van Parys, Parl.St. Kamer, 2000–2001*(1076), 001.

Schaanning, E. (2009). *Den tilsiktede smerten.* Oslo Academic Press.

Shammas, V. L. (2014). The pains of freedom: Assessing the ambiguity of Scandinavian penal exceptionalism on Norway's Prison Island. *Punishment & Society, 16*(1), 104–123.

Snacken, S. (2005). Forms of violence and regimes in prison: Report of research in Belgian prisons. In A. Liebling & S. Maruna (Eds.), *The effects of imprisonment* (pp. 306–339). Willan Publishing.

Sykes, G. (2007). *The society of captives: A study of a maximum security prison* (First Princeton classic ed., Princeton classic editions). Princeton University Press.

van Zyl Smit, D., & Snacken, S. (2009). *Principles of European prison law and policy. Penology and human rights.* Oxford University Press.

6

Emancipation Versus Forced Social Education: Normalizing the Social Dimension in Prison

For a human being, living a normal life is only possible by maintaining interpersonal contacts in an essentially social environment. This is as true inside prison as it is outside. Prison, however, is a very different context from the world outside. It is characterized by power and deprivation, and prisoners face more psychological, social, health and financial problems than the general population (Beyens et al., 2014; Gunter et al., 2008; Skarðhamar, 2003). As Liebling (2004: 258) points out, this makes for a social climate full of tension and conflict: '*There are two contrasting truisms relating to prison life: first, that prison is full of tensions and conflict; and secondly, that prison life is all about relationship*'. Essentially, the normalization of the social environment in prison thus comes down to creating a context in which entering into and maintaining normal social interactions are possible. This social environment includes prisoners, prison staff and external visitors, each of these groups playing their own role in the potential normalization of this environment. This also means that the social environment is more than just a clear-cut, observable aspect that can be normalized directly. It is one thing to normalize, for example, the cooking facilities in prison by providing a well-equipped

H. De Vos, *Beyond Scandinavian Exceptionalism*, Palgrave Studies in Prisons and Penology, https://doi.org/10.1007/978-3-031-28635-3_6

kitchen, but it is something entirely different to normalize an environment that depends more on informal, emotional and social feelings and capacities than on practical or technical skills or resources. Any effort to normalize the social environment of a prison is inevitably more of an attempt to set the right atmosphere, indirectly providing the right context for meaningful and normal relationships to thrive.

While the normalization literature seems to have given more attention to material prison conditions, the wider prison research has produced an enormous amount of studies on all aspects of social life in prison. It is not my aim here to 'redo' a full sociological study of the four prisons under scrutiny, but instead to outline to what extent and in which ways the normalization of the social environment has been reflected in Belgian and Norwegian prison legislation, and how the social environment of these four prisons is being normalized in practice.

6.1 The Distinct Social Environment in Prison

The ever-growing body of prison sociological literature shows that the social environment in prison differs significantly from that of society at large. As summarized by Piacentini (2015: 81), '*the prison is one of the very few institutions where pain, suffering and power are depressed into the entire infrastructure and social fabric*'. As far back as 1940, Donald Clemmer was one of the first prison sociologists to identify the distinct dynamics of this social environment, and in particular the informal structures and prison culture. He found that all prisoners are susceptible to a certain degree of '*prisonization*', a process he defined as '*the taking on in greater or less degree of the folkways, mores, customs, and general culture of the penitentiary*' (Clemmer, 1940/1958: 299). Clemmer contended that the degree to which prisoners are affected by this process depends on the following seven determinants: (1) the duration of the prison sentence, (2) the nature of relationships before incarceration, (3) the nature of relationships maintained during incarceration, (4) the level of integration in dominant groups, (5) the level of adopting the prison codes, (6) the relationships with prisoners who are not integrated in the prison culture and (7) the aversion to abnormal sexual behaviour and excessive gambling (Clemmer, 1940/1958: 301–302). The speed of the prisonization process, he argued, differs according to prisoners' personality, age, offence and intelligence (Clemmer, 1940/1958: 302). Despite his observation of prisoners' adaptation processes and the formation of various informal social groups, Clemmer concluded that the '*social world of the prison*' is atomized, and that cohesion among prisoners is instrumental rather than genuine:

> *The prisoner's world is an atomized world. [...] There are no definite communal objectives. There is no consensus for a common goal. The inmates' conflict with officialdom and opposition towards society is only slightly greater in degree than conflict and opposition among themselves. Trickery and dishonesty overshadow sympathy and coöperation* [sic]. *Such coöperation as exists is largely symbiotic in nature. [...] It is a world of individuals whose daily relationships are impersonalized. It is a world of "I", "me", and "mine" rather than "ours", "theirs", and "his".* (Clemmer, 1940/1958: 297–298)

About two decades later, Sykes (1958/2007) identified similar adaptation processes to the prison environment as well as a '*system of social roles*' or so-called '*argot roles*':

> *The* rat, *the* center man, *the* wolf, *the* punk, *the* fag, *the* gorilla, *the* merchant, *the* ball buster, tough, *and the* hipster *– all are social roles in which, generally speaking, the inmate attempts to reduce the rigors of prison life at the expense of fellow prisoners and the individual pursues his own interests, his own needs, without regard for the needs, rights, and opinion of others.* (Sykes, 1958/2007: 106–107, emphasis in original)

While both prison sociologists provided a detailed understanding of the social structures and dynamics in prison, Sykes turned the focus more explicitly to the origins of these social rules and structures. In his view, the informal social structures result from the deprivations inherent to any prison, or '*pains of imprisonment*', and prisoners' coping with these deprivations.

Despite having their origins in the prison practice of two American maximum-security prisons of over sixty years ago, many of the elements that made up the distinct prison environment described by Clemmer and Sykes are still found in more recent studies and across various jurisdictions (see, e.g., Crewe, 2006, 2009 [UK]; Jewkes, 2002, 2005 [UK]; Ugelvik, 2014b [Norway]; Vegrichtová, 2018 [Czech Republic]; Vianello, 2015 [Italy]). Impression management, masking vulnerabilities and showing the ability to defend oneself are common survival strategies in a 'hyper-masculine' prison environment (Crewe, 2009; de Viggiani, 2012; Jewkes, 2005). It is nevertheless generally acknowledged now that prisons differ in terms of deprivations, '*moral performance*' and '*survivability*' (Liebling, 2004, 2011) and that many prisons are now more open towards society than sixty years ago (Crewe, 2016; van Zyl Smit & Snacken, 2009). Accordingly, prison cultures evolve over time and differ between institutions, and even within institutions (Crewe, 2016). The increasing multi-ethnicity (Vianello, 2015) and drugs in prison (Crewe, 2005; Jewkes, 2005) are among the factors that influence current evolutions in prison cultures. Yet it remains true that prisoners' adaptation processes to the prison culture differ greatly between individuals (Clemmer, 1940/1958; Crewe, 2016; Sykes, 1958).

Since this distinctive social environment has been associated with harmful effects on prisoners' well-being and reduced chances of successful rehabilitation and reintegration, normalizing the social interactions between prisoners is relevant from both an intrinsic and an instrumental perspective to normalization. Clemmer (1940/1958: 300) argued that a high level of prisonization would render '*a happy adjustment in any community [...] next to impossible*', suggesting a problematic reintegration after release. Even though this statement needs to be qualified since research also shows that prisoners tend to re-adjust to their pre-prison values and norms towards the end of their sentence or after release (Wheeler [1961] and Goffman [1961] in Crewe, 2016: 84–85), it is true that prisons tend to be criminogenic. Based on a review of the existing evidence in this respect, Cullen et al., (2011: 60) concluded that '*On balance, the evidence tilts in the direction of those proposing that the social experiences of imprisonment are likely crime generating*'. As for the effects on prisoners' well-being, both direct victimization and the perceived quality of the relationships between prisoners correlate with their well-being during imprisonment (van Ginneken et al., 2019). Prisoners who rated their relationships with other prisoners more positively were found to report higher levels of subjective well-being (i.e. the correlation at individual level), and the units in which prisoners reported lower levels of psychological distress were also the units in which prisoners rated their relationships with other prisoners more positively (i.e. the correlation at unit level) (van Ginneken et al., 2019: 1396).

Contrary to what Sykes claimed in 1958, the origins of any subculture in prison are best explained by combining the deprivation and importation theories (Clemmer, 1940/1958; Crewe, 2016; Hochstetler & DeLisi, 2005; Huey Dye, 2010; Mjåland, 2016; Paterline & Peterson, 1999; Penado-Abilleira & Rodicio-García, 2020; Velarde, 2001). Whereas the deprivation theory states that the distinct prison subculture is caused by the adjustment of prisoners to the deprivations in prison, as argued by Sykes (1958), the importation theory emphasizes the role of prisoners' pre-prison characteristics, values and experiences, which they then *import* into prison, as argued by Irwin and Cressey (1962) among others. The combined role of prison and pre-prison factors in shaping the social environment has at least three implications for its normalization. First, in order to normalize the social environment in prison, the deprivations or 'pains' experienced by prisoners need to be reduced. These 'pains' include being deprived of social interaction with family and friends, and frustrations in the context of the interactions that do occur, as well as in the context of security measures, material conditions, autonomy, privacy and activities—hence the need for a holistic approach to normalization. Second, the extent to which *imported* factors, such as pre-prison values, attitudes and behaviour, will be addressed by the normalization process depends on the approach adopted in relation to the subjective dimension of normalization. In other words, it depends on whose perspective is chosen to define 'normal' social interaction. When this is defined by the prison, some pre-prison factors will be addressed by the normalization process to make them fit the desired social interaction patterns. This will be the case for the aspects of the criminal subculture imported into prison:

> much of the inmate behavior classified as part of the prison culture is not peculiar to the prison at all. On the contrary, it is the fine distinction between 'prison culture' and 'criminal subculture' which seems to make understandable the fine distinction between behavior patterns of various categories of inmates. (Irwin & Cressey, 1962: 142)

When the normalization process is intended to reduce the differences between inside and outside prison *as experienced* by the individual prisoner, by contrast, the imported factors will provide the reference point for what is to be considered 'normal' in this context. It should be noted that this reasoning cannot simply be refuted by the argument that the normalization principle is not intended to introduce negative aspects of life in society into prison, and that the imported aspects of the criminal subculture can therefore not serve as a reference point for normalizing the living conditions in prison. The degree to which principles of loyalty, minding one's own business and distrusting authorities, which constitute the criminal subculture, can be considered negative aspects of life outside prison is at least debatable.

Third, the determinants of the distinct social environment in prison that fall beyond the scope of the normalization process should nevertheless be *taken into account* when normalizing the social environment. That is, at least when the normalized social environment is also intended to be *experienced* as such. For instance, the prison population differs from the general population. Unlike the general population, the vast majority of prisoners are men, and they are convicted for or suspected of a criminal offence. These aspects are inherent to the prison population and fall therefore beyond the scope of the normalization process. Prisoners also face more psychological, social and financial problems than the general population (Beyens et al., 2014; Bouverne-De Bie, 2002; Dufaux, 2010; Kelk, 2008; Skarðhamar, 2003; van Zyl Smit & Snacken, 2009) and their subjective well-being is significantly lower (Ginneken et al., 2019). Moreover, there is an overrepresentation of prisoners who do not hold the nationality of the country in which they are incarcerated (Aebi et al., 2019). Prisoners with different social and cultural backgrounds will import different social and cultural values and norms. Given that multiculturality and multilingualism are more prominent in prison than outside, and *if* the aim is to normalize the social environment in such a way that it is also *experienced* as normalized, such a normalization process will require, for instance, active facilitation of communication between people who cannot understand each other's languages but live nevertheless very closely together.

In addition to prisoners, prison officers also play an important role in shaping the social environment in prison and thus in normalizing this environment. Through their interaction with prisoners, they can worsen or mitigate the deprivation and pressures experienced by prisoners (Crewe, 2011a, 2011b; Crewe et al., 2011, 2014; Fredwall, 2017b; Kruttschnitt & Dirkzwager, 2011; Liebling, 2004; Molleman & Leeuw, 2012). Research shows that, like the above-mentioned prison cultures, also prison officers' attitudes and cultures differ between jurisdictions (Kruttschnitt & Dirkzwager, 2011; Liebling et al., 2021), between prisons or prison units (Crewe et al., 2011, 2014; Molleman & Leeuw, 2012), and over time (Crewe, 2011b). Based on a survey conducted with 1750 staff members and 4673 prisoners in all 48 Dutch prisons, Molleman and Leeuw (2012) found that prisoners' perceptions of the prison conditions were more positive in prison units where staff had a supportive orientation, i.e. helpful and motivating in their interaction with prisoners. This is in line with Liebling's (2004, 2011) earlier findings that the quality of prison life, as perceived by prisoners, differs between prisons, and that this is disproportionately influenced by prisoner-prison staff relationships and the underlying values of respect, humanity, trust, support and fairness. As already explained in Chapter 5, the most legitimate form of prison officers' power is '*light*', i.e. relaxed, cooperative and approachable, and at the same time '*present*', i.e. visible/available, interventionist and confident/authoritative (Crewe et al., 2014). Moreover, from an instrumental point of view to normalization, it is important to note that higher levels of the perceived quality of life in prison correlate with reduced misconduct in prison and with reoffending after release (Auty & Liebling, 2020; van Ginneken & Nieuwbeerta, 2020).

In addition to prisoners and prison officers, external visitors also shape the social environment in prison. This group includes prisoners' relatives and friends as well as professional service providers who enter prison to provide prisoners with the same services as citizens outside prison (based on the 'import model' explained in Chapters 3 and 4). Being deprived of the usual contact with family and friends is generally considered one of the most painful aspects of prison life (Rocheleau, 2013: 361; Sykes, 1958: 65). It entails not only reduced support from loved ones but also reduced opportunities to support them (Jones, 2007). This relates to the process of '*role dispossession*' described by Goffman (1961: 24–25), involving the reduction of the multitude of a person's social roles (spouse, father, brother, employee, neighbour, etc.) to one: the role of prisoner. In a situation of dependency, this prisoner role is associated with '*the terror of feeling radically demoted in the age-grading system*' (Goffman, 1961: 47, referring to Sykes, 1958; but also Knight, 2016; Ugelvik, 2014b). Some of these social roles can be resumed after release, but others are irrevocably lost (Goffman, 1961: 25). The latter is especially painful for imprisoned parents (Enos, 1998; Soffer & Ajzenstadt, 2010; Ugelvik, 2014a). Based on surveys conducted with 4538 prisoners housed in 28 Dutch prisons, van Ginneken et al. (2019: 1398–1399) found that prisoners who were satisfied with the frequency with which they received visits experienced higher levels of well-being. Moreover, the quality of visits, letters, phone calls and prison leave impacts not only the prison experience (Jones, 2007: 208; Knight, 2016), but also life after release. Thus, normalizing the contact with the outside world is relevant both from an intrinsic approach to normalization (to protect the right to private and family life as a fundamental right) and from an instrumental approach (to reduce the painful and harmful effects of detention, to increase prisoners' sense of responsibility and to facilitate their reintegration).

In sum, the social environment in prison, shaped by the formal and informal interactions between prisoners, prison staff and visitors, is complex. It is all the more so because the social dimension of prison life cannot be fully understood without also considering the material, security and time dimensions in which the social interactions take place. Therefore, normalizing the social environment in prison is arguably even more challenging than normalizing the material conditions. Let us turn now to the ways in which the normalization of the social environment has been reflected in Belgian and Norwegian legislation.

6.2 The Normalization of the Social Environment as Reflected in Belgian and Norwegian Legislation

Although Belgian and Norwegian legislations cover similar aspects of the social environment in prison, the focus in the two countries is different. Whereas the Belgian Prison Act seeks to facilitate the contact between prisoners and their social network outside prison, the Norwegian Act on the Execution of Sentences seems to value the relationships inside prison over the contact with family and friends, thereby heavily restricting the opportunities for visits and phone calls.

The fact that the Belgian Prison Act has a stronger focus on the social relationships of prisoners with people *from outside* than on their relationships *within* prison makes sense from the Belgian point of view, since maintaining contact with one's social network, in particular with family, is a fundamental right of which prisoners must not be deprived (Prison Action Commission, 2001: 135). This intrinsic argument is complemented with several instrumental purposes, including facilitating prisoners' reintegration and reducing the harmful effects that are caused by the prison's '*total character*' and the related process of '*role dispossession*' (Prison Act Commission, 2001: 135–137, building on Goffman's work [1961]). The Prison Act Commission argued that visits in particular address prisoners in their different social roles, not just as 'prisoner', and encourage them to take up their responsibilities as parent or partner (Prison Action Commission, 2001: 137). These views have been translated into several enforceable rights in the Prison Act (art. 53–64) and are generally covered by article 53: '*the prisoner is entitled to contact with the outside world within the limits set by or under the law*'.

More specifically, the Belgian Prison Act stipulates that prisoners have the right to make daily phone calls to whomever they want (art. 64–65) and to send and receive letters without limitation and without the letters being read by staff members (art. 54–57). Unsurprisingly, these rights can be restricted for security and organizational reasons by the prison's internal regulations or by the prison governor (e.g. art. 64 §1 and §3). Nevertheless, the balance that the Prison Act Commission sought to strike between prisoners' fundamental rights on the one hand, and security, order and the interests of victims, on the other (Prison Act Commission, 2001: 135), is still reflected in the relevant articles of the Prison Act. For example, in their daily calls, prisoners have to use the prison's phone and their personal caller number, so that the numbers they call can be registered, stored and linked to the prisoner who made the call (art. 64§5). Another example of this balance is that the Act does *not* allow security checks of the different forms of communication with people from outside prison unless they are deemed necessary. Exceptionally, communication between remand prisoners and specific persons can be prohibited if this is necessary for the judicial investigation (art. 179).

In addition to letters and phone calls, the Belgian Prison Act also entitles prisoners to receive visitors (art. 58–63). Remand prisoners who are still considered innocent (art. 10) are in principle entitled to daily visits (art. 58§1), and other prisoners to at least three visits of at least one hour a week (art. 58§2 and 58§3). The Act further stipulates that the conditions in the visitors' room should support the affective relationships, especially when young people (under the age of 18) are visiting their parents (art. 60§2). The latter is not only intended to protect the prisoner's right, but also the child's right to stay in touch with his or her parent (Prison Act Commission, 2001: 233). As a general rule, prisoners have direct contact with their visitors, but they can be separated with a transparent panel for security reasons or when prisoners or visitors request this alternative (art. 60§3). Family members and partners are automatically allowed to visit and can only temporarily be denied access in the event of serious security risks (art. 59§1). Other visitors will be allowed with permission of the prison governor, which can only be denied when these visitors cannot demonstrate a legitimate interest or when there are indications that the visit of these individuals will pose a risk to order and security (art. 59§2). While the regular visits take place collectively in the visitors' room and are supervised by prison officers (art. 62), prisoners are also entitled to at least one visit a month without supervision in a separate 'family room'. To be allowed these unsupervised visits, the visitors should have an affective relationship with the prisoner, such as family members or partner (art. 58§4). If the prisoner and his or her partner are not married or were not living together, the partner should '*have shown interest in the prisoner for at least 6 months which indicates the sincerity of the relationship*' (internal regulations of the prisons). These visits are intended to respect the prisoner and visitor's right to private life, intimacy and sexuality. Normalizing this aspect of prison life is also intended to reduce the harmful effects of detention and to facilitate prisoners' reintegration (Prison Act Commission, 2001: 138–139).

In Norway, by contrast, contact with prisoners' personal social network is heavily restricted by the Norwegian Act on the Execution of Sentences. The Act provides similar opportunities for sending and receiving letters to the Belgian Prison Act, but is much more restrictive when it comes to phone calls and visits. However, these restrictions differ according to the prison's security level. In prisons with a high or very high security level, all letters can be opened and read by prison staff, while in a low-security prison the letters are not read by prison staff unless this is deemed necessary for security reasons (art. 30). This applies to regular as well as electronic communication, which the Correctional Service can allow in some cases (art. 30). The phone calls in high-security prisons are limited to twenty minutes per week, which can be divided over several calls (art. 3–29 Regulations relating to the Execution of Sentences). These phone calls are listened to by a prison officer, which also means that prisoners are required to speak a language that this prison officer understands (art. 32 Act). Exceptions to this rule are possible when the prisoner or his or her relatives do not master any other language, or when the prisoner has very little or no other contact with his or her family. In these cases, the conversation can be recorded instead (Guidelines concerning the Act on the Execution of Sentences and the Regulations). In low-security prisons, by contrast, the time limit of twenty minutes does not apply and phone calls are only listened to when this is considered necessary for security reasons. However, the latter does not require suspicion of a specific person, which means that these security measures can be applied randomly (art. 32 of the Act; art. 3–29 Regulations and Guidelines). As a general rule, prisoners in Norwegian prisons pay for their own phone calls, like Belgian prisoners.

When it comes to visitors, the focus of the Norwegian Act on the Execution of Sentences is on the security measures that apply to these visits rather than on facilitating the contact with family and friends (art. 31). Norwegian prisoners are asked to list four people from whom they want to receive visits. Closest relatives, including partner, children, parents, grandparents, brothers and sisters, count as one person (see Guidelines). These four people can be replaced later on (art. 3–28 Regulations). In any case, a person who has been convicted for a drug-related crime or who is serving a sentence at the time will generally not be allowed to visit. Exceptions are possible when this visit is of particular importance to the prisoner (Guidelines). The Norwegian Act does not specify the frequency or duration of the visits, which again contrasts with the rights-approach of the Belgian Act. Instead, this is decided by the prison governor, but as far as practically possible, prisoners should be allowed at least one weekly visit of at least one hour (as stipulated by the Guidelines, not by the Act itself). The Norwegian Act further stipulates the various ways to monitor the visits in high-security prisons: the visits can be visually supervised by a staff member, the conversation can be listened to by a staff member (in this case, the prisoner and visitor can be required to speak a language that the staff member can understand), physical contact can be prohibited, or the prisoner and visitor can be separated by a glass panel (art. 31). In low-security prisons, visits are only supervised when this is deemed necessary for security reasons (art. 31).

The intention to normalize the contact with people from outside emerges more clearly in two specific cases in Norway: visits by children and visits by '*regular visitors*'. These regular visitors, often Red Cross volunteers, are invited by prison staff to visit individual prisoners in order to support them during their prison term and prepare them for their reintegration (again, as stipulated in the Guidelines, not in the Act itself). The general restrictions regarding the frequency and duration do not apply to these visits. More remarkable is that these visits are explicitly expected to help with prisoners' reintegration, while this purpose is not mentioned in the context of visits by relatives—either because the latter is considered self-evident and therefore not worth mentioning, or because people who are selected for this purpose are expected to contribute more effectively to prisoners' reintegration. With regard to the child visits, article 31 of the Norwegian Act stipulates that these must take place in a '*considerate*' way. This applies to the material conditions of the visitors' room, but also to prison staff behaviour and security measures (Ot. Prp. no. 5). Even though both Belgian and Norwegian legislations protect the child's best interest in this context, this plays a more prominent role in the Norwegian prison policy as evident from article 3 of the Act and the comprehensive regulations concerning the child visits.

Another way in which the 'outside world' is present in prison is through what is known as the import model. Both the Belgian and the Norwegian Prison Act stipulate that the Prison Service should collaborate with service providers from society, including teachers, psychologists and social workers, to provide prisoners with the same services as other citizens (art. 4. of the Norwegian Act on the Execution of Sentences; art. 76 and 103 of the Belgian Prison Act, together with art. 5 of the Special Law of 8 August 1980 on institutional reforms; the Flemish Decree of 8 March 2013 concerning the Organisation of Social Assistance and Services for Detainees; Strategic Plan Flemish Government 2015–2020: 14). This import model has already been explained in the context of the material environment (in Chapter 4) and will be discussed in more detail in the context of the activities and services organized in prison (in Chapter 7), since it affects the material, time-use and social dimensions of the prisons. Indeed, this collaboration with community and municipal service providers entails the professionals and volunteers involved in these community and municipal organizations taking part in the social environment in prison, alongside prison staff and prisoners.

When it comes to the day-to-day interactions inside prison, both countries' legislations promote a communal regime to normalize the social interactions between prisoners. Article 17 of the Norwegian Act contains the general rule that prisoners participate *collectively* in work, education, 'other programmes' (see Chapter 7) and leisure activities, but are allowed their own cells to sleep in. The Guidelines add that prisoners should also have the opportunity to eat together (Guidelines 17.1). For security reasons, staff members must supervise these social gatherings at all times, at least in high-security prisons (art. 3–9 Regulations). The main aim of this communal regime is to reduce the harmful effects of isolation. Both the preparatory works of the Act (Ot. Prp. no. 5,

2000–2001: 98, 229–230) and the Regulations state that the exclusion of prisoners from this communal regime must be compensated by increased contact with staff members and satisfying activities. Moreover, according to the Correctional Service, living together in a communal regime is also intended to create a context in which prisoners can improve their social skills and in which '*employees of the prison and of the other public agencies serve as role models for good behaviour and provide prisoners with feedback in a way similar to what they would encounter in society*' (St. meld. no. 37: 108, see also Drægebø, 2006). More generally, the 'social-context work' is a method applied by prison officers in Norwegian prisons which is considered a '*good tool for creating a community with clear structures, routines, activities and credible relationships*' (St. meld. no. 37: 108, see also Drægebø, 2006).

Articles 48 to 52 of the Belgian Prison Act contain the 'conditions of cohabitation' in Belgian prisons and sound very similar to the relevant articles of the Norwegian Act. Articles 49 and 51 define the two standard regimes: the communal regime and the *restricted* communal regime. While prisoners in a communal regime spend most of the day in the common living and working areas, prisoners in a *restricted* communal regime stay inside their cells when not participating in organized activities. The latter is meant as an alternative for prisoners who do not function well in group or for pre-trial prisoners who *prefer* to distance themselves from convicted prisoners (art. 52; Prison Act Commission, 2001: 227). Like in Norway, these standard regimes are intended to reduce the harmful effects of isolation. In earlier drafts of the Belgian Prison Act, the communal regime was combined with the right to an individual cell in order to also ensure prisoners' privacy in this regime (Prison Act Commission, 2001: 132). As already mentioned, however, this right was not included in the final text of the Prison Act. Moreover, despite the similarities between the relevant articles of the Belgian and the Norwegian Act, not all of the Belgian articles had entered into force at the time of the observations. These difficulties with implementation are not surprising since the material conditions of most Belgian prisons were not designed for this kind of communal regime. Importantly, this again points out the need to address the normalization process holistically.

In addition to the communal regime, two other notions are promoted by the two countries' prison policies with the view of supporting the normalization of social interaction in prison: first, dynamic security and second, the principles of participation and responsibility. Dynamic security, as discussed in the previous chapter, always relates to an instrumental approach to normalization since it means that close interaction between prisoners and staff is *instrumentalized* to foster security in prison. While this is clearly promoted by the Belgian and Norwegian prison policy, it is only mentioned briefly or indirectly in their respective Acts. In Norway, the importance attached to dynamic security is explicitly mentioned in various policy documents of the Correctional Service (see St. Meld no. 37; Bronebakk, 2006; årsrapport 2019 for Correctional Service) but not in the Act itself. In Belgium, article 105 of the Prison Act stipulates that '*Maintaining order and security implies a dynamic interaction between prison staff and prisoners*' without further defining this dynamic interaction. The Prison Act Commission explained in this respect that the relationships between prisoners and prison officers should be based on reciprocity (Prison Act Commission, 2001: 177 and 188) adding that '*prison officers do not pick on every little detail and that they [prisoners] are not treated like children*' (Prison Act Commission, 2001: 188). Nevertheless, the wording of article 106 of the Prison Act, which defines the 'general code of conduct' for prisoners, does not reflect this reciprocal character, as it reads as follows: '*The prisoner must [...] follow the orders or instructions of prison staff when it comes to order and safety*' (art. 106, §2).

As for the principles of participation and responsibility, both principles are covered in the Norwegian and Belgian legislation in very similar ways. In Belgium, article 7 of the Prison Act stipulates that every prison must strive for a climate of consultation and that consultative bodies must be founded to this end. More specifically, these consultative bodies must allow prisoners to give their input in '*matters of common interest that may require their cooperation*' (art. 7 §1 Prison Act), including '*the products on the canteen list and their prices, the educational activities, opportunities for exercise/sport, etc.*' (Prison Act Commission, 2001: 207). Additionally, article 9§3 deals with the 'individual detention plan' and states that '*the convicted person is given the opportunity to cooperate constructively in the implementation of the individual detention plan [...] which is drawn up with a view to a harm-reducing, restorative, reintegration-oriented and safe implementation of the prison sentence*'. Article 38 of the Act confirms that this 'individual detention plan' is drawn up '*in consultation and with the cooperation of the convicted person*'. The nature of this 'individual plan' will be discussed in Chapter 7 as it is linked to the way in which the time in prison is used and normalized.

In Norway, article 25 of the Act on the Execution of Sentences stipulates that the prison *can* establish consultative bodies with representatives of prisoners and staff *if* prisoners want this, and with the aim of discussing issues important for prisoners' daily life, but not individual prisoners, staff members or security measures. Additionally, the Norwegian Act also promotes a more structural collaboration between prisoners and staff in the framework of the 'future plan'. The Guidelines regarding Future Planning stipulate in this respect that:

> The quality of the planning process must be a priority. This means that the quality of the cooperation in this context between the convicted person, the prison service and other partners is valued over a comprehensive planning document.

Like the Belgian 'individual detention plan', this 'future plan' must include the activities and measures that are most suited for the individual prisoner. The nature of the 'future plan' will therefore be discussed in more detail in Chapter 7, yet two main differences with the Belgian plan are relevant with respect to normalizing the social interaction in prison. First, in Norway, this plan is drafted with the support of the prisoner's 'contact officer', a role that does not exist in Belgian prisons. Contact officers are the prison officers who are linked to individual prisoners and are responsible for informing them about the prison and their rights and duties, supporting and motivating them, supporting the 'future planning process' and assisting with requests for external services, among other things (see Guidelines regarding the Work of Contact Officers). All prisoners must be provided a contact officer, and all trained prison officers do in principle fulfil this role of contact officer (Guidelines regarding the

Work of Contact Officers; Guidelines concerning the Act on the Execution of Sentences and the Regulations). The Guidelines regarding the Work of Contact Officers explain this as follows, thereby endorsing the instrumental approach to normalization:

> A main objective of the Correctional Service is to create the conditions for prisoners to make their own efforts to counteract criminal behaviour patterns. The contact officer has an important function in assisting prisoners in this work, and must collaborate actively with the prisoner in a motivation and change process. [...]
>
> The contact officers have a special responsibility to take care of social needs and provide practical assistance to remand prisoners who have been excluded from letters and visits.

Second, the 'future planning' is only mentioned in the Norwegian Guidelines concerning the Act on the Execution of Sentences and the Regulations and in the Guidelines regarding Future Planning and not in the Act itself. This means that Norwegian prisoners do not have the same legal basis as Belgian prisoners with which to enforce their right to such an individual plan. This difference suggests that Norwegian prisoners depend more on the goodwill of staff members than Belgian prisoners do, while the social interactions in Belgian prisons are laid down by law, providing prisoners with opportunities to file formal complaints (see also Snacken, 2015). Strengthening the legal position of prisoners was indeed one of the main objectives of the Prison Act Commission and is not only reflected in the context of the individual plan (Prison Act Commission, 2001). To this end, the Belgian Prison Act also stipulates that the reasons for all decisions taken within the framework of the Act must be provided, except in some exceptional cases (art. 8). Such a provision is lacking in the Norwegian Act.

This example beautifully reflects the two different approaches to normalization of the social environment. In Belgium, the rights-based approach intends to recognize prisoners as 'full legal citizens' in their various social roles and in so doing, to reduce the harmful effects of detention, although translating normal interaction among prisoners and staff into enforceable rights is more complex and perhaps also less desirable, since it results in over-juridification of these interactions (see also Snacken, 2015). In Norway, the instrumental approach means that it is not so much the legislation itself that extensively describes the normalization process, though covering similar aspects of the social environment compared to Belgium, but rather the Correctional Service policy documents (e.g. St. Meld. no. 37; Guidelines regarding the Work of Contact Officers; see also Drægebø, 2006). It is interesting to find out, in the section, which of the two approaches leads to more normal interactions in practice.

6.3 Setting the Right Conditions for Normal Social Interaction in Practice

The observation that the social environment in prison differs from that in society at large means that people in prison interact differently and take on other social roles than they would do outside prison. As explained above, this is due to a combination of imported and prison-specific factors. The role of prisoner tends to become predominant and to affect all other social roles, such as parent, friend, son/daughter, brother/sister, colleague, member of a sports team or of a spiritual community (see Goffman, 1961). Each social role is defined in relation to other members of a social group and is associated with role-related behaviour. Setting the right conditions so that normal interaction can thrive means then, creating, or not restricting, the opportunities for exercising a variety of social roles in ways that resemble the social interaction outside prison (see also Snacken, 2002). In what follows, the focus is on how the conditions in the four prisons were organized so that they enabled prisoners to take on various social roles in ways that resembled social interaction outside prison. This is closely linked to a person's identity, self-perception and agency (see, e.g., Bosworth, 1999; Crewe, 2009; Rowe, 2011; Ugelvik, 2014b), but the analysis presented here will only mention these individual processes insofar they provide a better understanding of the social environment in prison and its normalization.

6.3.1 Enabling Various Social Roles in the Two Belgian Prisons

All prisoners in Hoogstraten were in the last stage of their sentence, Dutch-speaking, and risked being sent back to a closed prison when they violated the prison rules. In Leuven, by contrast, about forty per cent of the prisoners was pre-trial, which involved more trial-related stress, more incoming prisoners and a rapidly changing population, more overcrowding and more nationalities and languages than in Hoogstraten prison. Despite these differences, the two Belgian prisons were similar in terms of normalizing the social interaction and will therefore be discussed together in this section. According to prison officers in both prisons, Leuven and Hoogstraten had a more relaxed social climate than other Belgian prisons, and I witnessed only a few aggression incidents. This fairly relaxed climate was commonly contrasted to that of 'real' prisons. Especially in Hoogstraten, this was very present in the discourse of prisoners and prison officers, many of whom had prior experiences with the same closed prison and shared their aversion to the violence and abuses they witnessed there.

> Bob [prison officer] explains that many things happen behind closed doors that are not supposed to get public. Most disturbingly, the excessive use of violence against prisoners. Tuur [prison officer] confirms this by saying that some of their former colleagues [in the other prison] were just very frustrated and used violence against prisoners for no reason. But as a colleague there is little you can do about this. Bart [prisoner] joined this conversation and said that he had seen things that he would never forget. For instance, when he had to clean the punishment cell after use. He never knew what exactly had happened in there, but he had to clean feces and blood from the walls. (Field notes 5 November 2014, Hoogstraten prison)

This was the usual reference point used by prisoners and prison officers to assess the 'normalized' interaction in prisons like Hoogstraten and Leuven. However, just as normalizing the material conditions is not the same as improving those conditions, so is normalized social interaction not the same as non-violent or friendly interaction. The following paragraphs will show that normalized social interaction occurred in these two prisons when prisoners took on another social role than the 'inmate role' in interaction with people from outside prison, and in particular with people who were *not* part of their own social network.

At the risk of oversimplifying the complex social interaction in prison, it could be argued that, in the two Belgian prisons, the role of prisoner and that of prison officer were one-dimensional, focused around order and safety, and mirrored each other. This observation does not say anything about the subjective experiences of the various aspects of these roles, or about all types of resistance or coping strategies that occurred, but simply points out the social roles that are 'produced' by the social setting of these prisons. The social role of prison officer was shaped by the task to supervise and enable daily life activities in prison. Counting prisoners at fixed times, day and night, and thus preventing escapes, was considered their key task. The prisoner role involved following the rules and instructions, ideally politely and obediently, and in fact institutionalized. Most interactions between prisoners and prison officers were short and instrumental to the daily operation of the prison. They had limited expectations of each other, and prisoners were generally satisfied with short polite interactions, when prison officers opened and closed the doors on time, and acted decisively when needed.

> *Senne:* Yeah they [prison officers] are really great. [....] I am always polite: 'thank you' and so and so. I am always polite to them, they are polite to me too. And if it continues like this, there is no problem for me. (Interview Senne, Leuven prison)

***

> *Jef [prison officer]*: This is how things work: they disturb me as little as possible and I won't disturb them. So I address the men friendly, so that they are calm towards me. (Field notes 22 October 2014, Hoogstraten prison)

The role of prison officer was hierarchically superior to that of prisoner, not in professional but in social terms, and this determined the social interaction between them. Prisoners' dependency on prison officers for the most basic human needs reinforced this dynamic. For instance, prisoners could indicate that they had a request (e.g. that they would like to make a phone call, or, in Hoogstraten, that they needed to go to the toilet) by turning on the light above their cell door. Prison officers had to keep an eye on these lights, and could react promptly, but could also delay their reaction when they had to do other things first, or for no particular reason, which some of them tended to do under peer pressure.

> *Maarten [prisoner]*: I'll say, over the years I have learned to... that it is a game you play. I know that the guards like me. If a guard gives me a disciplinary report, I will never change my attitude towards him. He'll never hear about it again. Because I know very well, those blue ones, I still need them to get anything. So actually, you put on a mask, not with everyone, but with some, you know. You familiarize yourself with it. If you keep pounding on your door, they won't open it, so what do you do? You put on that light, and you wait. And then, if they open the door, you thank them, because those small words contribute to the fact that they will like you, which is probably the reason why I already got a job after two months. So you have to play the game. (Interview Maarten, Leuven prison)

In both prisons, the distinction between these two social groups was made visible through the prison uniforms, but also more subtly, through separate menus for staff and prisoners, separate toilets and well-meant advice not to use a coffee cup that could have been touched by a prisoner. Yet surprisingly, the 'we versus them'-feeling was more strongly present in prison officers' discourse than in that of prisoners, in the sense that prison officers more regularly stressed that they needed to have each other's back. In Leuven, this distinction was also marked by the staff tradition to shake hands at the start of each shift and by the way in which prisoners and prison officers were generally addressed. Prison officers were usually called 'chief', and prisoners were usually called by their last name, cell number or 'job description'. I was told, for instance, not to worry about my used coffee cup, because '*the servant will do the dishes*', referring to the man who was cleaning the corridor. When talking about prison officers' tasks, prisoners were also referred to as 'something':

'*is there still something to be unlocked at your section?*' In Hoogstraten prison, on the other hand, first names were used for prisoners and prison staff (i.e. prison officers, social workers, teachers, psychologists, but not for prison governors, which indicated the hierarchy between governors and other staff members). The use of first names symbolically narrowed the distinction between the two groups, which is uncommon in Belgian prison and required a mentality shift from prison officers. Those who could not get used to this common practice in Hoogstraten prison would request a transfer to another prison. Hence, not only prisoners, but also prison officers were (self-)selected in this prison, which contributed to the more relaxed social climate in this prison.

> Pieter has applied for his transfer to [a closed prison]. He says that it is difficult for him to adapt to the working methods in Hoogstraten. … He is not convinced that prisoners should know his name, and therefore never wears his badge (which shows first name, last name and photo). 'I am just a chief in here, nothing else'. (Field notes 11 November 2014, Hoogstraten prison)

The need to distance themselves from prisoners also included peer pressure among prison officers not to sympathize too much with prisoners, either for security or practical reasons, or for reasons of principle, even to the extent that some prison officers felt the need to give a good excuse for assisting prisoners.

> Three prisoners have been waiting for over an hour in the two small, unventilated waiting cells for being registered, so that they could be sent to their own cell. They had been tapping the small window in the door, but most prison officers 'had no time' or 'did not hear them'. Eddy [prison officer] opens the doors to see what's the matter… One of them is having difficulty breathing. Eddy apologetically explains that the window of this cell cannot be opened. There is indeed uncomfortably little fresh air in this cell. Eddy offers this man some water and asks the other one if he also wants something to drink. A colleague who passes by and overhears this question, asks mockingly: 'So, are you pouring these men a beer or what?' Eddy fills two plastic cups with water. He then asks the prison officers in the central control room whether this prisoner can be

registered soon, because he has been waiting for a long time and is having difficulties breathing. 'You know, I don't want to be responsible for this man's death.' (Field notes Leuven prison, 5 November 2015)

Prisoners distanced themselves from prison officers in similar ways, but also from other prisoners, which resulted in a 'me versus them versus them'-discourse (similar to Clemmer's (1940/1958: 297–298) quote above). All interviewed prisoners stressed the need to present themselves as 'tough but not reckless' in relation to other prisoners. Despite these underlying interpersonal tensions, however, overt physical and verbal aggression did not occur often. On the contrary, most interactions appeared friendly, and small issues were solved with a quip or a joke. Indeed, it was considered beneficial to the smooth operation of the prison to avoid both hostile and genuine interaction. This was mentioned by prisoners and prison officers alike.

> *Viktor [prisoner]*: I got better in acting more friendly than I actually am. It is a social obligation in prison: if you're smart, you act friendly. And the same goes for the guards: they often come and talk to me, but they barely know me, so obviously that is fake as well. (Field notes 4 December 2014, Leuven prison)

* * *

> Lies [prison officer] explains that she is very good at switching off her emotions when she enters the prison. Nothing can hurt her emotionally, nothing that prisoners would shout at her. She says that she is not like this outside prison, but inside this is necessary. (Field notes 11 November 2015, Leuven prison)

The nature of the social interaction between prison officers and prisoners was different in the workshops, laundry service or library, where they interacted more closely with each other and knew each other better. Some experienced this as more normal interaction, for instance prisoners who appreciated the advice from prison officers which was based on common sense rather than expert advice, others experienced these close interactions as less normal, for instance prison officers who felt that prisoners were more manipulative in the workshops than on the sections. Yet overall, they still interacted in their respective roles as prisoner and prison officer. This means that prisoners still found themselves in a position of dependency that does not exist between colleagues or between employer and employee outside prison (where, if it exists, it is generally considered abusive). For instance, prisoners could lose their work for speaking disrespectfully to a prison officer, which is at odds with the idea of 'full legal citizen' underlying the Belgian Prison Act.

These observations once again point out that creating a normalized social environment can only be done when the environment is approached holistically. As with the other dimensions, normalizing separate aspects of the social dimension may not have the desired effect or even cause unwanted side effects. Against this background, it is not surprising, for instance, that prisoners were rather sceptic about the consultative bodies, which were supposed to have an emancipating effect: '*they organize this because they have to, they listen but what we say doesn't make a difference. It's more so they can say they had a meeting with prisoners*' (Field notes Leuven, 4 December 2015). Nor is it surprising that Viktor preferred to eat alone in his cell rather than with a group of prisoners who might attack him, or as he put it '*many prisoners want to eat comfortably, not gobbling their food with their back against the wall*' (Field notes Leuven prison, 4 November 2015).

From the side of prison officers, it is relevant to note here that, in both prisons, many prison officers had a low professional self-image. Some of them had been working for years but were still on the waiting list to start their training. This was seen as one of the many signs that their job was not taken seriously. In informal conversations about the operation of the prison, they would often conclude by saying '*we're only guards, you know, no one ever listens to us*'. The perception of being undervalued clashed with the implementation of a true rights-based approach in dealing with prisoners and led sometimes to the adoption of a very restrictive interpretation of these rights (i.e. sufficient nutrition and spending one hour outdoors).

> Brigitte talks about the fact that it was all easier in the past. Now prisoners only get rights, rights, rights... it sometimes looks more like a restaurant in here than like a prison. (Field notes Hoogstraten, 12 November 2014)

Does this mean that the interaction between people in their respective roles of prisoner and prison officers have no value for normalization? Of course not. Following the deprivation theory, normalizing the social environment does indeed require to reduce the deprivations inherent to the prison context, including the deprivation of security, dignity, respect, etc. Thus, the nature of these relationships is relevant for normalizing the prison conditions, even if in themselves they do not resemble usual social interaction outside prison, when they reduce harmful effects and interpersonal tensions, and facilitate the normalization of the other dimensions and of the other social interaction. It was not that the more relaxed climate in these prisons was not appreciated, it definitely was, but the observations in Leuven prison and Hoogstraten prison made it also very clear that *normalizing* social interactions requires more than just the rights protected by the Prison Act.

More specifically, it required interaction with people from outside prison, as this enabled them to take on various social roles, so more than just the one 'inmate role'. Contact with family was for many prisoners the most important and most meaningful interaction in prison, and was enabled through visits, phone calls and letters. At least, if they had family members with whom they were still in touch, if they could afford the phone calls, and if the family members were able and willing to come to the prison for a visit. Leuven prison is easily accessible, being located in the city centre and at walking distance from the train station; but that is not the case for Hoogstraten prison. Moreover, providing contact opportunities between prisoners and their family is one thing, but it does not automatically lead to normalized interaction with loved ones. A crucial difference was that, while in prison, it is hard to take up responsibilities inherent to the social role of father, grandfather or partner, which caused frustrations and concerns.

> *Marcel*: It's frustrating... Look, my wife cannot afford anything at home... I pay for the rent and all that, but they [the prison

> system] don't seem to think about that. (Interview Marcel, Leuven prison)

This contrasts with the policy aim of responsibilization: prisoners cannot take responsibility for their loved ones in the manifold ways they would want to (emotionally, practically, financially), but at the same time, they are supposed to show the system how 'responsible' they are in doing little prison tasks. Some prisoners found it too painful to keep in touch with family, either because they did not want them to see them in prison, and did not want to be a burden to their family, or because it made them more strongly and painfully aware what they were missing out. This made them sometimes cut off all contact with family as long as they were in prison.

> *Karim*: But yeah it's okay, I have accepted this… for me, I cross off every day… If everything goes well, ten more months, and then I can leave with a bracelet. Ten months, only ten months, I've been inside for two years now, so ten months is nothing. That is, in my head, I've closed myself off. I've closed myself off from the outside, I am really not thinking about outside. Only my sisters come to visit but that's all. I don't call anyone, or I don't have any contact. (Interview Karim, Leuven prison)

All this is not to suggest that contact opportunities are less meaningful or important than generally assumed. It is not only a fundamental human right; for some prisoners, family visits are the one thing that keeps them going. But the point is that these visits in themselves do not enable social interaction resembling the interaction of outside prison in any way.

An exception to that conclusion is the unsupervised visits and the child visits in Hoogstraten prison. These child visits take place once a month in a separate room, with a separate entrance so that children do not have to enter through the prison gate and are only supervised by social workers in civilian clothing (while regular visits are supervised by uniformed prison officers). These conditions encourage fathers and families to visit prison with children, to stay in touch and thus to make sure that the children still know their father when he gets out and comes home. It is at the request of some prisoners that the age of children who can participate in these visits has been raised to 18, which points out that the atmosphere during these visits is experienced as more normalized compared to the regular visits. Yet, in other instances, several aspects remind prisoners that, though aimed at normalizing the contact between fathers and their children, the child visits remain a prison activity. Prisoners are supposed to act as an engaged father and are not allowed, for example, to let their children play in the playground while talking to their girlfriend or wife who is accompanying the child, despite the normality of this situation outside prison.

Given the complexities of normalizing the social interactions with prisoners' personal network, the interactions that resembled those outside most closely were social interactions with teachers, sport coaches or volunteers (via the 'import model'). These people entered the prison only occasionally or a few times a week, and addressed prisoners in different social roles, such as student, sporter or conversation partner. Through these interactions, prisoners were sometimes pushed out of their 'inmate role'. This was enthusiastically noticed by a prisoner in Hoogstraten during a Sunday morning football game between the team of Hoogstraten prison and another local team. The prisoner in question acted as referee and was addressed in that capacity by the players from outside, and thus with 'sir', an apparent honour he did not want to let go unnoticed: '*Chief, did you hear that? He called me 'sir'!*' (Field notes Hoogstraten prison, 26 October 2014). In Leuven prison, similar interactions happened during conversation evenings called *Café combine*, organized in the visitors room and with a mixed group of participants from inside and outside prison. In these events, prisoners were addressed as participants and conversation partners, and not in their role of prisoner. The atmosphere and topics of conversation were very different from those inside prison, in such a way that one of the prisoners wrote on his evaluation post-it '*It was nice to feel normal again*' (Field notes Leuven prison, 17 November 2015).

One of the strengths of the import model is that people who enter prison only occasionally never stop using their reference points from outside prison. This is as true for material conditions as for social interaction. People who occasionally participate in activities, like the football players in Hoogstraten and conversation partners in Leuven, but also teachers and sports coaches, are generally people who give the same courses inside and outside prison, enter the prison to teach, and therefore approach and address prisoners in their role of student or participants in a sports activity. Unlike prisoners and prison officers, they continue to notice the 'abnormality' of the prison context and to express their confusion about some prison habits and routines. In so doing, they tend to irritate prison officers. For prisoners, however, it clearly demonstrates that these people are not part of the system, are not involved in any decision regarding the execution of the sentence and indeed are making the effort to enter prison for them. This kind of interactions, teacher-students or sport coach-participant, is most similar to their equivalent outside prison and enable prisoners to take on various social roles that resemble those outside prison. More than anything else in prison, it makes them feel normal again.

6.3.2 Living Together in a High-Security Prison: High Expectations and Many Frustrations

In Nermarka prison, the social interactions among prisoners and between prisoners and prison officers were normalized more proactively than in the two Belgian prisons. With the exception of the units A1 and A2, all prisoners were accommodated in living units with a capacity for twenty-two prisoners or less. From an observer perspective, the living units did indeed give a homelike impression, and the social interactions in these units seemed to be normalized: prisoners ate together, made food, played games, watched TV and could go to their own cell when they wanted to be alone. However, living together with about twenty other prisoners was not experienced as normalized as it seemed for an observer and for prison staff. In fact, the accounts of the prisoners in the E building were very much in line with findings of prison sociological research in other jurisdictions, which is remarkable given the significant differences in material prison facilities. Not only was '*living closely together with criminals*' considered one of the biggest differences between life inside and outside prison, it was also considered a source of painful and harmful effects. The painful effects were caused by the ongoing possibility of aggressive encounters, threats and pressure on 'weaker' and younger prisoners to hand over their medication or smuggle things inside; but also by the constant need for impression management to avoid victimization. For sex offenders and 'snitches', who were not accepted in this communal life, this social environment was even tougher. Some sex offenders would therefore self-isolate in the A building. Farid described the tensions in the living units as follows:

> *Farid*: So if somebody asks me to fight or if somebody tries to do something, I just make sure that we have finished with this problem right there. So I don't have to go around and hide, and make food in the corner or something like that... but many other people who is a little bit weaker, this is the problem, yeah... they take their food, or they take their cigarettes or... [....]
>
> *Me*: Also in here?
>
> *Farid*: You don't see it, because it's very sneaky [...] It is the threats... you know, psychological war... In here, you don't see so much violence, but you know, people are talking with ... the intention of hurting you or something like that. .... They, for example, ask: tomorrow you buy cigarettes for me, if not, I'm gonna fuck you up. And you tell them: why should I do this? No, you will see if you don't do it. (Interview Farid, Nermarka prison)

Another source of 'pains' was the superficiality of this social climate. Interactions and conversations with other prisoners often remained superficial and instrumental, not only because showing genuine emotions was avoided to mask anything that could be considered by others as vulnerabilities, but also because prisoners often found only a few people with whom they had shared interests or could have a meaningful conversation. A commonly mentioned strategy to thrive in this social environment was to 'deactivate' their usual social skills.

> *Fredrik*: I just play along. 'Yeah... okay... yeah yeah...', like that. But I don't discuss my problems with anyone you know... Just someone. So this is uh... the social agenda in the prison is very... random... (Interview Fredrik, Nermarka prison)

Prisoners feared that staying in this kind of social environment was harmful in the longer term. They were concerned that they would lose the social skills they needed outside prison, or that they would get involved in new criminal activities by socializing with criminals.

> *Olav*: Yes it does something with you. If you stay in that kind of environment long enough, it influences you. And when you get out, it's hard to just switch uh… it can be very easy for someone who doesn't have that social circle to just go completely off track…. (Interview Olav, Nermarka prison)

***

> *Steinar*: You know, in prison, it's a school of criminality… all kind of people from everywhere are in one place… many young people will get trained to do criminal things… If I want to, I can make a living by doing criminal things the rest of my life, because I have contacts now all over the world, after I've been in prison a couple of years. So it is only what you set your mind to. But it is easy to get manipulated to be a part of criminal things. (Interview Steinar, Nermarka prison)

Hence, the assumption that the social interactions in these living units would nicely resemble those outside prison does not take into account that prisoners do not necessarily want to, or feel comfortable to, live 'normally' together with other prisoners. This is all the more relevant because the coping strategies that prisoners apply in interacting with other prisoners contrast with the attitudes and behaviour they are expected to show in relation to prison officers and the prison system. Indeed, the social role of prisoner and prison officer, in relation to each other, reflects the instrumental interpretation of normalization. This means that both roles are defined by security as well as rehabilitation needs. These two elements do not only shape their social interaction but also the expectations towards each other. In Nermarka, a prisoner was expected to follow the prison rules as much as to work on his rehabilitation. The latter involved acknowledging his problems, the need for help or assistance, and the willingness to change. A prison officer was expected to ensure security inside prison and to prevent escapes, but also to support this rehabilitation process. These role-related expectations were present in both prisoners' and prison officers' discourse. Let's have a closer look.

Prison officers underlined the importance of close and constructive interaction with prisoners and of supporting prisoners' rehabilitation process, which they believed to contribute to the security in prison. The use of humour and the absence of 'we versus them'-tensions were often mentioned by prison officers to explain why there was so little violence in this prison. The 'we versus them'-distinction was indeed less sharp than in the two Belgian prisons, which became clear in many small gestures. For instance, when tables and chairs were put in place for an activity, prison officers and prisoners would typically do this together. Prison officers would also put their own plates and cutlery in the dishwasher and did not leave this task for a prisoner. They were physically present on the courtyard, and some spent a great deal of their time in the living units (reading a newspaper, chatting with prisoners or playing cards or chess) and ate together with prisoners. The latter was seen by prisoners as a sign of respect and of the fact that prisoners were not just security risks in the eyes of prison officers. First names were used, although this is less remarkable in Nermarka than in Hoogstraten prison, because in Norway, unlike in Belgium, it is common to use first names also for teachers and professors, for instance. It is also important to note here that the close and constructive interaction between prison officers and prisoners did not quite suggest equality between them.

Prisoners' expectations were very much in line with prison officers' discourse. The absence of prison officers' violence was taken for granted, hence not as much appreciated as in the Belgian prisons. Instead, Norwegian prisoners expected staff members to contribute to their personal security as well as to their rehabilitation process, including assistance with practical arrangements.

> *Anders*: I basically asked him, 'do me a favour', and he did. I asked him to send an email to a person and he did that. And when he got a response from the email, he gave that to me, and I think that was yesterday.
>
> *Me*: Okay, but that's good that you can ask something like that?

> *Anders*: Yeah yeah… well, if they don't do that … then what are they here for? That's how I feel. They're here to, you know, make sure that we don't do stupid shit and all that. Make sure that we get up and close and open the doors… I think they're here a bit to help us as well, yeah, if we have issues with anything or need information or… stuff like that. (Interview Anders, Nermarka prison)

At the same time, prisoners' high expectations, though very much in line with the Norwegian prison policy, also led to many frustrations, and somewhat paradoxically, prisoners in the E building generally advocated *more* interventions in terms of dynamic security and rehabilitation. Unlike prison officers, prisoners did not think that aggression in the living units was reduced thanks to the strong dynamic security in this prison. On the contrary, many of them believed that the tensions between prisoners would reduce when prison officers were more often present in the living units (i.e. '*light*' but more '*present*', in terms of the above-mentioned framework by Crewe et al. [2014]). Moreover, prisoners tended to attribute the constructive interaction with prison officers to their own ability to conform with their role expectations rather than to prison officers' constructive attitudes. Arguing or disagreeing with staff members was feared to be bad for their progress through the system. It was generally considered smarter to follow the rules obediently without thinking than to question the rules. At the same time, however, these conformist attitudes led to feelings of resignation and apathy. Emil illustrated this with a situation in which one of the staff members wanted to talk with him about the seriousness of his conviction: '*you just have to keep calm and let them shit on you. If you start arguing, you only get in trouble*' (Field notes 27 April 2016, Nermarka prison). A similar feeling was voiced by Olav:

> There are so many stupid rules in this prison, or unfair decisions, that you should not get frustrated about these things. Just try not to think too much about them, otherwise you go crazy. Just do what they tell you to do. (Field notes 11 May 2016, Nermarka prison)

Commonly heard frustrations regarding rehabilitation and support were caused by the experienced lack of suitable programmes or insufficient efforts done by staff members to support them. This was particularly frustrating because Norwegian prisons were in their view supposed to provide high-quality rehabilitation programmes. Farid and Emil expressed their frustrations as follows:

> *Farid*: I think they press me more down than that they build me up. And uh... psychologically I think I'm more angry when I go out than rehabilitated. ... So, that's the problem, you know, I get more angry when I'm here because nobody really... I feel like nobody really wants to help me, just press me down. (Interview Farid, Nermarka prison)

***

> *Emil*: Norway always pretends to be so good at everything, but its prisons are worthless. No energy is put in the rehabilitation of a prisoner. Well, maybe a little in those without training, they can take some classes, but otherwise prisoners are just locked up and kicked out after their time. All problems remain, and in many cases they only get worse. (Field notes 21 March 2016, Nermarka prison)

While showing prisoners' frustrations, these quotes also indicate that Norwegian prisoners still believe in the potential of the system, but are disappointed by the fact that it does not work the way it is supposed to work. It is telling that prisoners who were not familiar with the Norwegian system had different expectations and experiences. They did not trust their contact officer with personal information and were excluded from certain services, which they experienced as discriminating and made them identify strongly as 'foreign national'. At the same time, they noticed much more that the prison system was taking care of prisoners, and were even surprised about this good care: *'we are criminals, for god's sake!'* (Field notes 4 June 2016, Nermarka prison).

In *Modulen*, by contrast, the role-related expectations of prisoners and prison officers were more consistently implemented, which solved many of the above-mentioned frustrations. As already explained, the regime in *Modulen* is rehabilitation-orientated and demanding in terms of mandatory activities, counselling sessions and urine tests, but also more comfortable in terms of material conditions. The social environment was less tense than in the E units. This was due to a combination of factors, including the fact that prisoners had more privacy and more personal space, more meaningful activities, the stricter drug policy and the selection of prisoners and prison officers. However, the selection of prisoners played arguably only an indirect role. The prisoners who had been selected were often convicted for drug-related offences, some for many years, and most not for the first time. Therefore, it might have been the *idea* of being selected rather than the actual selection that contributed to the more relaxed atmosphere. They came from the E building and would not 'waste this chance' (i.e. self-discipline). In line with the instrumental policy view on normalization, working on prisoners' rehabilitation was deemed to increase security. Though also present in prison officers' discourse in the E building, it was much more apparent in the daily practice of *Modulen*. A prisoner who is transferred to *Modulen* is considered motivated and willing to work on his rehabilitation and therefore deserving of additional efforts from prison officers. His social role becomes that of prisoner-client, while prison officers take on the role of prison officer-social worker. The various layers of the prison officer's role enabled them to effectively ensure the dynamic security, or social control by prison officers. The subtle but extensive social control can be illustrated by this observation:

> I join Nils and Pål on the couch. They are watching the snooker game between Abdel [prisoner] and Per, a prison officer who is at the same time wearing headphones to listen in on a phone call from Emil. Per always wins, they say. Meanwhile they are laughing with Emil. He is on the toilet, calling with his mother. So, Per is winning this game, whilst via his headphones listening to the conversation that Emil is having with his mother on the toilet. (Field notes Nermarka prison, 30 May 2016)

During certain activities, the prisoner and the prison officer role in *Modulen* were almost equal: when playing cards, snooker, sports activities inside or outside prison. In these sports activities, prison officers did not wear their uniform, hence reducing the visible distinction between them. In daily life activities, the interaction was close and personal: prison officers were usually present in the living rooms, and they used the kitchen to make their own lunch and ate together with prisoners. In rehabilitation activities, however, the distinction between the prisoner role and the prison officer role became much more delineated, as prison officers were both supporters (e.g. arranging meetings with NAV or applying for a place in a rehabilitation centre) and controllers (regular urine tests, strip searches, room searches, listening in on prisoners' personal phone calls). All in all, this regime is very '*tight*', to use Crewe's (2011a) and Crewe and Ievins (2021) conceptualization: prison officers supervise daily activities and interaction, they know prisoners' hopes and wishes for the future, they have insight into family relationship by overhearing personal phone calls, and from all those perspectives, they discuss the progress of prisoners in terms of rehabilitation. For many prisoners, this is the best place to be in this prison: the best material conditions, the best chance to use their time meaningful and the best chance to get the support with rehabilitation and reintegration they expect from the system, but also the best way to get out of prison as quickly as possible, since they can 'show their progress'. In this light, Fredwall (2017a: 173) rightly wondered '*where the moral boundaries [are] drawn for how far officers should go in terms of doing "something about the living conditions and [...] offer measures that help transform the convicted persons themselves"*'. As Fredwall already found, there is no easy or straightforward conclusion to draw. Yes, the regime seems to be very intrusive indeed, and the daily life social environment in *Modulen* does not seem to resemble the 'normal' social environment outside prison at all. And yet, this social environment was experienced by prisoners as less painful and less harmful, as they expected and appreciated it to be intrusive and disciplinary.

So far, the social interactions discussed here only involved interaction between people in their respective role of prisoner and prison officer, even if these roles had a different nature in *Modulen* when compared to the E building. It is true that the proactive interventions to normalize the social environment in this prison only created a few opportunities for prisoners to take on various social roles. These opportunities were similar to those in the Belgian prisons and were created through the import model, the contact opportunities with family and friends (letters, phone calls and visits) and, in *Modulen*, also the activities outside of the prison walls. Two manifestations of the import model are particularly noteworthy in this context. First, the visits by Red Cross volunteers, who could visit prisoners inside their cells and were not bound by the regular visit arrangements. These visitors entered into interaction with their 'outsiders perspective', which led to conversations that were experienced as normal and private, and were highly valued by prisoners. Second, the 'service market', which was a regular informative event organized in the multifunctional room that made the import model concrete and tangible. Different service providers (from NAV, education and health care, and from Leira prison) were present in the multifunctional room and presented their information in such a way that prisoners could walk around the room to see which services were provided in the prison and ask service providers in person for more information. Thus, prisoners received this information in a similar way as they would have outside prison and were approached and addressed as client or student rather than prisoner.

Taking on the social role of family member or friend was enabled through the opportunities to receive visitors, to send and receive letters and to make phone calls. However, as was the case in the Belgian prisons, maintaining relationships with family or partners, and thus continuing to exercise those meaningful social roles were hard. In Nermarka prison, this was further complicated by the security restrictions that limited the duration of phone calls (20 minutes per week) and did not allow for private conversations. For some prisoners, receiving regular visits was all that mattered in prison, even if it meant weekly strip searches. For others staying in touch with family was too painful, either because they would miss their family even more, or because they did not want their family to see them in prison. These prisoners decided to put their role as father, grandfather or brother on hold for the time being, in the hope to resume this role after release. Yet another reason why the opportunities provided by the prison did not suffice to normalize the contact with family was that it was sometimes practically impossible to receive visitors from abroad or even from Oslo. Therefore, a common coping strategy was to cut off from family altogether while in prison.

Fredrik: Of course you get placed in a prison where there's available space and that is not always in your neighbourhood, it can be very far away. In my case, my family lives in Oslo and this is far away from here. So my mother has been here one time and ... I've not seen my family for two years. Not my sister, brother, father. I talked to my father once in the telephone, I think. (Interview Fredrik, Nermarka prison)

For child visits, a great deal of effort was made in Nermarka to make the conditions as child-friendly as possible. In terms of atmosphere and activities, these child visits were very similar to those in Hoogstraten, but they did not occur as often and the children had to enter through the regular prison gate. For the duration of this two-hour visit, the participating prisoners could really interact with their children as fathers. Of course, this activity is organized by the prison, meaning that, on the one hand, their behaviour as father was still being watched by the staff members who were present, and on the other hand, they were not expected to take many of the responsibilities that are usually related to the father role outside prison. At the same time, many of these children lived in a complicated situation and were not used to have a present father in their life. This shows again how difficult it is to normalize such social interactions: it does not make sense to reduce the differences between the living conditions inside and outside when the situation outside prison is not desirable at all.

As soon as the men entered the room, the children flew into their fathers' arms. They then started playing badminton, football, hockey, and Jenga. In the meantime, the two women staff members, Ida and Marit, were baking waffles, which filled the room with a delicious smell. The table was set. There was fruit juice, coffee, Cola, and toppings for the waffles: jam, cream, cheese and brunost, and many balloons. [...]

Ida explained that many of these children live in institutions and are very insecure, even though you may not see that right now. A little boy came closer to ask her if she could always come to pick him up at the gate when he comes to visit his daddy. When Ida did not answer immediately, the boy asked: 'Do you know what I mean? Just come to the gate and then come along with me.' She gently responds that she will think about

> it. When he is gone, she says that this is actually not possible because he is accompanied by his grandmother. But he clearly feels more comfortable with this staff member than with his own grandmother.
>
> At the end of the visit, the fathers help their children to get dressed again. It was very hot in this small room, which is the largest in the prison but still quite small to organize activities like this. When they are ready to leave, the children all get a balloon. A six-year old girl wants to give her dad the heart shaped balloon, but he insists that she keeps it. Then it is time to say goodbye. The children hug their dads. One of the boys has a hard time letting go of his daddy. The men return to the E building. The women accompany the children back to the gate. The kids keep looking and waving until their fathers are out of sight. (Field notes 30 March 2016, Nermarka prison)

This visit was a nice example of the normalizing efforts done in Nermarka prison. It is also very much in line with the policy to ensure children's right to stay in touch with their incarcerated parents. At the same time, it could also be argued that such interactions remain artificial when organized by and in the prison. For precisely this reason, many prisoners did not want to receive their children or grandchildren in prison. The normalization of the material environment, too, played an important role here. Some prisoners admitted that they would definitely consider letting their children visit if they were in Leira prison, where prisoners can meet with their family in a comfortable apartment in one of three separate buildings. Unlike the setting in Nermarka, this is not intimidating at all, as it looks like a normal apartment and there are no prison officers on watch.

The same bittersweet feeling came over some prisoners in *Modulen* when they participated in activities that took place outside of the prison, in the *normal* context. Even during these activities, prisoners still interacted at least partially from their role of prisoner and continued to perceive themselves as prisoners that were taken out of their 'normal' prison environment. This happened for example when three prisoners and a prison officer went to a nearby sports shop to buy themselves some sports clothing.

> Today, Trond has visited [a popular sports shop in Trondheim] to buy clothes for their trip next week. He was accompanied by a staff member and two other prisoners, but he felt very uncomfortable. He got really nervous and too hot. When I asked what made him so uncomfortable, he answered: the risk of meeting people that you know, the feeling that you have to justify yourself, or that you will end up in unpleasant situations. I answer that he shouldn't justify himself at all when meeting someone at the store, no one expects an explanation of where you come from and where you are going, that would be rather strange. 'Yeah, that's true… but still, it is strange, and people will notice when they hear us ask permission to buy a bar of chocolate or to go pay.' They laugh with the strange situation of grown men asking if they are allowed to buy some chocolate. People must surely think that we come from an institution, especially when they see how happy we are when we get permission to buy some chocolate. Trond also got annoyed when the other prisoner asked Per [prison officer] if he could take something to his 'cell'. When you talk about your cell in a shop, people will of course know that you're talking about prison! So he was more subtle himself and asked if he could get his drinking bottle when they're back 'at home'. This story made the other prisoners laugh out loud: 'People probably suspect something way worse than a regular prison when they meet you in a shop!' (Field notes 24 May 2016, Nermarka prison)

This example reaffirms the importance of providing prisoners with opportunities to take on various social roles, when aiming to normalize the social interactions, and in any case a social role that suits the situation. Even though this activity was highly, or even perfectly, normalized in terms of material conditions, going shopping with a guard whose permission is needed to buy some chocolate is not a normal situation for most adult people outside prison. Such security concerns did not limit the normalization efforts in Leira prison.

6.3.3 Multi-layered Roles of Prisoner and Prison Officer

In Leira prison, where the social environment was qualitatively different from that in the other three prisons, social interaction felt genuinely personal and constructive. Because of this personal interaction and because prisoners as well as prison staff did not wear prison uniforms, the distinction between staff and prisoners was not visible at first sight. Everyone was introduced to me in the same way, with his or her first name; they all ate together and participated together in work and leisure activities. The following sections will show that the distinct social environment in Leira prison did not only result from the smaller scale and lower security level, but also from the different social roles that people took on when socially interacting in this prison, which explicitly resulted from Leira's policy. Both the role of prisoner and the role of prison officer comprised more layers in this prison than in the other prisons. In relation to people from outside prison, prisoners were 'pushed' out of their prisoner role. This too had an impact on the general atmosphere in this prison. But the opposite occurred as well: some personal social roles (e.g. the role of father) were partially absorbed by the prisoner role when they were actively addressed by the prison's policy.

With its capacity for twenty-one convicted men and four convicted women, Leira prison is smaller than the other three prisons, and all prisoners are selected on the basis of their motivation for rehabilitation and reintegration. This facilitates the more personal approach in this prison. Moreover, prisoners are well aware of the fact that they can be sent back to a closed prison when they break the rules. This too plays a role. At the same time, however, Leira prison resembles the other prisons in the sense that the prisoners are living very closely together, and in the sense that the friendly interactions among them are not motivated by genuine trust or friendship. Adrian described this as follows:

Adrian: Some of them, I can call friends. But I know them for a long time. But you don't go to prison to get friends, because 80% of what people in prison say is a lie.

Me: Even here?

Adrian: Not…maybe not here, but it's like, you can't trust someone you don't know from before. It's difficult. (Interview Adrian, Leira prison)

Remarkably similar to observations in other prisons was the importance attached to 'impression management'. Jonas explained why prisoners should never take off their 'mask', not even in Leira prison:

> *Jonas*: Everyone has to believe that you have no feelings whatsoever. Because there is a big chance that you will meet those people again, and no one wants to do business with you if they think that you have weaknesses. That is why you should keep this mask even at Leira, to a lesser degree though. Because in Tunga [Nermarka prison], everyone wears several masks at the same time, trying to create a certain image, for instance by telling tough stories convincingly enough so that others will spread them for you. (Field notes 17 June 2015, Leira prison)

As explained in the first section of this chapter, imported factors like this kind of impression management are only addressed by the normalization process when the reference point for 'normal interaction' is defined from the prison's perspective, and not from the perspective of this individual prisoner for whom this is the normal way of interacting outside prison. Jonas identifies himself with what Irwin and Cressey (1962: 148) would call a '*hard core member of the thief subculture*', who '*seeks status in the broader criminal world of which prison is only a part*'. This was certainly not the case for all prisoners, but such attitudes tend to predominate the social environment in prison if not addressed. In Leira prison, the desired social interaction patterns, including behaviour and attitudes, were explicitly defined by the prison policy and enforced through close social control. On the one hand, it was not allowed for prisoners to self-identify as a criminal or as a member of a Motorcycle Club (MC) like Hells Angels. Not only was using threats or violence a reason to be sent back to a closed prison, but this was also the case for discussing one's crimes or wearing MC symbols (the latter was also forbidden in Nermarka prison). This policy was restricting and liberating at the same time, since it mitigated the pressure among prisoners to conform with the prison-like impression management. As a result, the low interpersonal trust and impression management did not determine the social interaction among prisoners to the same extent as it did in the other prisons. The more relaxed atmosphere, when compared to closed prisons, was one of the aspects that prisoners valued most in this prison.

> *Petter*: So in open [prison], you have uhm, more … more normal people, being here. More relaxed, and you can talk and you don't have to be afraid. So, in closed prison, I get very… anxious, restless… because of other prisoners and guards and everything. It's much fighting and … people steal, steal from each other…. And you have people who, who wants to fight you. (Interview Petter, Leira prison)

On the other hand, each prisoner was also expected to take on the following prosocial roles: co-worker or student, client (in counselling), cohabitant and active participant in the operation of this prison. Prisoners were not required to just participate in activities like work, drug counselling, sports and social activities, they were also asked to '*show a positive attitude towards work, activities, education and community life*' (Information booklet for prisoners at Leira: 2). Showing a negative attitude towards work and negatively influencing the social climate in this prison were reasons to be sent back to a closed prison (Idem: 17). In their role of 'cohabitant', for instance, prisoners were expected to be quiet between 16:00 and 17:00 in order to respect everyone's rest, to take off their outdoor shoes when entering the building and to keep the kitchen clean after use. Based on a rotating system, each week two prisoners were responsible for cleaning the kitchen at the end of the day and to prepare dinner on Saturday. Furthermore, all prisoners must take part in the general prison meetings each month, and staff members and prisoners had a shared responsibility for the maintenance of the prison's building and surroundings (as stipulated in the house rules). From the moment that prisoners were invited for their intake interview and guided tour, they were addressed as 'active participant' in this prison's operation. It was only after being informed about the rules and expectations that they signed the contract by which they formally confirmed that they would follow these rules. Mutual respect, open communication and being explicit about the consequences of their choices, including the choice to stay at Leira prison, were in line with the principles of the 'consequence pedagogy method', on which the functioning of this prison is based, both ideologically and practically. As described in Chapter 2, this method is aimed to strengthen prisoners' capacity to make their own choices in life and to enable them to live a life without crime (Information booklet for prisoners at Leira; Hammerlin & Larsen, 1997; Steiro et al., 2013). It starts from two premises: first, that every person is responsible for his or her actions and for the consequences of these actions, and second, that choosing the right actions will lead to positive consequences (Information booklet for prisoners at Leira: 3). These skills are developed through daily life social interaction, work and social activities (Information booklet for prisoners at Leira: 2–5). This philosophy is reflected in the above-mentioned prosocial roles expected of prisoners.

Whether this is normal can of course be questioned. Proactively addressing a person's social role is artificial and a kind of re-education that is at odds with common social interaction among adults in society (see also Engbo, 2017). It is also reminiscent of Wolfensberger's '*social role valorization*', which was criticized for wanting to normalize the person rather than the person's environment. Moreover, the above-mentioned roles are not to be considered as a variety of different social roles, but rather as multiple layers of the prisoner role. This conclusion is based on two arguments. First, different social roles are taken on in relation to members of different social groups, while the roles in Leira prison are all taken on in relation to the prison system and the people involved in this system. Second, taking on these prosocial roles was *mandatory* for each prisoner in Leira prison. The fact that prisoners took part in their mandatory counselling sessions as 'prisoner', and not just as 'client', became clear when they were careful about what they wanted to discuss and about not 'snitching' on other prisoners (as explained by one of the counsellors, Field notes 15 June 2015, Leira prison). Another example was that prisoners interacted in the same superficial way in their role of 'co-worker' as they did outside the working hours, based on the pragmatic logics: 'it is alright to be here, let's keep it as comfortable as possible for everyone; play cards, make jokes and do your time'. This superficiality was due to the combination of a lack of trust, the need for impression management and the prohibition to negatively affect the social atmosphere.

Jonas: I can't deny, I'm pretty tired of living with so many people. Because you haven't that much privacy, you know. And you always see the same fucking faces every day. Some people got years left, and people are cranky, pissed off, angry at the system. (Interview Jonas, Leira prison)

Furthermore, taking social responsibilities and making well-considered choices when deprived of their liberty are still experienced by many prisoners as conforming with the rules rather than taking real responsibilities.

Kristian concludes [his talk about Nermarka prison] by saying that they treat you as a five-years old child there. You have to ask everything and they can just say no. Here at Leira, they treat you like a ten-year old, which is already a bit better. (Field notes 8 June 2015, Leira prison)

It is fair to note, however, that some of these imposed roles were genuinely taken on by some prisoners. As discussed in the next chapter, some prisoners did genuinely feel proud of and responsible for the jobs they were expected to do.

Regardless of whether these prosocial roles, or rather prosocial layers of the prisoner role, were genuine or artificial, they *did* have a positive impact on the general atmosphere in prison. Living closely together with twenty-eight other convicted people for a considerable amount of time is in itself very different from usual living conditions outside. Therefore, proactively addressing the social role of 'prisoner', as described above, seems to lead to a more normal experience than not intervening with this social role at all. Many prisoners felt more comfortable knowing that other prisoners also had to comply with these rules, so that they did not have to watch their back the way they did in other prisons. Moreover, prisoners who genuinely wanted to work on their rehabilitation could do so in a drug-free and supportive environment. This is well-aligned with the instrumental approach to normalization.

Espen: I'm happy to be at Leira. This is a good prison to take a fresh start. In other prisons, the only thing you can think of is to get out of that fucking prison as quickly as possible. Here at Leira

> you've got the time to get back on track... I'm actually glad that I got a prison sentence, that is how I got rid of my drug issues. (Field notes 9 June 2015, Leira prison)

In turn, the multi-layered role of prisoners was mirrored and enabled by the multi-layered role of prison officer. In some respects, prison officers interacted with prisoners as equals, or at least almost equals. In their role of co-worker in the garden centre and fellow participant in some sports and leisure activities, the distinctions between the prisoner role and prison officer role were quite subtle. As co-workers in the garden centre, prison officers wore the same red t-shirts and sweaters as the prisoners working there, and they took breaks and ate lunch together with prisoners. The Friday tradition to eat waffles together with all co-workers, prisoners and prison staff alike, was one of the many examples of the personal interaction between prisoners and prison staff.

> It is Friday 2 o'clock in the afternoon. This means that there will be waffles soon. Everyone who has been working in the garden centre gathers around the picnic table, where we all sit together between 2 and half past 2. Lisa hands out ice creams, and the pile of waffles is high enough for everyone to eat as much as he or she likes. There is butter, jam and brunost. Afterwards, most of us stay outside to enjoy the sun. (Field notes 19 June 2015, Leira prison)

The only things that set prison officers apart were that only they participated in the daily staff meetings, took on coordination tasks and did the jobs for which a computer was needed, like ordering new flowers or plants and the accountancy. They were also trained to run a garden centre. The reason given for this distinction was the continuity, since staff members stayed much longer than prisoners.

In terms of participating in sports activities, some staff members used Leira's fitness room together with prisoners, and also the volleyball tournament was played with mixed teams where prisoners and staff played as one team and interacted at least for the duration of the match as equals. Like prisoners, prison officers could take initiative for activities and could participate. In these activities as well, the distinction between the role of prisoner and that of prison officer was subtle, apparent for instance by the fact that only staff members were allowed to drive the minivan to the activities.

The close interaction with prisoners does require particular professional and social skills from prison officers and a different mindset than in other prisons. Several prison officers at Nermarka prison, with whom I discussed Leira prison one year later, argued that they would not like to work so closely with prisoners, and that they preferred a clear distinction and liked their uniform. Laughingly they added: '*well, maybe when we're old*' (Field notes 21 March 2016, Nermarka prison). Prison officer Lisa, on the other hand, did not mind when customers of the garden centre would think that she was a prisoner.

> Lisa admits that she first thought that I was a new prisoner. That is usually the case when someone is new. It happened also to her, when she first started working here. A customer then asked her if she was new and if she had to stay for a long time. When she replied that she was going to stay for quite a long time, the customer recoiled a little. When Lisa bumped into the same customer on a day off, she was asked if her stay was over, but replied that she just had a day off. Lisa thought such situations were very funny. (Field notes 2 June 2015, Leira prison)

Since this close interaction is part of Leira's philosophy, as the consequence pedagogy method entails that acquiring professional and social skills is essentially done through social interaction, all staff members are trained in this methodology. This means that the philosophy is applied through the social interactions between prison staff and between prison staff and prisoners. It also means that these staff members have all chosen to work here, with these working methods, and to take this additional training.

The distinction between the role of prison officer and prisoner became more apparent in other aspects of the prison officer role. As 'contact officers', they were actively involved in a prisoner's reintegration preparations, in ways that resembled the work of a social worker. Prisoners did not have to write notes, like in other prisons, but could directly ask or discuss things with staff. This individualized and personal support was positively valued by prisoners. As Jonas pointed out, '*you get help with it from everybody, you don't have to do everything by yourself. Of course, it's a lot better to be here, of course'* (Interview Jonas, Leira prison). Finally, prison officers also supervised the implementation of the prison sentence and the compliance with the rules. They took randomized urine samples and checked at night if all prisoners were and stayed in their room. Prison officers also supervised prisoners' day-to-day behaviour and interactions and discussed these during staff meetings, together with other relevant information such as work performance or family matters. The close interaction enables strong and natural social control, which is a very effective way to establish dynamic security. Indeed, the various layers of the prison officer role taken together shaped a very efficient '*soft power*' (Crewe, 2011b): prison officers knew almost everything about the prisoners: past, present and future plans, and decisions were made about the execution of the sentence based on this information. Prisoners, on their part, knew that they were being watched and that prosocial attitudes and behaviour were important for the further execution of the sentence (be it early release, placement in a rehabilitation centre or electronic monitoring). This goes hand in hand with self-discipline and social control among prisoners.

In addition to the multi-layered prisoner role, situations occurred in which prisoners took on another social role than that of prisoner. In interaction with people from outside prison, they could even be 'pushed' in another social role. Thanks to the activities outside prison and the openness of the garden centre for people from outside prison, prisoners regularly interacted with people who did not realize they were prisoners. For instance, staff members at the store or library, who would address prisoners as clients; clients of the garden centre, who would address them as garden centre staff; or staff at the rallycross, who would address them as clients. In these events, prisoners were 'pushed' out of their role of prisoner and had to use their 'normal' social skills, including small talk, which are skills prisoners tend to—or at least, fear to—lose in prison. These social interactions with people from outside prison were not normalized, they were just normal. Interactions with clients from the garden centre, for instance, were of a professional nature, whether it be between client and staff member or prisoner. The shop was easily accessible for customers without them noticing that they entered the prison area, and even if they knew that the garden centre is part of the prison, they would not notice being assisted by a prisoner or by a staff member. Of course, the same goes for interactions with the librarian or cashier in the municipal library and store outside prison, and the teachers and students in the school where two prisoners followed classes several days a week. These kind of interactions forced people out of their role of 'prisoner' and into 'normal' conversation and small talk. Another example was the rallycross:

> We've arrived at the rally track, and enter the office to register the ones who will be driving and to pay. Because the prisoners don't dawdle and take responsibility seemingly without hesitation, the man of the rally can't possibly know that he is talking to prisoners. This becomes clear when he asks them at the end if they would like to volunteer at a rally event later this month. [...] The prisoners answer that they would be happy to do that, but that he should probably ask Vegard, because he is a staff member. (Field notes Leira prison, 11 June 2015)

In Leira prison, staff also helped re-establishing contact with relatives and provided opportunities to make phone calls, receive visitors and leave prison for a short period (which is more normalized than receiving visitors in prison). The social role of parent was most actively supported. As explained before, the Norwegian Act protects children's right to be with their imprisoned parent. In practice, a group course is organized for fathers to be a good father (by ICDP—International Child Development Programme). Fathers who follow this course can use the visitors' apartment for the visits of their children. For some prisoners, this meant that they could assume a social role in prison they had not been able to take on before their incarceration. Espen received a visit from his daughter, whom he had not seen in ten years.

> Espen says that ten years of his life have flown by without realizing it. He lost his job, started drinking, started taking drugs, and things got worse. Prison got him rid of that. His daughter grew up without realizing it, she was ten, now she is twenty. (Field notes 9 June 2015, Leira prison)

Addressing an individual's personal social roles can be experienced as emancipating and supportive but also as intrusive and distressing, depending on the individual and on how this is implemented in practice. But in any case, it is once again telling of the strong '*grip*' of Leira prison on its prisoners (Crewe, 2011a; Crewe & Ievins, 2021). When actively addressed by the prison's policy, a personal social role can even be partially absorbed by the prisoner role. Prisoners' behaviour as father can be discussed at staff meetings, together with his behaviour during work, social and other activities. Thus, the role of father is partially absorbed by the role of prisoner: performing as a good father can be beneficial for the further implementation of the sentence, and is a good reason for regular prison leave. By proactively intervening with prisoners' social roles, the social environment in Leira prison differed from that outside prison, but at the same time, this constructive climate resulted of and contributed to the consistent implementation of the instrumental normalization process that is intended to change their way of life and to live a crime-free life after release.

6.4 Conclusion

The social dimension of prison life is generally considered to contribute disproportionately to the prison experience (Liebling, 2004). At the same time, normalizing the social environment in terms of reducing the differences between social interactions inside and outside prison is more complicated than normalizing the activities or material conditions in prison. Because the prison population differs in many ways from the general population (see e.g. Beyens et al., 2014; Skarðhamar, 2003), and because prisoners are involuntarily living together, the following paradoxical situation arises: refraining from intervening in the social interactions leads to abnormal, potentially harmful, situations (see also Mathiassen, 2017), but also intervening in prisoners' social roles could be said to *increase* the differences between inside and outside prison rather than reducing them. Building on the intrinsic perspective to normalization, a rather defensive approach was adopted in the two Belgian prisons (for '*proactive*' and '*defensive*' approach, see Engbo, 2017). The intention was to intervene as little as possible in the contact opportunities with people from outside prison, so that prisoners could continue to exercise other social roles than that of 'prisoner'. While this defensive approach was valuable for contacts with people from outside and did create opportunities for occupying various social roles, at least to some extent and for the limited duration of certain activities (e.g. phone calls, visits, sports or educational activities), the vast majority of day-to-day interactions were left unaddressed by this normalization process.

The day-to-day interactions between prisoners and prisons staff nevertheless predominantly shape the social environment in prison. Living and working in a tense social environment characterized by mistrust, threats and impression management were not only reported to be painful during imprisonment (in line with prison sociological research in other jurisdictions: Clemmer, 1940/1958; Crewe, 2009; de Viggiani, 2012; Jewkes, 2005), but also feared to cause harmful effects that would continue after release. Feeling safe enough is also necessary to shift focus from surviving daily life in prison to preparing for life after release (see also Crewe et al., 2014: 400), and arguably also to take on other social roles. Hence, a purely defensive approach seems to bracket the differences inherent to the social environment in prison, such as the 'criminal code' (Irwin & Cressey, 1962: 148), which was in some form imported into each of the four prisons. Such imported factors, in combination with the deprivations in prison, tend to dominate in the prison environment if not addressed proactively. It is crucial to bear in mind in this respect that prisoners greatly differ in their relation to such criminal code. While some prisoners import this into the prison, others are not at all familiar with this kind of interaction but nonetheless conform to this code (e.g. don't snitch) in prison in order to avoid victimization (see also Irwin & Cressey, 1962). For the latter group, the differences between inside and outside will be reduced by proactively addressing such imported factors.

In the Norwegian prisons, the social role of prisoner, or inmate role, was proactively normalized in the sense that role-related expectations were aligned with the instrumental interpretation of normalization. This was most consistently implemented in Leira prison and *Modulen*, but also most far-reaching and intrusively, by addressing prisoners' behaviour as well as attitudes. The proactive normalization of the social interactions here was combined with omnipresent '*soft power*' (Crewe, 2011b): through close interactions with prisoners, prison officers could subtly but firmly enforce the prison policies. The intended results of this normalization process were explicitly defined from the perspective of the prison (and not from that of the individual prisoner): prosocial roles that would lead to prosocial interaction in prison and after release. This is in line with Shammas' (2014: 107) observation that open prisons in Norway '*are meant to act as "socialization machines" gradually acclimatizing prisoned offenders to life on the outside*'. From a comparative perspective, it is relevant to note that this is completely at odds with the views of the Belgian legislator (Prison Act Commission, 2001: 73; see also Chapter 3). The well-intended interventions fit nevertheless well within Smith and Ugelvik's (2017) understanding of the Norwegian welfare state, being inclined to interfere with citizens' lives '*for their own good*'. Accordingly, the consistent implementation of the instrumental approach to normalization resulted in prison policies that were inclined to interfere with prisoners' lives.

As mentioned before, such interventionist policies and practices raise questions as to '*where the moral boundaries [are] drawn for how far officers should go*' in supporting prisoners to change their way of life and to live a crime-free life after release (Fredwall, 2017a: 173). They tend to shift the focus from normalizing the prison conditions to normalizing the person of the prisoner, a shift for which Wolfensberger's '*social role valorization*' was strongly criticized some decades ago. Moreover, the firm 'grip' of the prison on the prisoner, which Crewe has conceptualized as '*tightness*' (Crewe, 2011a; Crewe & Ievins, 2021), has been associated with several new 'pains of imprisonment', such as the pain of psychological assessment and the pain of self-government (Crewe, 2011a). These findings suggest that such instrumental implementation of the normalization process would not reduce the pains of imprisonment, but rather create *different* pains. From the observations in Leira and *Modulen*, however, a different picture emerged: the '*tighter*', i.e. the *more* demanding and intrusive the regime, the *less* painful and harmful effects were mentioned by prisoners. Based on these observations, it could be argued that as far as the *social* environment of the prison is concerned, a proactive normalization process leads to a more normalized *experience* for prisoners and prison staff.

This conclusion seems very much in line with Crewe and Ievins' (2021) recent findings that adjust the original conclusions related to '*tightness*' in prison (in Crewe, 2011a), stating that '*prisoners often welcome institutional attention – including certain forms of oversight and intervention – when it is supportive rather than coercive, and where it recognises and maintains the integrity of the individual through authentic engagement with his or her full personhood*' (Crewe & Ievins, 2021: 65). Nevertheless, Crewe and his colleagues (Crewe & Ievins, 2021; Ievins & Mjåland, 2021) did not find this in Norwegian prisons. On the contrary, they concluded that Norwegian prisons are characterized by a '*laissez-faire*' inclusive policy (Ievins & Mjåland, 2021). This different conclusion might be caused by Norwegian prisoners' high expectations in terms of rehabilitation interventions and their related frustrations in 'regular' units, like in the prisoners in the E building. Norwegian prisoners' expectations in this respect contrasted sharply to the expectation of foreign national prisoners in Nermarka prison, who were surprised and even suspicious of the care provided by the prison, but also to the low expectations of prisoners in the two Belgian prisons, who were satisfied when prison officers were polite, and opened the doors when they were supposed to. In any case, Ievins and Mjåland (2021) also found that Norwegian prisoners were in favour of *more* interventions on the part of prison staff or the prison system.

Before jumping to the conclusion that proactively normalizing the social environment in prison leads to better results in practice, let us first contextualize these findings through a holistic lens, to see which preconditions need to be in place for this statement to be true. First, Norwegian prisoners expected state interventions and trusted that the system, *if* it works the way it is supposed to, would support their rehabilitation with their best interest in mind. This would not necessarily be the case for Belgian prisoners, as they had little confidence in the Belgian prison system. Second, in Leira prison, many of the deprivations related to material conditions, autonomy, privacy and time-use were reduced as well, thus contributing to the normalization of the prison climate, according to the deprivation-importation model. Third, the small scale of Leira and *Modulen* enabled prisoners and prison staff to know each other and communicate directly. In the larger prisons, prison staff did not really know each other, or each other's job description. Fourth, in *Modulen* and in Leira, prison officers had deliberately chosen to work in these units and to actively support prisoners with their rehabilitation and reintegration, and in Leira prison, all staff members were trained in the consequence pedagogy method. Moreover, staff members were also seen by prisoners as genuinely doing efforts to support them, not unimportant since the impact of staff's supportive attitudes for the social climate in prison pointed out by previous research (Kruttschnitt & Dirkzwager, 2011; Liebling, 2004). Fifth, the interventionist approach was a good fit with the rehabilitation philosophy underlying the regimes in Leira and *Modulen*. The role-related expectations of prisoners and prison officers were consistent with the instrumental interpretation of normalization (see also Fredwall, 2017a, 2017b) and were also consistently implemented. Moreover, prisoners had applied to be transferred to Leira or *Modulen* and had been informed about (and consented to) the rules and rehabilitation interventions before their transfer. Finally, the extent to which such a proactively normalized social environment can be considered 'normal' at all is still open to debate. The answer will vary according to our approach to normalization: whether prisoners' *experiences* are decisive in this assessment, and whether normalization is approached instrumentally or intrinsically—and it is clear that the Belgian and Norwegian prison policies differ at this point.

A striking similarity between the two countries, on the other hand, was the importance attached to the import model, based on which service providers from the community enter the prison to provide prisoners with the same services as other citizens. Since social roles are defined in relation to other members of a social group, widening the range of people with whom prisoners have contact has the potential of widening the variety of his or her social roles. It was indeed the interaction with people from outside, who were not part of prisoners' personal network (e.g. customers of the garden centre; volunteers; teachers and sports coaches) that resembled most closely equivalent interactions outside prison. The most meaningful social roles were those in relation to relatives and friends, but those were also the most complicated to exercise while in prison (and sometimes too painful), and challenging to address by the prison policy. But despite being complicated and challenging, the observations showed that some prison policies and practices did impact the way in which prisoners could exercise these social roles. The child-friendly conditions in Hoogstraten did encourage prisoners to receive their children in prison, while the strict security restrictions in Nermarka seriously hampered the opportunities to take on these meaningful social roles. By limiting the phone calls to 20 minutes a week, and by listening in on all of these calls, the possibility to stay in touch with family and friends was hampered or even undermined. It is also questionable whether these security measures are 'the lowest as strictly necessary', as the normalization principle requires. Contact with one's personal social network is nevertheless important from an intrinsic and instrumental approach to normalization. But from a comparative perspective, it is also fair to note here that prison stays are on average much shorter in Norway than in Belgium, which facilitates the resuming of some social roles after release. This time dimension is the last of the four broad dimensions that together provide a holistic image of the living conditions in prison and will be discussed in Chapter 7.

References

Aebi, M. F., Berger-Kolopp, L., Burkhardt, C., Chopin, J., Hashimoto, Y. Z., & Tiago, M. M. (2019). *Foreign offenders in prison and on probation in Europe—Trends from 2005 to 2015 (inmates) and situation in 2015 (inmates and probationers)*. Strasbourg: Council of Europe.

Auty, K. M., & Liebling, A. (2020). Exploring the relationship between prison social climate and reoffending*. *Justice Quarterly, 37*(2), 358–381.

Beyens, K., Dirkzwager, A., & Korf, D. (2014). Detentie en gevolgen van detentie. *Tijdschrift Voor Criminologie, 56*(2), 1–22.

Bosworth, M. (1999). *Engendering resistance: Agency and power in women's prisons* (Advances in Criminology). Ashgate.

Bouverne-De Bie, M. (2002). Historische en actuele ontwikkelingen in de relatie tussen strafuitvoering en hulpverlening. In M. Bouverne-De Bie, K.

Kloeck, W. Meyvis, R. Roose, & J. Vanacker (Eds.), *Handboek forensisch welzijnswerk* (pp. 275–298). Academia.

Bronebakk Bølgen, K. (2006). *Kriminalomsorgens sikkerhetsstrategi 2006–2010 Trygghet for samfunnet, domfelte, innsatte og tilsatte*. Kriminalomsorgen.

Clemmer, D. (1958). *The prison community*. Holt, Rinehart and Winston.

Crewe, B. (2005). Prisoner society in the era of hard drugs. *Punishment & Society, 7*(4), 457–481.

Crewe, B. (2006). Prison drug dealing and the ethnographic lens. *The Howard Journal, 45*(4), 347–368.

Crewe, B. (2009). *The prisoner society: Power, adaptation, and social life in an English prison* (Clarendon Studies in Criminology). Oxford University Press.

Crewe, B. (2011a). Depth, weight, tightness: Revisiting the pains of imprisonment. *Punishment & Society, 13*(5), 509–529.

Crewe, B. (2011b). Soft power in prison: Implications for staff–prisoner relationships, liberty and legitimacy. *European Journal of Criminology, 8*(6), 455–468.

Crewe, B. (2016). The sociology of imprisonment. In Y. Jewkes, J. Bennett, & B. Crewe (Eds.), *Handbook on prisons* (2nd ed., pp. 77–100). Routledge.

Crewe, B., & Ievins, A. (2021). 'Tightness', recognition and penal power. *Punishment & Society, 23*(1), 47–68.

Crewe, B., Liebling, A., & Hulley, S. (2011). Staff culture, use of authority and prisoner quality of life in public and private sector prisons. *Australian & New Zealand Journal of Criminology, 44*(1), 94–115.

Crewe, B., Liebling, A., & Hulley, S. (2014). Heavy-light, absent-present: Rethinking the 'weight' of imprisonment. *The British Journal of Sociology, 65*(3), 387–410.

Cullen, F. T., Jonson, C. L., & Nagin, D. S. (2011). Prisons do not reduce recidivism. *The Prison Journal, 91*(3), 48S-65S.

De Viggiani, N. (2012). Trying to be something you are not: Masculine performances within a prison setting. *Men and Masculinities, 15*(3), 271–291.

Drægebø, H. (2006). *Miljøarbeid i fengsel*. KRUS.

Dufaux, F. (2010). L'emploi des personnes incarcérées en prison: pénurie, flexibilité et précuriat. Une normalisation? *Déviance et Société, 34* (3), 299–324.

Engbo, H. J. (2017). Normalisation in Nordic prisons—From a prison governor's perspective. In T. Ugelvik & P. S. Smith (Eds.), *Scandinavian penal history, culture and prison practice: Embraced by the welfare state?* (pp. 327–352). Palgrave Macmillan.

Enos, S. (1998). Managing motherhood in prison: The impact of race and ethnicity on child placements. *Women & Therapy, 20*(4), 57–73.

Fredwall, T. E. (2017a). Guarding, guiding, gate opening Prison officer work in a Norwegian welfare context. In T. Ugelvik & P.S. Smith (eds.), *Scandinavian penal history, culture and prison practice: Embraced by the welfare state?* (pp. 157–176). Palgrave Macmillan.

Fredwall, T. E. (2017b). Straff som pine. *Retfærd: Nordisk juridisk tidsskrift, 40*(3–4), 24–37.

Goffman, E. (1961). *Asylums. Essays on the social situation of mental patients and other inmates*. Penguin Books Ltd.

Gunter, T. D., Arndt, S., Wenman, G., Allen, J., Loveless, P., Sieleni, B., & Black, D. W. (2008). Frequency of mental and addictive disorders among 320 men and women entering the Iowa prison system: Use of the MINI-Plus. *Journal of the American Academy of Psychiatry and the Law, 36*(1), 27–34.

Hammerlin, Y., & Larsen, E. (1997). Konsekvenspedagogikken. *KRUS Småskrift, 2*, 1–37.

Hochstetler, A., & DeLisi, M. (2005). Importation, deprivation, and varieties of serving time: An integrated-lifestyle-exposure model of prison offending. *Journal of Criminal Justice, 33*(3), 257–266.

Huey Dye, M. (2010). Deprivation, importation, and prison suicide: Combined effects of institutional conditions and inmate composition. *Journal of Criminal Justice, 38*(4), 796–806.

Ievins, A., & Mjåland, K. (2021). Laissez-faire inclusion and authoritarian exclusion: Comparing the experiences of men convicted of sex offences in England & Wales and Norway. *Criminology, 59*(3), 454–479.

Irwin, J. & Cressey, D. R. (1962). Thieves, convicts and the inmate culture. *Social Problems (Berkeley, Calif.), 10*(2), 142–155.

Jewkes, Y. (2002). The use of media in constructing identities in the masculine environment of men's prisons. *European Journal of Communication, 17*(2), 205–225.

Jewkes, Y. (2005). Men behind bars 'doing' masculinity as an adaptation to imprisonment. *Men and Masculinities, 8*(1), 44–63.

Jones, H. L. (2007). *The pains of custody: How young men cope through the criminal justice system*. Thesis submitted for the Degree of Doctor of Philosophy in the University of Hull, UK.

Kelk, C. (2008). *Nederlands detentierecht*. Kluwer.

Knight, V. (2016). *Remote control: Television in prison* (1st ed.). Palgrave Macmillan UK.

Kruttschnitt, C., & Dirkzwager, A. (2011). Are there still contrasts in tolerance? Imprisonment in the Netherlands and England 20 years later. *Punishment & Society, 13*(3), 283–306.

Liebling, A., assisted by Arnold, H. (2004). *Prisons and their moral performance. A study of values, quality and prison life*. Oxford University Press.

Liebling, A. (2011). Moral performance, inhuman and degrading treatment and prison pain. *Punishment & Society, 13*(5), 530–550.

Liebling, A., Johnsen, B., Schmidt, B. E., Rokkan, T., Beyens, K., Boone, M., Kox, M., & Vanhouche, A.-S. (2021). Where two 'exceptional' prison cultures meet: Negotiating order in a transnational prison. *British Journal of Criminology, 61*(1), 41–60.

Mathiassen, C. (2017). Being a woman in mixed-gender prisons. In P. S. Smith. & T. Ugelvik (Eds.), *Embraced by the welfare state? Scandinavian penal history, culture and prison practice* (Palgrave Studies in Prisons and Penology) (pp. 377–404). Palgrave Macmillan UK.

Mjåland, K. (2016). Exploring prison drug use in the context of prison-based drug rehabilitation. *Drugs: Education, Prevention and Policy, 23* (2), 154–162.

Molleman, T., & Leeuw, F. L. (2012). The influence of prison staff on inmate conditions: A multilevel approach to staff and inmate surveys. *European Journal on Criminal Policy and Research, 18*(2), 217–233.

Paterline, B. A., & Petersen, D. M. (1999). Structural and social psychological determinants of prisonization. *Journal of Criminal Justice, 27*(5), 427–441.

Penado Abilleira, M., & Rodicio-García, M. L. (2020). A study of the inmate code of conduct in Spanish prison. *Deviant Behavior*, 1–18.

Piacentini, L. (2015). 'Get in, get out, go back?': Transitioning from prison ethnography to prison policy research in Russia. In D. H. Drake, R. Earle, & J. Sloan (Eds.), *The Palgrave handbook of prison ethnography* (Palgrave Studies in Prisons and Penology) (pp. 81–98). Palgrave Macmillan.

Prison Act Commission. (2001). Eindverslag van de commissie 'basiswet gevangeniswezen en rechtspositie van gedetineerden'. *Verslag namens de commissie voor de Justitie uitgebracht door de heren Vincent Decroly en Tony Van Parys, Parl.St. Kamer, 2000–2001*(1076), 001.

Rocheleau, A. M. (2013). An empirical exploration of the 'pains of imprisonment' and the level of prison misconduct and violence. *Criminal Justice Review, 38*(3), 354–374.

Rowe, A. (2011). Narratives of self and identity in women's prisons: Stigma and the struggle for self-definition in penal regimes. *Punishment & Society, 13*(5), 571–591.

Shammas, V. L. (2014). The pains of freedom: Assessing the ambiguity of Scandinavian penal exceptionalism on Norway's Prison Island. *Punishment & Society, 16*(1), 104–123.

Skarðhamar, T. (2003). Inmates' social background and living conditions. *Journal of Scandinavian Studies in Criminology and Crime Prevention, 4*(1), 39–56.

Smith, P. S., & Ugelvik, T. (2017). *Embraced by the welfare state? Scandinavian penal history, culture and prison practice* (Palgrave Studies in Prisons and Penology). Palgrave Macmillan UK.

Snacken, S. (2002). Normalisation en prison: concept et défis. In O. De Schutter & D. Kaminski (Eds.), *L'institution du droit pénitentiaire. Enjeux de la reconnaissance de droits aux détenus* (pp. 133–152). Librairie Générale de Droit et de Jurisprudence et Bruylant.

Snacken, S. (2015). Tien jaar Basiswet—'Back to basics'. In T. Daems, C. Hermans, F. Janssens, J. Millen, L. Robert, & V. Scheirs (Eds.), *Quo vadis?: Tien jaar basiswet gevangeniswezen en rechtspositie van gedetineerden* (pp. 179–203). Maklu.

Soffer, M., & Ajzenstadt, M. (2010). The multidimensionality of 'pains of imprisonment' among incarcerated women in Israel. *Women & Health, 50*(6), 491–505.

Steiro, T. J., Andersen, B., Olsvik, L. S., & Johansen, P. (2013). Balancing structure and learning in an open prison. *International Journal of Management, Knowledge and Learning, 2*(1), 101–121.

Sykes, G. (2007). *The society of captives: A study of a maximum security prison* (First Princeton classic ed., Princeton classic editions). Princeton University Press.

Ugelvik, T. (2014a). Paternal pains of imprisonment: Incarcerated fathers, ethnic minority masculinity and resistance narratives. *Punishment & Society, 16* (2), 152–168.

Ugelvik, T. (2014b). *Power and resistance in prison: Doing time, doing freedom* (Palgrave Studies in Prisons and Penology). Palgrave Macmillan.

van Ginneken, E. F. J. C., Palmen, H., Bosma, A. Q., & Sentse, M. (2019). Bearing the weight of imprisonment: The relationship between prison climate and well-being. *Criminal Justice and Behavior, 46*(10), 1385–1404.

van Ginneken, E. F. J. C., & Nieuwbeerta, P. (2020). Climate consensus: A multilevel study testing assumptions about prison climate. *Journal of Criminal Justice, 69*, 101693.

van Zyl Smit, D., & Snacken, S. (2009). *Principles of European prison law and policy. Penology and human rights*. Oxford University Press.

Vegrichtová, B. (2018). Nonverbal communication of prison subculture through criminal tattoo symbols. *Academic and Applied Research in Military and Public Management Science, 17*(3), 179–186.

Velarde, L. D. (2001). *Living in prison: Evaluating the deprivation and importation models of inmate adaptation.* Doctoral dissertation Louisiana Tech University Louisiana Tech Digital Commons, ProQuest Dissertations Publishing.

Vianello, F. (2015). Communauté carcérale et transformations de la prison. *Déviance Et Société, 39*(2), 151–169.

7

From Killing Time to Using Time: Normalizing the Time-Use in Prison

The saying 'time is money' commonly expresses the value of time in society. People are constantly 'busy', having too little time to do everything they need to do. Robinson and Godbey (1997, as cited in Gini, 2003: 3) even argue that '*being busy has become a status symbol*'. In prison, the value and meaning of time is different. Prison time is not used but *done*, *wasted* or *killed* (Knight, 2016; O'Donnell, 2014). This is partly because the time dimension is related to the *intended* pains imposed by the judge, in the sense that the severity of the prison sentence is expressed in time units, be it days, weeks, months or years. This time, as pointed out by O'Donnell (2014: 176), '*has been taken from them along with their freedom, but unlike liberty it can never be won back*'. However, also the way in which time is organized and used in day-to-day prison life greatly differs from what is common outside prison. Prisoners are '*removed from the natural rhythms of social life*' (Haney, 2003: 127) and largely lose autonomy over their time-use. Not only the nature of most daily activities is determined by the prison system, but also the timing, sequence and duration of these activities. This does not only impact the living

H. De Vos, *Beyond Scandinavian Exceptionalism*, Palgrave Studies in Prisons and Penology, https://doi.org/10.1007/978-3-031-28635-3_7

conditions in prison, the degree of institutionalization and the experienced pains of imprisonment, but can also hamper the reintegration after release (Irwin & Owen, 2005; Schinkel, 2014).

While the duration of the prison sentence can be seen as the intended pains that fall beyond the scope of the normalization principle, the *use* of that time in prison is being normalized in Norwegian and Belgian prisons. Normalization of this time-use is intended to ensure prisoners' rights, to reduce the harmful effects of detention, to facilitate prisoners' reintegration and to directly or indirectly reduce recidivism (art. 9 of the Belgian Prison Act; art. 4 Flemish Decree of 8 March 2013; art. 2 and 3 of the Norwegian Act on the Execution of Sentences). This chapter explores how time-use is being normalized by Belgian and Norwegian legislation and how this is reflected in the practice of the four prisons.

7.1 Prison Time: An Invisible Source of Pains

The duration of a prison stay has direct and indirect effects on the prison experience. A direct effect is caused by the psychological weight of the time that is still to be served. For many prisoners, but in particular for long-term and isolated prisoners, thinking about the time ahead leads to attacks of '*chronophobia*' (O'Donnell, 2014), or a '*sense of temporal vertigo – an overwhelming feeling of dizziness, resulting from the sense that time was warping and falling away*' (Wright et al., 2017: 232). A common coping strategy of long-term prisoners is therefore to refocus completely on the '*prison-present*', by avoiding thinking about past or future, and by avoiding living emotionally in two places at the same time (Irwin & Owen, 2005; O'Donnell, 2014; Schroeder, 1976 as cited in O'Donnell, 2014: 180; Zamble & Porporino, 1988). More indirectly, the amount of time spent in prison determines the degree to which prisoners are exposed to and affected by the prison environment. A longer stay relates to stronger adaptation to prison life; more confrontations with violence, threats and drugs; weakened ties with the outside world; reduced social and professional skills; stronger feelings of emotional numbness; and a considerable fear of mental deterioration (Cohen & Taylor, 1972; Crewe et al., 2017; Hulley et al., 2016; Irwin & Owen, 2005; Johnson et al.,

2016; Liebling, 2011; O'Donnell, 2014). Furthermore, existential questions are most pressing for long-term prisoners (Cohen & Taylor, 1972; Liebling, 2011; van Zyl Smit & Snacken, 2009). Moreover, the objective passage of time and the subjective time perception are two distinctive aspects of the time dimension, whose relationship varies depending on a person's state of mind (Crawford & Hutchinson, 2016; Flaherty, 1999: 13, as cited in O'Donnell, 2014: 181). This is true inside and outside prison, but both the time-use and people's state of mind are of course different in prison. All of this is relevant in the sense that the more normalization can mitigate the direct and indirect effects of prison duration (that is: the *unintended* pains thereof), the more it will arguably have a positive effect on prisoners' state of mind and, thus, their subjective time perception.

When considering day-to-day prison life, time manifests itself in three ways: activities, routines and 'empty time' (Johnsen, 2018; Knight, 2016; Middlemass & Smiley, 2016). Engaging in interesting activities, i.e. those requiring '*mental agility*' or '*physical dexterity*' (Knight, 2016: 60), is crucial to prisoners' self-esteem, offers opportunities to improve their lives and makes time in prison pass more quickly (Johnson et al., 2016; Knight, 2016; O'Donnell, 2014). In her study on distance learning, Hughes (2012) found that prisoners' motivation to engage in education was often rooted in the avoidance of boredom or an attempt to kill time. But this first motivation transformed into a positive choice for education, because participants welcomed the stimulation of the mind and the sense of achievement. Not only the nature of the activities, but also the perceived choice in terms of daytime activities, including work, education and leisure activities, is found to strongly affect the perceived quality of life in prison (van der Kaap-Deeder et al., 2017). Despite the known benefits of meaningful activities, however, research generally shows the lack of activities or the tedious and meaningless nature of activities in prison (Johnson et al., 2016; Knight, 2016; Rocheleau, 2013). This means that prison time is disproportionately defined by routines and 'empty time'.

Indeed, a great deal of prison time is 'empty time', characterized by inactivity, monotony, boredom, loss of mental stimulation and ongoing attempts to 'kill time' by watching television, sleeping or using drugs

(Jones, 2007; Knight, 2016; Mjåland, 2016; O'Donnell, 2014; Wener, 2012). Without any meaningful occupation, prisoners tend to focus on the passage of time, which makes it slow down. As articulated by one of Jones' (2007: 191) interviewees: '*I bought a clock – I had to chuck it in the bin – you keep watching it and it goes slower and slower*.' Prisoners are very aware of the dangers of boredom. This '*mental poison*', as it was called by a prisoner interviewed by Knight (2016: 121), is associated with negative emotions, serious misconduct and distressed caused by too much '*thinking time*' (Johnson et al., 2016: 85–86; Knight, 2016: 124; Rocheleau, 2013: 366; Shaffer et al., 1994). The limited access to educational or rehabilitation programmes, boredom and inactivity have been associated with suicidal feelings (Liebling, 1999). The slow passage of time is experienced as painful, yet paradoxically, the feeling of having lost this time is also painful (O'Donnell, 2014).

Prison routines, then, affect the prison experience in at least three way. First, the rigour of routines reduces prisoners' agency and autonomy in similar ways as physical restrictions do (Goffman, 1961; Irwin & Owen, 2005; Johnson et al., 2016; Jones, 2007; Knight, 2016; O'Donnell, 2014; Snacken, 2005). When the timing, duration and sequence of most activities are determined by the prison system, prisoners lose their '*'adult' self-determination*' and '*freedom of action*', which can induce '*the terror of feeling radically demoted in the age-grading system*' (Sykes, 1958: 73–76, as cited in Goffman, 1961: 43; see also O'Donnell, 2014: 194). Second, routines do not only lead to much waiting and boredom, but also imply predictability and sameness. This makes time pass more quickly in prison (O'Donnell, 2014; see also Shammas, 2014) and can even lead to '*an almost painlessly automatized existence*' (Serge, 1970: 116, as cited in O'Donnell, 2014: 200). Over a longer period, such institutionalized existence is likely to make the reintegration after release more difficult (Irwin & Owen, 2005; Schinkel, 2014). Third, routines '*offer certainty when much is uncertain*' (O'Donnell, 2014: 199). This is to be understood in the light of Giddens' conception of '*ontological security*' (Giddens, 1984: 60 as cited in Bottoms et al., 1990: 90), which refers to '*the need that most individuals have for a level of predictability in daily encounters*'. Applying this concept to the prison setting, Bottoms et al. (1990: 90–91) argue that, under certain conditions, '*The existence of some routines and predictability in prison life operates to reduce personal insecurity.*' Hence, routines can facilitate life inside prison, and thus reduce some pains, but cause at the same time harmful effects as they increase the level of institutionalization, which '*steadily erodes the skills prisoners will need to cope with life in the outside world with its relatively rapid pace, lack of structure and vast number of choices*' (Irwin & Owen, 2005: 100).

Even if the duration of the prison sentence, and the pains and frustrations directly caused by this duration are considered part of the *intended* punishment imposed by the judge, the way in which time is used in prison is still a crucial aspect of the prison conditions, and reducing the differences between the time-use inside and outside prison is relevant from an intrinsic and instrumental approach to normalization. Of course, outside the prison walls, too, life is built around routines and people are bored at times; yet they have, at least to a certain extent, the choice to rely on routines to get their life organised. And even if freedom outside prison walls is not at all absolute, in general citizens tend to have the liberty to take initiatives and to make their own choices. In addition to providing interesting and meaningful activities, the challenge for normalization would be to soften routines and to protect as much as possible prisoners' agency, even if this leads to less predictability. As became clear in the previous chapters, such attempts will affect and be affected by the normalization of the other dimensions of the prison context. The time-use and the material environment, for instance, are very intertwined (Johnsen, 2018; Moran, 2012, 2013). Before going on to explore the normalization in this respect in our Belgian and Norwegian prisons, we shall have a look to the relevant legislation.

7.2 Normalizing the Use of Time in Prison: A Legislative Perspective

From both a Belgian and a Norwegian policy perspective, the aims of normalizing the time spent in prison are to ensure prisoners' rights, to reduce the harmful effects of detention, to facilitate prisoners' reintegration and to directly or indirectly reduce recidivism (art. 9 of the Belgian Prison Act; art. 4 Flemish Decree of 8 March 2013; art. 2 and 3 of the Norwegian Act on the Execution of Sentences). The prison policies of both countries are also similar in that this normalization process is grounded in the concept of the individual plan and on the so-called import model, and in that prison labour, and its normalization, is considered crucial for a normalized time-use in prison.

7.2.1 Individualized Detention

The legislation in both Norway and Belgium considers the individual plan for each convicted prisoner as an instrument to organize the time spent in prison in a normalized way and in a way that contributes to the aims of the execution of the prison sentence. In Norway, this means enabling prisoners to live a crime-free life after release, while in Belgium, this means in the first place preventing the harmful effects of detention and preparing prisoners' reintegration in an individualized way. Both countries' legislations stress the shared responsibility of the prisoner and the prison system in developing and implementing this plan, but stipulate at the same time that the plan should be realistic in terms of practical possibilities. Note the paradox in this respect: an individual detention plan is in both countries considered the backbone of normalized time-use, while such a plan is typical of life *inside* and not outside prison. This is more evidence to the fact that the process of normalization in general might include aspects that do not, or at least not at first sight or without having the bigger picture, seem 'normal' at all.

In Belgium, the individual detention plan is explicitly defined as the cornerstone of the normalization of the time spent in prison. As explained in the preparatory works of the Prison Act, this plan is intended to individualize the harm reduction principle and to work towards the aims of the execution of the prison sentence, in particular the aim of preparing prisoners' reintegration in an individualized way (Dupont, 1998: 142–147; art. 9§2 Prison Act). The plan is to be prepared in consultation with the prisoner and on the basis of his needs (art. 38 Prison Act), but he or she also has the right to refuse such a plan (art. 35§2 Prison Act). Content-wise, it should include activities that focus on restoration, such as compensating the victim(s), and on reintegration, such as work, education and psychosocial or medical treatment programmes (art. 38§3 Prison Act). The idea that the prisoner plays a serious role in this respect is also indicated by article 38§4, which states that the 'collaboration agreement' is to be signed by the prisoner as well as the prison governor. This reflects the philosophy of normalization and of the associated principles of participation, respect and responsibilization: the prisoner has a say in the way in which his prison time is spent and how his reintegration is prepared, which involves shared responsibility. In practical terms, however, '*the detention plan will be drawn up taking into account the prisoner's potential and what is practicable in the penitentiary administration*' (art. 38§3 Prison Act). Moreover, despite being considered a cornerstone, the relevant articles of the Prison Act (art. 35 to 39) have only entered into force after the observation period of this research,[1] and after having been adjusted by the Act of 25 December 2016.[2]

In Norway, 'future planning' entails the mapping of the most suitable activities for each individual prisoner. These activities can include work, education, leisure activities and programmes that focus on the prisoner's social network, drug use, crime and social and practical skills needed for daily tasks (see Guidelines for the Correctional Service's 'future planning'). The aim is to organize the execution of the prison sentence in a goal-oriented way, implying that it should enable prisoners to change their criminal behaviour and to increase their chances to live a crime-free life after release. Additionally, in doing so, prisoners should get familiar with the social services they can use during and after their detention, and especially during the first period after release. These aims point out the instrumental approach to this normalization process.

---

[1] Royal Decree of 5 April 2019 determining the date of effect of Title IV of the Belgian Prison Act of 12 January 2005, *BS* 26 April 2019.

[2] Act of 25 December 2016 *amending the legal position of the prisoners and of supervision of prisons, with diverse stipulations for the Justice department:* Art. 35, §2 has been adjusted; Art. 36, §3 has been deleted; Art. 37 has been deleted; Art. 38, §2 and §5 have been deleted, Art. 40 has been deleted.

The prisoner's contact officer[3] is responsible for drafting this plan together with the prisoner in the beginning of his prison term, to motivate him throughout this process (but the prisoner can still decide not to make such a plan), to establish collaboration with relevant public agencies and to coordinate this collaboration (art. 18.2 of the Guidelines concerning the Act on the Execution of Sentences and the Regulations; Guidelines for the Correctional Service's 'future planning'). Additionally, the contact officer should help the prisoner to formulate specific objectives, and link these to specific measures, timing and collaborating partners. Although the plan is not legally binding for either the prison or the prisoner, the prison system should support the implementation of the plan as much as possible and take it into account in decisions concerning the prisoner's transfer to another prison (Guidelines for the Correctional Service's 'future planning'). At the same time, however, the relevant guidelines underline that the plan should be realistic and only include services that are provided by the Correctional Service or by collaborating partners in society, based on the import model that is explained below.

Finally, based on the principle that prisoners retain the same rights to social services as other Norwegian citizens, they are also entitled to an individual plan in the framework of the Social Services Act of 18 December 2009 and the Health Act of 24 June 2011. This individual plan is intended for persons with a need for long-term and coordinated services in the context of social and economic security and housing (art. 1 and art. 28 Social Services Act) as well as in the context of medical and psychological health care (art. 3–1 and 7–1 of the Health Act; *Forskrift om habilitering og rehabilitering, individuell plan og koordinator*). Although this individual plan does not create new rights for prisoners, it can help to manage their personal situation in a well-organized way (see www.tilbakeføring.no).

[3] Contact officer: prison officer who is linked to a particular prisoner in order to inform, motivate and assist this prisoner throughout his prison sentence (see *Retningslinjer for kontaktbetjentarbeidet*, KSF 02/2002, 06.06.2002).

7.2.2 Import Model

In both countries, the rationale underlying the import model is that prisoners have the same rights to social services as other citizens and that by involving community service providers from outside prison, prisoners get familiar with the services they can use after release, which is aimed at facilitating their reintegration. In Norway, municipal and other service providers, such as teachers, medical doctors, psychologists, priests, librarians and case managers of NAV, enter the prison to provide their services to prisoners (art. 4 of the Act on the Execution of Sentences; see also §3–9 Health Act of 24 June 201; Social Services Act of 18 December 2009; and the related Guidelines). In line with the normalization principle, this is aimed to contribute to '*a better continuity in the deliverance of services*' and '*involvement from the community with the prison system*' (www.kriminalomsorgen.no/index.php?cat=265199, original in English). Another advantage for the Correctional Service is that '*The services in questions* [sic] *are financed by other bodies as they are part of the rights of any inhabitant of Norway*' (www.kriminalomsorgen.no/index.php?cat=265199, original in English). The Correctional Service (at the regional level) is responsible for making available a wide range of activities for prisoners, while the prison governor is responsible for coordinating these activities in such a way that prisoners who work or go to school can still participate in other programmes as well (art. 18.1 and 18.3 Guidelines concerning the Act).

In Belgium, too, the import model underpins a wide variety of activities, including education, social assistance, well-being, culture, sports and other leisure activities. Since the state reforms of 1980 and 1988, the responsibilities regarding social assistance and services to prisoners have been transferred from the federal to the Flemish level (art. 5 of the Special Law of 8 August 1980 on institutional reforms). In doing so, the social services became more clearly separated from the execution of the sentence, which enabled a more welfare-oriented approach (Meyvis, 2002; Polfliet, 2015). In this context, the federal Prison Act stipulates the '*duty of the prison*' to enable the provision of these services (art 76–80 Prison Act), while the Flemish Decree of 8 March 2013 ensures '*the right of prisoners and their social network*' to high-quality social assistance and services. The actual provision of these services is organized by the service providers that are subsidized by the Flemish Community to provide all inhabitants of Flanders, including prisoners, with their services, for example the Centre for Mental Health Care (CGG), Centre for General Welfare (CAW), Adult Education Centre (CVO), Basic Education Centre (CBE), Flemish Service for Employment and Vocational Training (VDAB), Public Centre for Social Welfare (OCMW), Moderator (victim offender mediation), Vormingplus (cultural and educational activities for adults) and all sorts of other organizations (e.g. volunteering, theatre, sports). Like in Norway, this import model is not only intended to guarantee the quality of the services offered in prison, but also to facilitate prisoners' reintegration, since they can get familiar with the service providers on which they can also rely after release (Polfliet, 2015).

In practice, however, the import model means that these service providers depend on the prison system to offer their services in prison and that differences in perspectives and priorities can lead to difficulties in the implementation of social services. This has proven to be very difficult in some Belgian prisons (see e.g. Beyens et al., 2016) and was recognized in the Flemish Strategic Plan of 2015–2020:

> Which assistance and services are implemented, is after all dependent on many different factors, including the needs and wishes of the specific population, the presence of particular (weaker) groups, the available infrastructure, the efforts of personnel from various domains, the potential local partners for cooperation and the degree of overpopulation. Actually being able to offer the above is, of course, highly dependent on the cooperation with the prison management and the space created for it. (p. 7)

Despite being a Flemish responsibility, the Belgian (federal) Prison Act does stress the importance of these services and activities. More specifically, article 103 of the Prison Act protects prisoners' right to social assistance and services provided in the prison (§1), and stipulates the duty of the prison governor to take the measures necessary to enable service providers to offer their services in prison, '*with due regard for order and safety*' (§2). While this right is crucial in the light of the normalization of prison life, it should be noted that the intended result of this normalization process is restricted in two ways. First, order and safety considerations can result in serious practical restrictions of this right; second, prisoners have the right to the services that are '*provided in prison*', implying that their rights depend on what is made available in prison, which undermines the normalization idea. However, this word choice results from the fact that this is a Flemish, and not a federal, competence.[4]

The Belgian Prison Act also protects prisoners' right to education and training activities. Article 76 of the Act stipulates that the prison administration shall enable the *greatest possible access* to the whole of education programmes *offered in prison* (§1), including education, literacy, vocational training, social/cultural education, social skills training, creative and cultural activities and physical education (§2). Three aims are explicitly mentioned in this article: (1) stimulating prisoners' personal development; (2) providing prisoners with a meaningful way to spend their time and (3) increasing the chances of a successful reintegration. The intended result of this provision is again the greatest *possible* access to the services of the Flemish Community, which indicates the relativity of these provisions. Nevertheless, in the final report of the Prison Act Commission (2001), it was clearly stated that education is recognized as a subjective right, which can be enforced by prisoners on the basis of their individual detention plan. This is still reflected in article 78 of the Prison Act, which protects convicted prisoners' right to education, *if* they are '*willing and able*'. Along the same lines, the Prison Act guarantees access to the library facilities and to a satisfying selection of literature (art. 77), it stipulates the right to exercise for at least two hours a week (art. 79), the right to spend at least one hour a day outdoors and the right to participate in communal leisure activities. Finally, article 80 of the Prison Act allows prisoners to engage in non-profitable intellectual or artistic activities, *if* the prison governor allows it.

---

[4] The constitutionality of these federal articles were questioned by the Flemish Government, but the Constitutional Court argued that the federal Act can still refer to these Flemish responsibilities without violating the division of competences between the federal and the Flemish level (arrest Arbitragehof, 109/2006, see also Polfliet, 2015).

As for the aims of this normalization process, it is clear that the normalization of these services fits within the rights-based approach of the federal Prison Act, but the six additional aims expressed in article 4 of the Flemish Decree reveal a stronger instrumental approach to normalization: to (1) stimulate prisoners' self-development; (2) restore prisoners' social, relational and psychological balance; (3) reduce the harmful effects of detention for prisoners and their social network; (4) facilitate reintegration and participation in society after release; (5) stimulate restoration between offender, victim and society and (6) reduce recidivism. In order to achieve these objectives, the Flemish policy goes beyond the protection of prisoners' rights, and also aims at proactively motivating prisoners to participate in the activities, while at the same time building support inside and outside prison for providing these services (art. 5 of the Flemish Decree 8 March 2013).

7.2.3 The Right to Work Versus the Duty of Activity

When it comes to daytime activities, the most important difference between the two countries' legislation is that Belgian prisoners have the *right* to the work and education that is made available in prison, while convicted prisoners in Norway have a *duty* of activity. This difference clearly reflects the different views on normalization in the Belgian and the Norwegian prison policies. In Belgium, prisoners retain the right to work (art. 81 Prison Act), and as already explained above, the right to education (art. 76, 78 Prison Act and art. 3–5 Flemish Decree of 8 March 2013), the right to leisure activities and sports (art. 76, 77, 79, 80 Prison Act and art. 3–5 Flemish Decree), the right to social services (art. 103 Prison Act; art. 3–5 Flemish Decree) and the right to legal assistance (art. 104 Prison Act). Norwegian legislation stipulates that the Correctional Service shall provide prisoners with activities in the daytime (art. 18 Act on the Execution of Sentences), which is further elaborated in the corresponding Regulations and Guidelines. It is clear from these regulations and guidelines that these activities are to be understood in the light of prisoners' duty of activity (art. 3 Act on the Execution of Sentences). As already explained in chapter 3, the obligation of convicted prisoners to carry out an activity in daytime is considered '*central to the content of the sentence*' (Ot. prp. no. 5) and can involve work, education, specific programmes and other measures which are intended to facilitate a crime-free life after release or to reduce the potential harmful effects of detention (art. 18.4–18.8 Guidelines concerning the Act).

Prison labour in Belgium is seen as '*fully within the objectives of the execution of the sentence*' (Prison Act Commission, 2001). Article 82 of the Belgian Prison Act specifies five purposes of prison labour: (1) to '*spend the term of their sentence meaningfully*'; (2) '*to retain, further or acquire the suitability to hold an occupation after their release*'; (3) to '*mitigate their detention*'; (4) to '*take on responsibilities, if applicable with regard to their relatives and the victims*'; and (5) to pay off debts '*if there is just cause, partly or wholly [...], with an eye to restoration or reintegration*'. Although 'normal' labour is given an important role in the light of normalization of prison life and of the aims of imprisonment, only a few aspects of prison labour are formally part of the normalization process. The first, and in the Belgian view perhaps most fundamental aspect is the *right* to work. The idea behind this is that prisoners must not experience negative discrimination with regard to their right to work, which is safeguarded for all citizens including them by article 23 of the Constitution (Prison Act Commission, 2001). This is reflected in article 81 of the Prison Act, which gives prisoners the *right* to participate in the work '*available in the prison*' that is '*assigned by the governor*' (art. 84 Prison Act). The latter is of course a serious limitation to this 'right to work'. Nonetheless, the Act also provides a counterpart to the right for prisoners, namely the obligation of the prison administration to provide work (art. 82). The Belgian legislature consciously opted for the right to work and not an obligation to work, because '*the positive value of work is lessened when work becomes an aspect of the punishment*' (Prison Act Commission, 2001). In line with this, article 84§2 contains the phrase that '*the work assigned must not impair the prisoner's dignity nor may it have the character of a disciplinary punishment*'. Working conditions and working hours in prison, too, are subject to the normalization process, as demonstrated by art. 83 of the Prison Act: '*the employment of the prisoner in prison take place under conditions that, to the extent that the nature of the detention does not dictate otherwise, as much as possible correspond with those that characterize the same activities in free society*'. The second section of the same article stipulates that '*The duration of work and working hours shall be set in the internal regulations. In no event may the duration of working times exceed that for corresponding activities in free society determined by or under the law*'. Consequently, the internal regulations of Belgian prisons stipulate that prisoners may not work more than 8 hours a day and that they have the right to two days off per week.

Thus, the intended result of this normalization process is the right to work, with the labour conditions as much as possible comparable to those outside prison ('*to the extent that the nature of the detention does not dictate otherwise*', which is of course an elastic term). Additionally, some prison labour has been outsourced to the prison by external companies, which is based on the import model (see e.g. www.cellmade.be). Other aspects of prison labour are excluded from the normalization process: the nature of the work, the labour agreement, the income from work and the social security system. The exclusion of these aspects hampers the achievement of the five aims set out in article 82 of the Prison Act: if prisoners earn less than €1 an hour, the aim of restoration is compromised, which is also true for the opportunity to financially support their family or to save some money for after release. Along the same lines, if the nature of the work is not normalized, it is unlikely that prisoners will acquire professional skills that will prepare them for their jobs after release.

In Norway, the 'duty of activity' implies that convicted prisoners must participate in the prison work or equivalent activities, which in principle results in working days from 8:00 to 15:00, from Monday to Friday, although deviations are possible, if necessary, for a particular activity (Ot. prp. no. 5, 2000–2001; Regulations relating to the Execution of Sentences 3–12; art. 19.2 Guidelines concerning the Act). While prisoners cannot be forced to participate in education, programmes or other treatment measures, convicted prisoners will have to work if they refuse to participate in these other activities. Article 18.4 of the Guidelines stipulates that prison work should be organized in such a way that prisoners receive training, that they have *normal* working days and that they can work together with others. Still in line with the normalization principle, the working methods should resemble those of similar activities in society as much as possible. The aims of prison labour are to increase prisoners' chances of a job or education after release, to give prisoners work experience and to train their professional or social skills. The prison jobs can include joinery, car mechanics, domestic work (cleaning and work in the prison kitchen), and maintenance or repair work (www.kriminalomsorgen.no/arbeidsdrift-og-aktivitetstilbud.237884.no.html).

In addition to the prison labour, participation in education, '*programmes*' or '*other measures*' can also fulfil the requirement of the 'duty of activity' (art. 18.6–18.8 Guidelines). As for education, article 18.6 of the Guidelines protects prisoners' right to education, thereby referring to the Norwegian Act on Education. Young prisoners with a lack of education are strongly encouraged to participate in education. For this purpose, the prison collaborates with local schools, based on the import model. 'Programmes', then, are specific measures organized for convicted or remand prisoners that consist of teaching, skill training and/or structured conversations (art. 18.7). 'Other measures', finally, are defined as '*measures provided by the prison or partners [...] that are aimed at enabling the prisoner to live a crime-free life, or to reduce potential harmful effects of imprisonment*' (art. 18.8). These measures can include 'future planning' and psychological or medical treatment, as long as they are aimed at reducing recidivism. Other treatments, such as dental treatment, are not considered programmes or measures in the context of the 'duty of activity', but prisoners can get time off to attend these appointments.

Article 21 of the Act on the Execution of Sentences stipulates that the Correctional Service shall enable prisoners to participate in leisure activities including sports and cultural activities. When it comes to young prisoners, the responsibility of the prison goes beyond the mere provision of sport opportunities: young prisoners should be particularly motivated and encouraged to use these opportunities (art. 21.3 Guidelines). Other hobbies can be organized as well, if the organization does not cause practical or security problems (art. 21.4 Guidelines). Furthermore, and very similar to the Belgian legislation, prisoners should get access to a wide range of books (and the opportunity to borrow books from the municipal library to which the prison library is linked) and to a TV and radio, if practically possible (art. 21.2 and 21.5 Guidelines). Additionally, prisoners are allowed to go outside for at least one hour every day, as far as possible (art. 22 Act and art. 22.1 Guidelines). The aims of these leisure activities are to reduce the harmful effects of isolation (art. 21.1 Guidelines) and to ensure prisoners' right to leisure activities (see e.g. www.kriminalomsorgen.no/kulturarbeid.237973.no.html), even though most of these provisions are formulated as a duty of the prison system rather than as rights for prisoners.

Finally, the normalization of time-use in Norwegian prisons is also reflected in 'good' daily routines, and in the importance attached to the time spent in group. 'Good' daily routines simulate the rhythm of 'normal working days'. This is intended to facilitate prisoners' reintegration. At the same time, however, it is also acknowledged that these routines can worsen the institutionalization of prisoners, which is known to impede their reintegration (see e.g. St. meld. no. 37: 109). As for the time spent in group, Norwegian prisoners should not only spend time together during work or other organized activities, but also during meals and leisure time (art. 17 Act; art. 17.1 Guidelines). The reason for that is that social interaction with other prisoners and with staff members is considered important in the light of prisoners' rehabilitation and reintegration, and is particularly valued in the context of '*miljøarbeidet*' (i.e. skill training in daily social settings) (St. meld. no. 37). How this all works in practice, is discussed in the next section.

7.3 Normalizing the Use of Time in Prison Practice

When looking at actual prison practice, it is clear that the way in which the passage of time is used and structured is a salient factor affecting daily life in prison and the experience of prison life. Elaborating on the use of time in Hoogstraten, Leuven, Leira and Nermarka prison, the following sections demonstrate how time inside prison is shaped by routines, activities and periods of unstructured time. Although the number and nature of organized activities differ greatly between the prisons, prisoners in all four prisons generally associate the passage of time with prison routines, waiting and boredom, which in turn causes feelings of dependency on routines, loss of autonomy and a lack of intellectual stimulus. According to many prisoners, this is one of the greatest differences between prison life and their lives before incarceration, and in their opinion it is likely to impact their reintegration in a negative way. And yet, differences between Belgium and Norway already apparent in their policies, were even more striking when looking at the daily prison practice.

7.3.1 Education and Work as Intended Results

As indicated by its official name, the 'Penitentiary School Centre' of Hoogstraten provides prisoners with a variety of education and work programmes. In practice, this means that most prisoners have the opportunity to work or to participate in vocational training in the daytime, and additionally to participate in evening courses, such as language or computer courses. Thus, prison time in Hoogstraten prison consists for most prisoners of organized activities as well as routines, which determine the exact timing, duration and sequence of each activity. In what follows, the focus is first on these routines and then on the activities organized in this prison.

Structure and Waiting: Two Sides of the Same Coin

Daily life in Hoogstraten prison is strictly routinized from 6:10 until 21:50. From the time schedule below, it is clear that despite being an 'open' prison, it does not have much flexibility in terms of time-use. On the contrary, the timing and duration of most activities are determined by the prison. This is true for the activities of both prisoners and prison officers. Prisoners' autonomy over their time-use is limited to the choice to either apply for the available work, education programmes or leisure activities, or stay inside their cells. However, once they sign up for an activity, they are expected to attend it, and otherwise they are removed from the participants list.

Routines on weekdays[5]	
06:10	Prison officers' early shift starts Prisoners are counted
06:15	'Servants'[6] are awakened
06:30	All prisoners are awakened, night buckets are emptied, and coffee and hot water are distributed (as well as breakfast on 'breakfast days')
06:55	'Doctor's movement'[7] is unlocked
07:10	'Doctor's movement' leaves
07:15	'Work movement' is unlocked, prisoners leave their cells immediately and the prison governor is informed about any prisoners who are still in bed
08:30	Cells of prisoners who participate in other courses are unlocked
11:45	Lunch break, prisoners are locked inside their cells and counted. Food items are counted[8] and distributed
12:30	Servants do the dishes Prisoners who work or participate in other activities are unlocked
12:50	Walk for prisoners without job or other activity
13:45	End of the walk, prisoners are locked up inside their cells Prisoners are counted
14:00	End of prison officers' early shift Prisoners are counted Start of prison officers' late shift
15:55	Work movement from workshops to cells, prisoners are locked up inside their cells and counted
16:15	All prisoners can shower and take clean clothes
17:30	Food items are counted and distributed
18:45	Cells of prisoners who participate in evening classes are unlocked
19:00	Prisoners are unlocked for the evening walk Prisoners have access to the training room if they are on the list
20:10	Prisoners who choose to come inside after one hour are locked up inside their cells
21:00	All prisoners are locked up inside their cells and counted
21:50	Prisoners are counted again Prison officers' night shift starts

[5] The words used in these daily routines are literal translations. This is 'prison language' and does not always make sense in Dutch either.

[6] 'Servants': these prisoners' jobs include the cleaning of their section and the distribution of the food in their section.

[7] Doctor's movement: the prisoners who need to see the doctor walk together and under staff supervision from their cells to the doctor's office.

[8] Number of pieces of meat, cheese, fruit, desserts, … are counted before they get distributed.

These highly structured days in Hoogstraten prison are positively valued by prisoners and prison officers. This was expressed as follows by a young prisoner who spontaneously compared his stay in this prison with previous experiences in other prisons and with his life outside prison:

> The good thing about Hoogstraten is that they wake you up in the mornings, you have to get up. That's good, you learn what life is like as a working person. In other prisons you lay in bed all day. And outside of prison, I always overslept. (Field notes 30 October 2014, Hoogstraten prison)

This quote illustrates two important issues related to the normalization of the time-use in this prison. First, the main reference point to assess the routines and activities organized in Hoogstraten prison is the other Belgian prisons rather than the living conditions outside prison. Both prisoners and prison officers frequently and spontaneously mentioned the poor and disturbing prison conditions in what they called the 'real prisons' (i.e. closed Belgian prisons). This resulted in a relatively positive image of Hoogstraten prison. Second, like the young prisoner in this quote, many prisoners and prison officers seem to advocate a more disciplinary approach to normalization, which entails the imposition of routines in order to prepare prisoners for 'normal life' after release and to manage the prison in a well-organized way.

For example, Lorenzo, a 40-year-old prisoner with considerable prison experience, argued that strict prison routines are necessary for the smooth running of a prison:

> Can you imagine something so crazy as having 400 men and they all get to choose when they get to take a shower? You can't do that, can you? That doesn't make sense.... (Interview Lorenzo, Hoogstraten prison)

He is also confident that many prisoners, and in particular young prisoners who lack structure in their lives, benefit from the routines imposed in prison.

> And I see a lot of guys who think that's strange, yeah. [...] but that's because of their upbringing, that's for sure. And I think it's good that they

> carry it out so strictly, having chefs and like that, just drawing the lines ... I do think that can help, yeah, for some people, not for everybody. (Interview Lorenzo, Hoogstraten prison)

However, prison routines do not only provide structure, they also involve a lot of waiting: waiting for the next activity to start, waiting for a prison officer to open and close the cell doors before and after each activity, waiting for the next meal, waiting to be allowed to 'walk' outdoors, waiting to call or waiting to go to the toilet. Indeed, following the routines means that everything should happen at the *right* moment. Clean clothes, for instance, are to be taken during the 'shower routine'. If prisoners forget something, they will have to wait until the next 'shower routine' to get it, although some prison officers have more flexibility than others.

Weekend days and public holidays have similar routines, except that prisoners are awakened at 7:30 instead of 6:30, and that the workshops are closed. This means that prisoners spend a large part of the weekends inside their cells, apart from the 'walks' and a few other activities, such as the Catholic mass on Saturdays, football games on Sunday mornings and receiving visitors on Saturdays and Sundays. Although this could be seen as a way of 'normalizing' the weekly routines, in practice it results for most prisoners in more 'empty time' in the weekends. The same is true for prison officers, for whom Sundays and public holidays are also often boring.

The Prison's Pathways to Prisoners' Reintegration

Following the import model, more than twenty organizations provide activities in Hoogstraten prison, covering six domains: (1) education, such as cooking, gardening and Microsoft Excel courses; (2) culture, such as guitar classes and library access; (3) health care, such as drug and aggression treatment; (4) sports, such as gym workouts, 'start to run' and football; (5) well-being, including the 'child visits', Skype, debt assistance, individual counselling, victim offender mediation and voluntary work by the *core group* of prisoners; and (6) employment, including vocational training and counselling. Five vocational training courses are organized in this prison: bricklayer, painter, electrician, car mechanic and plasterer. These are full-time trainings for 6 to 9 months, followed by official testing at the local office of the Flemish Service for Employment and Vocational Training (VDAB). The main aim of these vocational trainings is to facilitate prisoners' reintegration in two ways: first, by teaching them the skills they need for a particular job after release; second, by providing them with an official certificate, which is exactly the same as the one they would obtain outside prison. This does not only mean that prisoners get the right certificate to qualify for a job, but also that they can at least partly fill in the gap in their CV caused by the prison term.

If not participating in one of these vocational trainings, most prisoners work in daytime. The jobs in this prison include producing and repairing pallets, carpentry, maintaining the prison buildings and surroundings, providing household services and working in the prison kitchen, bakery, print shop and farm. Both the work commissioned by external companies (e.g. the pallet workshop) and the involvement of prisoners in the daily operation of the prison (e.g. preparing the meals, baking the bread, cleaning, maintaining buildings and surroundings) are based on the principles of normalization and responsibilization. These principles are even more emphasized by prison staff in the context of 'trust positions', which are jobs that require a higher degree of responsibility and can therefore only be performed by 'trusted prisoners'. One of these jobs entails the opening and closing of the gate of the castle. Both the prison governor and several prison officers pointed out the responsibility that comes with this job. However, since staff members have their own keys to this gate and since the outer gate is permanently guarded by one or two prisoner officers, the real responsibility of this prisoner-gatekeeper is very limited. For the prisoner in question, this 'position of trust' involves standing or sitting next to the gate all day long, waiting for a person to enter or leave the castle. The fact that this job is considered to entail a relatively high degree of responsibility indicates at the same time the very low degree of responsibility involved in the 'regular' prison jobs. Neither this 'trust position' nor the regular jobs require prisoners to take real decisions. For this reason, it could be argued that the 'normalizing' value of involving prisoners in the operation of this prison is to be situated at the level of the prison (e.g. the food is made by prisoners, the buildings are cleaned by prisoners, the prison domain is maintained by prisoners…) rather than at the level of the individual prisoner. From the prisoners' point of view, the main reasons to participate in prison labour are to spend part of the day outside of the cell, to have social contact and to have something to do in the daytime. Even though it is questionable to what extent this kind of work contributes to the professional skills that prisoners will need after release, prisoners are clear about the fact that participating in prison work reduces the painful effects of detention. Again, these benefits were especially valued by prisoners who had experienced living conditions in other Belgian prisons.

Although prisoners generally valued the number of activities organized in this prison, especially when compared to other Belgian prisons, concerns were raised regarding the relationship between prisoners' participation in these activities and their chances of conditional release. Whereas prisoners seemed to favour a more disciplinary approach when it comes to the normalization of daily life in prison, the requirements for conditional release were considered excessively disciplining or almost impossible to meet. The salience of these concerns was reflected in two common topics of conversation among prisoners: first, frustrations about the psychological assessments by the psychosocial service (PSD); second, the disciplinary nature of the system of conditional release, which raises questions about the voluntary character of participation in these activities.

> *Lorenzo*: They put that in your file […] it's down on paper, everything, good and bad…uh…how many courses you've taken, the therapy groups, whatever. And they see that [when deciding about conditional release]: 'we think this guy will do fine'…or that's what prisoners say anyway, that it's better to do that… it's purely, only for that [conditional release]. (Interview Lorenzo, Hoogstraten prison)

Although it is quite possible that Lorenzo is more cynical about the system than prisoners with less prison experience, there is no doubt that conditional release is a huge concern and source of frustration for many prisoners in Hoogstraten prison. Maurice, for example, complains about the fact that he did not get the chance to participate in a therapy programme, which was in turn a reason to deny him a conditional release.

> The results of the personality assessment he had when he began his sentence are still being used, and he hasn't been tested since then. 'If they assume I'm not going to change, why am I being locked up for this many years?' He says that he has in fact changed, but he contradicts himself soon afterwards, saying that he doesn't believe that anyone becomes a better person here, because you don't get therapy. There is a 'therapy group', but it's not enough, and besides, only selected prisoners are allowed to participate. Maurice doesn't understand this, since everybody needs help, so some of them will go back out into the streets without having had any kind of therapy. Maurice will soon be ending his prison stay after having served his full sentence, and will be freed after six years without any conditions attached. (Field notes 28 November 2014, Hoogstraten prison)

Maurice's complaint points out two important issues related to the psychological services in Belgian prisons and their role in prisoners' reintegration process. First, there is a general lack of psychological treatment. Based on the import model, two service providers are responsible for the mental health care in Hoogstraten prison: the Centre for General Welfare (CAW) and the Centre for Mental Health Care (CGG). The task of the two CAW counsellors is to provide prisoners with information about all activities organized in Hoogstraten prison and to assist them with specific, mostly practical questions related to their reintegration. These counsellors work demand-driven, meaning that they work only with the prisoners who write them a 'report letter'. It is clear, however, that these two counsellors are not able to closely follow up each of the 170 prisoners. The same is true for the psychologists of the CGG, who are responsible for the actual psychological treatment in prison. For all prisons in Flanders, housing 7330 prisoners in 2014, there were 17.5 FTE psychologists providing psychological treatment to prisoners (see Strategic Plan of the Flemish government 2015–2020). Second, unlike these 17.5 FTE psychologists, most of the psychologists in Belgian prisons are federal employees with an advisory role in judicial decisions. This means that they inform the prison governor or the judge about the personality of and risks associated with the prisoner concerned. Because of this advisory role, prisoners know, or should know, that it is to their disadvantage to share personal problems or concerns with these psychologists. When considering these two issues related to the lack of adequate psychosocial counselling, it is clear that even in this open prison where the focus is on prisoners' reintegration, the implementation of the individual detention plan for each prisoner, which is intended to 'normalize' and meaningfully organize prison time at the individual level, is still a long way off.

This gap between policy and practice is equally relevant for the fact that prisoners are fully aware (yet frustrated) that their participation in activities is taken into account for conditional release, even with a lack of opportunities, which also makes this normalization process less rosy than would seem at first sight. This is also true for the disciplinary nature of the routines in this open prison: following strictly imposed routines in monotonous prison life might be a success of normalization compared to other prisons, but creating and maintaining their own routines in life outside prison is something else entirely. This begs the question whether, if possibilities and upsides on paper are weighed against frustrations and obstacles in practice, the effort of normalization still has any positive effect in this prison.

7.3.2 Empty Time and Boredom

Daily life in Leuven prison is structured along similar routines as the life in Hoogstraten prison. This means that the timing and duration of all activities are determined by the prison and that prisoners are locked inside their cells when they are not participating in organized activities. The main difference with Hoogstraten prison is that, due to the limited work available, only a minority of the prisoners can work in Leuven prison and therefore most spend the majority of their time inside their cell. For these prisoners, the days are structured by the food distributions and the 'walks', while the rest of the day consists largely of waiting and boredom, and any activity is a welcome change.

Boredom and Fear of Negative Thoughts

For most prisoners, the majority of time spent in Leuven prison is 'empty time', which entails being alone (or sometimes with one or two other prisoners) in a cell for almost 22 hours a day, with little opportunities for mental or physical activity. They associate this 'empty time' with boredom, waiting and looking for ways to 'kill time', and consider it a serious threat to their mental health. Although some prisoners appreciate time to think, having too much time to over-think everything is considered by many prisoners to be one of the most salient differences between life in Leuven prison and life outside prison:

> *Ali*: The biggest difference is the time, you know. In prison, you always stay inside, you always have nothing to do and you always get time to think [...] So, you use your mind for negative things and positive things at the same time, so at the end you become to be confused not to get any positive answer, because you combine negativity and positivity at the same time, so it's a big difference from outside life. [...] So it's ruining people, this Leuven prison, it's ruining people's mind because, if the mind can get not something to be busy with, it's always gonna end with stress or depression, things like that. (Interview Ali, Leuven prison)

Similarly, Senne, a 20-year-old prisoner, explains that daily life in this prison mainly consists of 'doing nothing'. Also in his view, this contrasts with life outside prison and is difficult to cope with.

> *Senne*: You have to ask for everything, you sit in your cell for 22 hours a day here... there aren't a lot of activities... that's not really easy for some people who can't really handle that [...] Some people are used to going out every day, ... being outside every day, doing what they want. And here they suddenly have to switch, just click, sitting in a cell for 22 hours a day. Sometimes we're even locked up 23 hours a day. [...]

> *Me*: So what do you do in your cell?
> *Senne*: yeah, watch TV… eat something, drink something, have a little snack… there's not much to do in the cell, is there? Not much at all.
> *Me*: And how do you feel about that?
> *Senne*: Yeah, after a while you can't stand it. Of course. Some people …. It's not so bad for me, for some people it's really bad, they get depressed and have to ask the doctor for pills so they can sleep… I don't have any trouble getting to sleep here. Just waiting in your cell and stuff… yeah, you're locked up, you can't… you can't just keep on complaining or making trouble. (Interview Senne, Leuven prison)

Even though most prisoners find ways to 'kill time' in an attempt to avoid negative thoughts, some prisoners face more difficulties than others, in particular prisoners with ADHD, with dyslexia or with lower levels of literacy. A prisoner with dyslexia explains that he has difficulties reading the books from the library and since he does not have a DVD player in his cell, he cannot watch movies either. Watching television and going outside for the 'walk' are therefore his only activities (Field notes 12 November 2015, Leuven prison). Another prisoner struggling with ADHD explains that it was very difficult for him to calm down in his cell at the beginning of his incarceration, sitting there for 22 hours a day every day. In addition to the distress directly caused by these periods of 'empty time', prisoners also raised concerns about their impact on their perception of time. Prisoners get used to a slower rhythm of life due to the functioning of this prison and their own strategies for 'killing' time. The unwanted side effect is that time outside prison seems to go too fast after release, making reintegration more difficult in their view.

Organized Activities: A Welcome Change to Isolation and Boredom

Since only a few prisoners can participate in the prison labour, these prisoners consider this a great 'privilege'. Prison labour is associated with mental distraction, being outside of the cell, having 'something to do' and getting structured days. Another advantage is being allowed to shower in the evening on days one has worked (or participated in sports), since as a general rule, prisoners can only shower every other day at 6:30 a.m. The fact that the opportunity to participate in prison labour is positively valued does not mean, however, that the work itself is considered interesting or even as a contribution to their professional skills.

> *Maarten*: And the work itself... Okay, what I have to do, that's not too bad [he cleans one of the sections], but like in the workshop, they shouldn't consider everybody a retard that belongs in a social project. [...] Here they generally assume okay, we're going to make a social project out of this and have everybody do little jobs that mentally retarded people do. While we can do a lot more. (Interview Maarten, Leuven prison)

The same applies to the positions of trust such as that position of 'gate servant'. This prisoner brings goods delivered to the prison from near the entrance gate to the cell section or kitchen. Since this job requires him to go up to the gate and thus almost onto the street, this prisoner needs to be trustworthy. This prisoner himself is rather sceptical about his job description and the trust that goes along with it.

> *Marcel*: The work itself? I have to do that at home too, don't I, tidy up a bit, clean up other people's rubbish, or my own rubbish ... We have to do that at home too. Those are everyday things. ... it's actually not a job, is it, it's actually just part of everyday life... I have to drive the cart there and [bring it back] full [...] They say it's a 'position of trust'... (Interview Marcel, Leuven prison)

Besides these limited work opportunities, prisoners can participate in the activities and services organized by the Flemish service providers, and in the daily 'walks', the religious services, and they can receive visitors. Based on the import model, teachers, trainers, social workers and psychologists of more than forty Flemish service providers organize activities in the following seven domains: (1) well-being, such as individual, social and psychological counselling, debt assistance, 'being a father in prison' for fathers with a drug addiction and 'child visits'; (2)

education, such as Dutch classes for non-native speakers, e-learning and general education (3) health, such as AA; (4) restoration, such as victim offender mediation; (5) culture, such as library access, guitar classes, circus training and the film festival; (6) sports, such as fitness, fitball and crossfit; and (7) employment, such as VDAB counselling. Despite the aim of and efforts towards having these activities fully resemble the same activities outside, material and security limitations create differences beyond the control of the service providers. One example of this is that the creative arts class is interrupted for the head count, the participants have to return to their cells to be counted when the class is halfway through. This can usually be avoided by planning activities in between the two headcounts, but this often makes these activities just too short to work on anything in much depth.

In general, prisoners are satisfied with the educational and recreational activities offered in this prison, although they find there is too little on offer and there is a lack of courses going beyond a basic level. The prisoners interviewed were very positive about the sports classes. However, Maarten did state that what is considered 'normal' in this context differs from person to person. For him personally, it is 'normal' to work out three to four times a week, which he cannot do in this prison. Interestingly, however, the positive rating of the activities on offer is partly due to their low expectations. As Victor and Marcel put it:

> *Victor*: We're in prison, not in school, and a lot of them do it just to be out of their cells for a bit. (Interview Victor, Leuven prison)
> *Marcel*: Those people [teachers] do their best to come here. Yeah, I think that's really nice that they want to come here. [...] And yeah, you can learn from everything, can't you... (Interview Marcel, Leuven prison)

Even though many prisoners have low expectations when it comes to the nature of the activities organized in prison and consider it a 'privilege' to be allowed to leave their cells in order to clean the section, some prisoners argue that activities can only be considered meaningful if they contribute to prisoners' reintegration. These prisoners tend to value a more instrumental and disciplinary approach to normalization in order to render imprisonment more 'useful'. Ali, for example, advocates compulsory participation in activities. In his view, this would reduce the risks of becoming depressed during detention, increase feelings of accomplishment and reduce recidivism. Indeed, he links education directly to what he considers the purpose of the prison sentence: the rehabilitation or 'correction' of prisoners.

> *Ali*: So, I think, the system should change [...] Because then you can say: okay, I was in prison but at least I did something in that time, I didn't waste all the time. Because [...] things are going on in outside world, time passes [...]

> The most important is not games, you know, the most important is to learn. That's the most important, because games, you have been playing games your whole life, that's why you maybe are here, because of that stupid time you have been playing, but when you learn and educate yourself or do something that will be beneficially here... (Interview Ali, Leuven prison)

Similarly, prisoners argue that psychological treatment, especially in the context of substance abuse, could be a meaningful way to spend prison time but is largely lacking in Leuven prison. Karim, for example, did not get the support he expected to rehabilitate from his drug addiction.

> *Karim*: You're left to your fate here. A lot of people complain about it, and they let them do it actually, like the users, 'OK, here's your methadone'... I'm kind of against that. I mean, they're here, in prison... They can cut down or stop using, but they don't have to ... and afterwards, they send them to a detox centre. No, no, do something about it HERE! Why are they here then? To sit around here? No, they're here to achieve something. That's missing here. (Interview Karim, Leuven prison)

This apparent lack of the meaningful use of the time spent in this prison also raised more fundamental questions about the purpose of imprisonment.

Marcel: The first few months, I just lay on my bed, I was just tired. That's resting, and actually, it's doing nothing. Then you wonder: yeah, just what is my punishment?
Me: What do you mean?
Marcel: Yeah, that doing nothing, just lying around, … so they're just shoving people aside, outside of society and then they don't do anything with them, then you wonder why are we punished this way? (Interview Marcel, Leuven prison)

7.3.3 Mandatory, Comfortable and Meaningful Activities

Since Leira prison is a 'drug management unit', or a 'life management unit' as Leira's manager prefers to call it, the time spent in this prison is dedicated to reintegration and rehabilitation, with a particular focus on drug abuse. In practice, this means that prisoners have to work or go to school in the daytime and additionally participate in several other activities, such as mandatory walks and group meetings. Besides these mandatory activities, however, prisoners are relatively 'free' to spend their spare time the way they want. Indeed, the higher degree of physical freedom in Leira prison also entails more autonomy over the use of time than in the three other prisons. In the following sections, these daytime activities will be discussed in more detail, including the mandatory and the 'free' time activities, after which the focus will turn to the distinction between a comfortable and a meaningful way to spend prison time.

Mandatory Activities

All prisoners in Leira prison have to work or participate in an education programme. As indicated by the schedule below, the working days are structured from 7:45 to 15:00, including coffee and lunch breaks.

Daily routines	
06.00–07:45	Breakfast
07:45	Start of the working day

(continued)

(continued)

Daily routines	
08:00	Activity list is finalized/posted
09:30	Morning meeting for staff members
09:30–09:45	Coffee break for prisoners
11:30–12:00	Lunch break
13:30–13:45	Coffee break (except on Fridays)
15:00	End of the working day (14:30 on Fridays)
15:15	Dinner
15:30–21:30	Prisoners can receive visitors (Monday-Wednesday-Friday) (Saturday & Sunday: 10:30–21:30)
17:00	On Tuesdays and Thursdays: compulsory trainings: short walk (40 min) or long walk (1 hour 30 min)
19:30	On Thursdays: prisoners' meeting
19:45	Meeting with prisoners' representatives
20:00	Every other Thursday: general meeting
21:30	All activities should be finished (on Saturday at 18:00 because of group dinner)
23:00	Pool games should be finished Kitchen and living rooms are checked for cleanliness
24:00	Women and men who live in the separate houses should leave the main building Outside doors are locked (Friday, Saturday and holidays at 01:00)

There are seven work places. First, the garden centre is where most prisoners work, along with some staff members. This work involves the growing and selling of a variety of plants, for which the garden centre is equipped with several greenhouses and a shop. Second, the maintenance of the prison buildings and surroundings, which involved gardening during the observation period, but is more about shovelling snow in the winter, and the maintenance of the equipment such as the tractors and lawn mowers. This work is done by four prisoners. Third, one prisoner is responsible for the caretaking of the horses, the owners of which have an agreement with Leira prison. Fourth, one prisoner does the laundry, which involves washing the clothes coming from Nermarka prison and local sport clubs. Fifth, one prisoner is responsible for the cleaning of the prison building. Sixth, four prisoners work in Leira's car repair shop, where they are supervised by a specialized teacher from a local secondary school and which is thus accredited for apprenticeships. And finally, two prisoners work in the kitchen and are responsible for preparing a buffet for lunch with freshly baked bread, vegetables, eggs and leftovers from the previous dinner, and to make sure that the dinner, which is prepared at Nermarka prison and brought to Leira, can be served on time. During the observation period, two prisoners were taking classes outside of the prison for several days a week and worked on the other days.

Prisoners' opinions about the prison work differed according to their personal interests, the specific tasks they had to do and their views on the objectives of prison work. While some prisoners experienced the work mainly as a way to pass time, others considered the work intrinsically meaningful and a good way to enhance their professional skills. Issam, for instance, who had experience working in a restaurant kitchen, took his work in Leira's kitchen very seriously and was genuinely satisfied when the others enjoyed his food (Field notes 9 June 2015, Leira prison). Along the same lines, Petter had been working as a professional landscaper before and therefore enjoyed his job in the garden centre. However, not all jobs lay within the prisoners' personal fields of interest. Many prisoners consider the work in the garden centre just a way to pass time, which is valued differently depending on their personal views on the objectives of prison work. While Adrian thought of the prison work as a comfortable way to pass time, Jonas argued that it should entail a minimum of responsibilities and intellectual challenges in order to be meaningful, which he missed in the work that he was doing in the garden centre:

> *Adrian*: I think the work is boring, but it's work. It's something I do and it's no problem, it's okay. It's like, the time goes when you work. It's not my favourite work, but it's okay, it's no problem. (Interview Adrian, Leira prison)

***

> *Jonas*: It's an open prison but the work mentality is still: you gotta do this, and you move plants from here to here, you don't think. So, if I were to organize this prison, I would organize it so that the prisoners would have to think themselves, you know. Maybe.... involve them more in the ... all the aspects of the work, you know, like having to take responsibility, so that they could feel that they are doing something meaningful and...because it's like,

> in a prison, the job-thing they make you do, makes you go in a sort of trance, almost. (Interview Jonas, Leira prison)

Besides participation in the work or classes, other mandatory activities are the walks on Tuesdays and Thursdays, the group meetings, the conversations based on the 'consequence pedagogy method' and participation in the team, rotating weekly, that cleans the kitchen and prepares dinner on Saturdays. The prisoners who were interviewed positively valued these mandatory activities, including the fact that they were mandatory. For example, Issam argued that obliging prisoners to take their responsibility and cook for the others helps them to develop necessary skills, which some of them would not have developed on their own. Similar views were expressed about the mandatory walks. These are fixed walking routes of 4 or 8 kilometres. Prisoners must check in when they depart and when they return, which must be within the agreed-upon time period, 40 minutes for 4 km and an hour and a half for 8 km. Although there were complaints in the group about these walks, especially on rainy days, most prisoners whom I asked explicitly about it, were positive about the fact that they were mandatory. Both Issam and Adrian were convinced that many prisoners would not participate in these walks if they were not mandatory, even though many of them complained about boredom and about having put on weight during their stay in Nermarka prison.

> *Issam*: I think...for me is perfect, I like it. I go even if it's not [mandatory] walking. I like to walk every day if it's nice weather. Yeah, so, I think it's very good, because people here don't do too much. [...] they like to stay and sit all the time. (Interview Issam, Leira prison)

***

> *Adrian*: Yes, I like the activities here. It's very important. Because if we hadn't had the walk and the activities, I think many people is going to ...they get unhealthy, you know, and they eat too much pizza...everything... so it's good for everyone.
>
> *Me*: And if it wasn't mandatory, then not everyone would do it?

Adrian: No, no, if you could choose, I think many people would not. (Interview Adrian, Leira prison)

These opinions reflect a rather disciplinary approach to normalization, which aims at preparing prisoners for a healthy, responsible and crime-free life after release. This tendency towards a disciplinary approach also emerged in prisoners' and staff's belief that staying in Leira prison requires more effort and a stronger motivation than staying in a closed prison, but at the same time it improves the chances for a successful reintegration.

Petter: So, I think open prison is good for people who want to do something with their life. And you have closed [prison] for the people who don't give a damn. Who don't want to change their life, they can stay in closed prison, just do the sentence and finish. Because, it's more work for people to be in open prison than it is in a closed prison. Maybe it sounds a bit wrong for you, but it is more … you must give more of yourself to be in open. If you don't want to change your life, you can just go away and do what you best can, but you will come back to prison. […] you can't be in open prison and don't do anything. […] It is not a holiday. It can seem to be very open and good, but it's much more you have to do. You have to work, you have to do your things, …. When you are in closed prison, you can say 'close me in' and you can try to, try to die, but they come in and give you food. So it's very easy, but it is harder when you come out. So people are getting damaged from being in closed prison for so long. (Interview Petter, Leira prison)

'Free' Time

Prisoners are relatively 'free' to spend their leisure time in the afternoons, evenings and weekends the way they want, largely but not exclusively on the prison premises. They can use the prison facilities, for example, to watch television, work out, cook and eat, play pool, video games, cards or chess, or go for the fixed walk of 4 or 8 kilometres (which is compulsory on Tuesdays and Thursdays, but optional on the other days), or they can choose to initiate a leisure activity or to participate in the leisure activities proposed by someone else. Petter describes the leisure time in this prison as follows:

> *Petter*: I think it's good here, because you must start to do something yourself. If the guards are saying, 'this day, all of you have to play football… this day, you have to play this, you have to do that', then it's these people who is making things for you. But here, you have something you have to do, these two walks, and after that, you must do it yourself. So, it's good. So, if you want to relax, you can relax. And if you want to do something, you just do it or you talk with other people and you do things together. (Interview Petter, Leira prison)

A variety of recreational activities are organized outside of the prison, and any prisoner or staff member can suggest one. These can take place any day except Tuesdays and Thursdays, although in principle day trips are only done on weekends. Suggestions for activities are written on the whiteboard in the prison's dining area (by 8:00 the same day), so that other prisoners can sign up. If at least three participants sign up, the activity takes place. Most activities are allowed, with a few exceptions, such as swimming in Trondheim's indoor water park, shopping and sunbathing on the beach. Participating prisoners pay for most activities themselves (unless they are free of charge), although the prison will contribute NOK 50 for certain sports activities. During my observation period, there was a barbecue at the edge of a lake, snooker, rally cross, football training, a trip to watch a football match in the Lerkendal stadium and a barbecue held in Leira with a volleyball tournament (with mixed teams of prisoners and staff) to which the neighbours were also invited.

These activities are highly valued by the prisoners who participate. Jonas is convinced that leisure activities outside of the prison contribute to prisoners' rehabilitation in a way that goes beyond the possibilities of the therapeutic conversations in prison.

> *Jonas*: I like it. It's a lot more like normal things you do when you are outside of prison. [...] Just like when we were out barbecuing yesterday.... we had a lot of good conversations around the bonfire, you know. And in my opinion, that is better than sitting for instance in a room and talk, something they like to call 'therapy'. Because, it's not. It's more therapy to get good, good balance of doing things that are normal... (Interview Jonas, Leira prison)

Paradoxically enough, the relative freedom over the use of time had the effect that time was experienced as passing more slowly in Leira prison than in Nermarka prison, where daily life is much more routinized. For many Leira prisoners, this 'free time' resulted in some kind of 'empty time', which made them complain of boredom and a lack of mental stimulation. Consequently, prisoners in this prison also had their own techniques to 'kill time'. Kjetil, for example, used a daily afternoon nap to make his days pass more quickly and tried to work on Saturdays too (the garden centre was open on Saturdays, but prisoners did not have to work on Saturdays). The same can be said for the most common leisure activities such as playing cards, playing pool or watching television. At first sight, these activities seem comfortable ways of spending one's spare time, yet, after a few observation days, it became clear that these were just other ways to 'kill time', or in the prisoners' words: '*always the same games with the same people*'.

When compared to Nermarka prison, prisoners assessed their autonomy over time and the nature of activities in Leira in a very positive way. The fact that time seemed to pass more slowly in Leira prison, was not decisive for their experience. However, prisoners underlined that the way in which time is used in Leira prison still differs fundamentally from the way it is used outside prison, due to the lack of real responsibilities. This was a commonly heard concern in Leira prison, as Kristian put it:

> *Kristian*: [In Nermarka prison] they treat you like a five-year-old. You have to ask permission for everything and they can always say 'no'. Here in Leira they treat you like a ten-year-old, that's already a little better. (Field notes 8 June 2015, Leira prison)

Indeed, even in Leira, prisoners did not have responsibilities in terms of time management: they work when they are told to do so, they go shopping when they are brought to the shop, and they clean the kitchen when it is their turn to do so. Jonas believed that this aspect of Leira prison should and could be improved.

> *Jonas*: I think the whole mentality and the whole mind of prisoners would work in a whole different way because, even if you are outside prison walls... we are here, but there are still walls, you know. You can't see the walls, but they are there. Because you ... still, you have lost your freedom, you're still put in a place that you're not supposed to think much for yourself, you've been told what to do. And I think, when you are from a closed to open prison, you should be given more responsibilities, because, look around, you're in open prison but you are not allowed to think for yourself yet. (Interview Jonas, Leira prison)

Increasing prisoners' sense of responsibility would in his view both change the atmosphere in prison and facilitate reintegration after release, which brings us to the distinction between comfortable and meaningful ways to spend time in prison.

Comfortable Versus Meaningful Time-Use in Prison

The distinction between a comfortable and a meaningful way to spend prison time emerged from the conversations with many prisoners at Leira prison, pointing out that they considered activities that contribute directly to their reintegration more meaningful than others. All prisoners agreed that serving their time at Leira prison was much less harmful and more comfortable than in Nermarka prison, thanks to, among other things, the mandatory and leisure activities organized in Leira prison. However, when reflecting on the *meaningful* use of time, prisoners did not refer to these activities in the first place, but rather to the help they received with their reintegration.

Several prisoners mentioned the support of staff members in Leira prison, which they considered crucial for a successful reintegration, and which contrasted with the poor assistance they had experienced in closed prisons.

> *Jonas*: In my opinion, if you go from closed prison to outside, you don't stand half the chance you got when you go to this place first. Because the transition would be smoother, you will get to get routines, a place [to live] before you are released and you get help with it from everybody, you don't have to do everything by yourself. Of course, it's a lot better to be here, of course. (Interview Jonas, Leira prison)

***

> *Petter*: To get a better life out of prison, you need a good place to live, without neighbours who is using drugs and everything. And you need something to do, some work, school or something. And you need friends. Friends and contact people. You must have these three different. ... so, the prison here, they are starting when you are in prison to get a good place to live and with contact people on the outside. (Interview Petter, Leira prison)

Along the same lines, Adrian explained the concept of *ansvargruppe*, a group of staff members that helped him with preparing his reintegration. This group consists of his contact prison officer, psychologist and NAV counsellor. He meets regularly with this group in prison.

> *Adrian*: I have a group around me, like I have one shrink care, I have one guard who is my officer, and I have a woman of NAV, you know NAV?
>
> *Me*: Yes
>
> *Adrian*: Yeah, that is my group and some people [other prisoners], they let…they do the work for them but I'm more like, I want to do it myself, and I can choose what I want her to do and what I want her to help me with. For me, it's very important that I can choose myself what I want to do. (Interview Adrian, Leira prison)

It should be noted, however, that time spent in Leira prison is usually limited to the last several months of the prison sentence. This may explain why prisoners experienced the practical preparation for their reintegration as more meaningful than the other daily activities. On the other hand, from the observations it is clear that the more 'comfortable' way to spend time (because of the activities organized as well as the material and social environment in Leira prison) is a precondition or a catalyst for the 'meaningful' use of time. Espen explained this as follows:

> I'm glad to be in Leira. This is a good prison if you want to make a fresh start. In other prisons, all you can do is think about how to get out of fucking prison. Here in Leira you have the time to put your life in order. Also, you aren't locked up, you can go outside whenever you like, you get fresh air and you can exercise. Actually I'm glad I got a prison sentence, because here I have the chance to get off those drugs. (Field notes 9 June 2015, Leira prison)

Indeed, the climate in Leira prison encourages prisoners to prioritize their reintegration, since they are no longer preoccupied with 'surviving' their prison term. Moreover, it is only because the time in Leira prison is generally considered 'comfortable' or at least 'okay', when compared to other prisons, that prisoners set higher standards for the use of time in prison, and thus point out this difference between a comfortable and a meaningful use of time.

7.3.4 Dictated by the Clock

The way in which time is used and structured in Nermarka prison differs between the various buildings. Most of the time spent in the A building, the most strict section in Nermarka, is 'empty time'. This means that prisoners spend most of the time alone inside their cells. For many prisoners, the lack of mental stimulation or distraction in the beginning of their incarceration is one of the most difficult aspects of detention in this prison (cf. Leuven prison). In the E building, by contrast, the time-use is structured by routines and activities. The latter is also the case for the M building (*Modulen*), but here prisoners also participate in organized activities both outside the prison walls and indoors, such as group meetings and individual sessions with drug therapists. In what follows, the focus will first be on the prison routines, then on the activities in the E building and finally on those in the M building.

Prison Routines

In the E and M buildings, the weekdays are structured along the routines listed below. All prisoners in these buildings have to participate in the work or education programmes, resulting in principle in working days from 8:00 to 15:00. Breakfast and dinner are eaten in the sections, and lunch at the workplaces (or in the sections if prisoners are for some reason there around lunch time). The spare time after work is mainly spent in the common area of the sections, which means that prisoners have the opportunity to eat together, cook, play games and use the showers and toilets. Between 17:15 and 18:15 prisoners can go to the yard outside. The weekend routines start at 10:00 with breakfast in the common area of each unit.

Daily routines	
07:05	Prisoners are awakened and have breakfast
07:55	'Bus' departure[9]
08:00	Start of working day
11:30–12:00	Lunch break (in common area or at work)
15:00	End of working day Dinner is served
15:00–16:00	Spare time in the common area of each unit
16:00–17:00	Break for staff members Prisoners are locked up inside their cells
17:15–18:15	'Having open air'
18:15–20:30	Spare time in the common area of each unit

These routines are defining for the experience of prison life. They are intended to make prisoners used to 'normal' working days and thus to prepare them for their reintegration, yet result in the clock being considered the driving force of prison life. On the one hand, routines give structure to the days, but on the other hand, they seriously reduce

[9] This is another prison term as there is no actual vehicle. Prisoners walk from their sections to the workplaces, closely monitored by prison officers (there is no bus involved in this action).

prisoners' feelings of autonomy and self-determination. This is considered a crucial difference between the living conditions inside and outside prison, which is believed to negatively impact their reintegration.

> *Fredrik*: Yeah, that is the worst thing. [...] From my point of view, ... it's very hard to be able to be human in prison. [...] Inside prison you are living against the ... along with the clock, the time. And I think that is the hardest. [...] you have this schedule, which is very.... very...what can I say? Not like the outside, you can manage your own day. But this is not possible inside. (Interview Fredrik, Nermarka prison, E building)

Due to the predominance of these routines, many prisoners even conclude that they could, or should, stop thinking for themselves and just follow the system.

> *Steinar*: It's only rules and uh... you don't get to use your brains as much, you know, everything is routine in here, every day at 7:00 we are locked out and... Inside... it's hard to... not thinking yourself, you know, everything is been thinking for you, everything... you can't decide nothing here. (Steinar, Interview Nermarka prison, E building)

***

> *Olav*: And it's also bad because you're not really thinking so much, you get like a robot... you're like: oh I go do this, go do that, go this. What's the time? Okay I go do that. Thirty minutes. I go do that. It's really .... you can turn off your brains completely... and just do what you're told. Eat now, okay, lock in, okay, sleep. So it gets very like uh... like I said: boring. You don't have to think... don't get any mental stimulation. [...] That I think is maybe the most negative part of the prison system in Norway. It's just go inside and turn off your brain, and you turn it on when you get out. (Interview Olav, Nermarka prison, E building)

The consequence of the strict routines and the repetitiveness of prison life is that time is passed less consciously and that it seems to pass more quickly. These two aspects together induce the feeling of what Fredrik calls being 'jail sick'.

> *Fredrik*: Actually, the days and the weekends go very fast. Because the day is the same every day. Not anything else happens than the day before. So, you get a little bit delusional. Because you cannot stimulate your brain the way you can outside. So, this makes people jail sick. (Fredrik, interview in Nermarka prison, E building)

The fact that these concerns are mainly raised by prisoners in the E building and not in the M building means that the nature of the activities prisoners can participate in also influence their experience of these routines. While daily life in both buildings is structured along similar routines, prisoners of the M building participate in more interesting and meaningful activities than those in the E building.

Lack of Mental Stimulation

The prisoners of the E and the M building have a duty of activity. As explained above, this means that they have to participate in the prison's work or equivalent programmes in the daytime. The education programmes in Nermarka prison are managed by a local school and include classes at the level of primary and secondary school, as well as specialized vocational trainings. Prisoners can also enrol in university programmes when the university supports distance learning. Additionally, the prison collaborates with NAV for the financing of studies, for internships and for work placement after release, and with *Stavne gård*[10] for work-oriented rehabilitation programmes. The labour in Nermarka prison includes cleaning the prison buildings, maintaining the prison area and working in the kitchen and in the carpentry workshop, the painting workshop and the machine shop.

Most prisoners are thankful to have a daytime activity, especially after the time spent in isolation in the first stage of their incarceration. The

[10] *Stavne gård* is a municipal organization (managed by the city of Trondheim) that organizes '*work-oriented rehabilitation measures for those who need assistance in various areas of life*' (https://sites.google.com/trondheim.kommune.no/stavne).

fact that the work is mandatory and often considered boring or meaningless, does not detract from prisoners' experience that it reduces the harmful effects of detention. Both Fredrik and Boriss explain that their prison term would have been more difficult without these mandatory daytime activities. Moreover, Boriss argues that the fact that prisoners can work in daytime makes life inside prison more similar to life outside prison, even when the nature of the prison work differs from that outside prison.

> *Fredrik*: I'm glad that I got work, because you get very depressed of isolation… [shakes his head] … every person will get sick of this. In this section [E building], you have to work. If you don't work here, you will be transferred to this A1, that's where you get a plastic knife and a plastic fork… [shakes his head again]. But that is not my goal, you know, to come there. So, I just stay here and do my things. (Interview Fredrik, Nermarka prison, E building)

***

> *Boriss*: If there was no work, then it was catastrophe. Then I don't know what to do here… but it's good that I work… then you know what to do. You come in this routine, you know, like outside: you have job, you come from job… it's like outside. Then you feel a little bit like you are not in prison. (Interview Boriss, Nermarka prison, E building)

The advantages of prison work mentioned by prisoners include opportunities to overcome boredom, to make time pass more quickly and to have contact with other people than the prisoners of their own section, and the fact that some particular jobs result in additional liberties. By contrast, neither earning money nor improving one's professional skills was spontaneously mentioned as an advantage of the work in Nermarka prison. This can be explained by the low salaries (NOK 65 per day) and the routine nature of some jobs. Jonas, Olav and Rafael describe a job that many Nermarka prisoners are doing. Jonas and Olav are very sceptical about the added value of this kind of work, which they both call 'zombie work' (independently of one another).

Jonas: And the kind of work is like, it's the same over and over again. For instance, we have some.... screws....you have to screw it half way into a plate in the machine. So, you just put the screw and just [makes sound of screwing], again... And in that kind of work, you don't think at all. You're just like... you're a machine using a machine [...] And you're not expected to think at all, you know. You just gotta walk around and be a machine or like a zombie almost. (Interview Jonas, interview in Leira prison about Nermarka prison)

***

Olav: But other guys there, I can see, they have extremely routine work [laughs]. Like uh... like zombie work, you can just put on... like a screw in a metal plate. Thousands of them. It's very boring work. [...] So they accepted that I will not accept to just sit and do zombie work... I like to use my brains... if they don't let me use my brains there, I can just go back in my cell, read a book or something. (Interview Olav, Nermarka prison, E building)

Rafael, on the other hand, explains that this routine job allows him to think of other things during his work.

Me: What Do You Think of the Work in the Prison?
Rafael: Uhm it's Good... it's Good to Work Because You Have Something to Do. You Fill up Your Time... and... When I Work, I ... I Think Better... When I Work.
Me: What Do You Mean?
Rafael: Uh... I don't Feel Pain... I Think Better Things...
Me: And What Kind of Work Are You Doing?
Rafael: Something boring... really boring... I sit and only do like this... [...] I don't think about my job when I'm doing this... I think about something else, because this is... this is boring job... and many people... nobody wants to do this job. But I must think positive... and I can do this job. (Interview Rafael, Nermarka prison, E building)

Daytime activities are experienced as more meaningful when prisoners have the feeling that they are being intellectually challenged or that they are learning things that will be useful after release. This is the case for some of the jobs, such as the work in the kitchen, and for most educational programmes. For example, some prisoners who had not finished secondary school managed to do so in prison.

In the afternoon, after the working day, prisoners spend most of the time in the section, where they can use the kitchen and living room with couches, television, board games and ping-pong table, or spend time in their rooms. Between 17:15 and 18:15, they are allowed to go to the outside yard. Additionally, they can participate in some organized leisure activities. During my observation period, there were two concerts (of which prisoners could attend one) with a pizza buffet organized by Red Cross volunteers, a film screening, bingo, several sports activities, such as a three-kilometre run with chocolate for prisoners who finished, and church services (including the Easter mass). Despite these activities, however, most of the time spent in the E building is considered a meaningless waste of time.

> *Olav*: But also, after the work, when the work is done, you go straight back to being zombie. There's nothing here to do. We have a ping-pong table, and chess and cards but that's it. And what kind of skills do you need outside to play ping-pong and chess and stuff like that? It's a good waste of time, that's all it is. It's a waste of time. And that's my main problem with this, it's just a waste of time. (Interview Olav, Nermarka prison, E building)

Indeed, most prisoners expressed feelings of boredom and having nothing to do in the afternoons, apart from preparing food, which was indeed the most common activity. While making food could be considered an aspect of prison life that has been 'normalized' to a certain extent, for the prisoners in the E building, it is mainly a way to overcome boredom. Other common ways to overcome boredom were trying to sleep a lot, using drugs and doing everything as slowly as possible. This makes many prisoners worry about their ability to adapt again to the rhythm of life after release.

> *Petter*: You do everything slowly. If you are going to the shower, you are using long time to shower because then you're getting out of your room. But when you are a free man, you can take a shower in fifteen minutes, when you're in closed prison, you can use fifty minutes, one hour. Just to be outside your room [...] But uhm, I have a friend of mine, he has been many years in prison and when he comes out, if I talk to him and maybe I go to meet, he will take two days before he comes, because he is so slow, he is taking so long time. So you get fucked up, I think, if you are being so much in closed. (Interview Petter, Leira prison, about Nermarka prison)

Furthermore, prisoners did not receive the help they expected, such as psychological treatment or learning problem-solving skills, in tackling the problems that had caused their incarceration, or problems caused by their incarceration. Arne, for example, explains that he can only start his drug rehabilitation after his release or when he gets transferred to the M building (Field notes 3 May 2016, Nermarka prison). Some prisoners of the E building even argue that regular meetings with a psychologist should be mandatory for all prisoners. Since the latter is the case in the M building, it is even more frustrating for them not to be transferred there.

Only a few prisoners in the E building mentioned the possibility of positive time investment. Steinar, for example, explains that he wants to obtain as many certificates as possible during his prison time. He looked online for the relevant educational programmes in all Norwegian prisons, and made a plan based on this information. When he has obtained all the useful certificates offered by a particular prison, he applies for a transfer to the next prison. The disadvantage of this plan, however, is that he does not receive any family visits because he spends his prison time far from home.

> *Steinar*: You know, I have a long sentence and sat down and I asked myself what I want to do and how is the best way to do it and take the most out of it, those years that I'm in prison. I want to have as much papers as possible when I finish. [...] So it's important to make a plan when you come in prison and you stick to

> it. Don't do nothing else, just stick to the plan. Because that plan, I made for myself but if the...I think it would have helped a lot if the prison have contacted each inmate and ask what they want and help them, you know, set a plan to the future, you know... maybe they want to school.. but they have to do something that means something, you know... they don't have to just take mathematics or something...and not using it outside. (Interview Steinar, Nermarka prison)

It is remarkable that the prisoners' concerns and complaints about the need for meaningful use of time in the E building are in fact very much in line with the prison's own view on normalization, namely to offer as much meaningful work and activities as possible. The cause of these frustrations is arguably a mix of both a different perception of the activities on offer between staff and prisoners (to many visitors and perhaps staff members, prisoners playing cards and leisure games do not *seem* to be bored, although they are just killing time), and a gap between what is desirable in theory and what is possible in practice (prison staff is aware that much of the available work is not very stimulating and thus not considered meaningful by prisoners). Moreover, the regime in the M building, which reflects a disciplinary approach to normalization, meets most of these concerns raised by prisoners in the E building.

Mandatory Activities and 'Tight' Follow-Up

The M building differs from the E building in terms of activities and prisoner supervision, which are both more intense in the M building as already became clear in the previous chapters. In addition to the mandatory work or educational programmes, these prisoners have to participate in the morning meetings of all prisoners and staff members, plus weekly group and individual meetings as part of drug rehabilitation, and have regular drug tests. Participation in the 'leisure' activities organized inside and outside of the prison is also mandatory for them, although they first need the administration's approval to leave the prison and deliver a clean drug test. During my observation period in the M building, these activities included an orientation run, a three-day trip somewhere outside of

Trondheim, preparations for this trip (such as buying sports clothes in a nearby shopping centre), football trainings and watching football games in Lerkendal stadium. All of the activities were organized without any form of static security. The mandatory participation reflects the disciplinary and instrumental approach to the normalization of the time-use, since preparing prisoners for a crime-free life even includes making them familiar with 'good ways' to spend their leisure time after release.

The idea with the M building is that these prisoners are willing to work on their rehabilitation and reintegration and are rewarded for their efforts. These rewards include the activity-rich regime itself, better living conditions and activities outside of the prison, as well as minor privileges such as spending some of the free time outside of the building when it is sunny (while prisoners of the E building can only *see* these privileges). Moreover, the 'tight' supervision also means that these prisoners have a greater chance of being granted prison leave or being transferred to an open prison or drug rehabilitation centre (see also Crewe & Ievins, 2021). The other side of the coin, however, is that upon every return from outside activities prisoners have to undergo strip searches, since *Modulen* is part of a high-security prison. This is more than just a side note since, as the previous chapters have hopefully firmly established, the normalization process (and certainly how it is experienced) it not just the normalization of one aspect that matters (in this case the outside activities) but also the way in which the context is—or rather, is not—normalized.

7.4 Conclusion

In both countries, the idea of normalizing the living conditions in prison builds on the acceptance that the deprivation of liberty should be the only intended punitive aspect of the prison sentence, and that the duration of this deprivation of liberty is to be proportional to the severity of the offence. This basic starting point implies that the 'pure' deprivation of liberty and its duration are the *intended* punishment and fall therefore beyond the scope of the normalization process. But this logic does not apply to the time-use in prison and to prisoners' autonomy over this time-use. In this sense, the deprivation of time cannot be considered an *intended* aim of the prison sentence. On the contrary, if the time-use in prison is successfully normalized, prisoners can use their time in a similar way as outside prison, while still being deprived of their liberty. The degree of this normalization process largely depends on the normalization of the other dimension, and hence, the time-use was most normalized in Leira prison. It is therefore not surprising that this was the only prison where prisoners spontaneously made a distinction between comfortable and meaningful activities.

Although time-use and its normalization differed greatly between the four prisons, all prisoners considered it crucial to their daily life in prison and agreed that empty time was most harmful. Most of the time spent in Leuven prison and in the A building of Nermarka prison is unstructured or 'empty' time. This means that prisoners are locked inside their cells with little mental stimulation or distraction. The idea that prisoners are not only deprived of their physical liberty but also of their time (Christie, 1982: 95; Middlemass & Smiley, 2016; O'Donnell, 2014, 2016) is most apparent in this kind of regime, and makes prisoners question the meaning of their imprisonment. While this individual regime is implemented intentionally in Nermarka prison at the beginning of prisoners' incarceration, in Leuven prison it is an unintended result of the lack of work available. Sleeping as much as possible and watching TV were common techniques for 'killing time' in Leuven and Nermarka. Remarkably, this was even the case in Leira prison, albeit to a much lesser extent. It is therefore not surprising that prisoners in Leuven had low expectations when it came to activities, and welcomed any and all activities that allowed them to leave their cells for a while. When the aim of normalizing the use of time is to reduce the harmful effects of detention, long periods of unstructured time are to be avoided. This means that all prisoners should get access to daytime activities that involve some mental distraction and social contact, even activities that are not considered meaningful in themselves. If, however, as Belgian and Norwegian prison policies stipulate, normalizing time-use is also aimed at providing opportunities for the *meaningful* use of time (be it on intrinsic or instrumental grounds) and to prepare prisoners for their reintegration (from an instrumental point of view), such activities will not be sufficient.

Activities were generally considered meaningful if they contributed directly to the reintegration. This includes three types of activities: first, practical help with the reintegration (e.g. finding a job and housing, and other administrative assistance); second, activities which are intellectually challenging and give them knowledge or skills that are useful after release (e.g. English courses, vocational trainings and other educational programmes that award the same certificates as outside prison); and third, treatment programmes related to drug abuse or other psychological problems. In this respect, it is striking that prisoners' views are very much in line with the Belgian and Norwegian policy views. However, Belgian prisoners and prison staff advocate a more disciplinary approach to the normalization of time-use than the approach underpinning the Belgian Prison Act, and favour more mandatory activities, such as education or regular meetings with a psychologist.

The daily and weekly routines in prison make time seem to pass more quickly, thereby reducing the painful effects of detention (see also O'Donnell, 2014; Shammas, 2014). This bitter sweet observation is in line with previous research findings (Irwin & Owen, 2005; O'Donnell, 2014; Shammas, 2014). While some would consider the reduction of painful effects by prison routines a normalization success, prisoners did worry about the harmful effects of this 'robot-like' existence in the longer term. The many concerns about not having to think for themselves and being expected to follow the clock show that prison routines fail to prepare prisoners for the rhythm of working life after release. It also reinforces a common finding in prison research, which Sykes (1958: 73–76) and Goffman (1961: 43) already identified as the '*terror of feeling radically demoted in the age-grading system*'. Telling is the fact that the same feeling was even regularly mentioned by prisoners in Leira.

The sense of autonomy over one's time-use requires at least some physical freedom. However, prisoners in the E building were relatively 'free' to use their spare time in the afternoon and were given the opportunity to eat together, to use the kitchen and make their own food, to play games or to watch TV. But instead of feeling an increased autonomy over time, they generally experienced this spare time as 'empty time' and expressed feelings of boredom and meaninglessness similar to those in Leuven prison. One possible explanation is that prisoners in Nermarka prison had higher expectations regarding activities and treatment than those in Leuven prison. They compared their own situation to the more favourable conditions in *Modulen*, while prisoners in Leuven had very low expectations of the system. A second possible explanation is that these prisoners also struggle with boredom when performing these daily life activities outside prison, since many prisoners have a high need for excitement and a low tolerance level for boredom (Shaffer et al., 1994). A third explanation is that prisoners might assess the meaningfulness of time-use in relation to their lives outside prison. While playing cards or chess with friends, and cooking and having dinner with family might be experienced as pleasant and meaningful ways to spend time, this is not the case for playing cards or chess and having dinner with fellow prisoners. This could explain why the 'free time' in Leira prison was also experienced as boring and being 'killed' by sleeping and playing cards, even though these prisoners had both a high degree of autonomy over the use of time and the freedom to initiate activities outside of the prison. It is therefore important to bear in mind, even when advocating an intrinsic approach to normalization, that what is considered a meaningful time-use in society might not be considered meaningful inside prison.

In *Modulen* and Leira prisons, the use of time was normalized in an instrumental and rather disciplinary way, at both the level of the sentence and that of everyday life. This means that time spent in these sections is supposed to prepare prisoners, under close supervision, for a crime and drug-free life after release. At the level of the sentence, this means that prisoners get access to rehabilitation programmes and practical help with their reintegration process. At the level of everyday life, this normalization process entails many mandatory activities, including work or education in the daytime as well as mandatory group conversations, individual sessions and sports activities. Participation in other leisure activities is also mandatory in *Modulen* but not in Leira prison. Instead of waiting for release, as described by the prisoners in other sections, prisoners in Leira and *Modulen* use their time to prepare for their release. From a rights-based approach to normalization, it could be argued that the right to these activities and services also entails the right *not* to make use of these services, while this instrumental approach to normalization in *Modulen* and Leira has turned many of these rights into duties. Nevertheless, this '*tight*' and at the same time '*shallow*' (Crewe, 2011, 2021; Crewe & Ievins, 2021) implementation of imprisonment was experienced as more meaningful than imprisonment in the other sections, and for some prisoners even a chance to make a new start in life, which might not have been possible without their being imprisoned.

References

Beyens, K., De Koster, K., Kloeck, K., Beckmann, M., Breuls, L., Scheirs, V., Snacken, S., & Vanhouche, A.-S. (2016, 7 May). Onze gevangenissen staan in brand. *De Morgen*. www.demorgen.be/nieuws/onze-gevangenissen-staan-in-brand~b20ecad3/. Last accessed on 7 August 2021.

Bottoms, A. E., Hay, W., & Sparks, J. R. (1990). Situational and social approaches to the prevention of disorder in long-term prisons. *The Prison Journal, 70*(1), 83–95.

Christie, N. (1982). *Limits to pain*. Robertson.

Cohen, S., & Taylor, L. (1972). *Psychological survival: The experience of long-term imprisonment*. Penguin.

Crawford, A., & Hutchinson, S. (2016). Mapping the contours of 'everyday security': Time, space and emotion. *British Journal of Criminology, 56*(6), 1184–1202.

Crewe, B. (2011). Depth, weight, tightness: Revisiting the pains of imprisonment. *Punishment & Society, 13*(5), 509–529.

Crewe, B. (2021). The depth of imprisonment. *Punishment & Society, 23*(3), 335–354. https://doi.org/10.1177/1462474520952153

Crewe, B., Hulley, S., & Wright, S. (2017). Swimming with the tide: Adapting to long-term imprisonment. *Justice Quarterly, 34*(3), 517–541.

Crewe, B., & Ievins, A. (2021). 'Tightness', recognition and penal power. *Punishment & Society, 23*(1), 47–68.

Dupont, L. (1998). *Proeve van een voorontwerp van beginselenwet gevangeniswezen en tenuitvoerlegging van vrijheidsstraffen: Basisteksten, 30 september 1997*. KU Leuven.

Gini, A. (2003). *The importance of being Lazy: In praise of play, leisure, and vacations*. Routledge.

Goffman, E. (1961). *Asylums. Essays on the social situation of mental patients and other inmates*. Penguin books ltd.

Haney, C. (2003). Mental health issues in long-term solitary and 'supermax' confinement. *Crime and Delinquency, 49*(1), 124–156.

Hughes, E. (2012). *Education in prison: Studying through distance learning*. Ashgate Publishing Limited.

Hulley, S., Crewe, B., & Wright, S. (2016). Re-examining the problems of long-term imprisonment. *The British Journal of Criminology, 56*(4), 769–792.

Irwin, J., & Owen, B. (2005). Harm and the contemporary prison. In. A. Liebling & S. Maruna (Eds.), *The effects of imprisonment* (pp. 94–117). Willan Publishing.

Johnsen, B. (2018). Movement in the prison landscape: Leisure activities—Inside, outside and in-between. In E. Fransson, F. Giofrè, & B. Johnsen (Eds.), *Prison, architecture and humans* (pp. 65–85). Cappelen Damm Akademisk/NOASP (Nordic Open Access Scholarly Publishing).

Johnson, R., Rocheleau, A. M., & Martin, A. B. (2016). *Hard time: A fresh look at understanding and reforming prison* (4th ed.). Wiley-Blackwell.

Jones, H. L. (2007). *The pains of custody: How young men cope through the criminal justice system* (Thesis submitted for the Degree of Doctor of Philosophy in the University of Hull, UK).

Knight, V. (2016). *Remote control: Television in prison* (1st ed.). Palgrave Macmillan.

Liebling, A. (1999). Prison suicide and prisoner coping. *Crime and Justice, 26*, 283–359 (Chicago, IL).

Liebling, A. (2011). Moral performance, inhuman and degrading treatment and prison pain. *Punishment & Society, 13*(5), 530–550.

Meyvis, W. (2002). Van private reclassering naar maatschappelijke dienstverlening aan justitiecliënteel. In M. Bouverne-De Bie, K. Kloeck, W. Meyvis, R. Roose, & J. Vanacker (Eds.), *Handboek Forensisch Welzijnswerk* (pp. 37–76). Academia Press.

Middlemass, K. M., & Smiley, C. J. (2016). Doing a bid. *The Prison Journal, 96*(6), 793–813 (Philadelphia, PA).

Mjåland, K. (2016). Exploring prison drug use in the context of prison-based drug rehabilitation. *Drugs: Education, Prevention and Policy, 23*(2), 154–162.

Moran, D. (2012). "Doing time" in carceral space: Timespace and carceral geography. *Geografiska Annaler. Series B, Human Geography, 94*(4), 305–316.

Moran, D. (2013). Between outside and inside? Prison visiting rooms as liminal carceral spaces. *GeoJournal, 78*(2), 339–351.
O'Donnell, I. (2014). *Prisoners, solitude, and time* (Clarendon Studies in Criminology). Oxford University Press.
O'Donnell, I. (2016). The aims of imprisonment. In Y. Jewkes, J. Bennett, & B. Crewe (Eds.), *Handbook on prisons* (2nd ed., pp. 39–54). Routledge.
Polfliet, K. (2015). De Vlaamse hulp- en dienstvelening en de federale Basiswet: twee handen op één buik?! In T. Daems, C. Hermans, F. Janssens, J. Millen, L. Robert, & V. Scheirs (Eds.), *Quo vadis? Tien jaar basiswet gevangeniswezen en rechtspositie van gedetineerden* (pp. 79–104). Maklu.
Rocheleau, A. M. (2013). An empirical exploration of the 'pains of imprisonment' and the level of prison misconduct and violence. *Criminal Justice Review, 38*(3), 354–374.
Schinkel, M. (2014). *Being imprisoned: Punishment, Adaptation and Desistance* (Palgrave Studies in Prisons and Penology). Palgrave Macmillan.
Shaffer, C., Waters, W., & Adams, S. (1994). Dangerousness: Assessing the risk of violent behavior. *Journal of Consulting and Clinical Psychology, 62*(5), 1064–1068.
Shammas, V. L. (2014). The pains of freedom: Assessing the ambiguity of Scandinavian penal exceptionalism on Norway's Prison Island. *Punishment & Society, 16*(1), 104–123.
Shea, E. (2005). Les paradoxes de la normalisation du travail pénitentiaire en France et en Allemagne. *Déviance et Société, 29*(3), 349–365.
Snacken, S. (2005). Forms of violence and regimes in prison: Report of research in Belgian prisons. In A. Liebling & S. Maruna (Eds.), *The effects of imprisonment* (pp. 306–339). Willan Publishing.
Sykes, G. (1958). *The society of captives: A study of a maximum security prison.* Princeton University Press.
van der Kaap-Deeder, J., Audenaert, E., Vandevelde, S., Soenens, B., Van Mastrigt, S., Mabbe, E., & Vansteenkiste, M. (2017). Choosing when choices are limited: The role of perceived afforded choice and autonomy in prisoners' well-being. *Law and Human Behavior, 41*(6), 567–578.

van Zyl Smit, D., & Snacken, S. (2009). *Principles of European Prison Law and policy. Penology and human rights*. Oxford University Press.

Wener, R. E. (2012). *The Environmental Psychology of Prisons and Jails: Creating Humane Spaces in Secure Settings*. Cambridge University Press.

Wright, S., Crewe, B., & Hulley, S. (2017). Suppression, denial, sublimation: Defending against the initial pains of very long life sentences. *Theoretical Criminology, 21*(2), 225–246.

Zamble, E., &. Porporino, F. J. (1988). *Coping, behavior, and adaptation in prison inmates*. Springer.

8

Normalization, Punishment and Exceptionalism: What Do Normalized Prison Conditions Teach Us About Societies?

For all its conceptual complexities and practical challenges, one basic truth about studying normalization is that it tells us something about life in prison as much as about life outside prison. The concept both reveals how society perceives and portrays itself and provides a deeper understanding of prison policies and practices. Hence, normalization is a complex and above all revealing concept to study in a comparative perspective. The previous chapters have discussed the normalization of various dimensions of prison life (material environment, security, social environment and time-use) and have done so by focusing on the policy intentions and their 'translation' into legislation and into daily practices in two Belgian and two Norwegian prisons. Two fundamental findings underpinned the design of those chapters: first, only a holistic approach taking into account all dimensions of prison life can lead to a proper understanding of normalization, and, second, the combination of analysing law and policy on the one hand and looking to the prison practice on the other is of utmost importance for this purpose. This concluding chapter will now zoom out and consider the role of normalization in the wider macro-level debate in comparative penology.

H. De Vos, *Beyond Scandinavian Exceptionalism*, Palgrave Studies in Prisons and Penology, https://doi.org/10.1007/978-3-031-28635-3_8

As presented in the introduction, Scandinavian countries have been labelled 'exceptional' for their relatively low detention rates and relatively humane prison conditions (Pratt, 2008a, 2008b; Pratt & Eriksson, 2013). These two statements are largely true in comparison with most Western countries, including Belgium. However, when explaining these exceptional characteristics in his well-known 2008 articles, John Pratt also argued that the humane conditions in Scandinavian prisons resulted from the recognition in these countries that '*prison [...] itself [is] the punishment for crime*' and that '*prison conditions can then approximate to life outside as far as possible*' (Pratt, 2008a: 119). In so doing, he linked the humane prison conditions in Scandinavian countries to the normalization principle. Again, there is some truth in this statement, but the previous chapters have shown that this understanding of normalization is oversimplified and therefore inaccurate. Even though such use of normalization is intuitive and common, it has limited analytical value for comparative research. The detailed comparisons in the previous chapters allowed to point out some inaccurate assumptions and over-generalizations that have characterized many macro-sociological comparisons. While Pratt suggested that the normalization principle is somehow characteristic of the Scandinavian prison policies, the principle is indeed also central to the Belgian prison policy and is in fact reflected much more prominently in the Belgian Prison Act than in the Norwegian. Moreover, Belgium, as a corporatist welfare state with a multiparty political system, is much more similar to the Scandinavian countries, including Norway, than the Anglo-Saxon countries that are commonly used as benchmarks in comparative penology. Trying to understand in what ways normalization is linked to the Scandinavian exceptionalism thesis or to resisting any rising punitiveness inevitably entails reflecting on the core features and starting points of the principle, as well as on the notion of punishment and society in general. For this purpose, this chapter aims to establish the link between the findings at micro-level, i.e. the level of the four prisons and the individuals involved, and the debate at macro-level, i.e. the level of societies.

8.1 Normalization as a Process: Insights from the Four Prisons in Comparative and Holistic Perspective

Normalization sounds misleadingly simple. This was already pointed out by Wolfensberger (1983/2011: 436), who stated that the vast majority of readers '*assume – usually wrongly – that they know "what it means"*'. While the normalization principle is commonly used to argue for better prison conditions or to explain the high material standards in Scandinavian prisons, normalizing the prison conditions is not the same as modernizing or improving these conditions. As explained and illustrated in the previous chapters, the normalization principle establishes the link between living conditions inside and outside prison. In this sense, normalization can be compared to a mirror. When looking in a mirror, we see a reflection of reality. This reflection differs depending on the qualities of the mirror, the part of reality that has been reflected and the perspective from which we look at the mirror. At an abstract level, it is quite easy to assert that the living conditions in prison should resemble those outside prison as much as possible, or, as stipulated in the European Prison Rules, '*approximate as closely as possible the positive aspects of life in the community*'. At a more concrete level, however, it becomes clear that only parts of the living conditions outside prison are reflected inside prison, and that only parts of the prison conditions are included in the normalization process. This partial reflection is inevitable since, unlike people outside prison, prisoners are deprived of their liberty, and this liberty deprivation takes place in a penal institution. Without these restrictions, the normalization principle would lose its meaning. Normalization is therefore best understood as the process of making prison life, or certain aspects of prison life (i.e. the 'focus areas'), approximate as closely as possible the reference points from outside prison that were chosen for this purpose (i.e. the intended results of the normalization process). Given that this process is both relative and subjective, this seemingly simple notion leads to quite diverging policy, legislative and practical 'translations' in different jurisdictions. This also explains why Pratt's reference to normalization did not strengthen his case for the exceptional character of Nordic prisons.

8.1.1 Normalization Is Essentially Relative and Subjective

Since normalization always assumes a reference to the living conditions in prison in relation to those in society, the principle is *relative* in essence. Hence, comparing the normalization of prison conditions in Belgium and Norway de facto entails a relative comparison of the relationship between the living conditions in Belgian prisons and those in Belgian society, on the one hand, and the relationship between living conditions in Norwegian prisons and those in Norwegian society, on the other. This relative dimension also entails that normalization is an ongoing process, since the living conditions in society evolve quickly, especially in terms of technology and digitalization (Engbo, 2017; Liebling, 2004; Smith, 2012). For such relative comparison, it is important to bear in mind that there are cultural differences between the two countries, such as different eating practices, but also that the living standards in the Norwegian society are generally higher than those in the Belgian. In 2018, Norway had the world's highest Human Development Index, while Belgium was listed 17th in this world ranking of the UN (UNDP, 2019). This difference was also reflected in the subjective life satisfaction of their respective inhabitants. According to the most recent OECD report on this topic, Norwegians gave their general life satisfaction a 7.6 on a scale from 0 to 10, while Belgians gave it a 6.9 on average (OECD, 2020). Without discussing these numbers any further, they suggest that applying the same normalization process in both countries would result in higher living standards in the Norwegian prisons than in the Belgian. The bare corridors of Leuven and Hoogstraten prison did indeed contrast with the homey-looking living units in Nermarka and Leira prison, equipped with living rooms and kitchens. At the same time, this comparison also showed that the gap between the material conditions inside and outside prison was much wider in Belgium. The two Belgian prisons were built over 150 years ago, making it challenging to provide material comfort in terms of thermal and sound insulation, ventilation and hygiene. Moreover, these buildings were neither designed nor structurally converted with the view of normalizing the living conditions inside, as was the case for the two Norwegian prisons.

Considering these major differences between the Belgian and Norwegian prisons, it is worth repeating that the four prisons of this study were considered case studies and not representative for all prisons in the two countries. The only selection criterion was the security level, assuming that the conditions in low-security or open prisons would be more normalized than those in high-security or closed prisons. Without generalizing to all prisons in the two countries, the *material* living conditions in the two Norwegian prisons were undeniably more normalized than those in the two Belgian prisons. Of course, materiality is only one dimension of prison life, and scholars who have identified the most painful aspects of prison life, or the aspects that 'matter most', have pointed to the social dimension rather than the material conditions (Liebling, 2004, 2011; Rocheleau, 2013). Hancock and Jewkes (2011) even warned for the downsides of highly modern material conditions, such as '*near-constant surveillance*' and high demands in terms of self-discipline. Nevertheless, the comparison of these four prisons showed that the material environment is crucial for the normalization of prison life, as it literally provides the framework within which a normalized life can be given form. Not in the sense of high-tech security or material luxury, but in the sense of a material context that supports the normalization of the other dimensions. This was much more the case in the Norwegian prisons than in the Belgian. For instance, while officially being an open prison with a 'communal regime', Hoogstraten prison did not have living rooms or kitchens for common use, which seriously limited the opportunities to establish a community life in this prison. This was also the case for Leuven prison, where the nineteenth-century building was not equipped with living units or adequate workshops which could have supported the normalization of the social interactions and activities in this prison. This demonstrates that, given the interdependence of these dimensions, it is not possible to normalize only those aspects of the prison conditions that are identified as most painful or most relevant. Social interactions may well be a dimension of prison life that matters most, but if the basic materiality does not provide for any occasion of social interaction or other material conditions hamper interactions in more subtle ways, the efforts to normalize the social environment will matter much less or even not at all. And this is just one example. Hence the need to normalize these dimensions together and with respect for the entire prison context, including the material one.

In terms of social contact with family and friends, the Belgian prisons were actually more normalized than the Norwegian. The difference was most striking with respect to incoming prisoners. While incoming prisoners in Nermarka were socially isolated for several weeks for the purpose of the criminal investigation, those in Leuven were entitled to daily visits in order to respect the presumption of innocence. Of course, it could be the case that family support is considered more important in the Belgian society than in the Norwegian, and that the observed difference thus resulted from the relative nature of normalization. A recent European comparison of the responsibilities of adult children towards their parents and vice-versa indeed showed that the Norwegian respondents had the lowest sense of family responsibilities out of the thirteen European countries involved in the study. However, the Belgians' sense of responsibility towards family was found to be only slightly higher (Herlofson et al., 2019). Perhaps more relevant in this context is that 'more normalized' means here that the visits and phone calls in Belgium were less restricted in terms of frequency and variety of people that could visit or be called; that the phone calls were generally not listened to; that under certain conditions, prisoners, including remand prisoners, were entitled to unsupervised visits (conjugal or family visits); and that prisoners could enforce their legal rights in this context. It does not mean, however, that prisoners in Leuven and Hoogstraten could actually maintain contact with their loved ones in a similar way as they would do outside prison. Moreover, an important side note is that the rules concerning phone calls were less restricting in Leira than in Nermarka, and that prisoners in Leira were more regularly allowed to leave the prison for five hours or for the weekend, enabling them to maintain contact with relatives even without regular visits or phone calls in prison. This side note only reinforces the fact that the relative character of normalization does not entail that all prisons in a given society are normalized in the same way or to the same degree. The differences between prisons in one jurisdiction were already pointed out before (e.g. Drake et al., 2015; Johnsen & Granheim, 2012; Liebling, 2004, 2011), but the comparison of these four prisons also showed that the way in which and degree to which some dimensions of prison life were normalized in practice differed more strongly between the two prisons in the same country than between prisons in the two different countries. This further nuances the idea that Scandinavian prisons are generally more normalized.

Hoogstraten and Leuven prison differed significantly in terms of daytime activities. While most prisoners in Hoogstraten could participate in professional or educational programmes in daytime, and additionally in various courses or sports activities in the evening, which is common outside prison, most prisoners in Leuven spent the vast majority of time inside their cells, watching TV or doing nothing at all. Having too much time on their hands was one of the main concerns of prisoners in Leuven, as they feared for negative effects on their mental health in the shorter and longer term. As a consequence, the differences with the living conditions in society were in this prison predominantly determined by the time dimension. This was strikingly similar to the stories about the A building of Nermarka prison. The main difference between the regimes in Leuven and the A building was that the latter resulted from a deliberate policy to isolate prisoners at the start of their incarceration period (with the criminal investigation in mind), whereas the isolation in Leuven prison largely resulted from inadequate material context and limited resources to organize meaningful professional and educational programmes for all prisoners. The monotonous routines in Hoogstraten prison, on the other hand, were strikingly similar to those in the E building of Nermarka prison. While prisoners in the E building seemed to have more autonomy over the use of time in the afternoons, thanks to the living room and kitchen at their disposal, the routines still made them live, in their words, like '*zombies*', '*on autopilot*' and '*brainlessly*'.

A notable similarity between all four prisons was the way in which social services were normalized, both in legislation and in practice. Based on the so-called import model, service providers such as teachers, social assistants and psychologists entered the prisons to provide prisoners with the same services as other citizens. This was noted by Pratt (2008a: 120) as one of the remarkable features of Scandinavian prison conditions, but this is organized in a very similar way in Belgium. In both countries, the underlying idea is that prisoners are still entitled to these services and that this way of working facilitates the reintegration. In practice, this means that teachers, for instance, give the same classes inside and outside prison. As a result, they use their classes outside prison as reference point for *normal* classes, including teaching materials, the content, level and duration of the classes, the teacher-student interaction and the interaction among the students. Thus, the import model has two major benefits for normalization. Firstly, the fact that external service providers continue to use their services outside prison as benchmarks for normal services makes it easier for them to resemble the services from outside prison. Prisoners and prison staff, by contrast, who had become used to the restrictions of the prison context, had the tendency to assess the 'relatively' normalized conditions in one prison in the light of the highly abnormal living conditions in another or argued that interrupting a class half-way for a head count, for instance, was 'normal in prison'. Secondly, a stable level of normalization requires the living conditions in prison to evolve at the same pace as those outside prison. When service providers work both inside and outside prison, they will notice when developments in society are not being followed inside prison, and will try to reduce the growing discrepancies if this is practically possible. Thus, the import model really embodies the relative character of the normalization principle. It should be noted, however, that these benefits diminish when these 'external' service providers are in practice working full-time inside the prison.

Besides being relative, normalization is also *subjective*. The more concrete the process becomes, the more apparent its subjective character. In fact, there are two distinct ways in which normalization is subjective. I will explain both using the mirror metaphor again. Firstly, the reflection in the mirror will differ according to which part of reality was placed in front of the mirror. Similarly, the normalized prison conditions will differ according to which living conditions from outside prison were used as benchmarks. This always involves a subjective assessment, since the variety of the living conditions that are considered normal outside prison cannot entirely be implemented inside prison. Is it more normal, for instance, to eat together than to eat alone? For people who live alone, which is more than one-third of all Belgians (statbel, 2020) and about one-fifth of all Norwegians (Statistisk Sentralbyrå, 2020), eating alone will arguably be more normal than eating collectively. For others, it is arguably more normal to eat with people from their household, but even then, eating collectively with other prisoners or prison staff is somewhat artificial and not necessarily experienced as 'normal'. In both prison policy and practice, choices are made, and these choices are made from a *subjective* point of view. This is still true when policymakers have defined these 'normal conditions' based on allegedly generally accepted standards, or when this is done pragmatically rather than deliberately.

Secondly, the reflection in the mirror will differ according to the perspective from which one looks at the mirror, i.e. the perspective from which the prison conditions are perceived or experienced. This is of course also subjective: the same conditions can be considered normal by one individual and abnormal by another. As a general rule, the greater the autonomy, for instance to decide on the time budget or on cooking, the bigger the group of prisoners who can experience the prison conditions as resembling those outside. The question whether or not the subjective perspective of the individual prisoner should be taken into account is at heart of the debate between *subjectivists* (like Ashworth, 2011; Bronsteen et al., 2009; Kolber, 2009; Neumann, 2012; Raaijmakers et al., 2014) and *objectivists* (like Markel et al., 2011; Pratt & Eriksson, 2012). The answer will depend on the aims associated with the normalization process. When the main aim is to reduce the painful and harmful effects of detention, as advocated by the Belgian prison policy, the subjective experience of individual prisoners is very relevant indeed. Because common meals, for instance, can reduce the distress of isolation for some prisoners, but increase distress for those who fear physical victimization, the best way to reduce painful and harmful effects is to give prisoners the choice (but in the two Belgian prisons, prisoners ate alone in their cell). Yet, if normalization is aimed to create the right conditions to encourage prisoners to change their way of life, as advocated by Norwegian prison policy, it becomes less relevant whether or not individual prisoners experience these conditions as normal. Common meals or other group activities will then be considered a successful implementation of the normalization process, as they provide prisoners with an opportunity to improve their social skills, also, and in fact even more so, when these moments cause distress to less socially-minded individuals. Both in Belgium and in Norway, policymakers defining normalized prison conditions take into account a framework of societal norms and standards, consciously or unconsciously, and prisoners experience the degree of normalization in relation to their own framework of norms and standards. This is the key difficulty of normalization, and it is also the main reason why normalization should always be studied combining policy goals and its legislative and practical translations.

8.1.2 Normalization Is the Interplay Between Policy and Practice

The study of policy documents and legislation in Chapter 3 showed that the Belgian Prison Act reflects the normalization principle much more systematically than the Norwegian, providing prisoners with a legal basis to formally enforce their rights. Indeed, it explicitly and specifically defines prisoners' rights in terms of material conditions, activities, social services and contact with people outside prison, even though some of these rights are restricted to such an extent that the normalizing value is being undermined. The Norwegian Act on the Execution of Sentences, by contrast, does not repeat the intention to normalize the prison conditions for each aspect, nor to systematically protect prisoners' rights. On the contrary, the security restrictions are made more explicit than the intention to normalize the living conditions. In fact, if one of the two penal philosophies were to be called 'exceptional', it would be the Belgian one. However, this philosophy has only partly been translated into the Prison Act of 12 January 2005, with regular amendments to the original bill over the years and its implementation facing many difficulties (see Daems, 2010; Snacken, 2015). The Norwegian normalization principle, on the other hand, is left more implicit in the Act, but is at the same time more deeply embedded in the prison policy and social policy. This appears to have proven relevant for its implementation in practice. Indeed, the prison practice showed another picture. The discrepancies between the intended results of the normalization process and the results in practice were much greater in the two Belgian than in the two Norwegian prisons. The far-reaching philosophical policy principles underlying the Belgian Prison Act were met with a sobering awareness of major practical and security restrictions, while the more pragmatic approach in Norway was implemented more consistently in the prison practice.

Just this short review reveals how important the combination of policy and practice was for a thorough and nuanced view of normalization in both countries. It shows that the conclusions of this research on normalization would have been fundamentally different without that combination of policy, legislation and practice. Focusing on policy and legislation alone could have resulted in jumping to the conclusion that Belgium is far more ambitious—or even 'exceptional'—when it comes to normalization compared to Norway. Focusing on prison practice alone could have further reinforced the caricature of Belgium lagging behind with normalization because of centuries-old prisons and a lack of resources. Combining both made for nuance and depth in the picture of normalization as a process, translating a principle into reality. The combination made it clear that normalization does not just exist on a policy level and on a practical level, but that it exists also in the interplay between both. Let us have a look at the two main examples of that interplay.

First, in the ideal situation, prison policy largely shapes the prison practice and consequently the experiences with the prison practice. Since the policy interpretation of normalization differs significantly between Belgium and Norway, comparing the practices as if they existed in a vacuum would only tell us part of the story. The fact that normalization is in Norway understood as a principle that contributes directly and proactively to the punishment aims helps for a consistent implementation of the principle in practice. It means that prison officers are supposed to actively contribute to the normalization of prison life (through social interaction and activities) and at the same time to the punishment aims to reduce recidivism and ensure public safety. This is a simple logic: normalization leads to better results during and after imprisonment. This logic is more clearly reflected in the discourse of people in practice, than in the relevant legislation. In particular, in Leira and *Modulen*, prison officers play a crucial role in the normalization of prison life *and* in the implementation of the punishment aims. These normalized, but demanding, regimes are also most in line with prisoners's expectations of what prisons should look like in Norway.

Aligning the Belgian intrinsic approach to normalization with daily prison life and prison officers' work is built on a more abstract reasoning than the instrumental. For instance, the relative autonomy between the sentencing aims and the aims of the execution of the sentence entails that prison officers do not contribute to the implementation of the sentencing aims, but only to the aims of the execution of the punishment (i.e. reintegration, rehabilitation and restoration). On top of that, this intrinsic approach only relates *indirectly* to these aims, since creating a normalized context is considered an end in itself. Of course, the distinction between an intrinsic and an instrumental approach is an analytical distinction that is not found in its pure form in policy or practice, neither in Belgium nor in Norway. The rather intrinsic approach reflected in the Belgian policy documents has also many instrumental elements. The importance attached to dynamic security is one example, as it is the *instrumental* use of social interaction between prisoners and prison officers to increase the level of security in prison. Valuing such dynamic security over the use of static security is commonly seen as a way of normalizing prison life. It has also been linked to the quality of prison life, since Liebling (2004, 2011) found that the way in which prison staff uses its authority contributes *disproportionately* to prisoners' evaluation of fairness and ultimately to their well-being. Nevertheless, dynamic security fits very well within the consistent instrumental approach in Norway, but is less consistent with the largely intrinsic philosophy advocated by the Prison Act Commission and still reflected in the Belgian Prison Act. This requires Belgian prison officers to work in a less consistent framework than the Norwegian.

Moreover, the far-reaching philosophical policy principle underlying the Belgian Prison Act is also difficult to align with the reality prisoners and prison staff are confronted with. This gap between '*law in the books*' and '*law in action*' (Matthews, 2005; Nelken, 2003) affected the credibility of the prison policy and its normalization principle. Prisoners' rights are emphasized in a prison context in which it is impossible to ensure these rights due to practical difficulties that are (seemingly or actually) beyond anyone's control, such as the old buildings and limited financial resources. The emphasis is on *voluntary* participation in a wide range of activities, but participation turns out in their favour in the decision about conditional release. Furthermore, prisoners can legally enforce their rights, but this is to be done in writing while not all prisoners can write. Finally, some prison officers have the feeling that their rights are considered less important than those of prisoners. The strength and weakness of the intrinsic approach to normalization are that it is value-based: protecting human dignity and human rights as a purpose in itself. This also means that its value cannot be 'proven' to people who remain sceptical, for instance prisoners and prison staff who are confronted with these tensions or paradoxes in the prison practice. A prison officer summarized her views in this respect as follows: '*the Prison Act is a lot of blah blah, you know, it was written by criminologists who have never seen the inside of a prison*' (Field notes 4 November 2015, Leuven prison).

Second, because policy and legislation raise expectations in practice. Prisoners' expectations of prison life, and of normalized prison life, differ according to cultural, social and personal views and habits. But different policies also raise different expectations in prisoners. Unmet expectations can affect the prison experience negatively, regardless of the actual practices (Sexton, 2015). Similarly, experienced inconsistencies are a major cause of frustration (see also Crewe & Ievins, 2021), that is: experiences which go against one's expectations based on previous experiences, stories from others, or official policy or rules. Expectations and experiences vary from person to person, but overall Norwegian and Belgian prisoners had very different expectations about certain aspects of the prison system, such as the social interaction with prison officers. Norwegian prison officers, and in particular in their capacity as *contact officers*, are supposed to support prisoners with their reintegration. These specific tasks are not part of the job description of Belgian prison officers. In practice, prisoners in Belgium assessed these interactions positively when prison officers were polite and opened the doors at the right times. Norwegian prisoners, on the other hand, expected prison officers to actively assist them, for instance with communication with social services. Consequently, Norwegian prisoners were dissatisfied when staff members failed to support them effectively, and paradoxically, they complained more often about the prison officers, even though those in Norway were in general more supportive than those in Belgium. The same example also showed that prisoners who had been living in another country had different expectations of prison life. This became most clear in Nermarka prison, where the increasing proportion of foreign national prisoners did cause tensions on a daily basis. The tensions that I observed were rather minor, despite the many complaints by many Norwegian prisoners and prison staff about the increasingly violent atmosphere allegedly due to foreign national prisoners, and the many complaints by many foreign national prisoners about racism and discrimination. Foreign national prisoners were usually *more* satisfied with the material prison conditions, but other aspects, like the system of *contact officers*, caused misunderstandings. While Norwegian prisoners would only complain about their contact officers being not supportive or proactive enough, foreign national prisoners who were not used to this kind of support were sceptical about these prison officers who were in their opinion excessively intrusive, and therefore refused to share any personal information with them.

Taken together, all of the reflections above on the interplay between policy and practice might lead to three important conclusions. First, the way in which policymakers formulate normalization *as a principle* will affect the credibility and feasibility in practice. Second, making the policy approach to normalization and the related aims explicit will not only contribute to a good understanding of the normalization process itself, but is also necessary to understand the relationship between normalization and the punishment aims. And third, consistency between policy views and views of prison staff and prisoners might be one of the most important factors for successfully normalizing the prison conditions. An excellent example of these three conclusions was Leira prison, arguably the most normalized of the four prisons even when taking into account all of the similarities, differences and nuances between the prisons mentioned earlier. At least part of that success can be explained by the fact that its prison organization in general and its implementation of the normalization principle in specific were very much in tune with the explicitly instrumental interpretation of normalization in Norwegian policy and its legislative translations.

The living conditions in Leira prison came very close to those outside prison. In fact, its homey design, green and open surroundings, atmosphere, smells, sounds and individuals involved did not give a prison impression at all. At first sight, it was impossible to recognize this as a prison or to distinguish prison staff from prisoners, given the absence of static security measures and uniforms. Moreover, prisoners would regularly leave the prison premises for sports and leisure activities, shopping and library visits. Private customers, on their part, could buy their plants in the garden centre of Leira prison without noticing that it was located on the prison premises or that they were being assisted by prisoners or prison staff. Hence, these aspects of the living conditions did not just *resemble* those outside prison but *were* the conditions in society, including the small talk in the shop or library, and the Norwegian forests and mountains where some sports and leisure activities took place.

When looking more closely, however, this seemingly all-encompassing normalization process was indeed just a *partial* reflection of the Norwegian society. The 'focus areas' and intended results were chosen deliberately and implemented consistently to normalize the prison conditions instrumentally. Instrumentally in the sense that these normalized conditions served the punishment aims. The comfortable material conditions, close interaction among prisoners and staff, the relatively high degree of freedom of movement on the prison premises, and to some degree beyond, and the relatively high degree of autonomy over one's time-use were part of a broader policy. This policy also included mandatory participation in certain activities (work or education, group conversations and meetings, individual counselling, two-weekly walks and some other social activities), a very strict drug policy, and high levels of social control and self-discipline. All together, these normalized conditions were explicitly instrumental to provide prisoners with '*tools to live a crime and drug-free life after release*' and with insights into their own behavioural choices and into the consequences of these choices.

In short, the implementation of normalization in practice matched the punishment aims and the underlying policy goals of normalization, and prisoners' expectations of this type of instrumentally used open prisons, based at least partially on Norwegian penal policy, were met. Put differently, going back to my definition of normalization as a process, the start of the process (formulating policy aims, carefully and deliberately selecting 'focus areas', and identifying intended results) went smoothly on to its implementation in practice. This example of Leira prison might also constitute a good lesson for research on normalization: not only how important it is to investigate policy and practice and their interplay, but also how vital it is to flesh out the entire normalization process in its context down to the micro-level before making any claims about the punitiveness, mildness or humaneness of a certain penal system—as well as its supposed 'exceptional' nature, on which more below.

8.1.3 Normalization Is a Holistic Process Rather Than a Fixed Result

Leira also demonstrated how important the *holistic* implementation of this whole normalization process was. Holistic not in the sense that every single dimension of prison life had to be normalized in its own right, but rather in the sense that the normalization of each dimension mutually reinforced the normalization of the other dimensions and thus constituted a normalized experience as a whole. For instance, the normalization of the social interactions was supported by the small scale of the prison, so that prisoners and staff knew each other, and by the various living rooms and well-equipped kitchen that were used by prisoners and staff alike. The close social interactions allowed in turn for a high degree of dynamic security and social control/self-discipline among prisoners, to the extent that the static security became redundant, which contributed to, but was also stimulated by, the homey material environment. The material availability of the garden centre, car workshop and horse stable provided for daytime activities for all prisoners, which were generally assessed more positively by prisoners than those in Nermarka prison. Future-oriented activities were considered most meaningful by prisoners, but their implementation was enabled by the fact that prisoners felt safe and comfortable enough to reflect upon their life after release in concrete and practical terms (thus supported by the material and social environment). Hence, the time-use, social environment, material environment and security were all normalized as a whole for the purpose of preparing a crime and drug-free life after release.

The comparison with the other prisons has shown that, if not addressed holistically, 'normalized' aspects could cause unwanted side effects in practice or even lead to more 'abnormal' practices. While the practice of eating together (prisoners and prison staff) contributed to a relaxed and constructive atmosphere in Leira prison (and also in *Modulen* in Nermarka prison), prisoners in Leuven ate individually inside their cells and also preferred it that way, since they feared that eating collectively would increase interpersonal tensions and distress in the given context. The same was observed in the context of security. Leira was the only prison where security and normalization went smoothly hand in hand and mutually reinforced each other. That is: security based on low levels of static security in combination with high levels of dynamic and organizational security as well as self-discipline, and an interpretation of normalization that is instrumental and rather disciplinary. The instrumental use of normalization in Leira led to and built on the effective self-discipline of and by prisoners, since they were well aware that they would be sent back to a high-security prison if they violated the prison rules. This played a less important role in Hoogstraten because it did not differ as much from the closed prisons as Leira prison did. The reduced level of static security in Hoogstraten prison, by contrast, was seen by prisoners and prison officers as security flaws or as indications that security was not taken very seriously, and was compensated by security routines and checks. Dynamic security was also important in the two Belgian prisons, but this *instrumental* use of social interaction to increase security and feelings of security did not match as well with the policies and the practices in Hoogstraten as it did in Leira.

The far-reaching, consistent and holistic implementation of the normalization process in Leira prison does not only stand out in comparison with the other prisons in Belgium and Norway. It is also revealing on a more fundamental level as it raises some key questions about punishment and liberty deprivation as *intended pain*.

8.2 Deprivation of Liberty as Punishment

Normalization builds on the acceptance that the deprivation of liberty should be the only intended punitive aspect of the prison sentence that causes the only intended painful effects. Prisoners therefore are to retain all their rights aside with the exception of the right to liberty, and their living conditions should resemble those outside prison as much as possible. In other words: normalization is the correction towards this 'pure' deprivation of liberty. It is an attempt to reduce the additional painful and harmful effects of imprisonment that are *not* directly or inextricably linked to the liberty deprivation. This also means that the liberty deprivation itself and its inevitable consequences lie *beyond* the scope of the normalization principle. The idea of a 'pure' deprivation of liberty, however, is a theoretical understanding of imprisonment that is not easily implemented in practice. Confinement *to* and *within* a penal institution by definition entails forced living together and being forced out of one's own social environment. So where does the 'pure' deprivation of liberty end, and do the additional, unintended pains of imprisonment begin? And this is not the only challenge. Some of the typical frustrations experienced in prison, it must be reminded, are not necessarily due to either the 'pure' deprivation of liberty or the practical implementation of imprisonment. In life outside prison, people also have frustrations, and 'complete freedom' is an illusion at least to a certain extent. Even the most liberal society sets limits to the 'freedom' of its citizens, and the similarities between prisons and other institutions in society have been pointed out (Foucault, 1977; Goffman, 1961). If citizens outside prison are frustrated about the long waiting lists for psychological help, or if they experience boredom or meaninglessness, similar frustrations in prison might not be intended 'pains' of the liberty deprivation but neither additional pains that should be prevented. Drawing a clear line between the 'intended painful effects' and 'unintended harmful effects' becomes even more complicated when taking into account all different policy objectives behind the punishment. Indeed, various punishment aims are linked to the prison sentence and thus shape the way in which the deprivation of liberty is given shape, without necessarily the intention to intensify or alleviate the *intended* pains. Long story short: it is still unclear which painful effects are directly and inextricably linked to the deprivation of liberty, and fall therefore beyond the scope of the normalization process.

And yet, for all the theoretical difficulty to define this 'pure' deprivation of liberty in academic debate, Leira prison offered a remarkable example. Based on the case of Leira, it is clear that many painful and harmful effects are not as 'inextricably linked' to the deprivation of liberty as often assumed or argued. At the same time, this case also shows which painful effects are indeed directly linked to the liberty deprivation and therefore *intended* pains. Crewe's concepts '*depth*' (Crewe, 2011a, 2021) and '*tightness*' (Crewe, 2011a; Crewe & Ievins, 2021) are helpful to understand the ways in which Leira prison is normalized and how this relates to the deprivation of liberty. The 'depth of imprisonment' refers to the '*distance from freedom*' and the '*impact of security and control measures on the prisoner's sense of autonomy and the remoteness of their existence*' (Crewe, 2021: 4). Applied to Leira prison, it is quite straightforward that this prison is meant to be '*shallow*' from a policy perspective, and that it is also experienced as such by the people involved: the distance to freedom is short, in physical and in temporal terms. Apart from the outside doors being locked at night, static security measures are completely absent, prisoners also regularly leave the prison premises in group and individually, and the garden centre is freely accessible to customers. As mentioned above, this means that some aspects of the living conditions of these prisoners do not just approximate those of other citizens but are exactly the same (e.g. the garden centre, shop, library, sports fields).

This closeness to freedom does not mean that the liberty deprivation is not felt by these prisoners. On the contrary, the more visible the freedom, the more tangible the liberty deprivation. As observed in other open prisons in Norway (Neumann, 2012; Shammas, 2014), the ongoing confrontations with freedom cause frustrations that do not exist in closed prisons (except in *Modulen*), i.e. frustrations caused by seeing life outside prison without being able to fully partake: prisoners continuously see what they are missing out on (e.g. drinking alcohol) and require a high level of self-discipline (prisoners cannot rely on physical walls to keep them inside). For instance, the bus that drives to the city centre has a stop right in front of Leira prison, and there is nothing but prisoners' self-discipline that stops them from getting on this bus. As prisoners would argue: '*In an open prison, there is an invisible fence*'. In closed prisons, by contrast, prisoners can close themselves in, focus on the prison-present and let time pass until they get released. At the same time, these confrontations with freedom prevent prisoners from losing touch with the outside world, including the small talk with strangers and the pace of life, which are hard to imitate in a closed institution but important after release. While Neumann (2012) and Shammas (2014) have convincingly argued that open prisons cause *different* pains rather than *less* pains, I argue here that a '*shallow*' prison like Leira, in which prisoners continue to be confronted with freedom, manages to focus on the *intended* pains of the liberty deprivation while limiting the *unintended* harmful effects: deprivation of liberty becomes really tangible (i.e. intended pain) and prisoners do not estrange as much as they do in deep-end prison (i.e. avoiding additional painful and harmful effects). In this sense, normalization has come close to its ultimate goal.

However, Leira prison is not only open or *shallow*, but also demanding and *tight*. Crewe and Ievins (2021: 48) have defined '*tightness*' as the grip of the prison on the prisoner. Starting from the prison system in England and Wales, the authors link this in the first place to high demands in terms of risk assessment and to '*soft power*' or the '*power of the pen*' (see also Crewe, 2011b). In Leira prison, the demands in terms of self-discipline are high and the social control and 'soft power' omnipresent and quite intrusive. As a consequence, staying in Leira was experienced as more demanding than staying in a closed prison. But these high demands did not emerge from actuarial risk assessment, as described by Crewe and Ievins (2021), and were not at odds with normalization. On the contrary, they smoothly merged with the way in which the living conditions were normalized in Leira prison and in Norwegian policy. Indeed, normalizing the prison conditions with the view of providing the right conditions for prisoners to change their way of life (rehabilitation) and to live a crime-free and drug-free life after release (reintegration) comes close to normalizing the 'deviant' person instead of the prison conditions. Ideally, prisoners are not just law-abiding citizens when they leave Leira prison, but also citizens who have a job, do sport, wear adequate clothing for each activity, know how to make a decent meal, have good contact with family and enjoy spending part of the weekend in the forests or mountains. Such proactive approach to normalization has been criticized for being paternalistic and '*forced social education*' (Engbo, 2017: 344). This may well be the case, and it is indeed debatable whether such conditions can be considered normal, but prisoners in Leira did not experience this interventionism as a source of additional pains. On the contrary, the demanding regimes of *Modulen* and Leira prison were experienced as less painful and less harmful than the less interventionist regimes of Nermarka prison. Staying in a shallow prison, like Leira, is and remains a prison sentence, and pretending that it is not, by refraining from intervening in people's current and future lives, does not make it any more normal. Equally important is that these experiences also indicate that prisoners believed that the interventions were in their best interest, and that staff and management, together with prisoners, had succeeded to create a safe and constructive atmosphere.

If this comes close to the best result that normalization can achieve in a penal institution, and thus to the 'pure' liberty deprivation, could and should these practices then be used as an example for the Belgian context too? Since I have argued that the consistency between policy views and views of prison staff and prisoners is one of the most important factors for this successful normalization process in Leira, it is unlikely that this would be equally successful in the Belgian context. Such tight and intrusive interventions do not fit well in the Belgian rights-based approach, and Belgian prisoners might experience such intrusion and self-discipline as additional pains, which would then be unintended pains additional to the liberty deprivation. This should not come as a surprise. This research has shown how important the context is when considering normalization, how all dimensions are interrelated and should be looked at holistically, making normalization not an easily transferable process. Nevertheless, Leira has served as excellent example to better understand the relationship between normalization and the 'pure' deprivation of liberty. It is only in a well-functioning ecosystem of normalization (*consistently* normalizing *all* dimensions of prison life) that the deprivation of liberty itself is experienced as the actual source of pains and frustrations, which are indeed *intended*, and not all kinds of institutional worries and concerns, which are too often the source of frustrations and pains in other prisons. This can also work in Belgium, as long as the normalization process is both conceived and implemented consistently.

8.3 'Scandinavian Exceptionalism' Through the Prism of Normalization

Considering all the above, what then is the role of the normalization principle in relation to the Scandinavian exceptionalism and the rising punitiveness? This is of course a tricky question since the use of both concepts 'Scandinavian exceptionalism' and 'punitiveness' has been challenged. Bearing in mind all legitimate questions and doubts raised concerning these concepts, the question I would rather address is what the normalization principle tells about society and its prison system, in a comparative perspective. Given the relative and subjective dimension of normalization, the results of the normalization process will only be as 'exceptional' or 'humane' as the society in which it is applied. Is the Norwegian society in any way more 'exceptional' or 'humane' than the Belgian? Or is this just another caricature like the popular stories about violent Vikings?

Normalization does not only show how a society sees its prisoners and other citizens, but above all how this society likes to see itself in the 'mirror of normalization'. Hence, normalized prison conditions reveal a society's 'self-image'. The premise of normalization and limiting the punishment to the deprivation of liberty, as most severe punishment, is in itself an expression of a government that perceives, or at least portrays, itself as humane. This is what Belgium and Norway have in common: their self-image of a humane society. Portraying itself in the official website brochure '*Belgium in a nutshell*', the Belgian government explains that Belgium is located at the heart of Europe, and that '*Europe is very close to Belgians' hearts*'. Respecting and promoting the European fundamental rights and freedoms, as well as the European penal principles, fit well within this image. Respecting prisoners' human dignity and rights also reflects and strengthens Norway's international reputation of 'humanitarian superpower' (Horn & Ugelvik, 2017; Leonard & Small,

2003; Lohne, 2020). This international reputation was deliberately built around four 'stories', which together aim to cover the Norwegians' self-image: (1) humanitarian superpower; (2) living with nature; (3) equality; and (4) spirit of adventure (Leonard & Small, 2003). In their 2003 report on Norway's cultural and public diplomacy strategy, Leonard and Small suggested these four stories to express the Norwegian identity in order to overcome its international invisibility as a small country. Almost twenty years later, we know that this strategy has worked because these four 'stories' do reflect the international image that we have of Norway.

Moreover, normalization will be most meaningful in a strong welfare state. Norway and Belgium are both strong welfare states, albeit with different historical paths and different public structures (Moeys, 2017). They have both been characterized as community-oriented societies that seek to include all citizens (although this was most strongly evidenced in so-called social democracies like Norway) (Cavadino & Dignan, 2006). Recent Eurostat numbers show for instance that the percentage of total government expenditure (GDP) on social protection was 19.3% in Belgium and 19.1% in Norway, and on education 6.29% in Belgium and 6.94% in Norway. It has been argued that Nordic prisons might be exceptional in the sense that they are '*understood as integrated parts of the strong, inclusive and ambitious Nordic welfare states*' (Ugelvik, 2016: 389). This is to some extent also true for Belgium: thanks to the import model, prisoners have in principle access to the same social services as other citizens (such as education, social assistance, mental health care). But the two welfare states are linked to different legal cultural traditions. The Belgian legal tradition was strongly impacted by the fact that today's Belgium became part of France in 1795, only a few years after the start of the French Revolution (Stevens, 1988). This has led to a strong legal culture of individual rights, local government and voluntary initiative that protect citizens *against* state intrusion. Norway, on the other hand, tends to present itself as protector of citizens and citizenship. In line with this image, the Norwegian government allegedly knows and does what is best for its citizens (Smith & Ugelvik, 2017). Norwegian citizens, on their part, like other Scandinavians, have generally more trust in the authorities of their countries than other Europeans (Lappi-Seppälä, 2008). Normalizing the prison conditions in order to prepare prisoners for their release as 'law-abiding citizens', fits well within this image of a welfare-oriented government that is not reluctant to interfere with its citizens' lives for their own good (Smith & Ugelvik, 2017).

According to Pratt, the Scandinavian 'cultures of equality', which he identified as the roots of 'Scandinavian exceptionalism', emerged in the late nineteenth and early twentieth centuries, when '*the 'sameness' between citizens ensured that the conduct of everyday life reflected passivity, consensus and an emphasis on collective rather than individual interests*' (Pratt, 2008a: 125). In this sense, these 'cultures of equality' observed in the Nordic societies do play a role in the implementation of normalization, because they make it easier to define what normal living conditions are outside, and consequently inside, prison. However, this common notion of Norway being a homogeneous society is in itself a persistent self-image that is not entirely consistent with reality (Ryymin, 2019). Based on nineteenth-century statistics, Ryymin (2019) explains that the presence of ethnic minorities like Sámi, Kvens and Romani, as well as 'foreign-borns', contradicts this notion of homogeneous Norway. The category of 'foreign-borns' was very small, consisting of less than 2% of the population, but this was still slightly *higher* than the average percentage of 'foreign-borns' in other European countries at the time. Ryymin (2019: 23) therefore concludes that

> We might best interpret Kiærs' [Director at Statistics Norway in the late 19th century] statement of "uncommon homogeneity" as an expression of a wish or a goal for how the population of Norway should be — that is, "racially" and nationally unified. (emphasis in original)

One of the explanations that Ryymin gives for what he calls a '*particularly persistent myth in Norway*' (2019: 22) is that these statements about Norway being a homogeneous society are no '*genuine attempts at accurate historical description*', but '*rhetorical commonplaces (loci communes) serving quite different functions than accurate description*' (Ryymin, 2019: 31). Despite being a 'myth', the self-image of homogeneous Norwegian culture and apparent national consensus about everyday life habits and practices still persists and makes it easier for policymakers to define the intended results of normalizing the prison conditions. The downside of this strong sense of in-group inclusion is the exclusion of 'others', such as foreign nationals and foreign national prisoners. Already in 2008, some years before the refugee crisis in Europe (see, e.g., Horning et al., 2020), Pratt wrote about '*the decline of homogeneity and solidarity*', pointing to the growing proportion of immigrants and growing intolerance towards immigration (Pratt, 2008b: 282–284). This argument was elaborated more thoroughly by Scandinavian scholars who understood this tendency to exclude 'others' as the *dark side* of the Scandinavian penal systems (Mathiesen, 2012; Smith & Ugelvik, 2017; Ugelvik, 2012).

The proportion of inhabitants who were born in another country is more or less the same in Belgium and Norway. In 2015, 13% of all inhabitants of Norway was born in another country (most of them in Poland, Lithuania and Sweden [Statistisk Sentralbyrå, 2015a, 2015b]) and 14% of all inhabitants of Belgium was born in another country (most of them in Morocco, France and The Netherlands [Lafleur & Marfouk, 2018: 33; Myria, 2016]). In the same year, on 1 September 2015, 40.1% of the Belgian prison population and 33.4% of the Norwegian prison population did not hold the Belgian or Norwegian nationality. Over the period between 2005 and 2015, this proportion has remained more or less the same in Belgium from 41.2%, in 2005, to 40.1% in 2015. In Norway, however, the proportion has almost doubled: from 17.8% in 2005 to 33.4% in 2015 (Aebi et al., 2019). This rapidly growing multiculturalism in Norwegian prisons does challenge the Norwegian consensus about 'normal' customs and habits, or self-evident 'normality'. In Belgium, defining 'normality' or normal living conditions seems more artificial, but this also means that individual differences and diversity seem less of a threat to 'the system' and to the intention to *normalize* the living conditions in prison. Of course, this is not to say that in *practice* multiculturalism, and especially multilingualism, is not challenging in Belgian prisons. But the point is, if Norway's self-perceived homogeneity might have contributed to a more consistent and easy implementation of normalization, it might also be more vulnerable to cracks in that self-image, even though those cracks are—again—more perception than reality.

We can conclude by arguing that the two countries do not only differ in what they consider normal living conditions and the ease with which this normality is defined, but also in *how* these normal living conditions are implemented in prison. Let us return to the mirror metaphor to make this clear. When looking at the reflection in a mirror, we do not only see part of reality, but we also gain an understanding of the qualities of the mirror. When the reflection appears bigger or smaller than reality, the surface of the mirror is curved inwards or outwards. In a similar way, we can gain an understanding of the aims associated with the normalization process by looking at the aspects of prison life that are selected to be normalized, and *how* they are normalized (in practice) or to be normalized (in policy and legislation). If normalization were a mirror, the mirror 'made in Belgium' and the one 'made in Norway' would be curved differently. Moreover, it could be argued that the Belgian mirror has a rougher surface than the Norwegian, leading to a more diffused and broken reflection of the 'normal' living conditions outside prison. Whether this is due to a lack of resources, as commonly argued, or whether it is simply too difficult to implement a vision that is principally consistent, but not pragmatically in line with the very idea of punishment, are questions for further research. But based on the comparisons, it is likely to be a combination of these factors.

References

Aebi, M. F., Berger-Kolopp, L., Burkhardt, C., Chopin, J., Hashimoto, Y. Z., & Tiago, M. M. (2019). *Foreign offenders in prison and on probation in Europe—Trends from 2005 to 2015 (inmates) and situation in 2015 (inmates and probationers)*. Council of Europe.

Ashworth, A. (2011). Re-evaluating the justification for aggravation and mitigation at sentencing. In J. V. Roberts (Ed.), *Mitigation and aggravation at sentencing* (pp. 21–39). Cambridge University Press.

Bronsteen, J., Buccafusco, C., & Masur, J. (2009). Happiness and punishment. *The University of Chicago Law Review, 76*(3), 1037–1082.

Cavadino, M., & Dignan, J. (2006). *Penal systems. A comparative approach*. Sage.

Crewe, B. (2011a). Depth, weight, tightness: Revisiting the pains of imprisonment. *Punishment & Society, 13*(5), 509–529.

Crewe, B. (2011b). Soft power in prison: Implications for staff–prisoner relationships, liberty and legitimacy. *European Journal of Criminology, 8*(6), 455–468.

Crewe, B. (2021). The depth of imprisonment. *Punishment & Society, 23*(3), 335–354. https://doi.org/10.1177/1462474520952153

Crewe, B., & Ievins, A. (2021). 'Tightness', recognition and penal power. *Punishment & Society, 23*(1), 47–68.

Daems, T. (2010). Toeters noch bellen: vijf jaar basiswet gevangeniswezen en rechtspositie van gedetineerden. *Fatik, Tijdschrift voor Strafbeleid en Gevangeniswezen, 28*(125), 23–25.

Drake, D. H., Earle, R., & Sloan, J. (2015). General introduction: What ethnography tells us about prisons. In D. H. Drake, R. Earle, & J. Sloan (Eds.), *The Palgrave handbook of prison ethnography* (pp. 1–16). Palgrave Macmillan.

Engbo, H. J. (2017). Normalisation in Nordic prisons—From a prison governor's perspective. In T. Ugelvik & P. S. Smith (Eds.), *Scandinavian penal history, culture and prison practice: Embraced by the welfare state?* (pp. 327–352). Palgrave Macmillan.

Foucault, M. (1977). *Discipline and punish: The birth of the prison.* Pantheon Books.

Goffman, E. (1961). *Asylums. Essays on the social situation of mental patients and other inmates.* Penguin Books Ltd.

Hancock, P., & Jewkes, Y. (2011). Architectures of incarceration: The spatial pains of imprisonment. *Punishment & Society, 13*(5), 611–629.

Herlofson, K., Daatland, S. O., & Veenstra, M. (2019). Generasjoner imellom: Holdninger til familiens ansvar øst og vest i Europa. *Nordisk østforum, 33,* 34–53.

Horning, A., Jordenö, S. V., & Savoie, N. (2020). Double-edged risk: Unaccompanied minor refugees (UMRs) in Sweden and their search for safety. *Journal of Refugee Studies, 33*(2), 390–415.

Horn, T., & Ugelvik, T. (2017). Best in class? Norwegian incarceration and the pragmatic production of legitimacy. In T. Daems & L. Robert (Eds.), *Europe in prisons: Assessing the impact of European institutions on national prison systems* (Series: Palgrave Studies in Prisons and Penology) (pp. 231–253). Palgrave Macmillan.

Johnsen, B., & Granheim, P. K. (2012). Prison size and the quality of life in Norwegian closed prisons in late modernity. In T. Ugelvik & J. Dullum

(Eds.), *Penal exceptionalism? Nordic prison policy and practice* (pp. 199–214). Routledge.

Kolber, A. J. (2009). The subjective experience of punishment. *Columbia Law Review, 109*(1), 182–236.

Lafleur, J., & Marfouk, A. (with collaboration of Fadil, N.) (2018). *Migratie in België in 21 vragen en antwoorden.* Universitaire Pers Leuven.

Lappi-Seppälä, T. (2008). Trust, welfare, and political culture: Explaining differences in national penal policies. *Crime and Justice, 37*(1), 313–387.

Leonard, M., & Small, A. (2003). *Norwegian public diplomacy.* https://www.regjeringen.no/globalassets/upload/ud/vedlegg/public.pdf. Last accessed on 5 January 2021.

Liebling, A. (2011). Moral performance, inhuman and degrading treatment and prison pain. *Punishment & Society, 13*(5), 530–550.

Liebling, A., assisted by Arnold, H. (2004). *Prisons and their moral performance. A study of values, quality and prison life.* Oxford University Press.

Lohne, K. (2020). Penal humanitarianism beyond the nation state: An analysis of international criminal justice. *Theoretical Criminology, 24*(2), 145–162.

Markel, D., Flanders, C., & Gray, D. (2011). Beyond experience: Getting retributive justice right. *California Law Review, 99*(2), 605–628.

Mathiesen, T. (2012). Scandinavian exceptionalism in penal matters. Reality or wishful thinking? In T. Ugelvik & J. Dullum (Eds.), *Penal exceptionalism? Nordic prison policy and practice* (pp. 13–37). Routledge.

Matthews, R. (2005). The myth of punitiveness. *Theoretical Criminology, 9*(2), 175–201.

Moeys, H. (2017). *Subsidiary social provision before the welfare state. Political theory and social policy in nineteenth-century Belgium* (Unpublished doctoral dissertation). KU Leuven, Leuven.

Myria—Federaal Migratiecentrum. (2016). *Migratie in cijfers en in rechten.* Myria. https://www.myria.be/files/MIGRA16_NL_AS-NEW.pdf

Nelken, D. (2003). Comparatists and transferability. In P. Legrand & R. Munday (Eds.), *Comparative legal studies: Traditions and transitions* (pp. 437–466). Cambridge University Press.

Neumann, C. B. (2012). Imprisoning the soul. In T. Ugelvik & J. Dullum (Eds.), *Penal exceptionalism? Nordic prison policy and practice* (pp. 139–155). Routledge.

OECD. (2020). *How's life? 2020: Measuring well-being*. OECD Publishing.

Pratt, J. (2008a). Scandinavian exceptionalism in an era of penal excess, part I: The nature and roots of Scandinavian exceptionalism. *British Journal of Criminology, 48*(2), 119–137.

Pratt, J. (2008b). Scandinavian exceptionalism in an era of penal excess, part II: Does Scandinavian exceptionalism have a future? *British Journal of Criminology, 48*(3), 275–292.

Pratt, J., & Eriksson, A. (2012). In defence of Scandinavian exceptionalism. In T. Ugelvik & J. Dullum (Eds.), *Penal exceptionalism? Nordic prison policy and practice* (pp. 235–260). Routledge.

Pratt, J., & Eriksson, A. (2013). *Contrasts in punishment. An explanation of anglophone excess and Nordic exceptionalism.* Routledge.

Raaijmakers, E., de Keijser, J., Nieuwbeerta, P., Dirkzwager, A., & Reef, J. (2014). De subjectieve zwaarte van detentie. Een Empirisch Onderzoek. *Tijdschrift Voor Criminologie, 56*(1), 60–80.

Rocheleau, A. M. (2013). An empirical exploration of the 'pains of imprisonment' and the level of prison misconduct and violence. *Criminal Justice Review, 38*(3), 354–374.

Ryymin, T. (2019). Forgetting diversity? Norwegian narratives of ethnic and cultural homogeneity. In S. Keskinen, U. D. Skaptadóttir, & M. Toivanen (Eds.), *Undoing homogeneity in the Nordic region* (pp. 21–34). Routledge.

Sexton, L. (2015). Penal subjectivities: Developing a theoretical framework for penal consciousness. *Punishment & Society, 17*(1), 114–136.

Shammas, V. L. (2014). The pains of freedom: Assessing the ambiguity of Scandinavian penal exceptionalism on Norway's Prison Island. *Punishment & Society, 16*(1), 104–123.

Smith, P. S. (2012). Imprisonment and internet-access. Human rights, the principle of normalization and the question of prisoners access to digital communications technology. *Nordic Journal of Human Rights, 30*(4), 454–482.

Smith, P. S., & Ugelvik, T. (2017). *Embraced by the welfare state? Scandinavian penal history, culture and prison practice* (Palgrave Studies in Prisons and Penology). Palgrave Macmillan.

Snacken, S. (2015b). Tien jaar Basiswet—'Back to basics'. In T. Daems, C. Hermans, F. Janssens, J. Millen, L. Robert, & V. Scheirs. (Eds.), *Quo vadis?: Tien jaar basiswet gevangeniswezen en rechtspositie van gedetineerden* (pp. 179–203). Maklu.

Statbel. (2020). *Alleenwonenden en alleenstaande ouders maken 45% van de Belgische huishoudens uit*. https://statbel.fgov.be/nl/nieuws/alleenwonenden-en-alleenstaande-ouders-maken-45-van-de-belgische-huishoudens-uit. Last accessed on 3 January 2021.

Statistisk Sentralbyrå. (2015a). *Fakta om innvandring*. www.ssb.no/innvandring-og-innvandrere/faktaside/innvandring. Last accessed on 17 January 2021.

Statistisk Sentralbyrå. (2015b). *Antall og andel innvandrere og flyktninger 2015*. www.ssb.no/befolkning/artikler-og-publikasjoner/flyktninger-i-norge?tabell=243292. Last accessed on 17 January 2021.

Statistisk Sentralbyrå. (2020). *Flere bor alene*. https://www.ssb.no/befolkning/artikler-og-publikasjoner/flere-bor-alene. Last accessed on 3 January 2021.

Stevens, F. (1988). L'introduction de la législation révolutionnaire en Belgique. In *La Révolution et l'ordre juridique privé. Rationalité ou scandale?* (pp. 472–493). PUF.

Ugelvik, T. (2012). The dark side of a culture of equality: Reimagining communities in a Norwegian remand prison. In T. Ugelvik & J. Dullum (Eds.), *Penal exceptionalism? Nordic prison policy and practice* (pp. 121–138). Routledge.

Ugelvik, T. (2016). Prisons as welfare institutions? Punishment and the Nordic model. In Y. Jewkes, J. Bennett, & B. Crewe (Eds.), *Handbook on prisons* (2nd ed., pp. 388–402). Routledge.

UNDP. (2019). *Human development report 2019. Beyond income, beyond averages, beyond today: Inequalities in human development in the 21st century*. UNDP.

Wolfensberger, W. (2011). Social role valorization: A proposed new term for the principle of normalization. *Intellectual and Developmental Disabilities, 49*(6), 435–440.

Index

H. De Vos, *Beyond Scandinavian Exceptionalism*, Palgrave Studies in Prisons and Penology, https://doi.org/10.1007/978-3-031-28635-3

O